CONTESTED NATURES

Theory, Culture & Society

Theory, Culture & Society caters for the resurgence of interest in culture within contemporary social science and the humanities. Building on the heritage of classical social theory, the book series examines ways in which this tradition has been reshaped by a new generation of theorists. It will also publish theoretically informed analyses of everyday life, popular culture, and new intellectual movements.

EDITOR: Mike Featherstone, *Nottingham Trent University*

SERIES EDITORIAL BOARD
Roy Boyne, *University of Durham*
Mike Hepworth, *University of Aberdeen*
Scott Lash, *Lancaster University*
Roland Robertson, *University of Pittsburgh*
Bryan S. Turner, *Deakin University*

THE TCS CENTRE
The Theory, Culture & Society book series, the journals *Theory, Culture & Society* and *Body & Society*, and related conference, seminar and postgraduate programmes operate from the TCS Centre at Nottingham Trent University. For further details of the TCS Centre's activities please contact:

Centre Administrator
The TCS Centre, Room 175
Faculty of Humanities
Nottingham Trent University
Clifton Lane, Nottingham, NG11 8NS, UK e-mail: tcs@ntu.ac.uk

Recent volumes include:

Pierre Bourdieu and Cultural Theory
Critical Investigations
Bridget Fowler

Re-Forming the Body
Religion, Community and Modernity
Philip A. Mellor and Chris Shilling

The Shopping Experience
edited by Pasi Falk and Colin Campbell

Undoing Aesthetics
Wolfgang Welsch

Simmel on Culture: Selected Writings
edited by David Frisby and Mike Featherstone

CONTESTED NATURES

Phil Macnaghten and John Urry

SAGE Publications
London • Thousand Oaks • New Delhi

First published 1998

Reprinted 1999

SAGE Publications Ltd
6 Bonhill Street
London EC2A 4PU

SAGE Publications Inc
2455 Teller Road
Thousand Oaks, California 91320

SAGE Publications India Pvt Ltd
32, M-Block Market
Greater Kailash - I
New Delhi 110 048

Published in association with *Theory, Culture & Society*, Nottingham Trent University

British Library Cataloguing in Publication data

A catalogue record for this book is available from the British Library.

ISBN 0 7619 5312 4
ISBN 0 7619 5313 2 (pbk)

Library of Congress catalog card number 97-062443

To Miranda

In memory of Wilga Urry

CONTENTS

ACKNOWLEDGEMENTS

We would like to express our special thanks to Robin Grove-White and Greg Myers.

We would also like to thank Nick Abercrombie, Barbara Adam, Alison Anderson, Jacqui Burgess, Manuel Castells, Gordon Clark, Alan Costall, Carol Crawshaw, Éric Darier, Jan Darrall, Sarah Franklin, Ann Game, Ken Hahlo, Mike Jacobs, Kate Lamb, Scott Lash, Sue Mayer, Mike Michael, Martin O'Brien, Sue Penna, Graham Pinfield, Steve Reicher, John Scott, Simon Shackley, Peter Simmons, Jackie Stacey, Bron Szerszynski, Floris Tomasini, Mark Toogood, Sylvia Walby, Claire Waterton, Patrick Wright and Brian Wynne.

The book reports on quite a considerable body of research undertaken over the last three to four years. Chapter 2 benefited from a British Academy Postdoctoral Fellowship on 'The cultural significance of contemporary British environmentalism'; chapter 6 from an ESRC project on 'Tourism and the environment' and from a CPRE-sponsored project on 'Leisure landscapes'; and chapter 7 from an ESRC project on 'Public rhetorics of sustainability' and a Lancashire County Council sponsored project on 'Public perceptions and sustainability in Lancashire'. We are very grateful for this support.

For offering useful insights into the history of contemporary environmentalism we would especially like to thank Tom Burke, Sue Clifford, Nigel Haigh, Chris Hall, Peter Melchett, Jonathan Porritt and Chris Rose.

1

RETHINKING NATURE AND SOCIETY

In this book we seek to show that there is no singular 'nature' as such, only a diversity of contested natures; and that each such nature is constituted through a variety of socio-cultural processes from which such natures cannot be plausibly separated. We therefore argue against three doctrines which are widespread in current thinking about nature and the environment. We begin this introductory chapter by briefly outlining these before seeking to develop our own position.

The first, and most important for our subsequent argument, is the claim that the environment is essentially a 'real entity', which, in and of itself and substantially separate from social practices and human experience, has the power to produce unambiguous, observable and rectifiable outcomes. This doctrine will be termed that of 'environmental realism', one aspect of which is the way that the very notion of nature itself has been turned into a scientifically researchable 'environment'. Modern rational science can and will provide the understanding of that environment and the assessment of those measures which are necessary to rectify environmental bads. Social practices play a minor role in any such analysis since the realities which derive from scientific inquiry are held to transcend the more superficial and transitory patterns of everyday life.

The second doctrine is that of 'environmental idealism', which has partly developed as a critique of the first. This doctrine holds that the way to analyse nature and the environment is through identifying, critiquing and realising various 'values' which underpin or relate to the character, sense and quality of nature. Such values held by people about nature and the environment are treated as underlying, stable and consistent. They are abstracted both from the sheer messiness of the 'environment' and the diverse species which happen to inhabit the globe, and from the practices of specific social groupings in the wider society who may or may not articulate or adopt such values. This doctrine can coexist with the first.

The third doctrine specifically concerns the responses of individuals and groups to nature and the environment. It is concerned to explain appropriate human motivation to engage in environmentally sustainable practices and hence the resulting environmental goods or bads. It seeks to do this in terms of straightforwardly determined calculations of individual and/or collective interest (such as cost–benefit analysis and contingent valuation schemes).

This doctrine we will term 'environmental instrumentalism' and is importantly linked to a marketised naturalistic model of human behaviour, and its radical separation from non-human species.

Obviously all these three positions have something to contribute to the untangling of contemporary debates on the environment. But it will be our view that all three ignore/misrepresent/conceal aspects of contemporary environmental change and human engagement. Our approach will emphasise that it is specific social practices, especially of people's dwellings, which produce, reproduce and transform different natures and different values. It is through such practices that people respond, cognitively, aesthetically and hermeneutically, to what have been constructed as the signs and characteristics of nature. Such social practices embody their own forms of knowledge and understanding and undermine a simple demarcation between objective science and lay knowledge. These practices structure the responses of people to what is deemed to be the 'natural'. We thus seek to transcend the by now rather dull debate between 'realists' and 'constructivists' by emphasising the significance of embedded social practices.

Such social practices possess a number of constitutive principles. These practices are:

- discursively ordered (hence the importance of the analysis of everyday talk especially as it contrasts with official rhetorics and models such as sustainability);
- embodied (hence the significance of identifying the ways in which nature is differentially sensed by the body);
- spaced (hence the importance of the particular conflicting senses of the local, national and global dimensions of the environment);
- timed (hence the analysis of conflicting times in nature including the apparent efforts of states to plan for the uncertain future);
- and involve models of human activity, risk, agency and trust (which are often the opposite of or at a tangent to 'official' models of human action, and which may or may not be at odds with the interests of non-human animals).

Much of the book is concerned with showing the character and significance of such social practices. Overall we seek to show that responses to and engagement with nature are highly diverse, ambivalent and embedded in daily life. Such responses necessarily involve work in order that they develop and are sustained. This work is not just economic and organisational, but also cultural in often complex and ill-understood ways. These social practices are structured by the flows within and across national boundaries of signs, images, information, money, people, as well as noxious substances. Such global flows can reinforce or can undermine notions of agency and trust.

Such social practices stem from and feed into tacit notions of the human agent, nature, the future, and so on. These notions are often opposed to, or contradicted by, official bureaucratic, scientific and managerial discourses, such discourses often becoming part of the problem rather than the solution. They may reinforce further manifestations of political alienation and estrangement. It also follows that these complex social practices need to be researched by 'methodologies' which are able to represent and capture some of these ambivalent and multiple characteristics. We will subject much of the research in the environmental area to methodological critique and develop alternative modes of investigation appropriate to such complexities.

We will also go on to examine how global–local changes transform what it is to be a subject/citizen/stakeholder within contemporary societies. We shall outline a revised politics of the environment which is not based on a simple interest model but one which recognises how arguments about nature provide new and embryonic spaces for political exploration and self-discovery. Further, we shall not argue for abstract values disembodied from the world of everyday experience, but we do recognise that nature and the environment are hugely bound up with certain valuations of desirable and/or appropriate 'natures'. We thus examine the character and complexity of human responses to nature, of people's hopes, fears, concerns and sense of engagement, and how current unease and anxiety about nature connects to new tensions associated with living in global times. And we shall not suggest that environmental activism automatically follows from environmental 'damage'. It is mediated by signs, senses of agency and particular timings. But we do recognise that environments change, that such changes can in certain ways and via a variety of media be sensed, and that those sensings can crystallise at some defining moments into perceived threats to 'the environment' and hence to significant socio-political responses.

We will also consider what an appropriate politics of nature would be; one which stems from how people talk about, use and conceptualise nature and the environment in their day-to-day lives, in their localities and other 'communities'. Such talk takes place in the context of official and public discourses and of the ideas, money, information, signs and substances flowing across national borders and which bring into being some often very extended 'communities'. Moreover, people's sense of their power or powerlessness in relation to such flows, as well as the impact of such flows upon the details of everyday life, will be identified as crucial for understanding how people make sense of nature, including the existential experience of living with environmental risks of unknown proportions and unknowable consequences.

In that sense we will try to provide some more specific sociological grounding for recent communitarian philosophy, which on the face of it would seem to have a lot to offer to the environmental movement. But we will endeavour to connect such possible communities to some of the unutterably modernist processes which appear to envelop nature and from which these philosophies and practices cannot escape, as Szerszynski argues (1996; see also Eder 1996). We do not think that the discovery of nature and the identification of 'natural limits' resolves the modernist dilemma. Nature does not simply provide an objective ethics which tells us what to do. It is too ambivalent, contested and culturally paradoxical for that. But we will argue that emergent 'cultures of nature' may on occasions facilitate the kind of communities and traditions that provide an enormously significant sense of meaning and value in societies struggling to break from the modern world; communities and traditions that are socially embedded and embodied, and temporally and spatially structured.

Finally, there are three important points of clarification. First, this book principally concentrates upon the relationship between society and nature within the 'West' or what we prefer to call the North Atlantic Rim societies. We will not consider the cultures of nature as these are shaping the development of environmental issues in the Pacific Rim, in the developing world, or in what was known as 'Eastern Europe'. Second, the book deals mainly with what would normally be identified as 'environmental' rather than 'biological' issues (see on the biological issues, Benton 1993; Haraway 1991; Strathern 1992). However, even that distinction is difficult to justify or sustain since it in part derives from the very development of those specialised sciences through which nature has been tamed and transformed. Moreover, people's responses to 'nature' and hence to particular 'environments' are in part derived from the kinds of human and non-human species which inhabit or have inhabited or might have inhabited particular locales. Third, this book is selective and makes no claim to be an exhaustive survey of even current environmental issues or debates. It will focus upon a limited number of 'contested natures' and has little to say about debates on shallow and deep ecology, Gaia, biocentrism, the 'new age', ecocentrism, technocentrism, and other conceptualisations of new and more ecologically 'benign' paradigms or worldviews (although see chapter 3 below for a critique of how some of these concepts embody variants of the doctrines set out above).

Nature and sociology

We have argued that nature and the environment have been inappropriately analysed within the three doctrines outlined. In particular the 'social' dimensions of nature have been significantly under-examined. In this section we turn to the discipline which on the face of it should have engaged with such an agenda, namely, sociology. However, we suggest that the neglect of the 'social' in the environmental literature has partly stemmed from sociology's own trajectory of development. This trajectory has been based upon drawing a strong and undesirable distinction between 'society' and 'nature'.

The discursive development of sociology was the product of a particular historical moment, of industrial capitalism in Western Europe and North America. Sociology's key concept has been that of society, as opposed to those of capitalism or the division of labour which are central to historical materialism (see Dickens 1996). Sociology accepted certain *a priori* assumptions about the consequent relationship between nature and society. Taking for granted the success of such modern societies in their spectacular overcoming of nature, sociology has concentrated and specialised on what it has been good at, namely, describing and explaining the very character of modern societies. As such, sociology has generally accepted a presumed division of academic labour which partly stemmed from the Durkheimian desire to carve out a separate realm or sphere of the social which could be investigated and explained autonomously. In a way sociology employed the strategy of modelling itself on biology and arguing for a specific and autonomous realm of facts, in this case pertaining to the social or society. Such a realm of social facts presupposed its separation from, and antithesis to, nature (Dickens 1996: 47; Dunlap and Catton 1994; Durkheim 1952; Macnaghten and Urry 1995).

As a discipline sociology has until recently been that social science least concerned with the natural, in either its biological or environmental form. The dichotomy between the social and the natural has been most pronounced in the case of sociology. The other social sciences have enjoyed a more messy and confused relationship with the facts of nature. In sociology this academic division between a world of social facts and one of natural facts has been regarded as largely uncontentious. *Inter alia* it was reflected in the conceptualisation of time, where it was presumed that the times of nature and of society are quite distinct (see Adam 1990; Lash and Urry 1994: chap. 9). Moreover, this account made good sense as a strategy of professionalisation for sociology since it provided a clear and bounded sphere of investigation, a sphere parallel to but not challenging or confronting those physical sciences that unambiguously dealt with an apparently distinct and analysable nature. The competition between the different nascent disciplines, including sociology, led to new forms of scientific authority and elitism, with a striking disparagement of lay, implicit, tacit forms of knowledge. What people 'know' in their 'social practices' was devalued and marginalised (Dickens 1996: chap. 1).

An interesting exception to such sociological orthodoxy was that posed by the American sub-discipline of environmental sociology in the United States (Catton and Dunlap 1978; Dunlap and Catton 1979). Dunlap and Catton (1994) defined the field as 'the study of interaction between environment and society', and sought to highlight the inextricable relationship between the development of human societies and their use and exploitation of finite resources and life support systems. By highlighting these links, environmental sociologists have advocated a reorientation of sociology towards 'a more holistic perspective that would contextualise social processes within the context of the biosphere' (Buttel 1987: 466). Yet even such a sociology employs a division of labour between the natural sciences, which provide the hard and factual base of the state of nature, and the more subservient social sciences, which identify the impacts of physical nature upon society, and the impacts of society upon nature.

Moreover, it is this model of sociology and more generally of the social sciences which is most visible in current investigations of so-called 'global environmental change'. Roughly speaking, the role of the social scientist is seen as that of addressing the social causes, impacts and responses to environmental problems which have been initially and accurately described by the natural scientist – a kind of 'Biology and Science First' model (also see Grove-White and Szerszynski 1992). Such emphases can be identified in most major international research programmes on global environmental change (see Newby 1993; Wynne 1994). For example, in early formulations of the Intergovernmental Panel on Climate Change, environmental change is conceived of as a set of scientific problems essentially requiring techno-logical solutions. A linear model was outlined with working panels estab-lished on the scientific evidence (WG1), the environmental and socio-economic impacts (WG2), and the appropriate response strategies described in explicitly technical terms (WG3) (although see Shackley 1997 for recent reformulations).

A similar process can be located in the UK research framework on global environmental change. Following a number of significant events, including a wave of environmental public consciousness in the late 1980s and Margaret Thatcher's landmark speech to the Royal Society in 1988 (see chapter 2 below), a new research culture emerged in which to study environmental processes. Following international models, the focus of this research was largely global and natural science-oriented (see Grove-White 1996a). Thus, when the UK Inter-Agency Committee on Global Environment Change was formed in 1990 to link all UK environmental research, the first report in April 1991 was unmistakably natural science in orientation. Moreover, when social science research became more prominent, propelled by the Govern-ment funding of a Global Environmental Change programme started in 1990, it operated in a political climate where considerable expectations and policy commitments became invested in the role of the social sciences as secondary, as formulating appropriate responses to the problems embodied in mounting natural scientific evidence (ESRC 1990).

Thus the role of the social scientist in the analysis of global environmental change has been largely seen as that of a social engineer, as someone who manipulates and 'fixes' society so as to facilitate the implementation of a sustainable society specified in essentially technical terms (based on varia-tions of doctrines 1 and 3 outlined above). In such an analysis instrumen-talist social science disciplines such as economics and geography have been particularly significant in forming and addressing an environmental agenda.

However, in the last few years there has been the development of some alternative thinking and research about nature and the environment. Such new wave thinking has been found within various disciplines, including anthropology (see Douglas 1992; Milton 1993a, 1996), archaeology (Bender 1993), cultural history (Arnold 1996; Robertson et al. 1996; Ross 1994; Schama 1995; Wilson 1992; Wright 1996), geography (Barnes and Duncan

1992; Cloke et al. 1994; Fitzsimmons 1989), literary studies (Wheeler 1995), the analyses of modernity and post-modernity (Lash et al. 1996), philosophy (O'Neill 1993), politics (Dobson 1990; McCormick 1991a, 1995), sociology (Beck 1992b, 1996b; Benton 1993; Dickens 1992, 1996; Eder 1996; Martell 1994; Redclift and Benton 1994), the sociology of science (Yearley 1991, 1996), and women's studies (Haraway 1991; Merchant 1982; Shiva 1988, 1991, 1994). These have begun to resonate with each other and to have begun the development of what we will loosely take to be a more socio-culturally embedded analysis of nature. In this book we seek to reflect these interlinking developments and to develop them further within the context of particular environmental topics. And by connecting such developments to those social practices through which nature becomes produced and consumed, we shall in a sense seek to repopulate environmental issues as they are lived, sensed and encoded in contemporary societies.

We turn now to a brief account of the history of the relationship between nature and society, in order to understand better how historically the social and the natural were torn apart and some of the different forms taken by this dichotomisation. This is not to provide anything more than a brief schematic account of certain moments in the changing relationship of 'nature' and 'society'.

Nature and society – historical context

In historical terms the juxtaposition of society and nature reached its fullest development in the nineteenth century in the 'West'. Nature came to be degraded into a realm of unfreedom and hostility that needed to be subdued and controlled. Modernity involved the belief that human progress should be measured and evaluated in terms of the domination of nature, rather than through any attempt to transform the relationship between humans and nature. This view that nature should be dominated presupposed the doctrine of human exceptionalism: that humans are fundamentally different from and superior to all other species; that people can determine their own destinies and learn whatever is necessary to achieve them; that the world is vast and presents unlimited opportunities; and that the history of human society is one of unending progress (also see Dunlap and Catton 1979).

This dichotomisation of nature and society possesses a number of deficiencies and has been subject to various kinds of critique. The following deficiencies should be noted: the dichotomisation has led to exceptional levels of exploitation and degradation of land and landscapes and of other animal species which many humans now find intolerable; humans have themselves suffered from being relatively estranged from these 'natural' processes; and there is no simple entity which we can designate as 'nature' which is to be regarded as waiting to be subject to enlightened human mastery. Indeed, the very idea of nature has been analysed as having multiple and even oppositional meanings: it can refer to the essential quality or character of something; the underlying force which lies behind events in the world; the entirety of animate and inanimate objects, and especially those which are threatened; the primitive or original condition existing prior to human society; the physical as opposed to the human environment and its particular ecology; and the rural or countryside (as opposed to the town or city) and its particular visual or recreational properties (see Strathern 1992: 172; Szerszynski 1993; Williams 1976: 219).

We now provide a brief historical sketch of the changing interpretations of human/nature relations; an exercise designed to show the multiple, contested and differentially embedded notions of nature even within the West during the high point of the doctrine of human exceptionalism. This delineation of some of the key transformations of people's understandings and relationships to nature in the West is usefully outlined by Williams (1972, 1976; and see Foucault 1970; Glacken 1966, 1967; Koestler 1964; Lewis 1964; Lovejoy 1936; Merchant 1982; Schama 1995; Short 1991; Thomas 1984; amongst numerous sources). He argues that the term 'nature' is perhaps the most complex and difficult word in the English language; that the idea of nature contains an enormous amount of human history; and that our current understandings of nature derive from an immensely complicated array of ideas, linked to many of the key concepts of western thought, such as God, Idealism, Democracy, Modernity, Society, the Enlightenment, Romanticism, and so on.

However, it is the abstraction of a singular nature from the multiplicity of lived experiences (starting over two thousand years ago) that was to prove so critical for subsequent human responses to the physical world. Indeed, the ways in which nature has historically been made singular, abstract and then personified provides key insights as to how people thought about themselves, their place in the world, their relationships with each other and with the land, and their sense of general power and powerlessness in shaping their lifeworlds. Starting with mediaeval cosmology, Williams identifies the social significance of the formation of a series of abstracted, singular and personified natures. Thus, first as a goddess, then as a divine mother, an absolute monarch, a minister, a constitutional lawyer, and finally a selective breeder, the appeal to a singular nature defined respectively the changing and often bitterly contested relationships between a state of nature, a state of God, and humanity. Indeed, once the idea of a singular nature became established, it then became possible to consider whether human activities did or did not fit into such a pre-existing and pre-ordained natural order. Williams argues:

> For, of course, to speak of man [sic] 'intervening' in natural processes is to suppose that he might find it possible not to do so, or to decide not to do so. Nature has to be thought of, that is to say, as separate from man, before any question of intervention or command, and the method or ethics of either, can arise. (1972: 154)

C.S. Lewis suggests that it was the pre-Socratic Greek philosophers who invented the first singular and abstracted nature. It was they who first had the idea that the 'great variety of phenomena which surrounds us could all be impounded under a name and talked about as a single object' (1964: 37). Then, and only then, could nature be personified, starting with nature as Goddess. However, the idea of nature was soon seen not to cover everything, and in not covering everything nature came to locate itself in relationship with humans and with God. In the mediaeval European idea, for example, nature was believed to have 'her' own particular place in the grand scheme of things:

> She had her proper place, below the moon. She had her appointed duties as God's vicegerent in that area. Her own lawful subjects, stimulated by rebel angels, might disobey her and become 'unnatural'. There were things above her, and things below. It is precisely this limitation and sub-ordination of Nature which sets her free for her triumphant poetical career. By surrendering the dull claim to be everything, she becomes somebody. Yet all the while she is, for the medievals, only a personification. (Lewis 1964: 39)

Within this grand design people too had their precise and pre-ordained place in the scheme of things, a place distinct yet bounded and connected to that of nature. In such a world nature was commonly portrayed as God's creation, and as reflecting a divine and perfect order in which everything had its right place, its home, its sense of belonging. Or, as Lovejoy says: 'the men of the fifteenth century still lived in a walled universe as well as in walled towns' (1936: 101). The mediaeval relationship between God and nature was often described through the analogy of nature as a book, requiring attentive reading. Glacken describes in scholarly detail how much of mediaeval theology was concerned with the two books in which God revealed himself: through the Bible (the ultimate book of revelation), and through the book of nature (through which the work and artisanship of God could be revealed; 1967: 176–253). Moreover, as Williams points out, the inclusion of people within nature was not static:

> The idea of a place in the order implied a destiny. The constitution of nature declared its purpose. By knowing the whole world, beginning with the four elements [i.e. earth, water, fire and air], man [sic] would come to know his own important place in it, and the definition of this importance was in discovering his relation to God. (1972: 153)

Such a perspective on nature, Williams argues, produced a quite considerable tension concerning the appropriate limits of physical inquiry and thus of human ethical action. To inquire too deeply could be construed as transcending one's allocated place, as an attempt to intervene 'unnaturally' in God's work. Such views of one's relationship to nature led to vigorous study of, and reverence towards, the visible world of creation (see also Merchant 1982; Ovitt 1987). Indeed, although during the Middle Ages there was substantial intervention in physical nature – from the clearance of forests and woodland for agriculture, to the quarrying of millions of stone for cathedrals and building – progress and intervention in nature were predominantly conceived in spiritual terms, in terms of discovering God's providential design and in constructing artefacts designed to express the perfectibility of God's order (Ovitt 1987: 200).

Yet, even in mediaeval times, there was ambiguity in people's relationship to nature, an ambiguity captured in two singular and largely competing personifications: that of nature as God's absolute monarch who possesses such powers of destiny we cannot escape; and that of nature as God's minister or even mother earth, who nurtures and provides for the needs of humanity. Williams (1976) argues that such singular natures helped make sense of the uncertainties in everyday life. When times were good, nature was personified as a mother, a provider, a goddess who sustained and nurtured; whereas in times of famine and plague, nature became personified as a jealous and capricious monarch.

As described above, pre-modern cosmology involved the idea of an overarching order within which humanity, nature and God were inextricably bound together in the Great Chain of Being (Lovejoy 1936). Moral judgement was then largely understood in terms of whether human action conformed to this 'natural' God-given order.

Two crucial transformations took place from the sixteenth and seventeenth centuries onwards, both dependent upon the separation and abstraction of a 'state of nature' from that of humanity and God, both effectively denying the possibility of an all-inclusive cosmological order. The first transformation involved the deadening of the state of nature from a life-giving force to dead matter, from spirit to machine. In effect, through the new sciences of physics, astronomy and mathematics, the study of nature became the study of how nature is materially constituted. Nature became a set of laws, cases and conventions, discoverable through the new rules of inquiry; forms of inquiry which could be carried out in their own terms without any recourse to a divine purpose or design (see Williams 1972).

Such a transformation was pioneered by the mechanists, and in particular by the physicalist ontology provided by Galileo, by the philosophy of Descartes which removed everyday *sensed* reality from nature (through distinguishing the world of science and primary qualities from the world of appearance and secondary qualities), and later by the scientific 'world picture' put in place by Newton. The scientific method no longer required teleological explanation. By contrast, the basic forces controlling creation could be described in mathematical or geometrical terms (Glacken 1967: 505; see also Whitehead 1926: chap. 3). God no longer had to be conceived *within* nature, but could now be detached from nature, placed in the heavens overlooking 'His' mechanical creation, intervening periodically with the occasional miracle. Such detachment is reflected in Kepler's clockwork analogy of the universe:

> My aim is to show that the heavenly machine is not a kind of divine, living being, but a kind of clockwork (and he who believes that a clock has a soul, attributes the maker's glory to the work), insofar as nearly all the manifold motions are caused by a single, magnetic, and material force, just as all motions of the clock are caused by a simple weight. And I also show how these physical causes are to be given numerical and geometrical expression. (Kepler 1605, cited Koestler 1964: 340)

The second transformation involved the contrast between a state of primeval nature and a formed human state with laws and conventions. Mythologies of an original state of nature, of a golden age in which humans and nature were in a state of balance and harmony, have been commonplace since the ancient Greeks. They have often coincided with the myth of Eden, of 'man' before the fall. However, such mythologies themselves have been ambivalent, based on a tension between nature as a state of innocence (nature as the state before the fall), and nature as the wild, untouched and savage places metaphorically outside the garden (the fall from innocence as a fall into wild and savage nature). Two variants of this idea evolved broadly into what we now term the Enlightenment and Romanticism. These two variants were grounded in the dispute over whether this 'pre-social state of nature' was the source of original sin or of original innocence. An early articulation of this dispute can be seen in Hobbes and Locke. While Hobbes famously described the pre-social state of nature as 'solitary, poor, nasty, brutish, and short', Locke described this state as one of 'peace, goodwill, mutual assistance and co-operation'. As such Hobbes argued that the basis of civilised society lay in overcoming 'natural disadvantages', while for Locke the basis of a just society lay in organising society around 'natural laws'. These novel constructions of nature had major consequences for the relationship between forms of social activity and a state of nature.

Indeed, the effect of the new abstract and geometrical 'natures' of the Enlightenment tradition legitimated not only theoretical inquiry – 'a separated mind looking at separated matter', 'man looking at nature' – but also new applications. Williams (1972) argues that the separation of nature from society was a prerequisite for practices dependent on constituting nature instrumentally: as a set of passive *objects* to be used and worked on by people (the doctrine of 'environmental instrumentalism' we set out at the beginning of the chapter). The morality used to justify the enormous interference which occurred from the eighteenth century onwards arose from this construction of a separate nature, whose laws became the laws of physics. And since these were considered God's laws, physical interference came to represent the continuation of God's creation. Indeed, it led to systems of thought where it became considered fundamentally purposeful for people to interfere on a massive scale for human use, first in the field of agricultural innovation, and later in the industrial revolution. It also led not only to arguments proclaiming the 'naturalness' of interference, but also to the argument that interference in and on nature was so inevitable that any criticism of the argument itself became classified as unwarranted interference in the mastery of nature. Hence a particular version of the socio-economic order, that involving a Hobbesian vision of struggle, of self-interest, and of the sanctity of physical intervention on nature for human use, came to be read as an extension of nature and of a naturalised order.

However, the formulation of 'natural laws' in the eighteenth century, alongside a renewal of interest in the state of the natural as original innocence (Rousseau), was closely aligned to the rise in popularity of natural history. Such interest itself arose partly from the life sciences, where the mechanical doctrines had not effectively supplanted the much older idea of the earth as a divinely designed environment, reflected in the very same sensory qualities (its beauty, form, smells and colour) that had been dismissed by the mechanists as unimportant and secondary. For those interested in the variety and complexity of *life*, the new scientific methodology appeared limited and abstract, and ultimately dissatisfying:

> Many men [in the eighteenth century] were dissatisfied with the knowledge of nature and natural laws which mathematics (and especially geometry) had yielded. The philosophy of Descartes, for example, was too removed from reality, from the nature as observed by travellers in all parts of the world. Where in Descartes were the fragrances, stinks, blossoms, colors? Nature was too rich, too luxurious, too complex to be understood by mathematical deduction from first principles. (Glacken 1966: 357)

Such interest in natural history was to prefigure the development of a new and important idea of nature in the late eighteenth and early nineteenth centuries. Just as the 'improvers' of nature were claiming the inevitability of their actions and their transformations of nature, so many people began to experience the turmoil which followed from this massive interference in 'nature'. From work-houses to smog-filled factories, from child chimney sweeps to the destruction of the countryside, from tuberculosis to syphilis, these processes rapidly became criticised as inhumane, unjust and, most relevant here, 'unnatural'. However, as Williams (1972) argues, while these many negative impacts of industrialisation were relatively easy to identify, it was much harder to imagine and to articulate a coherent 'natural' alternative.

Two of the most distinctive contributors in England to this Romantic critique were Wordsworth and Ruskin, who have both been viewed as early environmentalists (see Bate 1991 on Wordsworth; Wheeler 1995 on Ruskin). Ruskin's views were probably the most developed. He argued that good design in industry depends upon appropriate organisation, that this in turn depends upon the proper structuring of society, and that this in turn depends upon how faithful it is to the natural form. Ruskin particularly criticises the ways in which industrial society produced forms of social organisation that were not organic and functional as in nature, but involved competition, individual achievement and the division of labour. At much the same time Carlyle coined the phrase 'industrialism', and said that 'cash was becoming the sole nexus between man and man . . . while there are so many things [for] which cash will not pay' (cited Haigh 1986: 77). The division of labour is particularly criticised by Ruskin. It is, he says, not strictly speaking the labour which is divided by the 'division of labour', but people who are 'broken into small fragments and crumbs of life' (Ruskin 1985: 87). Some of the 'unnatural' phenomena that Ruskin critiqued included the railway, industrial pollution, litter, water reservoirs, cast or machine-made objects, industrial cities, suburban housing, plate glass, and so on (see Wheeler 1995).

Ruskin, though, stood out in his condemnation of the effects of the market. For most nineteenth-century commentators it was the market which was taken to be natural. As it and the associated division of labour were increasingly institutionalised in society, it became difficult both to criticise the mechanism which was identified as the creator of wealth, prosperity, profits and liberal democracy, and to devise a coherent alternative that did not entail the domination of nature (most socialist and Marxist alternatives equally implied the 'death of nature'). Indeed thanks to the utilitarians and late nineteenth-century neo-classical economics, the market itself and the associated division of labour rapidly came to be understood as 'natural'. The laws of the market were viewed as analogous to the laws of the natural world, and therefore not to be interfered with or contested. Williams argues:

> The new natural economic laws, the natural liberty of the entrepreneur to go ahead without interference, had its own projection of the market as the natural [sic] regulator. . . a remnant . . . of the more abstract ideas of social harmony, within which self-interest and the common interest might ideally coincide. (1972: 158)

This naturalising of the market strikingly showed how the restructuring of nature as 'natural science' was to cast its baleful influence over humanity and the social world. All kinds of inquiry became subject to the same search for natural laws.

The alternative conception of nature which did emerge in the nineteenth century, from the Romantic rather than the Enlightenment tradition, was more escapist than visionary (see Bate 1991; Williams 1972). Instead of efforts to reinvoke a morality and ethics within nature by thinking through new ways to rework nature *into* the social, nature sustained 'her' separation by departing from the predominant human sphere to the margins of modern industrial society. Nature was increasingly taken to exist on those margins, away from the centre of industrial society:

> Nature in any other sense than that of the improvers indeed fled to the margins: to the remote, the inaccessible, the relatively barren areas. Nature was where industry was not, and then in that real but limited sense had very little to say about the operations on nature that were proceeding elsewhere. (Williams 1972: 159)

In the eighteenth and nineteenth centuries in Europe one feature of nature that became especially valued was the sea, and especially its wild, untamed and immense quality; it seemed to be nature in a quite unmediated and directly sensed fashion (Corbin 1992). Nature was thus valued right at the margins of the civilised land, or perhaps where nature and civilisation came into direct and sustained contestation. And yet of course the sea too became subject to pretty rapid domestication and taming during the course of the nineteenth century. Piers and promenades, beaches and bungalows, swimsuits and swimming soon exerted the mastery of nature on the margins of society (see Shields 1991 on the beach as a marginal zone; and Sprawson 1992 on swimming). This was part of a general development in much of Europe to develop a much more managed conception of nature. In Britain it was exemplified in the campaigns by Wordsworth and later Ruskin to 'conserve' the Lake District and elsewhere, as places or enclaves distant and protected from science, industry and the operation of power (see chapter 6 below; Cannadine 1995 on the history of the National Trust in England, which has played an exemplary role in fostering such a managed nature; Wheeler 1995 on Ruskin).

In the USA many national parks were established, beginning with Yosemite in 1864. These were places where a particular conception of nature as managed wilderness was found. Thus the division between nature and society increasingly came to take a spatial form, with society in and at the centre and nature as the 'other' pushed out to the margins. And even at the margins there was increasing regulation and intervention so as to ensure that there was still a (managed) nature out there to sense (as will be discussed in chapter 4 below).

Seeing nature as the other, as on the margins of society, also relates to the ways in which nature is often presumed to be female (and God to be male). This we now know has been a characteristic conception, that nature has often been constructed as female, as a goddess or as a divine mother (see Yanagisako and Delaney 1995: 3). Further it often claimed that the taming of nature through the industrial economy, reason and science involves its 'mastery' and a form of domination analogous to how men master women, both directly and through the power of the 'look'. Implicit, then, in certain notions of nature have been male sexualised conceptions of the raping and pillaging of nature, akin to men's treatment of women. Central in many such accounts is the similar priority apparently given to the malevolent power of the visual sense (see chapter 4 below). Moreover, in some versions of eco-feminism it is claimed that women are in some sense more 'natural' and closer to 'nature' than are men; and this is particularly because of their role in childbirth and reproduction. It is also argued that women are often the 'guardians of biodiversity' since in developing countries they often know more about local farming practices, the soil, weather, and so on (Shiva 1988). Many feminist utopias have been built around an all-female society which lives at peace with itself and with the natural world (Merchant 1982; Plumwood 1993). Some of the discourses surrounding recent environmental politics have particularly emphasised the way that women 'naturally' will be more concerned to protect and conserve the environment, partly it is said because they will be more likely to take into account the interests of their children (and their children's children and so on; see Roseneil 1995 on the Greenham Common protest against cruise missiles). However, other recent theoretical formulations have criticised what can be seen as essentialist conceptions of men and women, society and nature (Haraway 1991).

It should also be noted that the history of nature further needs to account for how colonialism and racial oppression have also been premised upon a separate nature which is there to be exploited by and for the West (which in total now takes on the character of society). This nature has been seen to consist both of separate 'virgin' territories of often extraordinary natural abundance, and of peoples who are seen as more 'natural' as workers and later as objects of the colonising tourist gaze (Arnold 1996; Grove 1990; McClintock 1995; Shiva 1991, 1994). Plumwood neatly summarises the effects for social groups of thus being presumed to be natural, as located actually or imaginatively away from the centres of reason and science:

> To be defined as 'nature' . . . is to be defined as passive, as non-agent and non-subject, as the 'environment' or invisible background conditions against which the 'foreground' achievements of reason or culture . . . take place. It is to be defined as . . . a resource empty of its own purposes or meanings, and hence available to be annexed for the purposes of those supposedly identified with reason or intellect. (1993: 4)

The conclusion of this brief historical account is that there is no singular nature as such, only natures. And such natures are historically, geographically and socially constituted. Hence there are no simple natural limits as such. They are not fixed and eternal but depend on particular historical and geographical determinations, as well as on the very processes by which nature and the natural is culturally constructed and sustained, particularly by reference to what is taken to be the 'other' (see Arnold 1996: chap. 8 on the invention of 'Tropicality'). Moreover, once we acknowledge that ideas of nature both have been, and currently are, fundamentally intertwined with dominant ideas of society, we need to address what ideas of society and of its ordering become reproduced, legitimated, excluded, validated, and so on, through appeals to nature or the natural. And the project of determining what is a natural impact becomes as much a social and cultural project as it is 'purely' scientific.

We turn now to a brief account of some areas where we will develop analyses of nature and the environment in the succeeding chapters. These in part arise from how the 'social' and the 'natural' are being radically reconstructed in contemporary societies. In this we outline a tentative agenda for the social analysis of nature and the environment, focusing on four interrelated areas: a sociology of environmental knowledges; the cultural reading of 'natures'; environmental bads; and a more general account of the relationship between environmentalism and society.

A sociology of environmental knowledges

In many ways the current role ascribed for the social sciences presupposes a particularly modernist account of nature. Even though the planet is now largely acknowledged as having finite limits and thus no longer identified as offering endless bounty, scientific research programmes still operate under a number of highly modernist assumptions concerning the physicality of the world, its accessibility through scientific and rationalistic inquiry, and the fundamental separation of people and human culture from the physical environment. One implication of this agenda lies in the assumption, currently largely shared in social scientific accounts of the environment, that nature sets clear and measurable *limits* to what humans can achieve. The emphasis on absolute limits, typically defined by ecological science, has passed from the agenda of a few visionaries in the 1960s and 1970s into a commonly shared post-Rio agenda (see Newby 1990a; Redclift 1987, 1993, 1995; Yearley 1996). This is most apparent in current official moves and initiatives aimed at promoting sustainable development, including key inter-governmental documents whose primary aim is to identify ways to limit human activity so that economic and social development can proceed within the finite ecological capabilities of the planet (see, for example, CEC 1992b; IUCN 1980; LGMB 1993; UK Government 1994; UNCED 1992; WCED 1987). Such foci have been particularly organised around the identification, agreement and monitoring of a huge panoply of measurable indicators (see Macnaghten and Jacobs 1997; WWF and NEF 1994). In chapter 7 we examine how a global discourse of sustainability has recently come to organise the emerging environmental agenda, including the role ascribed to sustainability indicators. But what is most striking here is how all these approaches rest upon what we have termed the doctrine of environmental realism: that the realm of nature is separate and distinct from that of culture. In the rest of the book we seek to counter such a thesis.

There are various ways in which this doctrine can be seen to be misleading. First, it ignores the way in which nature should not be viewed as simply setting limits, as subjecting humans to constraint. In other words, nature can be not only constraining but also enabling. The enabling aspects are perhaps most visible when one conceives of nature as the lifeworld in which the social life takes place, rather than simply as a set of finite physical resources available for human exploitation. In chapter 2 we see how the popular appeal to ecology and the environment arose only occasionally through the direct findings of scientific inquiry. By contrast, we examine how public concern about and engagement in environmental issues resulted from specific contestations about instances of nature (involving government bodies, the media and the increasingly potent environmental groups) which came to symbolise a wider unease with the modern world. We will also examine how such concern has reflected aspirations for more meaningful collective engagement and moral renewal and thus a different basis to society, often in marked opposition to the spread of market-based doctrines and their associated model of instrumental human relations (doctrine 3). 'Nature' is not then something that only has to be tamed or 'mastered', or something that is necessarily at odds with human endeavour.

Indeed, to reify such an emphasis on limits, implemented with a series of don'ts, or do less, can promote the belief that environmental responsibility is something that is ultimately restrictive and disciplinary, a matter of Fou-cauldian normalisation. In chapter 6 we examine the ways in which the emerging environmental policy agenda in the English countryside is asso-ciated with a paradoxical increase in the disciplinary regulation of visitors (such as the 'Country Code'). Moreover, by defining limits in terms of physical quantities, the political focus lies in achieving commitments to limit economic behaviours, as opposed to the more fundamental questions con-cerning the very relationship between the natural and the social upon which current economic behaviour resides. Dickens (1991, 1996) has usefully set out how such disciplinary relations (such as ones which do not allow the realisation of intrinsic human potentialities) can be seen as a product of living in late capitalist societies, societies in which human/nature relations become commodified, abstracted by the division of labour, alienated from the sphere of productive labour, and how this forecloses possibilities for emancipation (see also Bookchin 1980 for a sustained critique of the notion of hierarchy in human society). In a parallel fashion we too seek to reconfigure nature/social relations. Instead of identifying current 'environmental knowledges' as setting the parameters for social action, we seek to explore the social origins involved in the production of such knowledges and their impacts in shaping the diverse subsequent debates.

Some of the implications of this can also be seen in relationship to risk (Royal Society 1992). Traditionally the role of the social scientist in public risk perceptions has been in developing techniques that purport to quantify public risk perceptions, in the face of what are taken to be objective accounts of the real risks of particular dangerous or hazardous technologies (nuclear technologies being perhaps the prime example). However, a more explicitly sociological approach is emerging, critical both of the methodologies (such as cost–benefit analysis, decision analysis and mathematical risk analysis) which are used to determine risk perceptions, and of the value-laden judgements upon which they rest.

An early challenge was proposed by Douglas (1966, 1985, 1990, 1992; Douglas and Wildavsky 1982). Douglas argues that individual risk perceptions need to be situated culturally in a network of social and institutional relationships which set concrete constraints and obligations to social behaviour. Risks are to be understood as inscribed in forms of life. All risks are primarily social constructionisms. They are a question of 'purity and danger' in which something is out of place and someone is to blame. Such risks are then analysed in terms of Douglas' categories of grid and group. Her typology aims to capture four idealised ways in which people conceive of their involvement and incorporation in society. Group refers to people's sense of their group solidarity; grid to their sense of control over their own lives. Schwarz and Thomson (1990) have recently used cultural theory in the realm of environmental change, arguing that perceptions of environmental risk depend on the moral commitment of particular communities to particular 'myths of nature' (also see Adams 1995; Harrison and Burgess 1994; Thomson et al. 1990). Four primary myths of nature are then mapped onto the grid–group typology, each representing a distinct cultural filter through which people make sense of the same environmental information. Thus Schwarz and Thomson propose that egalitarians support a view of 'nature ephemeral', hierarchists one of 'nature perverse', individualists one of 'nature benign', and fatalists one of 'nature capricious'. However, this analysis of risk has been criticised as being essentialist, oversimplifying more complex shades of social difference, and ignoring the more general causes of the growth of risk lying at the very centre of contemporary societies (see Johnson 1987; Lash 1995; Shackley et al. 1996).

A less deterministic framework for exploring the social framing of risk perceptions has been developed by Wynne (1982, 1989, 1992a) and Jasanoff (1987). They argue that we have to take into account the wider social and cultural dimensions articulated in people's concerns about risk. Focusing on the assumptions which experts make in setting the framework for the evaluation and assessment of risk, such as trust, ambivalence and uncertainty, Wynne (1992b) argues that these often radically conflict with the views of the lay public and that therefore the so-called experts misunderstand how people actually relate to their risk-laden environments. Public assessments of risk essentially involve judgements about the behaviour and trustworthiness of expert institutions, especially of those that are meant to be controlling the risky processes involved. Thus risks are what he terms 'social relational', and involve judgements of the quality of institutions and of one's relationship to such institutions. Such a view also emphasises that the lay public do not simply respond to risks and assessments of risks which are simply 'out there'. The responses of the public are partly generated by the very threats to their identity which arise from the inadequate conception of the human which is deployed within and by the objectivist or expert science which is supposedly there protecting the public against such risks (Wynne 1996a). We return to this issue in chapter 3 below and provide new empirical material on risk perceptions to illuminate such an approach in chapter 7.

Wynne (1996a) develops a further point here, namely, that in much discussion of risk there is a diminished view of the fluidity and constructed character of the boundaries between objective science and lay knowledge. What counts as authoritative scientific knowledge is, to a considerable degree, a product of active processes of interaction and negotiation between scientists and policy makers. For example, models of global climate change, central to international policy responses to threats of global warming, implicitly rely on questionable assumptions about human, institutional and market behaviour (see Shackley and Wynne 1995b). Yearley (1996: chap. 4) also examines the negotiations between supposedly universal discourses of science and the formation of policy in the fields of ozone depletion, global warming, biodiversity and sustainable development (see also Waterton et al. 1995). He suggests that in different ways standardising discourses of science can actually conceal unwarranted political assumptions, ignore local and cultural difference, and at times mask self-interest, especially for the benefit of the North (see also Agarwal and Narain 1991).

It is also possible to show that on occasions the analysis of 'local knowledges and practices' can challenge the explanatory power of the technical and natural sciences rather more generally. Such sciences often rest upon social assumptions which in the 'real world' mean that the predictions of the theory derived from the laboratory do not always work out in particular 'lived' circumstances. The laboratory is after all a very particular social and natural setting and the lay public may be better informed about the scientific understandings which will apply in their place of work or residence (see Latour and Woolgar 1986 on the laboratory). They may be in that sense better scientists.

This point is well shown in the case of the effects of the fallout from Chernobyl on sheep farming in the English Lake District. Wynne summarises:

> Although the farmers accepted the need for restrictions, they could not accept the experts' apparent ignorance of their approach on the normally flexible and informal system of hill farm management. The experts assumed that scientific knowledge could be applied to hill farming without adjusting to local circumstances . . . Experts were ignorant of the realities of farming and neglected local knowledge. (1991: 45; see also Wynne 1996a)

What this shows is the importance of identifying and analysing social practices, often in some sense based on local knowledges, which mediate forms of scientific knowledge. It is clear that implicit in western models of science is a process of standardisation, which almost certainly means that scientists will ignore the particular local conditions and the forms of local knowledge which are relevant to the appropriate assessments of risk.

Developing categories of analysis to make sense of such localised social practices and forms of knowledge is a key task of this book (see especially chapters 4 and 5 below). Such an endeavour also forces us to reflect further about appropriate methods of research (see chapter 3 below).

Cultural readings of natures

We begin here by noting that the social and cultural sciences can help to illuminate the socially varied ways in which an environment can be seen, interpreted and evaluated. What is viewed and criticised as unnatural or environmentally damaging in one era or one society is not necessarily viewed as such in another. The rows of terraced housing thrown up during nineteenth-century capitalist industrialisation in Britain are now viewed not as an environmental eyesore, but as quaint, traditional and harbouring patterns of human activity well worth preserving. The shifts in reading are even more remarkable in the case of the steam engine in Britain, whose belching smoke is now almost universally viewed as natural, as almost part of the environment. More generally there has been a striking shift in how the railway is viewed (see Richards 1995). Some 'man-made' features become 'naturalised', as almost part of nature, and would be very hard to demolish (plate 1.1). The reading and production of nature is something that is learnt. It is a cultural process and varies greatly between different societies, different periods and different social groupings within any society (see Barnes and Duncan 1992).

Furthermore, it is necessary to analyse and understand the complex social processes which give rise to certain issues being taken collectively as 'environmental'. We argue against the first and third doctrines outlined at

Plate 1.1   *View of Ribblehead Viaduct, Yorkshire Dales National Park: man-made objects becoming part of nature (source: John Urry)*

the beginning of this chapter in which it is assumed that environmental issues progressively come to light via the extension of scientific under-standings into the state of the environment. Rather it is necessary to identify the social and cultural context out of which environmental understandings are sensed and articulated *and* are seen as collectively 'environmental' (this is well shown in the case of various nineteenth-century environmental controversies in Wheeler 1995; see also Hajer 1995 for a social contructivist account of the 1980s acid rain controversy in the UK and the Nether-lands).

The social and political threads of contemporary environmentalism are complex and we will only consider here a couple of points. Contemporary environmentalism is linked both to the emergence of various other social movements, and to certain processes of globalisation (see Eyerman and Jamison 1991; Lash and Urry 1994; Melucci 1989). Theorists have argued that environmentalism is a new field of struggle against the 'self-defeating process of modernization' (Eder 1990, 1996). Environmentalism thus appears to stem from an emerging critique of a globally planned society, something initially reflected in the counter-culture of the 1960s which led into various other social movements as well as links to the 'enterprise culture' of the 1980s. But something else is involved here. Grove-White (1991a) argues that the very symbols and concepts that currently constitute the environmental agenda involve a process of active construction by environmental groups in the 1970s and 1980s, in response to rather more general concerns about the character of contemporary society. Using the examples in Britain of motorways, nuclear power, agriculture and conservation, Grove-White argues that the particular forms of environmental protest were related as much to widespread public unease with a highly technocratic and unresponsive political culture, as with any specific evaluation of the precise threats to the health of the physical, non-human environment. This argument is examined in some detail in chapter 2 below, in relation to the 'invention' and discursive construction of the contemporary environmental agenda in the UK.

So the environment as a problem came to be created or 'invented' through issues and politics which were apparently not directly concerned with a single unambiguous environment as such. Szerszynski (1993) notes that two preconditions had therefore to develop. First, it was necessary that a range of empirical phenomena came to be regarded as environmental *problems* rather than as simply demonstrating environmental change. So motorways or nuclear power had to be viewed as novel and disruptive, and not merely as further changes which were in a sense 'naturally' part of the modern project (as much fossil fuel energy continued to be so regarded; Szerszynski 1993: 4). And second, there had to be gathering up of a whole series of issues so that they became viewed as part of an overarching environmental crisis, in which a striking array of different problems and issues come to be regarded as part of 'the environment' and subject to similar threats (also see Porritt 1984; Rubin 1989). In chapter 2 we examine the ways in which movements emerge at particular defining moments which are almost always constructed through certain key images and signs. Such key symbolic moments in the UK include the 1976 Windscale inquiry on nuclear reprocessing, the 1981 Wildlife and Countryside Act, Margaret Thatcher's speech to the Royal Society in 1988, and the 1992 direct action protests over the building of the M3 at Twyford Down.

It will also be necessary to analyse those more widespread social practices that facilitate the reading of the physical world as environmentally damaged. This is particularly the focus of chapter 4, when we consider how different senses combine together to generate different 'natures' and different forms in which the environment appears to be 'polluted'. We consider especially the social practices of travel, since on occasions they provide people with the cultural capital to compare and evaluate different environments and to develop that sense of what is 'natural' and hence what appears to be environmentally damaged. It may have been the lack of travel in what was 'Eastern Europe' which partly explains the apparent blindness to the many kinds of environmental damage that we now know were occurring throughout the region. Other social processes which may be contributing to an emerging sense of the environment under threat include the widespread distrust of science and technology, and the perceived lack of agency of individuals when confronted with large-scale (often global) organisations operating within contemporary societies. This last point is to be examined in some detail in chapter 7, where we analyse how ordinary people talk about, value and make sense of nature in daily life, and how people's sense of their engagement in and responsibility towards nature is mediated by their longer-standing trust relations with public institutions.

Interestingly, though, while environmentalism can be seen as mostly in contradiction with modernity, there are other aspects of the latter which have facilitated a greater environmental sensibility, especially to the reading of nature as increasingly global. Thus, the emergence of global institutions such as the United Nations and the World Bank, the globalising of environmental groups such as the World Wildlife Fund, Greenpeace and Friends of the Earth, and the emergence of global media conglomerates have all helped to foster something of a new global identity in which environmental processes are increasingly identified as global and planetary. However, we will go on to consider whether these processes are really more global than many previous environmental crises which have tended to be seen as local or national. And although we will see that the 'global' in global environmental change is partially a political and cultural construction (see Wynne 1994), we also examine in chapter 7 the multiple senses of the global through which people comprehend their involvement in environmental change.

We thus take for granted that strictly speaking there is no such thing as nature, only natures. Such different natures both derive from and provide resources for various kinds of contestation over and objections to trans-formations of the 'natural'. Recently Szerszynski (1993) elaborated two distinctive ways in which nature has been conceptualised (and see Dickens 1992 for some mass observation data). First, there is the notion of nature as threatened. This sense can be seen in a variety of forms: in the panics over rare and endangered species, especially those which are spectacular and aesthetically pleasing; in the perception of nature as a set of exhaustible resources which should be stewarded for future generations; in the sense of nature as a collection of rights-bearing subjects, especially animals but also some plants (Benton 1993; Porritt 1984); and in the notion of nature as a healthy and pure body under threat from pollution, a nature which, according to Carson (1962), is fast becoming a 'sea of carcinogens' (see Szerszynski 1993: 19–20; also see chapter 2 below).

The second set of representations of nature construct it as an expressive realm of purity and moral power, to be enjoyed or worshipped. Nature may be seen as having sacred properties. There are again a number of alternative forms taken: nature as an object of spectacle, beauty or the sublime; as a recreational space to be roamed across; as a state of pre-social abundance and goodness reflected in the notion of 'natural' healing (see Coward 1989; Stacey 1997); as representing a return from alienating modern society to an organic community; and as a holistic ecosystem which should be preserved in its diversity and interdependence, as in the notion of Gaia (Lovelock 1988).

Both these conceptualisations of nature have of course long and turbulent histories (see Pepper 1984, 1996; Worster 1985). They also provide cultural

resources for the development of the contemporary environmental movement, although we have also argued that they could only function in this way
when the 'environment' as such had been discovered. Moreover, different
notions of nature have fed into different responses to perceived threats to
such natures. Hays (1959) notes the differences of approach in the early US
conservation movement between scientific experts, 'apostles of efficiency',
and wilderness-seeking urbanites (see. Hajer 1996). The former group saw
nature as a resource which needed to be developed in the name of efficiency
and thus they had little sympathy for a sentimental conception of the
American wilderness. But it was this very wilderness which American city-
dwellers increasingly regarded as the iconic demonstration of the moral
superiority of nature to the industrial and urban form. The progressivists
wanted to develop nature; the urbanites to preserve it. As Hays makes clear,
the former, under the rhetoric of conservation, succeeded in transforming
nature through a comprehensive scheme of 'scientific resource management'. Thus in that, as in later periods, there is no simple 'environmentalism', but rather a coalition of groups and discourses with contrasting
interests (see also Burningham and O'Brien 1994). There is no nature simply
waiting to be conserved, but, rather all forms of its conservation entail
judgements as to what indeed is nature (see Kwa 1987; Macnaghten et al.
1992; Milton 1993b; Olwig 1989; Toogood 1995). Later we shall consider
the particular contemporary progressivist take on conservation, namely
'ecological modernisation' and its claims that society can and should
modernise itself out of the environmental crisis and hence bring about a new
round of economic investment in clean technologies, environmentally sound
insulation, new tram systems, and so on (Hajer 1996).
 Many of the 'natures' which were especially threatened or indeed treasured were initially conceptualised within the context of each nation-state.
Arguments for conservation, preservation, recreation, and so on, were
couched in terms of national resources that could be planned and managed.
Again contemporary environmentalism has had to 'invent' the entire globe
or the one earth, which in its entirety is seen as under threat, or alternatively
through a oneness with nature which is viewed as a moral source. We will
consider whether it has been the modernist processes of globalisation which
have laid the structural conditions for the emergence of this 'global'
discourse around nature, or whether the viewing of the environment as
subject to 'global' threats is much more the product of discursive shifts
effected by movement intellectuals employing ideas and images, such as the
blue earth, which are increasingly mobile in the global 'economy of signs'
(see chapter 8 below; as well as Lash and Urry 1994; Szerszynski 1993:
chap. 1).

Environmental bads

A further way in which the analysis of social practices can contribute to the
understanding of environmental processes lies in describing the social

processes which currently produce what comes to be recognised as environmental damage. Many of these social processes are currently theorised in the social sciences, but rarely in terms of their environmental implications (examples include consumerism, tourism and globalisation). Almost all 'environmental' problems result from particular social patterns which are associated with the doctrine of human exceptionalism and the long-established division between 'nature' and 'society' discussed above.

Consumerism is a particularly significant social pattern here. It is reasonably well established that there has been something of a shift in the structuring of contemporary societies such that aspects of the pattern of mass production and mass consumption have been transformed. This is not to suggest that all economic activity was once 'Fordist' – much service industry was not – nor that there are not very significant elements of 'Fordist' production today. However, what are important are four structural shifts in the significance and nature of consumption: first, a huge increase in the range of goods and services which are currently available, as markets and tastes have been significantly internationalised; second, the increasing semiotisation of products so that sign- rather than use-value becomes the key element in consumption; third, the breaking down of some 'traditionalised' institutions and structures so that consumer tastes become more fluid and open; and, fourth, the increasing importance of consumption patterns to the forming of identity and hence some shift from producer power to consumer power (Lash and Urry 1994; Lury 1996; see the sceptical comments in Warde 1994).

Bauman's analysis is relevant here. He argues that:

> in present day society, consumer conduct (consumer freedom geared to the consumer market) moves steadily into the position of, simultaneously, the cognitive and moral focus of life, the integrative bond of the society. . . . In other words, it moves into the self-same position which in the past – during the 'modern' phase of capitalist society – was occupied by work. (1992: 49)

And as such the pleasure principle becomes dominant. Pleasure seeking is a duty since the consumption of goods and services becomes the structural basis of western societies (see also Lury 1996). Social integration thus takes place less through the principles of normalisation, confinement and disciplinary power, as described by Foucault or indeed by Bauman (1989) in the case of the Holocaust. Instead it takes place through the 'seduction' of the market-place, through the mix of feeling and emotions generated by seeing, holding, hearing, testing, smelling, and moving through the extraordinary array of goods and services, places and environments that characterise contemporary consumerism organised around a particular 'culture of nature' (see Wilson 1992). This contemporary consumerism for the affluent two-thirds in the major western countries entails the rapid churning of demand for different products, services and places. Contemporary markets thrive on change, variety and diversity, on the undermining of tradition and uniformity, on products, services and places going out of fashion almost as quickly as they come into fashion.

There is of course little doubt that some of these patterns of contemporary consumerism have had disastrous consequences for the environment. This is reflected in holes in the ozone layer, global warming, acid rain, nuclear power accidents and the destruction of many local environments. Taken to its extreme, consumerism can also involve obtaining or purchasing new parts for the human body, a process which undermines a clear sense of the natural body inside as opposed to the unnatural body outside (see Strathern 1992).

Such western consumerism in which 'nature seems turned into a mere artefact of consumer choice' has been extensively critiqued by the environmental movement (Devall and Sessions 1985; Irvine and Pontin 1988; McKibben 1990; Porritt 1984; Porritt and Winner 1988). And this in turn can be seen as part of the wider critique of modernity itself (Strathern 1992: 197). But there is a further paradox here. This is that the very development of consumerism has itself helped to generate the current critique of environmental degradation and the cultural focus upon nature. Environmentalism might be represented as presupposing a certain kind of consumerism. This is because one element of consumerism is a heightened reflexivity about the places and environments, the goods and services that are 'consumed', literally, through a social encounter, or through visual consumption (see Urry 1995b). As people reflect upon such consumption they develop not only a duty to consume but also certain rights, including the rights of the citizen as a consumer. Such rights include the belief that people are entitled to certain qualities of the environment, of air, water, sound and scenery, and that these should extend into the future and to other populations. Contemporary western societies have begun to shift the basis of citizenship from political rights to consumer rights, and within the bundle of the latter, environmental rights, especially linked to conceptions of nature as spectacle and recreation, are increasingly significant. Some such rights also come to be seen as international since with mass tourism people in the West are increasingly consumers of environments outside their own national territory, and as such develop systematic expectations of such environments and of the quality of air, water, scenery, and so on. Indeed part of the imposition of such expectations about a non-polluted environment is a contemporary form of economic and cultural imperialism (the contradictions in all of this are well shown in the journal *Tourism in Focus*). We examine in chapter 2 below the effects of a recent cross-European consumer boycott in relation to the *Brent Spar* controversy, and in chapter 8 we assess further the political implications of a new and embryonic ethical consumer movement, as part of cosmopolitan civil society.

Such reflexivity in the field of consumption is clearly connected to recent institutional developments, including what has been characterised as the emergent 'audit society' (Power 1994) in which organisations have to justify their accountability to the public (and to consumers) through an explosion of audits, especially in the public sector. Power has raised doubts as to whether such audits, typically in the form of quantifiable, economistic measures, actually result in more accountable forms of governance. Another related

arena for such institutional reflexivity is through the commissioning by
formal organisations of increasing quantities of surveys and polls designed
to ascertain what people really think and feel about the environment. Here
again, as we analyse in chapter 3 below, the answers revealed through such
a 'polling culture' are both partial and problematic.

However, the processes of intensification involved in commodifying
almost all aspects of social life have at the same time produced a corresponding intensification of non-market forms of behaviour and social
relations building on impulses of perhaps a more 'classical' human kind
(such as people trying to lead relatively altruistic, unselfish lives, operating
in more relational, interdependent non-market behaviours).The result is an
emerging set of tensions between conflicting market and non-market ration-
alities (see Berking 1996; MacIntyre 1985; Marquand 1988). Indeed, in
extreme forms, these social critiques of consumer-oriented society have led
to new forms of social organisation (in contrast to the consumer-oriented
groups as outlined above), whose social identity lies in explicit tension with
consumer principles – a point which will be expanded in the following
section on new social responses. These new social movements, often formed
as a response to perceived threats of environmental abuse (such as 'hunt
saboteurs', 'animal rights' groups, 'Earth First!' actions, and other direct
action groups), and having moved outside the legitimate sphere of state
regulated consumer-orientated action, are currently experiencing more overt
repression (such as the UK's Criminal Justice Act, specifically targeted at
these 'problem' groups). We examine these groupings as cultural forms of
environmental protest in chapter 2 below. A future topic for research is what
one might call the causes and consequences of 'environmental deviance'.

Environmentalism and society

In this final section we try to identify the role that the environmental agenda
is playing in the structural formation and cultural transformation of contemporary societies. First and most obviously, environmentalism has hugely
figured in current debates about the risk society and reflexivity. Giddens, for
example, argues that in modernity reflexivity consists of social practices
being constantly examined and reformed in the light of incoming information received about those very practices, thus altering their constitution. He
says that 'only in the era of modernity is the revision of convention
radicalised to apply (in principle) to all aspects of human life, including
technological intervention into the material world' (1990: 38–9). This
reflexivity is leading the methods of western science, the embodiment of
modernity, to be constructed as no more legitimate an activity than many
other social activities, each of which involves different forms of judgement.
Science is not viewed as having a necessarily civilising, progressive and
emancipatory role in revealing what nature is like. In many cases science
and its associated technologies are seen as the problem and not the solution.
This is especially the case where there are in effect massive and uncontrolled

scientific experiments which treat the entire globe (or a fair part of it) as its laboratory (as with toxic waste, agro-chemicals, nuclear power, and so on). In the risk society science is seen as producing most of the risks, although these are largely invisible to our senses (see Adam 1995a; Beck 1992b; chapter 4 below). This is also explored in chapter 8 below in relation to the UK Government's appeals to 'good science' in the BSE (or 'mad cow disease') controversy.

At the same time, science's loss of automatic social authority weakens the legitimacy even of the environmental (and medical) 'sciences'. The very identification of risk depends upon such science because of the 'disempowerment of the senses' that chemical and nuclear contamination produce (Beck 1987: 156; Douglas and Wildavsky 1982; and chapter 4 below on 'sensing nature'). This in turn causes problems for the green movement since such sciences have become central to many of the campaigns conducted by environmental NGOs, even though NGOs have hitherto tended to make tactical use of science in environmental campaigning, perhaps instinctively focusing on the indeterminacy and softness inherent in particular sciences (see Wynne and Mayer 1993; Yearley 1991).

These dynamics suggest that the processes mentioned above are to be viewed as much wider symptoms of the cultural processes of individualisation and detraditionalisation (see Beck 1992b, 1993; Giddens 1990; Heelas et al. 1996; Lash and Urry 1994). It is argued that such processes are leading to the emergence of less institutionalised forms of identity and social arrangement. Institutions such as science, the church, the monarchy, the nuclear family and formal structures of government are appearing to be delegitimated, and increasingly seen as part of the problem rather than the solution. Such processes have led to new, looser forms of social arrangement, including the development of new social movements or, what we prefer, 'new sociations' (see Clark et al. 1994a). Indeed, the emergence of a new sphere of the political in the form of looser, non-party-based and self-organising affiliations and associations, often in the form of self-help groups, community groups and voluntary organisations, link to what Beck (1993) has described as a new dynamic of 'sub-politicalization', whereby the state is confronted by an increasingly diverse and heterogeneous array of groups and minority sociations.

There are a number of characteristics of such sociations (Hetherington 1993; Urry 1995b). First, they are not like those of traditional communities since they are joined out of choice and people are free to leave. Second, people remain members in part because of the emotional satisfaction that they derive from common goals or shared social experiences. And third, since membership is from choice, many people will enter and leave such sociations with considerable rapidity. These characteristics effectively locate sociations as contemporary sites whereby new kinds of social identity can be experimented with. They may empower people, providing relatively safe places for identity-testing and the context for the learning of new skills. Such new detraditionalised sociations can be classified as to the degree of decentralisation of power from the centre, the degree of formal specification of the organisational structure, the level and forms of participation at the local level, the types of action entered into by the membership, and the degree to which the membership is reflexive about the organisation. We consider below in chapters 2 and 8 the significance of this new style of social organisation; the extent of its political impact in contributing to a new realm of the political; and its implications for current research on environmentalism as a so-called 'new social movement'. The emergence of new sociations in the sphere of the environment suggests that particular forms of social identity are emerging which imply the breaking down of the relatively separate spheres of society and nature, and in forming a kind of reconstituted civil society (Eder 1996; Jacques 1994; and see Dickens 1992: chap. 7 for some mass observation material on the processes of becoming 'green').

There are, moreover, some interesting and unexpected connections between such new sociations and what we discussed earlier, namely, the perception of the environmental crisis as global. Evidence for the global and holistic view of nature can be seen in the array of inter-governmental and governmental conventions, treaties and documents arising from the current focus on sustainability. Examples which have helped to foster the idea of a 'global' nature include the WWF-inspired *World Conservation Strategy* (IUCN 1980), the UNCED Brundtland Report *Our Common Future* (WCED 1987), the Rio-inspired UNCED *Agenda 21* (UNCED 1992) and the EU's *Fifth Environmental Action Programme for the Environment and Sustainable Development* (CEC 1992b). The Brundtland Report talks of 'our common future', partly because of the apparently global character of certain of the threats posed to nature, beginning with the nuclear threat. This global perception has been assisted by the development of global mass media which has generated an imagined community of all societies which appear to inhabit 'one earth' (hence of course Friends of the Earth). In chapters 7 and 8 we further differentiate the appeals to global environmental citizenship, and demarcate how especially younger people may now be appealing to a 'moral' global identity in contradistinction to more technical and detached global identities prevalent in official literatures. However, alongside this astonishing array of globalising processes lies a new set of concerns with culturally situated local environments (such as the Common Ground approach to environmentalism). There are an extraordinary range of local concerns around which mobilisation can occur: examples in the north of England include efforts to conserve a slag heap in Lancashire, a campaign to prevent the painting of yellow lines on some of the roads in Buttermere in the English Lake District, and intense opposition to the resiting of a burnt-down market in Lancaster.

Thus there are multiple environmental identities, the local as well as the global; the rationalistic as well as the expressive; landscape-oriented as well as use-oriented, and so on (for much more detail, see Szerszynski 1993). And further, these multiple identities appear to be of increasing salience in post-modern societies. We examine in chapter 7 below the apparently increasing significance of these diverse 'environmental identities' in contemporary societies, identities which often entail a complex intermingling of global and local concerns. For the present we can just note some statistical evidence for the importance of such environmental identities from the huge increases experienced across nearly all environmental organisations in the 1980s and 1990s. Mid-1996 UK membership of the more recognised environmental organisations include Greenpeace with 400,000 supporters, Friends of the Earth with 250,000 members, the National Trust with over 2,400,000 members, the RSPB with over 925,000 members, and the Royal Society for Nature Conservation with over 260,000 members.

Conclusion

We have thus set out some of the tasks of our approach to nature and the environment. It is a complex agenda which embraces questions of culture, political economy, the state, gender, science, new sociations, the 'other'. And in particular the reassessment of nature will throw particular light on the topics of time and space which have so much entered recent social scientific debate. Adam (1990) has powerfully demonstrated the unsustainability of the conventional distinction between natural time and social time. It is a commonplace to say that social time involves change, progress and decay, while natural phenomena are either timeless or can operate with a conception of reversible time. But the innovations of twentieth-century science have rendered the distinction between natural and social time as invalid and lead us yet again to conclude that there is no simple and sustainable distinction between nature and society. They are ineluctably intertwined. There are therefore many different times (as indeed there are different spaces) and it is not possible to identify an unambiguous social time separate from natural time (see chapter 5 below).

This relates to our more general project: to demonstrate the variety of 'natures'. Strathern (1992) points out a significant paradox about such contemporary developments. It is clear that in most western societies there is a greatly enhanced focus being placed upon the importance of nature and valuing the natural; upon purchasing natural products (and even natural products made more 'natural' such as decaffeinated coffee); upon employing images of the 'natural' in marketing products, policies and organisations; and upon joining and supporting organisations concerned with the conservation of nature. She summarises:

> With the elision between nature and biology, bodily functions have long been regarded as the special province of nature; what is new is the scale on which a natural style to certain aspects of living is presented as consumer choice. Indeed, the duty of the consumer to purchase is reinforced in the idea . . . that one is helping the environment by buying particular products. (Strathern 1992: 173)

But Strathern argues all these emphases upon nature are fundamentally mediated by cultural processes. In other words, culture has been necessary to rescue nature. Strathern argues that this produces 'the conceptual collapse of the differences between nature and culture when Nature cannot survive without Cultural intervention' (1992: 174). Therefore, if it needs culture for its nurturance, so to speak, is there any 'real' nature left? In the past the strength of nature lay in the way in which its cultural construction was in fact hidden from view (see Latour 1993 for such an account). But in the contemporary world of uncertainty and reflexive modernity, this no longer seems to be true. A major task for the social sciences will be to decipher the social implications of what has always been the case, namely, a nature elaborately entangled and fundamentally bound up with social practices and their characteristic modes of cultural representation (see Beck 1996b). A bold and convincing attempt to dissolve the nature/social divide recently has been provided by Ingold (1996) in which he sets out a framework where embodied human relations can be re-embedded within the continuum of organic life.

There are a number of conclusions that follow on from this. First, if there is no longer a nature which is somehow wholly bounded and separate from culture, then the sciences of nature no longer possess a distinct subject-matter with clear and convincingly policed boundaries. And partly because of this an alternative term for the subject-matter of certain of such sciences has developed over the past few decades, namely, the 'environment'. This term involves a particular way of representing space as sets of observable and measurable dimensions and forces. It has come to be widely used as nature and culture dissolve into one another. The 'environmental sciences' themselves date from the 1960s (see Jamison 1996; Worster 1985). Rather more generally, Haraway has dramatically shown this undermining of the subject-matter of biology; she says that the 'dichotomies between mind and body, animal and human, organism and machine, public and private, nature and culture, men and women, primitive and civilized are all in question ideologically' (1991: 163). In particular the social relations of science and technology are 'recrafting our bodies' as communication sciences and modern biologies are transforming the world into coded information (Haraway 1991: 164). And that information is subject to extraordinary levels of miniaturization which further dissolve the distinctiveness of humans and their biologies since they can now be implanted with new or corrected information, or use 'machines' which are extensions of themselves. In such a cyborg-world the 'machines' become increasingly smart and display some of the characteristics of what have been historically thought of as human (Haraway 1991; as with the computer virus, Strathern 1992: 198).

Second, if nature is no longer viewable as simply 'natural' but is socially and culturally constructed, then nature does not and cannot provide, as has often been argued, the simple and unmediated ethical or moral foundation for the good life. This undermining of an ethics of a singular nature results from the following processes: the realisation that there are many 'natures' and not just one; the complex interconnections between human and material practice so that it is hard to attribute moral value to Haraway's cyborgs

(1991); the undermining of the authority of the privileged arbiters of nature, the scientists, as well as those concerned with aesthetic value rather than media popularity; and the transforming of nature into style and therefore into something that is endlessly copyable and where intellectual property may be invested in the sign rather than in material nature (see Lury 1993).

Third, the 'social' itself is not unchanging since a variety of apparently globalising processes have recently come to the fore. These include the astonishing transformations of finance and money markets in which more foreign exchange changes in a day than goods are traded in a year; new forms of global culture including satellite technologies and new massive media conglomerates which 'collapse space and time' (Brunn and Leinbach 1990); the development of international travel and of 'small worlds' little connected to nation-state relationships; the increasing numbers of international agencies and institutions; the development of global competitions and prizes; the emergence of a small number of languages of communication, most notably English; the development of more widely shared notions of citizenship and of political democracy; and the proliferation of environmental 'bads' that appear to know no national frontiers (see Appadurai 1990; Lash and Urry 1994; but see Arnold 1996: chaps 4 and 5, on the fourteenth-century Black Death brought about by trans-oceanic exchanges causing 'bacteriological genocide').

These flows transform the nature of the 'social', which shifts from being principally composed of 'national social structures' to consisting of putatively globalising information and communicational flows. Such global flows criss-cross national borders, disrupting the organised coherence of individual national societies. Such flows exhibit spatial unevenness and temporal diversity, as we examine in chapters 5 and 8. Beck (1996b) describes this as a world risk society.

Fourth, this means that nature becomes less intertwined with each individual national society, with a national 'community of fate', and is much more interdependent with these putatively global relations, including the extraordinary range of informational and communicational structures that criss-cross the globe in ever-more elaborate and 'unnatural' shapes, evading certain constraints of time and space, but not necessarily generating cultural homogenisation. This is why we may increasingly live not in a risk *society*, which implies the fixities of institution and social order, but rather in an indeterminant, ambivalent and semiotic risk *culture* where the risks are in part generated by the declining powers of the nation-state in the face of multitudinous global flows (Giddens 1995; Lash 1995).

It is the implications of these conclusions that we explore in depth in the following chapters, beginning with the very idea of the 'environment' itself.

2

INVENTING NATURE

In the previous chapter we argued against the doctrine of environmental realism, in particular claiming that the 'environment' does not simply exist out there but had to be in a sense 'invented'. There is no simple linear process which would inevitably culminate in contemporary environmentalism. In this chapter we examine this complex and uneven invention of the 'environment', of how nature became the 'environment'. We detail the main events which have discursively constituted the contemporary environmental agenda. We consider this new agenda and analyse how this has been driven, not only by the emergent findings of science and by various processes in which the healthy body appears to be invaded by environmental bads, but by wider cultural and political developments. We examine just what processes led contemporary environmentalism to be constituted as a major public preoccupation, and the respective role played in this by various states (local, national and international), by the media (increasingly global and deploying global imagery), by the huge plethora of environmental groups (increasingly media-wise and inflected by their own 'enterprise culture'), and by more general cultural transformations (reflected through notions of risk, globalisation, reflexivity, detraditionalisation and post-modernisation).

We examine the recent post-war historical evolution of environmental issues and concerns. Our examination of the dynamics of contemporary environmentalism will principally focus on Britain but briefly takes into account the emergence of ideas, events and movements in the USA and Western Europe. The focus on Britain is mainly because it has the 'oldest, strongest, best-organised and most widely supported environmental lobby in the world' (McCormick 1991a: 34). We will note how the historical development of environmental issues and ideas in Britain is broadly representative of other western democracies, but we will show too how the permeation of environmental ideas into British institutional life took place in culturally distinctive forms. However, by contrast with most contemporary historical accounts, our account will focus more on the symbolic, invented and produced dimensions that contributed towards the emergence of contemporary environmentalism out of preceding conceptions of nature (see Bramwell 1989, 1994; McCormick 1991a, 1995; Pepper 1996).

In this chapter we differentiate the history of the invention of contemporary environmentalism into four phases of development, each of which corresponds to a broadly distinctive characterisation of nature and its relationship to modernity. The first phase focuses on post-war concern with nature up until the late 1960s, although we also take into account past traditions, and the dominant frameworks that evolved to ensure that concerns about nature were kept separate from and marginal to wider considerations of modernity. The second phase assesses the emergence of the discourse of nature as environment that took place beginning around 1962. We here examine the novel perception of the emergent 'environmental threat' as being of global proportions, and linked to the dominant values of modernisation and technological progress. In the third phase we look at how these general processes of transforming nature into environment worked out within Britain, such that by the late 1980s the global environmental challenge had been recognised by state institutions and the principle of linking development with environment had been endorsed. And in the final section we outline recent developments in the 1990s, as environmentalism became entangled with wider cultural processes of globalisation and detraditionalisation, and how a new and embryonic agenda can be identified in connection with direct action environmental protest.

Post-war reconstruction and rational nature

Bramwell (1989, 1994) argues that while post-war environmentalism was established in the late 1960s, its emergence needs to be situated in the wider and more diverse culture of the immediate post-war era. The 1950s and early 1960s are often considered a time of general reconstruction and growth. Especially in the US, but also in Europe, political priorities were apparently geared towards growing capitalist industrialisation, modernisation and technological progress. It is within these modernistic priorities that the post-war construction of nature should be situated.

For example, modern environmentalism in Germany (FRG) only became a public issue in the late 1960s. Before then discussion of nature, holism or harmony was considered politically suspect, as tainted by the lasting odours of a Nazi past. As Bramwell says: 'The "biologic" point of view that saw man [sic] as one with nature had been part of the tradition encouraged by the Nazis' (1994: 43). Indeed, 1920s and 1930s Germany was a hotbed of organic ideas, 'back to the land' movements, biodynamic experiments in farming, and youth movements. Much of this energy was devoted to an 'organic vision' of character and spirit, of a revitalised countryside of self-supporting communities in which a new order could counter the deadening forces of industrialism and city life. However, as Wright aptly points out, by the early 1930s there was 'too much blood, not enough soil' (1996: 187), and the rhetoric of 'folk, blood and soil' became a central tenet of the emerging racial creed of national socialism (Bramwell 1989; and see Schama 1995 on the role of forests within Nazi mythology). These dynamics helped to ensure that post-war Germany, as part of its cleansing and guilt-ridden 'blank page' approach to the past, was keen to marginalise pre-war traditions of organicism and stewardship which were deemed at best irrelevant. Previous literary associations of 'folk' and 'land' were also cast

aside. The academic discipline of biology too became stripped of any
emotional association of 'nature loving', and was transformed into a dry and
exacting modern science. As Bramwell (1994: 43) points out, the intense
drive of reconstituting Germany after the Second World War created a
political framework in which there was no political or cultural space for
environmental concerns. In this largely unsympathetic setting, only a few
isolated and largely conservative thinkers rejected the move towards rapid
industrialisation and its associated values, and sought a more organic and
pastoral Germany.

While American and New World environmentalism have roots within the
Romantic tradition, they also have a highly developed sense of 'wilderness'
(Merchant 1982; Tuan 1974; Wilson 1992; Worster 1985; and see chapter 6
below). The 'civilisation' of such New World nation-states has often been
framed as the cultivation of a 'country' out of 'native' forest and grassland
(Short 1991). This transformation of wilderness enjoys a special place in the
sense of national identity. However, the relationship between wilderness and
national identity is ambivalent. On the one hand, there is the classical or
Enlightenment mentality where such a 'savage' wilderness had to be tamed,
subdued and cultivated through human reason; while, on the other hand,
there is the more Romantic sense of reverence towards untouched and
unmanaged wilderness (see chapter 1 above). This ambiguity is of enormous
historical and cultural complexity. Moreover, it has had profound implications for the attitudes to indigenous peoples, the formation of national parks,
the containment of cities, landscape design, painting, literature, and so on
(for more detail, see Glacken 1967; Marx 1964; Thomas 1984).

Post-war American concern with nature reflected such ambivalent
attitudes to the land, but specifically in the form of a tension between a
'preservationist' desire to preserve nature in its original, untouched state
(building on the teachings of Thoreau, Walden and Muir), and a more
utilitarian 'conservationist' desire to regulate nature through rational and
efficient management (Hays 1959; and chapter 6 below on the development
of American conceptions of wilderness). This tension was captured in the
challenge posed by Leopold's *A Sand County Almanac* to the Pinchot school
of progressive conservation which had proposed the efficient conservation of
land for human use (Leopold 1949). Leopold had previously been an
advocate of the progressive school. However, in the *Almanac* he advocated
the preservation of untouched nature for its own sake and even suggested
that such experiences of wilderness were the source of the spirit that
characterised American democracy and its unique way of life. This rationale
was used by post-war ecologists and conservationists to justify the protection of nature irrespective of its instrumental use.

The post-war concern with nature in Britain was conceived of in distinct
and largely unrelated sets of issues of amenity, aesthetics, pollution control
and scientific nature conservation (Healey and Shaw 1994; Lowe 1983;
Newby 1979). Similar to Germany, these concerns were seen as secondary

to an assessment of Britain's problems and priorities. Modernisation permeated British policy in public housing, city centre development, a preoccupation with science and technological improvement, and Keynesian aspirations of permanent full employment and steady economic growth. Encapsulated in Harold Wilson's later phrase, 'the white heat of the technological revolution', concerns about the impacts of modernisation upon nature were seen to be backward, nostalgic, reactionary and irrelevant to public policy. Indeed, it was through attempts to preserve the integrity of the countryside in the face of development and modernising pressures that 'environmental' concerns entered the public consciousness; attempts which were commonly portrayed as 'the selfish response of a threatened landowner class' (Bramwell 1994: 49). But this is somewhat overstated since the post-war period also saw the establishment of national parks, the creation of the Civic Trust and countless amenity societies, and a comprehensive town and country planning system. However, such concerns saw nature as a 'setting' for rational exploitation, or as a 'backcloth' to be safeguarded for public leisure enjoyment (Healey and Shaw 1994: 427–8). These conceptions were premised upon the relative separation of nature from modernisation and technological progress that could happen elsewhere, in the centre.

Thus in their different ways, Germany (the FRG), the US and Britain presented relatively unfavourable contexts for the emergence of the kinds of environmental discourse and movements that did in fact emerge. We now interrogate in detail the British case in order to see how nature did in fact come to be reinvented and eventually placed at the centre-stage of civil society and to some degree the British state. To understand the emergence of this environmental dynamic we first will 'dig deeper' into its roots by initially examining past traditions of 'nature' and 'the rural' within Britain (and see chapter 6 below).

Traditions of nature

The first national voluntary organisations devoted to the causes of conservation and amenity were established during the latter stages of the last century, largely because of perceived concerns about the negative impacts of industrialism and urban growth (Haigh 1986; Lowe and Goyder 1983). In 1865 the very first national amenity society, the Commons Preservation Society, was formed to protect London commons from urban development and to protect open space for public recreation (Haigh 1986: 17). This was followed by the Society for the Protection of Ancient Buildings (established 1877), the Selborne Society for the Protection of Birds, Plants and Pleasant Places (established 1885), the Society for the Protection of Birds (established 1889), the National Trust for Places of Historic Interest and Natural Beauty (established 1895), the Garden Cities Association (established 1899), and the Coal Smoke Abatement Society (established 1899).

The emergence of preservationist movements was not simply a reaction to the alarming rate of natural destruction caused by urban growth and industrial expansion, but was also a result of a changing intellectual discourse. Preservationism was a Victorian reaction against the Enlightenment mentality which assumed that nature was to be improved through human reason and interference. Eminent social philosophers William Morris, John Ruskin and John Stuart Mill were active members of popular movements. Such reactions took many forms: from desires to improve the city through parks and better sanitation, to proposals for new Garden Cities, to preserving bits of England that had not yet been corrupted, to even setting up alternative rural communities (see Hardy 1979; Howard 1965; Williams 1973). Anti-pollution legislation was also enacted as a response to mounting public concern with deteriorating urban air quality: the Smoke Nuisance Abatement Act in 1853, and the more wide ranging-and pioneering Alkali Act of 1863 which led to the creation of the first government department to deal with pollution, the Alkali Inspectorate the following year.

However, the early preservationist movement was progressive in outlook just as much as it was nostalgic, driven by utopian ideals to connect social improvement with the safeguarding and protection of the common heritage through a philosophy of care and respect (Haigh 1976: 18). Rejecting the ugliness of the industrial revolution, preservationists sought to restore links with the past, and through the preservation of 'relics' and national 'monuments' to reinvigorate a spiritual relationship to place and country:

> Tangible relics of previous epochs and of the natural world served similar functions. Both provided evidence, however incomplete, of what 'progress' had destroyed. As constants in a changing world, they stood for continuity, stability and tradition, against the restless and rootless stirrings of industrial capitalism. . . . As disillusionment with industrial progress mounted, the essential national spirit was seen to reside not in British commerce and industry but in the past and in the country. (Lowe and Goyder 1983: 20; see also Wiener 1981)

The quest to save relics of the past and of nature thus came to represent a quest to save an integral part of English identity. Octavia Hill, one of the founders of the National Trust, famously said of the Trust's property that it was 'a bit of England belonging to the English in a very special way' (cited Lowe 1983: 340; see Cannadine 1995 on the history of the National Trust). Preservationism became part of a wider reconfiguration of 'Englishness', one which rejected aspirations for industrial progress and technological development and which looked to the English countryside and the past for a more harmonious order (see also Thomas 1984; Wiener 1981; Williams 1973; and see chapter 6 below).

After a brief lull between the turn of the century and the end of the First World War, the next national bodies to be established were the Ancient Monuments Society (established 1924), the Council for the Preservation of Rural England (CPRE) (established 1926), the National Trust for Scotland (established 1931) and the Ramblers Association (established 1935). In England, although the National Trust had become a formidable organisation in the acquisition of land and property, it was clear to preservationists that a different kind of organisation was required to protect the wider countryside from the onslaught of urbanism, suburbanisation and new industry. The CPRE was set up largely at the instigation of the planner Patrick Abercrombie as a 'literal council', made up of diverse organisations concerned with rural preservation (Matless 1990: 179–80). Abercrombie remarked: 'the greatest historical monument we possess, the most essential thing which is England, is the Countryside, the Market Town, the Village, the Hedgerow Trees, the Lanes, the Copses, the Streams and the Farmsteads' (cited Lowe and Goyder 1983: 18). The metaphors through which early CPRE activists operated are especially revealing: towns were conceived as 'beasts', or as 'octopuses' threatening to engulf 'unspoilt' England with urban sprawl (Williams-Ellis 1928, 1938). The CPRE soon became active in its campaigns to preserve the countryside especially from visually unattractive ribbon development.

One particularly resonant conflict was over the 4,000-mile National Grid, which had been given legislative blessing by Baldwin's government in 1926 (Luckham 1990). A number of set-piece conflicts ensued between 'triumphalists', who believed the Grid would reduce unemployment and boost the economy, and the preservationist 'Anti-Pylon Movement', who pointed to the 'scarring' threatened by the 'march of the pylons' upon the natural landscape and amenity. The pylon as symbol for the loss of 'old' England became a powerful mobilising force. Protest groups were set up in the South Downs, the Lake District, the New Forest and London; eminent writers and intellectuals such as Kipling, Belloc and Keynes became actively involved; and *The Times* began to coordinate anti-pylon news and features helping to engender a national debate. On the surface the argument appeared to be about economic modernisation pitted against the desire to protect and preserve nature and amenity. For example, Colonel Gwynne, Mayor of Eastbourne declared:

> When we contemplate the fair face of the Sussex Downs, scarred with masts and cables, and the placid beauty of the Pevensey Marshes slashed with a line of steel towers, we think that this is the type of progress we could do without. (cited Luckham 1990: 96)

However, the argument was sometimes more subtle, not so much about old England versus new England, or about urban versus rural, or even tradition versus modernity, but rather about order and disorder. Even Abercrombie (1933) recognised the beauty in pylons, especially with regard to their clarity of form (see also Cornish 1930; Peach and Carrington 1930; Williams-Ellis 1938). In the 1930s preservationism became less a critique of modernisation in the face of tradition, and more a 'modernist' concern to regulate boundaries, especially between town and country, by contrast with uncontrolled laissez-faire development (Matless 1990). Indeed, from the outset, the CPRE (and the Town and Country Planning Association (TCPA) formerly the Garden Cities Association) became increasingly concerned with the lack of planning and development control, and began to demand an integrated planning system to manage development, including the provision of new towns, and to establish specially designated national parks in areas of

wildness and exceptional natural beauty. In chapter 6 we will see that the
demarcation of the countryside from the town became a particular concern
of interwar campaigning.

The preservationist movement highlighted 'nature' as the 'unspoilt' other,
as embodied in the relics, customs and mystery of the English countryside.
Such a nature was no longer viewed as robust but as vulnerable, threatened
by urban growth and industrial expansion, and in need of the *state* for
protection in the collective interest. Traditionally, the preservationist movement in England had worked within or alongside the social and political
establishment, and comprised people from the same classes who saw
themselves for the most part as sharing more or less the same interests as the
rural landowners (Cannadine 1995; McCrone et al. 1995 on Scotland;
Shoard 1987: 111).

However, the inter-war years had also seen the widening of concern for
nature and the countryside, particularly through the emergence of the open-
air movements and the widespread practice of leisurely walking (Hall 1976).
Partly due to greater levels of affluence among the professional and white-
collar classes, the enhanced mobility provided by the railways, the new
passion for the 'great outdoors', and the increased power of socialist and
communist ideals, questions of access became increasingly significant. One
might even describe this as a kind of class struggle – between the
landowners and farmers, on the one side, and the urban middle classes and
later the industrial working class, on the other, who sought access to rural
roads and paths, forests and fields (see Urry 1995a for further analysis of the
class struggles within the English countryside). Especially after the First
World War, growing numbers of people felt entitled to the freedom of the
hills and valleys and to be increasingly resentful over the lack of public
access to much of the countryside. Such class disputes were particularly
marked in the north of England. Resentment led to a number of highly
publicised mass trespasses, most notably over Kinder Scout in 1932, and
contributed to a political demand for greater access to the overwhelmingly
privately owned countryside (Shoard 1987: 114; see McCrone et al. 1995 on
the even greater power and status of landlords within Scotland).

A final influence upon debates about nature was that of science and in
particular the birth of scientific ecology. In 1913 the British Ecological
Society was formed, partly as a reaction to what Lowe (1976) describes as
the obsession with novelty and rarity that characterised much of the
Victorian natural history societies. Ecologists concerned themselves with the
functions and dynamics of ecosystems and this led to a shift in concern from
individual species to habitats (Szerszynski 1995). Such emphases led to
important tensions, reflected particularly in the work of the Society for the
Promotion of Nature Reserves (established 1912), between preservationists,
who desired to leave nature in its original wild state, and ecologists, who
were apt to regard nature and nature reserves as open-air laboratories for
scientific inquiry (Lowe 1983: 341). However, the inter-war period proved
largely barren years for nature conservation and wildlife protection.

Paradoxically, the Second World War provided a more favourable context both for the discourse of conservation and for the perceived need and effectiveness of state regulation. In line with the post-war mood for reconstruction, amenity, wildlife and conservation issues came to be incorporated within the new rational, planned order (Bramwell 1989). We now trace the dominant frameworks through which the Attlee Government responded to inter-war controversies, and how these frameworks helped structure the public expression and articulation of British post-war discourses on nature.

Post-war frameworks

Much of the inter-war legislation aimed at curbing development on agricultural land had been ineffective. Preservationist pressure had led to the appointment of the Barlow Commission in 1937, a Royal Commission set up with the twin objectives of containing urban growth, especially of London, and redirecting growth and industrial renewal to the depressed regions. The subsequent 1940 Barlow Report set up the philosophical basis of the post-war planning system: a humane desire to improve the living conditions of the city, combined with a strict preservationist approach to the countryside (Hall 1973; Newby 1979). A very significant figure in this was Abercrombie, whose vision of a rigid distinction between town and country was to prove highly influential:

> The essence of the aesthetic of town and country consists in the frank recognition of those two elements, *town* and *country*, as representing opposite but complementary poles of influence. . . . With these two sites constantly in view, a great deal of confused thinking and acting is washed away: the town should indeed be frankly artificial; the country natural, rural. (cited Newby 1979: 230)

The subsequent Scott Report reinforced this philosophy and put forward a new planning principle whereby prospective developers would now have to demonstrate 'need' before planning permission would be granted for development in rural areas, thus incorporating into planning practice the general presumption of a rural 'status quo' (Newby 1979: 231). The drive to strengthen the planning system was further boosted by the desire to *plan* for the reconstruction of cities bombed during the war. Indeed, the post-war drive for reconstruction was both idealistic and optimistic. The war had shown just how much the state could achieve.

The 1947 Town and Country Planning Act put in place the modern land-use planning system, which was to prove influential and durable in shaping the modern landscape and the Government's response to post-war nature and conservation issues (Hall 1973: 109). The 1947 Act provided a framework to protect town and country distinctions, and to retain 'nature as a refuge from modern life' (Healey and Shaw 1994: 427). The Act was thus in theory a radical reform of the pre-war laissez-faire approach to land-use and to the *unsightly* ribbon development and urban sprawl attributed to unrestricted market forces (Newby 1979: 237). Later, the town and country distinctions were further reinforced by the introduction of Duncan Sandys' 'Green Belts' circular, enabling county councils to designate areas of land whose prime purpose was to limit urban expansion and the growth of suburbs. Healey and Shaw state that 1940s and 1950s planning reflected three competing constructions of nature:

> around the notion of the countryside as a resource for agriculture production, as an aesthetic landscape to be conserved, and as a place for recreation. . . . The planning tradition . . . embodies a peculiarly British marriage between economic modernisation and a romantic nostalgia for a particular ideal of rural life and landscape. (1994: 428)

The 1947 Act restricted the development of agricultural land for industrial and residential purposes. However, agriculture and forestry were excluded as forms of development and were not subject to planning control. By contrast, throughout the post-war period, agriculture was encouraged to become more intensive, more efficient and more modern, under government support policies designed to increase production yields. Indeed, the ruinous effects of such a policy on wildlife and landscape were to remain largely hidden until the passage of the 1981 Wildlife and Countryside Act. How did this occur? To begin with, the memories of pre-war agricultural depressions and those of the German U-boat blockade had left an indelible mark on Whitehall, and had helped to ensure that post-war agricultural policy became centred on a drive towards basic food production. But also at the time farmers were perceived as the undisputed and self-evident guardians of nature and the English countryside, and thus it was seen as politically and morally implausible to question the authority and judgement of the farming community to safeguard nature. This image was to remain largely intact up until the 1980s. Indeed, the mythology of the yeoman farmer and of a countryside stocked with wildlife has been carefully crafted through the BBC rural soap-opera *The Archers*, a radio soap specifically designed in the early post-war years to improve the public perception of farming:

> Epitomized by the late Dan Archer, he [the yeoman farmer] is seen as working long hours for little financial reward. He is, however, compensated for a lack of material comforts by the close contact he enjoys with the sights and sounds of nature and country life, which to him, bluff and manly figure though he is, are dear indeed. He is trustworthy and reliable, and, were the countryside to reside in his hands, we need have no fears for its future. (Shoard 1987: 143)

A second highly influential piece of legislation in the immediate post-war years was the 1949 National Parks and Access to the Countryside Act, which led to the designation of 10 national parks in England and Wales (none in Scotland); two new landscape designations; and a set of National Nature Reserves and Sites of Special Scientific Interest to be administered by the newly formed Nature Conservancy. The Act was a combination of romantic and scientific ideals. The aim of the national parks was that the 'characteristic landscape beauty should be strictly preserved', an objective which led to particularly strict development control (Newby 1979: 234). However, the Act also sought to guarantee public access in the wider countryside. Indeed, after the heated conflicts between ramblers and landowners in the 1930s it was generally regarded that more public access needed to be underwritten by the state. A committee was set up by the war-time coalition, chaired by Sir Arthur Hobhouse and including representatives of the Ramblers Association, to look into the feasibility of national parks, and to consider the issues of footpaths and access to the countryside. Acknowledging the centrality of issues of science and ecology within national parks, a related committee was set up under Julian Huxley.

At the time, the idea of American-style national parks which would be owned and managed by the state fitted into the post-war mood for national reconstruction. Indeed, Hugh Dalton, Chancellor of the Exchequer and champion of the Ramblers Association, had set aside £50 million in the National Land Fund to nationalise land for the proposed national parks. The 1945 Dower report proposed national parks closely aligned to the American model. The subsequent 1947 Hobhouse Report not only sought to extend the existing public footpath network but also advocated a general public 'right to roam' across wild, open land.

However, both the 'right to roam' principle and the proposals for public ownership of land were written out during the passage of the Bill. Max Nicholson, long-time advocate of nature conservation, who was at the time in Herbert Morrison's department, recalls what happened:

> But unfortunately Hobhouse and co. opened their mouths so wide, they frightened the guts out of the county councils and the county councils rallied round and completely emasculated the Bill – except for Part Three, which was the nature conservation thing, which went through. Everybody said 'nature conservation, don't know anything about that, let's turn over'. And so our powers of compulsory purchase and everything went through; all the similar powers for the national parks were emasculated. (1989: 10)

Hence, due to the lobbying of the County Council Association (who would have seen their power reduced in place of the proposed Parks Commission), and the untimely demise of Dalton (who lost his job at the Exchequer), the National Parks were set up *within* existing land tenure arrangements. Lewis Silkin, then Minister of Town and Country Planning, accepted the need to open up the countryside for recreation, but the 1949 Act opted for a less radical option advocating wider access only where local authorities had made special agreement. However, Part 3 of the Act on nature conservation did provide considerable powers to the newly formed Nature Conservancy and this reflected in part the enhanced prominence and status of ecological science.

Nature conservation became much more prominent in the post-war era. During the war ecologists had acquired enhanced status as trusty managers planning nature along scientific principles (Nicholson 1987). Ecologists gradually began to set themselves up as leaders of the conservation movement and calls to preserve wildlife came to be identified as an integral part of countryside preservation (Cherry 1975; Lowe 1983: 342). Indeed, the idea of government-protected nature reserves was concurrent with an emerging commitment to a comprehensive planning land-use system, and the 1947 Huxley committee drew up a national list of proposed nature reserves for adoption based upon earlier surveys by naturalist organisations. The Nature Conservancy was set up under the 1949 Act as a government agency with considerable autonomy to manage nature reserves, and to conduct scientific research on the conservation and control of natural flora and fauna with powers of grant giving. This twin role was to prove influential in the development of the Nature Conservancy, both in its philosophy of managing reserves along principles of scientific ecology, and in the primacy given to academic research and training. The Nature Conservancy also helped foster an 'ecological aesthetic' – a new aesthetic appreciation of the ecological complexity of conserved nature made visible through scientific inquiry (Toogood 1997).

Thus, the 1947 and 1949 Acts provided the core framework through which post-war concerns about nature were conceived within policy making. The third part of the framework was provided by the UK Government's approach to pollution. Even though the British Alkali Inspectorate had been established as early as 1864, the pollution of air and water had traditionally received little political attention in the UK (Hajer 1995; see also Ashby and Anderson 1981 for a comprehensive history of air pollution in Britain). Indeed, the general approach to pollution control that prevailed in the post-war era was characterised by a decentralised regulatory culture where pollution control was carried out via local government or regional inspectorates, a pragmatic and discretionary civil service flexible to local conditions and the vested interests of industry or public corporations, and a general appeal to science and to Britain's long and proud record in pollution control (see Ashby and Anderson 1981; Grove-White 1991b; Haigh 1987; Weale 1992; Wynne and Crouch 1991). Such an internal policy culture ensured that pollution concerns were conceived in technical rather than cultural terms, and also as separate from amenity and nature conservation.

In organisational terms the period following the war was characterised by continuity and stability. The voluntary organisations, so influential in the late nineteenth century and inter-war years, settled into an establishment role *within* the state, as guardians of the very reforms that they had helped to secure. Lowe and Goyder illustrate this continuity through the amazing long-term service of some of the leading individuals in the key organisations:

> Monica Dance was assistant secretary of the SPAB [Society for the Protection of Ancient Buildings] from 1931 to 1941 and then secretary until 1978. Lawrence Chubb remained secretary of the Commons, Open Spaces and Footpaths Preservation Society for a staggering 52 years, from 1896 to 1948. The Royal Society for the Protection of Birds had the same chairman, Montagu Sharp, from 1895 to 1942. When he retired in 1965, Herbert Griffin had been general secretary of the Council for the Protection of Rural England for 39 years, since its inception. Tim Foley was secretary and then chairman of the Pedestrians' Association from 1929 to 1970. (1983: 24–5)

In the immediate post-war era nature conservation continued to concentrate upon the setting up of nature reserves. The Nature Conservancy, especially under Max Nicholson as Director-General, applied an active policy of buying, leasing, managing and designating nature reserves, taking full advantage of cheap land prices and their state powers to buy land. By 1953 1,098 Sites of Special Scientific Interest (SSSIs) had been designated and the impetus to designate National Nature Reserves soon followed (Toogood 1997). By 1963 47 reserves had been designated, rising to 140 by 1975 and covering over 280,000 acres (Rose 1984: 33). The preoccupation with acquiring reserves was also shared by conservation groups: by 1975 the Royal Society for the Protection of Birds had 48 reserves totalling 32,000 acres; the acreage of reserves owned by the National Trust rose from 4,000 in 1960 to 58,000 in 1975; while by 1981 the 43 County Trusts managed 1,300 nature reserves covering over 45,000 acres. Such figures illustrate the efforts dedicated by post-war conservation bodies to the creation of wildlife sanctuaries, and a discourse whereby wildlife groups conceived of conservation and indeed nature as limited to special sites and cloistered from the wider town and countryside. One might characterise this as the 'ghettoisation of nature'.

The period between the late 1950s and early 1960s saw the formation of the Civic Trust, the Council for Nature (established 1957), the Victorian Society (established 1958), the British Trust for Nature Conservation (established 1965), and the rapid growth in county naturalists' trusts. There was also an enormous expansion in the number of local amenity societies and of organised voluntary activity. Professionals such as architects, planners, biologists and lawyers became active participants in voluntary societies dedicated to the preservation of village life and places of historic and natural interest. Amenity societies grew in stature and became valuable sources of information and expertise to local authorities (Lowe and Goyder 1983: 91). The Civic Trust provided a national forum for local societies dedicated to protecting and preserving their locality. It provided a framework in which people were encouraged to protect and care for their 'place' as a whole. It helped to promote a new discourse of nature encapsulated by the notion of 'fit' and 'character'. This discourse found its fullest expression in the 1967 Civic Amenities Act, which created a statutory duty on local authorities to designate conservation areas in places of character. Such places should be subject to planning control such that their character should be conserved and enhanced. As Haigh comments, such legislation subtly changed 'the presumption that the new must be inherently better than what existed . . . and has helped pave the way for a new emphasis on rehabilitation in urban areas rather than wholesale clearance and reconstruction' (1976: 20).

Although ostensibly concerned with the built form, the growth of amenity societies reflected, in part, the increasing significance of rural life in post-war Britain. The 1960s were the decade in which the pattern of rural–urban migration became reversed for the first time (Newby 1979: 22; Urry 1995a). With increasing affluence and especially car ownership, the affluent middle classes were able to realise their 'dream' of a house in the country. The old town and country distinctions became further accentuated at the cultural

level: cities representing squalor, atomism and dislocation; the village
representing social cohesion, community and a more natural order. Newby
explains how concerns over the fragility of social order and cohesion
became reflected in heightened desires to preserve the *look* of villages,
especially within the new emphases on 'aesthetics' provided in development
control planning legislation:

> Ideas about the English countryside as a *visual* phenomenon and ideas about the
> English countryside as a *social* phenomenon have therefore merged together. A
> locality which looks right must also, it is assumed, support a desirable way of life.
> In this way rural aesthetics and ideas about rural society have become closely
> intertwined. Little wonder, then, that there has been a movement to preserve this
> apparently fragile social *and* visual creation from the ever-present threat of alien
> encroachment and eventual destruction – and little wonder, also, that there is so
> much contemporary concern for the vitality of village life. (1979: 23; and see
> chapter 4 below on the significance of visuality)

Growing public concern and interest in the countryside during the 1960s
also focused on issues of recreation and public access. By the 1960s
conservation concerns increasingly came to be seen as in conflict with
aspirations for wider public access and countryside recreation. People came
to be viewed as a threat to the countryside, in terms of their impact both on
fragile landscapes and on vulnerable wildlife habitats. A 'keep out' school
developed among the middle-class County Naturalist Trusts, where reserves
came to be justified in terms of science and with relatively little regard given
to their wider public appeal (Rose 1984: 31). This dilemma was forcibly
reflected in the 1968 Countryside Act, and in particular in the establishment
of Country Parks, an initiative designed to channel the urban masses into
deliberately contrived honeypots aimed at relieving 'pressure' on the wider
remote and as yet 'unspoilt' countryside (Newby 1987: 118).

Thus post-war British (and especially English) policy was dominated by
aspirations to contain urban growth; by the preservation of the landscape
through land-use development control; by the protection of the character of
local places; by *ad hoc* pollution control arrangements; and by the protection
of wildlife through the provision of specific nature reserves and the
application of scientific ecology. The post-war desire to preserve the
countryside through the containment of the urban form later became
extended to a wider desire to preserve the countryside through control and
regulation of 'the urban masses'. Public concern for amenity and wildlife
conservation grew, but the resulting activity was largely confined to nature
reserves and to the conservation of amenity. Thus post-war policies were
framed within the three durable discourses of aesthetics, amenity and
science. Concerns about nature were perceived as largely distinct and
separate from each other, as well as from broader economic considerations
of progress and modernisation. As argued in chapter 1, nature was seen to
exist away from cities and sites of production. It is significant that these
priorities were embedded both in media and policy discourses and they
remained largely unquestioned by the public. However, as we argue in the
next section, a new discourse centred on what has become known as 'the

environment' was rapidly emerging on the horizon in the early 1960s, particularly within North America.

To nature as environment

By all accounts Rachel Carson's *Silent Spring* (1962) was a major landmark in the emergence of modern environmentalism (although see McCormick 1995 on the importance of even earlier texts such as Osborn's *The Plundered Planet* in 1948, and the role of Huxley and Nicholson from the conservation movement throughout the 1940s and 1950s). The book charted with relentless detail the effects of pesticides (most notably organochloride insecticides such as DDT, aldrin, isodrin, entrin and dieldrin) on the wildlife of the countryside, and their potentially catastrophic long-term effects on life support systems as toxic poisons worked their way up the food chain. McCormick points to the success of the book, which sold 500,000 copies and remained a bestseller for 31 weeks, as marking the beginning of what he calls the New Environmentalism:

> if nature protection had been a moral crusade centred on the non-human environment, and conservation a utilitarian movement based on the rational management of natural resources, New Environmentalism addressed the entire human environment. For protectionists, the issue was wildlife and habitats; for conservationists, the issue was natural resources; for the New Environmentalists, human survival itself was at stake. (1995: 56)

By contrast with Leopold's optimistic view of the wilderness as the embodiment of American democracy, Carson painted a picture of a world in mortal danger, a danger systematically and cynically produced by the greed and self-interest of the pesticides industry. Even more significant was the diagnosis that these 'elixirs of death' which entered the human body were a direct by-product of the post-war zeal for modernisation and technological improvement. While previous concerns had centred on the aesthetics of suburbanisation, or local pollution incidents, or the loss of particular habitats, Carson's critique centred on a representation of nature as systematically threatened by modern industrial processes. She graphically illustrated the increasing porousness of the borders around the natural body. The body had become subject to invasion by dangerous agents which could not be properly sensed, let alone repelled.

Carson was the first of a succession of academic scientists who by the late 1960s had come to prominence within the nascent environmental movement. Described as 'the prophets of doom', these scientists focused on issues of pollution, technology and population (Maddox 1972: 1).

Ehrlich (1968) highlighted neo-Malthusian concerns about population growth and the need for population control, especially in the so-called Third World. He predicted that under current conditions hundreds of millions of people would face starvation in the 1970s and 1980s, that attempts through technology to increase food production would further deteriorate soil conditions, and that all this would lead to famine, plague and nuclear war.

Hardin's 'The tragedy of the commons' (1968) argued that global destruction was an inevitable tragedy resulting from the destruction of communal
resources by individual self-interest, and that survival could only be achieved through 'mutual coercion', especially with regard to population
control. Commoner was more concerned with the symptomatic and destructive effect of technology, and in particular how 'ecologically faulty technology' in the form of synthetics, pesticides, heavy metals and plastics could
no longer be accommodated by 'the self-purifying capabilities of the natural
system' (1972: 123). To Commoner the problem lay in technologies driven
by greed and profit, and he pointed to a new range of dangerous substances
such as radioactive material which could no longer be sensed and whose
effects transcended natural biological cycles (see also chapters 4 and 5
below on the sensed and timed dimensions of nature).

Such predictions of global catastrophe also captured the imagination of
industrialists and technocrats. In 1968 Aurelio Peccei, President of Olivetti,
convened a group of scientists, industrialists and politicians to foster
understanding of the dynamics of 'the global system', a system of such
complexity as to be beyond the competence of individual institutions. The
emergent 'Club of Rome' set up a computer-simulated global model in 1970
which aimed to determine the effects of existing trends in world population,
pollution, industrialisation, food production and resource depletion. This
resulted in the influential *Limits to Growth* Report, which suggested that
aspirations of exponential growth lay at the heart of the environmental crisis,
predicting severe food shortages, famine and resource depletion by the end
of the century (Meadows et al. 1972).

The subsequent 1972 United Nations Stockholm Conference on the
Human Environment contributed to the political recognition of environmental issues as increasingly global. The Stockholm Conference had four major
effects: first, it consolidated an emphasis on the human environment and for
the need for rational management of the world's resources; second, it sought
to connect environmental issues with development issues – the inclusion of
less developed countries being a significant feature of the conference; third,
it recognised the role of NGOs as key players; and last, it led to the creation
of the United Nations Environment Programme, a body devoted in theory to
generating global solutions to global problems (McCormick 1995).

By 1970, the effects of popular environmental scientists such as Commoner and Ehrlich lecturing widely across the US, combined with increasing
public concern with problems such as nuclear fallout and oil pollution, led to
increased sensitivity to the environmental critique and to a new sense of a
global environmental crisis. This not only stimulated the growth of conservation groups such as the Sierra Club, but also led to Earth Day on 22
April 1970 when 300,000 people across the US took part in what has been
described as 'the largest environmental demonstration in history' (McCormick 1995: 79). The sense of planetary fragility was further reinforced by a
single widely circulated image of the Earth as seen from space, the Blue
Planet – an image which became especially salient after the 1969 moon

landing. The idea of the fragile and vulnerable one earth had entered political discourse in 1965 when the US ambassador Adlai Stevenson had referred to the earth 'as a single spaceship on which we travel together, dependent on its vulnerable supplies of air and soil' (cited Ward and Dubos 1972: 31). By Earth Day in 1970 the image of 'the Earth' had become the visual shorthand – a commonplace used by the media, politicians as well as environmentalists – of the new sense of global fragility and interconnectivity (Sachs 1994; Wilson 1992: 167).

Such debates and images contributed to the notion of the earth as a common home which needs care and maintenance, as in Ward and Dubos' *Only One Earth* (published in 1972 as a key text to the Stockholm conference). These developments provided much of the vocabulary that still pervades global environmental discourse, especially the focus on 'limits' defined in scientific and technical terms which impose fundamental constraints on human action, and the emphasis upon rational planning and management as the appropriate response. It is also very significant that the debates were predominantly carried out by experts in scientific and technical disciplines with little space granted for social scientific intervention. Thus the ecological debate of the early 1970s was often conducted between those seeking to impose limits on industrialisation and progress, and those who were optimistic about the role of technology and human ingenuity to solve social problems (O'Riordan 1976). John Maddox, then editor of the journal *Nature*, is usually credited to be the main 'doom critic' (McCormick 1995), although there were numerous attacks from others in the scientific establishment who saw science and technology as core and benign elements of the modernising project. Indeed, although the actual *Limits to Growth* projections were rightly criticised as naïve and misleading, the 'limits' arguments were to prove a symbolic landmark, providing a discourse which informed subsequent governmental and inter-governmental approaches and understandings of environmental issues.

However, to assume that the energy and dynamism of contemporary environmentalism originated in 'science' is to overlook the wider cultural critique of which the New Environmentalism was merely one part. By 1970 the world did indeed look more vulnerable and threatened, and a sense of the 'environmental crisis' as having global proportions was increasingly salient. However, this sense of crisis was itself part of a wider cultural shift beginning in the US that was reflected in the late 1960s student and counter-cultural movements. Bramwell (1994: 59) describes how a surprising number of environmental activists in the early 1970s had been veterans of the student protest movement. She suggests that environmental issues came to be understood within a liberation framework heavily influenced by the social criticism articulated by Marcuse and the emergent New Left. The environment became a key manifestation of the counter-culture, and environmental lifestyle a way of resisting an alienating and destructive culture apparently bent on self-destruction. Invested in the campus explosions of 1968 was mounting disaffection with old values of which modernisation was one aspect. The counter-culture represented a new cultural style – an expressive set of values, assumptions and ways of living in opposition to the values of materialism and technological progress (Martin 1981: 15).

A number of writers acquired iconic status, redefining environmentalism as the counter to the emptiness of consumer materialism and the iron cage of rationality (Bramwell 1994: 60). Reich (1970) expressed the alienation of young people from corporate America and of a lifestyle which was perceived to be personally as well as environmentally destructive. Illich (1973) also made a huge impact as a critic of 'the system', and in particular of modern and alienating state institutions. He advocated small-scale social arrangements, especially in schooling, and a human-oriented approach to technology (see also Illich 1975). The critique of bigness and statism was shared by fellow counter-cultural icons Schumacher (1974) and Roszak (1970, 1981). They criticised modern technocratic society and pointed to a future society based not on profit and greed, but upon the pursuit of human happiness, health, beauty and the conservation of the planet. Elsewhere we have argued that one explanation of such developments was the collapse of 'organised capitalism' and the development of diverse indicators of 'disorganisation', including various non-class social movements, especially feminism (Lash and Urry 1987).

The counter-culture provided an intellectual critique of the sickness of 'the [organised capitalist] system', including especially its embedded values of materialism, individual achievement and technological progress; its emphasis upon fixed roles, borders and boundaries, especially of sex and gender; its valuation of dull and predictable sources of pleasure mainly housed within the family; and its prioritisation of the interests and concerns of the generation that had 'won the war' and which was determined to exploit the earth's resources to enjoy the victory (the story is of course somewhat different in Germany, Italy and Japan).

This coming to an end of organised capitalism and the growth of a counter-culture posed a serious threat to the older and more established conservation and amenity movements, first in the US and subsequently in Britain. In 1969 David Brower, having been forced to resign as executive director of the Sierra Club, founded a new and overtly more activist organisation which he aptly named 'Friends of the Earth' (or FoE). The organisation was designed to inject the activism of the student protest movement into the politics of the environment (Pearce 1991). National organisations were set up in other countries as autonomous groups. They were loosely linked by certain shared principles: to respect biological diversity, to conserve resources, to protect wildlife, to limit pollution, and to effect changes in legislation (McCormick 1995). Offices were established in San Francisco in 1969, Paris and London in 1970 and Sweden in 1971. These organisations not only campaigned on a wider and more inclusive set of issues but also adopted a new expressivist style. By contrast with the hierarchical and conservative practices of the conservation movement, these new groups were egalitarian, passionate, expressive and artistic. They aimed their campaigns at *social* practices which were thought to be environmentally destructive rather than seeking the preservation of threatened *natural* sites and species (Szerszynski 1995: 8). Unlike more traditional groups which worked within the state, FoE engaged the public (or at least some younger parts of it) more directly, often through the use of media stunts which had been learnt from the very recent student movement.

Greenpeace was also formed in reaction to the conservatism that still pervaded much of the conservation movement. Set up in 1969 (initially named as the Don't Make a Wave Committee) to protest against nuclear testing, Greenpeace started using non-violent direct action as a strategy for change. By-passing traditional state procedures and more formal lobbying practices, Greenpeace initiated campaigns against nuclear testing, the waste trade and toxics, and whaling. Over the next two decades activists would sail their boats into test sites, obstruct whaling harpooners, organise boycotts and grassroots rallies, and ensure high-profile publicity in carefully planned media stunts. Using the Quaker tradition of bearing personal witness to atrocities, Greenpeace bore witness to corporate greed and the destructive practices of states, and sought to promote a higher moral creed of protecting species and various life forms (Merchant 1992: 176).

We will now see how these general processes of transforming nature into the environment worked out within Britain. We do not aim to be wholly inclusive but rather to examine certain processes which led to the contemporary environmental agenda. In particular we will stress the changing styles of NGO political engagement, the creative attempts by NGOs to reconfigure nature as environment in largely unsympathetic institutional frameworks, the increasing involvement of Europe and the media, and the symbolic character of particular events and incidents. It was the combination of these processes that was to give potency to the environmental movement, to add to a sense of shared identity, and to contribute to the formal recognition of a global environmental discourse within Britain.

Inventing British environmentalism

A symbolic landmark event in the emergence of the UK environmental discourse was the 1967 *Torrey Canyon* oil pollution disaster off the Cornwall coast, involving contamination to hundreds of miles of the Cornish coastline. The spillage dramatically showed the vulnerability of ecosystems within one country to contamination by the forces of supposed progress, and the surprising inability of existing environmental protection arrangements to deal with a pollution incident of such *international* dimensions. This was graphically illustrated when the untested detergents designed to break up the oil only appeared to accentuate further the ecological damage.

At about the same time abroad, a number of pollution incidents also began to make the headlines. These included a highly publicised blowout at a Union Oil Company platform off the coast of Santa Barbara, California; new and disturbing evidence of chemical and oil pollution of the Great Lakes;

and mercury poisoning at Minimata Bay, Japan (see McCormick 1995: 68–72). By 1970 public attention, both in Britain and abroad, began to be drawn to a much wider range of problems threatening the environment, concerns not simply over wildlife conservation and amenity, but now including nuclear radiation, pesticide use, vehicle emissions and other systemic forms of air and water pollution. These events began to generate an awakening sense of a more general crisis of environmental bads, moving across national borders and potentially invading everyone's body, rather than more sporadic and isolated excesses (Wynne and Crouch 1991: 15).

In Britain, anxieties over pollution and resources in the late 1960s had resulted in the creation of the UK Department of the Environment in 1970, and a new permanent Royal Commission on Environmental Pollution. The UK Government's approach to environmental issues can be best understood through the three durable discourses of amenity, aesthetics and science highlighted above. The new Department conceived of environmental change largely within these discourses, in terms of three broad categories of issue: land-use planning, pollution control and rural/nature conservation (Grove-White 1991b: 17). These three categories, institutionalised into long-established and distinct 'baronies' within the new Department, helped constitute the dominant discourses and frameworks within which the UK state still formulates environmental policy and understands environmental issues. Hence, in the early 1970s, concerns over more global and systemic environmental issues did not find a vehicle for public expression, since both environmental groups and government agencies still conceived of nature within the older vocabularies of rural preservation and amenity. This produced a tacit but prevailing consensus that concerns over nature were largely irrelevant to public policy development aimed at further modernisation of such areas as agriculture, energy supply, transport infrastructure and nuclear power stations, over and above their impact on landscape and amenity. Furthermore, in considering issues of pollution, Britain stood by its record in science and pollution control, and its belief in the commensurability of industrial expansion and the preservation of the natural and built heritage.

An early and largely intellectual challenge to such orthodoxy was posed by the now defunct Conservation Society, established in 1966 with the stated objectives of 'making people more aware of the effects on the environment of the unwise use of technology and the population explosion' (Hettena and Syer 1971). Other influential UK texts were Rattray Taylor's *The Doomsday Book* (1970) and the Ecologist's *Blueprint for Survival*, published in 1972 shortly before the *Limits to Growth* report. However, while these texts stimulated debate among scientists and the British conservation movement on the global dimensions of environment, they had little *immediate* effect on policy, because the concerns they expressed transcended the institutional discourses operating within the British state.

Through the 1970s and early 1980s a succession of 'issues' emerged which became constituents of an 'environmental agenda'. These were the proliferation of chemicals in the 1960s, resource and energy scarcity in the early 1970s, nuclear power and motorways in the late 1970s, agriculture and countryside issues in the early 1980s, and more recently acid rain, ozone depletion, biodiversity and global warming (Grove-White 1991a; Hajer 1995; chapter 1 above). Chris Rose, currently deputy executive director of Greenpeace UK and long-time environmental activist, describes the environmental movement of the 1970s and 1980s as 'essentially engaged in a struggle for proof, progressively raising the stakes of diagnosis to show critical damage not just at an individual level or a community level or locally or even regionally, but nationally, internationally, and finally globally' (1993: 287).

We now describe the process by which environmental groups 'struggled' to prove that certain issues were indeed part of a common environmental agenda. Such struggle involved what we term 'cultural work'. This meant that environmental groups worked opportunistically within the limiting institutional frameworks outlined above and sought to change the terms of reference, both 'spatially' and 'temporally', of what is the environment. These groups also sought to give expression to wider disillusionment with the nature of modern societies, to articulate what is often now characterised as the post-modern. This account of the invention of nature as the environment is informed by research interviews with most of the key activists working within Britain during this period.

Up until the early 1970s the main non-governmental organisations concerned with nature were the Royal Society for the Protection of Birds (RSPB), the World Wildlife Fund (WWF), the Royal Society for Nature Conservation (RSNC), the Council for the Preservation of Rural England (CPRE), the National Trust (NT), the Town and Country Planning Association (TCPA) and the Civic Trust. All except the NT were groups with small staffs who acted more or less independently of each other and with little sense of a common identity. These organisations tended to be involved in a fairly close and 'gentlemanly' dialogue with the state, relying on formal consultation procedures and private negotiations with officials. Conflict was mostly avoided and little challenge was made either to the principle of particular patterns of development, or to the dynamic that was seen to be creating environmental damage. Nature conservation bodies were preoccupied with the buying and managing of reserves, and planning-oriented organisations were consulted with respect to major proposed developments such as motorways, housing developments and mineral extractions. Indeed, when an organisation such as the CPRE did oppose particular set-piece development proposals, as for example in public inquiries into a third London airport and various new motorways, it operated as a witness rather than as a fully fledged campaigning organisation.

It is within this context that we should situate the early development of FoE. Grove-White and Burke both recall the chaotic and anarchic nature of the early FoE, its naïveté about the British political system, its disrespect towards orthodox institutions, and its tremendous sense of 'can do'. Many of the early activists had been engaged in radical student politics and fed an anti-establishment ethos into its campaigning zeal, with an intellectual programme partly informed by the more sedate Conservation Society. As Barclay Inglis was to state 'Friends of the Earth was an explosion waiting to happen' (Burke 1996: interview). Two early campaigns were against Rio Tinto-Zinc proposals to extract copper in the Snowdonia National Park in Wales, and a campaign to stop Cadbury-Schweppes from switching from returnable to non-returnable bottles. Both campaigns illustrate a concern not just over individual threatened sites, but with the social practices that were seen to be systematically accelerating waste in industrial society. Walt Patterson describes how this campaign struck a chord with the public, aided by a powerful visual image:

> On a sunny Saturday in May 1971 a procession of a hundred friends returned 1,500 non-returnable bottles to Schweppes headquarters. The striking visual metaphor – a forecourt entirely covered with discarded glassware – received press and TV coverage not only nationally but internationally. . . . In the ensuing weeks groups calling themselves 'Friends of the Earth' suddenly sprang up all over the UK. (1984: 141)

Tom Burke describes how such campaigns were focused, well researched, innovative and conducted with a tremendous 'density of energy' (1996: interview). Perhaps not surprisingly this type of activity had substantial effects on the style of more established groups. For Grove-White, this radicalism was part of a new context which encouraged the CPRE to become more overtly concerned with the underlying processes driving development in the countryside, which at the time were not available for public debate.

Grove-White argues that much of 1970s environmental campaigning was driven by a strong concern to expose and contest the often hidden assumptions of undifferentiated growth which apparently drove social and technological change within organised capitalism. By 1973 John Adams, geography lecturer at University College London, was advising FoE at motorway inquiries. He articulated an argument that current development pressures arose largely from what he later called a 'predict and provide' model of public policy (Adams 1981). This implied that predictions of future demand for roads were more or less self-fulfilling, in that it was the provision of supply (as in the form of new airports, roads and reservoirs), rather than any underlying need, that created future demand.

Campaigns often found expression through the land-use planning system since this was one arena where participation was actively encouraged (especially following the 1969 Skeffingham Committee on Public Participation in Planning). This was by contrast with, for example, the secrecy attached to pollution considerations. The public inquiry system played a pivotal role in which environmental pressure groups could challenge the assumptions and tacit commitments driving modernisation in public policy. Grove-White himself became an expert and lay advocate on the inquiry system, on how to mobilise evidence, on pre-inquiry tactics, on how to manipulate expertise. However, the usefulness of the inquiry system also lay in its theatre and sense of drama, where activists could argue the significance of particular cases as symbols of much wider debates:

> Indeed, the processes of tactical planning, intellectual preparation and increasingly sophisticated forensic argumentation entailed in this exploitation of the opportunities afforded by the public inquiry system over the period can be said to have played a significant role in the self-definition of the UK's environmental movement. . . . It became a key vehicle through which, in the context of Britain's particular political and administrative culture, an agenda of environmental issues – amongst them, nuclear power, motorways, urban development of rural land, and minerals extraction – was able to become explicit between 1975 and 1989. (Grove-White 1992: 38–9)

One illustration of this process was the 1976 inquiry into the Thorp reprocessing plant at Windscale on the Cumbrian coast (what is now known as Sellafield) and its effect on FoE, on the construction of nuclear power as an environmental issue, and on bringing out new identities amongst the protesting groups. Until 1976 overt public opposition to nuclear power had been relatively low-key. Indeed, even when Britain experienced its first serious nuclear incident when a fire broke out at the Windscale nuclear power plant, public and media reaction was muted (Hall 1986). Unlike continental Europe, where early 1970s opposition to nuclear power was more vocal and at times violent, Britain had retained a superficial climate of quiet faith in nuclear power as a benign application of science (Hall 1986: 137). Thus, when an application was made by British Nuclear Fuels to expand reprocessing at Windscale, few people in government expected more than local opposition, albeit of a quite pronounced sort. However, FoE spotted the application, and ran an article describing how the proposal would make Windscale one of the world's main radioactive dustbins. Patterson describes how the *Daily Mirror* picked up the story some months later and ran the front page headline 'PLAN TO MAKE WORLD'S NUCLEAR DUSTBIN' (1984: 149).

At about the same time, Michael Flood and Grove-White wrote a pamphlet entitled *Nuclear Prospects* (1976) which set out a moral and technical critique of nuclear power. One especially salient argument concerned how long-term dependency on a fast-breeder programme using plutonium as a fuel would inevitably lead to significant restrictions on civil liberties. Interestingly, *Nuclear Prospects* was a joint publication by FoE, the CPRE and the National Council for Civil Liberties (NCCL). It attracted widespread attention, not least in the form of leader articles in *The Times* and *Nature*. Its arguments were reinforced by the fact that five months earlier an armed police force had been set up with wide-ranging powers to guard Britain's nuclear power installations and its plutonium (Hall 1986: 143). These events, coupled with a controversial report by the Royal Commission on *Nuclear Power and the Environment* (1976), created enough public and political pressure to persuade the Labour Government to hold a public inquiry, and to lever open the consensus about the supposed benefits of nuclear power which up to that time had been largely shared by scientists, industry, trade unions, MPs and the media. As Hall points out:

> What was new was the outcry they caused. Newspapers, TV, radio and parliament
> all became interested in Windscale. And the debate about the benefits of it now
> began for real. (1986: 148)

Moreover, the drama of the inquiry and the accompanied media coverage
were both significant in constituting a new sense of a British environment
movement, of common ground and an embryonic shared identity between
different environmental groups. It also undoubtedly gave FoE an enormous
sense of collective confidence and presence.

Debates over nuclear power had by the early 1980s a much wider
resonance than concerns over public safety or landscape. With the resurgence of the Campaign for Nuclear Disarmament (CND), the sense of
unease with Western responses to the Cold War, and the election of
Margaret Thatcher, opposition to both civil and military aspects of nuclear
power came to reflect wider public opposition to a politics apparently geared
to economic self-interest. At the time, the political imperative to expand
nuclear power and to control energy supply away from coalminers was
paramount. Even the CPRE decided to run a high-profile campaign against
the Government's plans to build 10 nuclear pressurised water reactors
(PWRs) within the next 12 years. The Sizewell inquiry lasted two years, and
controversy was further exacerbated by tensions within the nuclear establishment over the safety and efficiency record of the proposed American-
designed PWR. Anti-nuclear sentiment throughout the 1980s was also
expressed outside the public inquiry system: from mostly Labour-controlled
local authorities refusing to implement the Government's civil defence
programmes and declaring themselves 'Nuclear-Free Zones', to key challenges within the Labour and Liberal parties to scrap nuclear power, to a
number of official inquiries addressing the possible link between nuclear
installations and leukaemia clusters, to highly vocal and largely successful
local campaigns to curtail government proposals to develop new low-level
radioactive waste dumps.

In a rather different way the 1981 Wildlife and Countryside Act was
significant in giving potency to the environment movement as a distinct
force in British politics. When the Tories came to power in 1979 the
Government found itself having to implement a European Community Birds
Directive. Having various other concerns over disappearing moorlands and
the like, they took over the previous Wildlife and Countryside Bill from
Labour, made it more favourable to farmers, and sent it to the Lords in 1980.
Peter Melchett, the former Labour minister, provides a useful insight into
how he thinks the Bill was perceived by the new Conservative Govern-
ment:

> I think for parliament, you know, this wildlife stuff was really a complete joke.
> Absolutely irrelevant to politics, nobody knew much about it and it was felt . . .
> House of Lords, lots of landowners, they'll know what they're talking about, bang
> it in there. (1996: interview)

However, quite fortuitously, conservation had suddenly become much
more controversial. In the days before the first delayed debate on the Bill in

the House of Lords, Marion Shoard, former campaigner in the CPRE, published her landmark book *The Theft of the Countryside* (1980). Chris Rose, then countryside campaigner at FoE, describes its impact on the political debate:

> The farming press and the NFU [National Farming Union] raged in complaint but she had expressed and clarified a mounting wave of concern, shared by millions of people. Reviewers loved it: 'A good story . . . the facts are plain . . . the system is insane' proclaimed *The Times*, while another wrote: 'Marion Shoard has decided, at long last, to break through the stifling consensus and spell out the truth about the scale of financial support given to agriculture and the purposes to which money is put'. (1984: 40)

The fate of the countryside became particularly contested during the 1980s. Controversy continued over the implementation of the 1981 Act, as the system of paying farmers not to engage in intensive farming came to be seen as costly and inequitable. Largely through the innovation of such groups as the Ramblers, FoE, the CPRE and the WWF, a new discourse of the countryside began to permeate public consciousness. Farmers were no longer identified as the self-evident guardians of the countryside, but were now seen to pose a threat to nature just as with any other industry. No longer were 'people' perceived as the main threat to the conservation of the countryside (as in the 1960s), and policies to 'keep people out' began to be regarded as self-interested attempts by landowners and conservation bodies to consolidate their own interests.

The early 1980s were also a time of mounting affluence, and this became translated into large increases in demand for housing within rural areas, especially in the south-east. In response Patrick Jenkin, Secretary of State for the Environment, introduced two circulars in 1983 designed to ease restrictions in the planning system within rural areas. Grove-White (1992: 40–2) describes how this produced an effective piece of CPRE campaigning. Building on a tension within the Tory Party between a dislike of regulation and a deep love for the countryside, the CPRE in association with the Civic Trust persuaded 60 Tory MPs from south-east constituencies to sign an Early Day motion objecting to the Government's proposals. Then sharing a joint platform with an array of countryside interest groups all of whom objected to the draft circular (albeit for different reasons), the CPRE left the Government with no choice but to withdraw both the Green Belt circular and another draft circular on housing land. Grove-White suggests that this event marked a changing point in the CPRE's relationship with the Government of the 1980s.

In the mid-1980s a number of Tory backbenchers within southern marginals started writing pamphlets on the environment, particularly focusing upon the countryside. They increasingly interpreted the fate of the English (southern) countryside as raising environmental issues, and this too helped extend the environmental agenda from an unlikely source. This political concern was itself partly as a reaction to the political threat from the newly formed Social Democratic Party (SDP), who were actively campaigning on countryside issues, on which they perceived Tory policy to be especially vulnerable. Simultaneously Geoff Lean committed the *Observer* newspaper to a year-long campaign on the countryside. By 1987 Michael Heseltine, then temporarily out of government following the Westland affair, was making speeches on planning and the countryside. Following a meeting with Tom Burke and Nigel Haigh (then director of the Institute for European Environment Policy), Heseltine was persuaded to make a speech on pollution to the annual dinner of the Chemical Industry Association. Soon Burke was writing Heseltine's speeches on the environment, which were seen as helping to develop the critique of laissez-faire policies within the Conservative Party. Indeed, throughout much of the 1980s the Green Alliance (with Burke as director) started a race between the political parties to 'green' themselves. Burke wrote David Owen's (then leader of the Social Democratic Party) speech on 'green growth', a phrase that Chris Patten as Secretary of State for the Environment later employed.

This critique of laissez-faire policies was reinforced at FoE, where Jonathan Porritt had just become Director. His formidable communications skills and his book *Seeing Green* (1984) helped crystallise the environmental movement as 'Green', even though both the Green Alliance (established 1978) and various green parties (especially the German Greens) had also contributed to such a perception. A cultural lifestyle began to emerge comprising vegetarian diets, concern for animals, wholefood shops, open-air festivals, cycling, hiking and rallies; what Strathern described as a cultural intervention to save nature (see chapter 1 above; as well as Savage et al. 1992). Partly as a consequence of this, and partly in response to the widely perceived intransigence of conventional politics to address core elements of contemporary concern, environmental NGOs grew in size and stature. Public concern mounted after the explosion of a nuclear reactor at Chernobyl in May 1986 – a spectacular example of how technology would bring almost instantaneous and widespread contamination; and during 1987 when public concern focused on the hole in the ozone layer – partly shaped by media coverage of scientific discussion, partly as a result of a successful campaign instigated by FoE against CFC producers. The increasing realisation of the instantaneous nature of new technologies helped to augment this sense that the environment was peculiarly threatened by extraordinary rapid ecological disasters that ironically would take many decades or even centuries to undo (see chapter 5 below). In the case of CFCs this realisation was driven home in the message that everyday and apparently benign consumer products (aerosol sprays and fridges) could damage the long-term health of the planet.

However, just as environmental groups were becoming increasingly adept at operating within the formal idioms of policy and science, there was concern that such increasing professionalism might be endangering the excitement that had sparked off the modern environment movement in the early 1970s. Common Ground was formed in 1983 to explore the subjective, imaginative, emotional and spiritual links between people and their local environments. It has sought to counterbalance the scientific with the personal, the rare with the everyday, the spectacular with the ordinary, the global with the local, abstract space with particular places, the general public with people who have complex, ambivalent identities and histories. This has taken place though art exhibitions; books (Clifford and King 1993; King and Clifford 1985; Mabey et al. 1984); encouraging people through the concept of parish maps to map out their place in terms of particular cherished uses (we further discuss the temporal dimensions of parish maps in chapter 5); devising a set of ground rules for 'local distinctiveness'; initiating projects symbolising aspects of nature particularly important to our historical identities, including Trees, Orchards and, most recently, Soil; setting up projects like the New Milestones project where sculptors work with local communities; and setting up new festive days on the calendar such as Tree Dressing Day and Apple Day.

But while the Government stood by its long and 'proud record' in pollution control, NGOs across Europe increasingly presented the UK as 'The Dirty Man of Europe'. Helped by media coverage and coinciding with public unease with the state's perceived intransigence on environmental and other matters, the label appeared to stick. Opportunities were afforded by Britain's membership of the European Community, not only through particular environmental policies and now five Environmental Action Plans, but also through the European Environment Bureau (EEB), a coalition of NGOs with a direct channel of access to the European Community institutions. Nigel Haigh (1987; first published 1984) in particular played a significant role in highlighting opportunities for NGOs to use European law and institutions against the UK Government and contributed, amongst numerous others, to the Environmental Sensitive Areas scheme (a programme where farmers are paid to do low-intensive agriculture), and to the formation of the National Rivers Authority, an independent pollution control body set up to regulate the privatised water industry.

Interestingly, up until the 1980s Britain had approved EC environmental Directives with little hesitation, including those on bathing water (1976), birds (1979), drinking water (1980) and impact assessment (1980). At the time Britain stood by its record as one of the more environmentally conscious countries in Europe, assuming that the five-year implementation period would be more than sufficient to make any necessary adjustments (Haigh and Lanigan 1995: 22). However, as noted, Britain had become labelled as 'The Dirty Man of Europe' by the late 1980s. Haigh and Lanigan (1995) explain the emergence of such a label through developments in the way European environmental policy was handled. Throughout the 1980s the Directorate Générale responsible for the environment (DGX1) grew in stature and prestige. Encouraged by mounting public concern for the environment, the emergence of Green Parties, and the arrival in 1989 of Carlo Ripa di Meana in the post of Environmental Commissioner, DGX1 began to adopt a 'maximalist' approach to the interpretation of environmental directives – in other words, an interpretation that Directives 'should be interpreted and then enforced in ways which maximise benefits for the environment' (Haigh and Lanigan 1995: 24). Such an approach brought the European Community in conflict with the UK, which had traditionally identified Directives more flexibly, as instruments whose implementation could take into account considerations of time, finance and vested interests. Such differences in interpretation provided considerable opportunities for British and European NGOs to accuse the UK Government of dragging its feet on a number of highly controversial issues: including its purported failure to carry out impact assessments on the controversial road proposals at Twyford Down and Oxleas Woods, and in issues of air quality, bathing water and water quality. All these were strategically used by national NGOs to foster the negative image of Britain's environmental credentials.

Finally, the last two decades have been characterised by the 'mediatisation' of social life. During this period the mass media have come to occupy centre-stage in the emergence of the discourse of 'the environment' (see Anderson 1997; Hansen 1993). Throughout the 1980s pressure groups used increasingly complex visual symbols to command public attention. Greenham women and other anti-nuclear protesters used peace camps and the encirclement of nuclear bases as powerful symbols of peaceful resistance (Roseneil 1995). FoE used the symbol of a nuclear explosion and 'nuclear power – no thanks', translated into numerous languages, to symbolise international opposition to nuclear power. Greenpeace used the *Rainbow Warrior* as a heroic symbol of resistance to corporate greed and the clear disregard for nature. Such symbols were novel, dramatic, heroic, fascinating and bizarre. Why would people risk their lives to stop dumping of toxic waste at sea, or spend years of their lives in a peace camp? Pressure groups, and *par excellence* Greenpeace, became increasingly adept at packaging powerful images for the national and international media, reflexive to the media requirements for novelty, human interest and drama.

In turn, by the mid-1980s the quality press began to instigate more regular coverage of environmental issues. One interesting development was the arrival of Max Hastings as editor of the *Daily Telegraph* in 1986, who was of the opinion that 'the countryside faced appalling dangers' (Porritt and Winner 1988: 95). Other newspapers also began to cover environmental issues, but with different emphases in tune with the orientations of their readerships. Thus, while the *Telegraph* focused on countryside issues, *The Times* tended to cover issues from the perspective of Whitehall, while *The Guardian* emphasised nuclear and whaling issues (Anderson 1997).

Media interest reached fever point in the summer of 1988 with widely reported news stories of seal epidemics in the North Sea. The *Daily Mail*, long standing supporter of the Conservative Party, used the seals story to attack the Government for alleged complacency. Other newspapers followed, in the tabloid as well as in the quality press. Indeed, the *Daily Mail*'s coverage of the seals epidemic was the culmination of a series of 'DOOM-WATCH' reports – reports accompanied with the logo 'The environment: the newspaper that cares' (Anderson 1997). The coverage of the seals was largely due to the appeal of 'cuddly animals' as dying victims of North Sea pollution, in a political climate where the Government was identified as largely complacent over the environment. Very shortly afterwards, a high-profile media campaign led by the *Daily Mirror*, alongside an alliance of environmental groups and trade unions, was undertaken to prevent Britain from accepting highly toxic heavy metal cargo from *Karen B*. The rhetoric presented was of a government aiding and abetting the dumping of toxic waste for profit, thus apparently showing wanton disregard and complacency in the face of the worsening environment.

We have thus traced some of the factors that led to the invention and perceived legitimacy of the idea of 'the environment' in contemporary British politics. There are two comparative aspects which are worth noting. First, successive UK governments have since at least the 1970s proved slow to respond to public opinion on the environment, certainly compared with the legislative and regulatory efforts of the US until the Reagan years. This was due partly to the persistence of the traditional view of British policy makers as servants of the executive, to Britain's first-past-the-post electoral system, and to institutional insensitivity to the wider social and historical context of particular concerns. Such factors contributed towards a strong executive with little receptivity towards radically new ideas, sensibilities or indeed political parties. Moreover, the pragmatic approach of voluntary compliance led to a preferred non-coercive approach to pollution, an approach which was to seriously backfire in the acid rain controversy (Hajer 1995), and in more recent controversies over BSE (see chapter 8).

Second, the lack of political influence of the British Green Party is notable compared with mainland Europe. In contrast, the emergence and significance of German environmentalism is more directly related to the rise of *Die Grünen* in the 1980s. The German Greens were particularly adept at being able to reflect the quite considerable array of alternative, anti-nuclear and leftist movements that arose in reaction to the post-war ethos of all-out industrialism (Parkin 1989). Their electoral success, notably in the 1983 European elections, brought a symbolic resonance for a new kind of politics by contrast with the rigidities of the Cold War.

By the late 1980s in Britain nature had been substantially reinvented as the environment; and such an environment had become firmly established as a major issue of British politics and culture. In September 1988 came the highly publicised conversion of Margaret Thatcher in her speech to the Royal Society in which she argued that global environmental issues were of critical importance. A key figure behind this apparent conversion was Sir Crispin Tickell, former UK ambassador to the United Nations. Importantly, though, her focus was not on *local* or *national* environmental issues such as the countryside but on *global* issues, and in particular on ozone, acid pollution and climate change. The speech generated considerable media coverage and led to the rapid appointment of environment correspondents and a search for 'expert' spokespeople who could cast judgement. For the leading environmental NGOs the effect was dramatic. No longer did NGOs play the role of activists seeking to persuade the rest of the world of the importance of environmental issues. Now the rest of the world appeared to share their agenda and was looking to NGOs for the next move. The state formally classified the environment as a priority, and thus politically some action was anticipated. The effect of the speech was to ensure that the environment was firmly established on the political agenda. One consequence was that large numbers of people joined environmental groups which were perceived to have long voiced the same message of global danger, especially those with high media profiles. Between 1985 and 1989, Greenpeace's UK membership grew from 50,000 to 320,000, and FoE's from 27,000 to 120,000. By 1990, the British environment movement had 4.5 million members, making it, after the trade unions, the largest mass movement in British history (McCormick 1991a).

Also in 1988, Elkington and Hailes published *The Green Consumer Guide*. Within a year the *Guide* had been through 11 impressions and had sold 350,000 copies (McCormick 1991a: 107). Throughout 1989 green consumerism became one of the most fashionable concepts in public life, shared by media, supermarkets, political parties and industry. McCormick describes how companies began to boast their 'green' credentials:

> Among the products promoted as green were unleaded petrol (Shell and Esso), batteries (Panasonic and Varta), chlorine-free disposable nappies (Peaudouce and Procter & Gamble), 'environmentally friendly' cars (Volkswagen, Audi and Vauxhall) and supermarket chains (Tesco and the Co-op). (1991a: 111)

The growth of green consumerism was part of a more general process of normalising the environment. In terms of international politics following the 'end' of the Cold War in 1989, 'the environment' became internationally established as part of the new world order. It was constituted as a set of concerns shared by both East and West, North and South. The concepts of sustainability and sustainable development emerged as the bases of a new officially backed discourse in which global corporations, states and environmental groups could all discuss environmental matters, and could all seek to participate in a post-Cold War agenda (this we discuss in chapter 7 below).

To understand the significance of the 1992 Earth Summit, we need to retrace briefly the history of global environmentalism since Stockholm in 1972. One output from the Stockholm conference was the formation of the United Nations Environment Programme (UNEP). The blueprint for UNEP was the Stockholm Action Plan, a highly rationalist programme in the mode of the *Limits to Growth* report, with a narrative of big science assessing the state of the environment and of determining environmental limits. A UN-sponsored body, Earthwatch, was set up to collect information from national governments and to assess global environmental trends, although in practice actual progress was uneven.

However, a number of reports through the 1970s and 1980s did foster the idea of a *global* environment. In 1977 President Carter commissioned a follow-up to the *Limits to Growth* report which resulted in the 1980 *Global 2000* report. In 1980 the International Union for the Conservation of Nature (IUCN) produced the *World Conservation Strategy* (WCS), which sought to identify the main threats to species and ecosystems. In 1980 the UN Brandt Commission produced the Brandt Report which identified growing economic and social inequities between North and South and how this threatened common security and survival. In 1987 the World Commission on Environment and Development produced the Brundtland Report, which popularised the term 'sustainability' and introduced the need to link the concept of the environment with that of development.

These reports and related international agreements provided the context for the 1992 United Nations Earth Summit at Rio. Rio represented the largest coming together of world leaders to discuss the environment and represents the pinnacle of *international* environmentalism and the beginning of a new phase of uncertainty. Here in the grand style of UN conferences, and representing a bigger and better version of Stockholm 1972, the principles of sustainability were agreed and global action plans endorsed (Rose 1993).

Since 1990 the UK Government has produced a White Paper, *This Common Inheritance*, the UK's first comprehensive policy document on the environment; an Environmental Protection Act in 1990; a formal policy response to the Earth Summit, *Sustainable Development: The UK Strategy* (1994); and a newly formed Environment Agency. This gamut of initiatives has 'consolidated the arrival of environment as a political language and concern' (Grove-White 1995: 269). One initiative intended to elevate environmental policy *within* the market discourse favoured by the Treasury was the appointment of Professor David Pearce as specialist advisor – the country's chief proponent of environmental economics and surrogate valuation methodologies (Grove-White 1997). The use of surrogate methodologies where monetary values would be attributed to environmental considerations promised a future where policy makers could weigh up the costs and benefits of proposed developments on an apparently rational and politically compelling basis – an approach which NGOs immediately attacked as misconceived.

The advocacy of cost–benefit approaches illustrates the rationalist approach favoured by the former Conservative Government to assess nature. Parallel techniques include those of formal risk assessment and eco-auditing (O'Riordan and Jordan 1995). Environmental issues are thus identified as a set of 'technological problems' requiring 'rational solutions', preferably through the use of science and economics. Since 1992 the UK Government has also launched a number of additional environmental initiatives reflecting its new commitments towards sustainability. These include: a high-ranking governmental advisory panel reporting directly to the Prime Minister, under the chair of Sir Crispin Tickell; a Round Table of 30 members from

business, local government, environmental NGOs and academia, aimed at
establishing consensus on issues of direct relevance to sustainability; and a
citizens' initiative scheme, 'Going for Green', aimed at encouraging environmentally friendly behaviours amongst the wider public. Such initiatives
reflect the new emphases on consensus building, and point to the claimed
aspiration to move towards sustainability in apparent *partnership* with
industry, environmental groups and the public.

As a result of these various developments since 1988, environmental
groups in Britain have struggled to redefine their role in a world in which
environmental discourses are now accepted as a legitimate part of a new
world order. The Rio Earth Summit proved a landmark event. But just when
environment groups had been invited to debate the environment, alongside
and occasionally in equal status with states and corporations, much of the
public had apparently become disappointed with and sceptical about the
results. In the next section we outline some very recent developments in the
post-Rio history of environmentalism, developments which seek to challenge the by now dominant environmental discourse. We begin with the
exceptional controversies generated by the road-building programme within
Britain.

Post-Rio environmentalism

Road rage

By February 1994, the scale of grassroots protest against the construction of
new roads had risen to such a level that Geoffrey Lean (1994), the doyen of
British environmental correspondents, described it as 'the most vigorous
new force in British environmentalism'. There are an estimated 250 anti-
road groups in the UK (Chaudhary 1994). The institutional context was the
Conservative Government's £23 billion proposed roads programme, which
was actively opposed by a wide consortium of environmental groups. By
contrast with previous campaigns, the tactic of non-violent direct action was
used by the anti-roads grassroots protesters.

Such non-violent campaigns drew partly of course on the extraordinary
experience of women who had lived in or visited the Greenham peace camp.
All through the 1980s the camp surrounding the perimeter of a USAF Cruise
Base had directed the world's attention to nuclear militarism as the symbol
of Cold War modernity. Roseneil graphically writes of the 'juxtaposition of
the colourful, domestic, ramshackle camp and the decorations of women's
symbols, doves, and handwritten messages hung on the fence with the rolls
of razor wire, watch towers, searchlights, and soldiers in fatigues' (1995:
115). Because of living in a liminal space in the open air many women were
led to rethink the 'environment', especially as they could see just how the
Base entailed the displacement of wildlife and the felling of hundreds of
trees (just as with road-building). The experience of living in the camp also
appears to have led many women to locate issues within more of a global

frame, to see the connections between the intensely local spatial practice of the camp and issues of worldwide militarism, patriarchy, development and the environment. More generally, Roseneil argues that the setting up of protest camps, the use of peaceful blockades and sabotage, and the general anti-modernist carnivalesque of the camp provided a new repertoire of collective action especially for those men and women who were to be engaged in the road campaigns in the 1990s.

The first of these occurred at Twyford Down. The decision to cut a road through one of Britain's most protected landscapes (home of two scheduled ancient monuments, several rare and protected species, and part of an Area of Outstanding Natural Beauty) had been decided following a public inquiry in 1985. However, it was not until 1992, following numerous injunctions, European Court rulings and other forms of objection, that construction work on this extension of the M3 was due to commence. By then the campaign run by local residents, national environmental groups and even the European Commission had more or less ceased. However, just as the more established and professional movement was accepting the end of a hotly fought but unsuccessful campaign, a new set of protesters was beginning to be involved. Throughout the summer of 1992, growing numbers of activists had come to set up camp on Twyford Down, preparing for a long campaign of active non-violent direct action. Composed of members of Earth First!, a hitherto American radical direct action group, and the newly formed

Plate 2.1 *Twyford Down: Donga tribe lament over the devastation of the countryside (source: with kind permission of Nigel Dickinson/Still Pictures)*

'Dongas' (a nomadic, back-to-the-earth tribe named after the Celtic track-ways which criss-cross the Down), a loose coalition of activists formed to prevent the road's construction.

The Dongas soon became a focal point of the protest (see plate 2.1). It had started in March 1992 when a young couple set up camp on the Dongas. Soon news spread and a growing band of people came to visit, some who joined the camp permanently. The camp before long evolved into what came to be the 'Donga Tribe'. One of the Dongas, Indra, describes her reasons for joining the tribe:

> We all felt completely frustrated by the way our environment is being destroyed. But as individuals, the idea of trying to change things was overwhelming. Where do you start? When we came together we realised that not only did we feel the same way but as a group we could do something about it. (cited Miss Pod 1993: 8)

Instead of becoming involved in existing environmental groups (such as the hitherto radical groups Greenpeace and Friends of the Earth), campaigners such as Indra were more inclined to join or to sympathise with the Dongas. The timing of the formation of the Dongas is interesting, since it occurred during the same summer as the 1992 Rio Earth Summit which had moved ecological issues to the top of the global agenda.

However, in this process, environmentalism appeared to have lost much of its critical voice as states, corporations and environmental groups all appeared to share the same language, the same commitments and the same appeal to management as the way to tackle global environmental problems (Sachs 1993; see also chapter 7 below). As environmentalists came to be seen as a legitimate part of the policy process, that very same process came to be critiqued as unlikely to achieve real environmental improvement. By the summer of 1992 especially younger activists began to think of main-stream environmental groups as having lost their radicalism and thus no longer the 'vehicle for agency' and empowerment that they had appeared to be only a few years earlier.

In this situation, the UK Government's roads programme symbolised the hollowness of its stated environmental credentials. Moreover, conventional campaigning tactics such as lobbying, public inquiries and pressure politics were perceived to be largely ineffective techniques to prevent the building of new roads. There was a general and shared perception that roads would be built despite the strength of local opinion, the ecological or landscape sensitivity of the site, or the damage to the social fabric of the community that would incur. Such considerations were largely beyond the frames of reference used in the formal assessment of costs and benefits and thus thought to be of little value. Indeed, in this context of general fatalism, the new and passionate attempts by the Dongas to prevent the physical construction of a road through one of Britain's most cherished sites became a catalyst for a new kind of environmental discourse. Welsh and McLeish (1996) provide an intriguing explanation for these forms of protest. Following Foucault's observations that all discipline ultimately is exercised upon the body, they provocatively suggest that anti-road activists offer their bodies to the state directly, symbolically gesturing the futility of more formal methods of participation and political protest.

Media attention focused on the Dongas when six members were jailed for breaching an injunction barring them from the site in July 1992. Throughout the autumn clashes between the protesters and security guards became common. Protesters invented a new array of practices to delay, sabotage, demonstrate, trespass and party upon the proposed site. Much of this was learnt from the experiences of Earth First!, who in America had developed an array of techniques of 'eco-sabotage'. However, it was the highly publicised skirmishes between the protesters and heavy-handed security guards in the so-called 'Battle of Twyford Down' on 9 December that brought the campaign to the public's attention. As Vidal points out: 'The powerful modern image of private money hand in hand with the machinery of the state rolling over the economically weakest to appropriate common resources was given perfect expression' (1994: 4).

Initially, both government bodies and environmental groups misread the significance of this new environmental protest, failing to realise its wider symbolic appeal. Friends of the Earth in 1992 warned its members not to have anything to do with Earth First!, believing that association with these radicals would lose them credibility. The UK Department of Transport responded to the battle with extensive policing (the cost of policing Twyford Down was an estimated £1.7 million); the hiring of private detectives to trace and photograph protesters (an estimated £250,000); and unsuccessful attempts to use the courts to make 76 protesters pay an estimated £1.2 million for delaying the work (Lezard 1993: 22; Vidal 1994: 4).

However, despite these official attempts to eliminate this new 'unlawful' protest, numerous anti-road groups were set up across the country within one year of Twyford, many of these formed under new umbrella alliances and information networks dedicated to the use of non-violent direct action (Vidal 1994: 4). Focal points of conflict moved to the M11 link road at Wanstead and Leytonstone in East London, and later to the M77 outside Glasgow, to the M65 in Lancashire, and to countless other proposed road sites in Newcastle, Bath, Skye, London, Oxford, Cornwall and, most recently, Newbury. In 1995 direct action protest moved to other forms of proposed development, including open-cast mining. The organisation 'Reclaim the Streets' also held street parties whereby groups of activists set out to take over streets, 'closing [them] to machines and opening [them] up for people' (Davis 1995: 5).

The array of direct actions has also diversified as protesters have become more expert, through the use of mass trespass, squatting in buildings and living in trees threatened by road programmes. They also have became more sophisticated in the use of new technologies, including mobile phones, video cameras and the Internet. This has enabled almost instantaneous dissemination to the media, as well as information about actions for a growing band of protesters prepared to travel up and down the country to protest against proposed developments (Travis 1994; Woolf 1995). Such developments have led to more 'efficient' actions: for example, in the first year alone, the 'No M11 Link Road' campaign cost the Government's newly formed Highways Agency an estimated £16 million (Penman 1995: 2).

Since 1992, there seems to have been considerable public support and sympathy for such actions, and there has been abundant media coverage across both the tabloid and quality press, growing support from more established environment groups, and surprising alliances made between radical activists and the wider population. Indeed, much has been made of the strange alliances between direct action protesters and their more mainstream counterparts, including establishment figures such as Princess Diana's step-brother Rupert Lege, the Marchioness of Worcester, the writer Bel Mooney, as well as the lollypop woman who played an active part in the M11 protests. Moreover, a recent June 1995 Gallup poll found that more than two-thirds of the British population agree with the proposition that 'there are times when protesters are justified in breaking the law, particularly in cases of environmental destruction' (Penman 1995: 2). And even with the latest announcement in July 1997 by the incoming Labour Government that it won't be proceeding with a number of the most sensitive road schemes (such as the Salisbury bypass), direct action anti-road protest appears to continue unabated.

Animal rage

The second most popular site for grassroots direct action environmental protest in the 1990s has centred on actions directed against perceived animal abuses (see Dickens 1996: chap. 2 for a powerful analysis of the 'alienated' nature of animal life within modern farming methods). Although public concern for animal welfare has been traditionally strong in Britain, non-violent direct action was rarely considered outside a small group of animal rights activists (most notably the largely underground animal rights organis-ation the Animal Liberation Front). However, from the middle of 1994 widespread public protest in many provincial English towns and cities has focused on the commercial export of live animals, most notably veal calves to Europe.

Before the Channel tunnel opened, the livestock export trade (involving an estimated 2 million calves and worth about £175 million) had been controlled by a small number of big ferry operators in major industrial ports such as Dover and Ramsgate. However, following the opening of the tunnel in 1994, the ferry operators disposed of the trade in live animals, sensitive to how the continuing presence of captive calves and livestock could drive away passengers in the new competitive market. Hence the trade in live animals moved to smaller ports and airports across England and Wales, where it rapidly became a hugely contested local issue. By the end of 1994 increasing numbers of people were demonstrating in the streets, angry and indignant over the inhumane conditions of calves in transport, the vested interests profiting from the export of live animals, and frustrated by the perceived intransigence and unresponsiveness of British institutions to stop the trade. Even Alan Clark, the former Tory minister, joined the demonstrations at Dover, clearly outraged and angry with the heavy policing he encountered:

> God knows what crimes are being committed while you are standing here watching defenceless animals being driven through this port. All this is a drain on police resources in support of a foul and repellent trade, which everyone in this country hates. All you are doing is pushing up the profits of a load of thugs in the haulage industry – congratulations! (cited Vallely 1995: 11)

By early 1995 protests against the export of live animals had focused on the sea ports of Dover in Kent, Brightlingsea in Essex, Plymouth in Devon, Shoreham in West Sussex, and the airports of Coventry and Swansea. In February 1995 Jill Phipps, an animal rights activist, died under the wheels of a delivery lorry as she tried to obstruct it. The death brought into focus the passion and intensity of the movement, as thousands flocked to the funeral at Coventry Cathedral, resulting in front-page media coverage.

Similar to the anti-roads protests, strange and diverse alliances were made, including those between animal rights activists, a broad green/left alliance of environmentalists and animal sympathisers, and local people, most of whom had previously never been involved in demonstrations (Erlichman et al. 1995; Vallely 1995). The new alliances of protesters led to considerable media coverage, with stories of 'how suburban housewives rubbed shoulders with new age travellers' (Gibbons 1995), and of 'the peaceful uprising of middle England against a cruel and immoral trade' (Heath 1995). By February 1995 the trade in live calves for European veal crates had been reduced to a mere 10,000 a month, as cross-channel ferries pulled out of the trade, and many small port authorities and regional airports began to enforce a ban on the export of live animals (Gibbons 1995). In response to such overt pressures, William Waldegrave as Agriculture Minister proposed that, notwithstanding his own personal distaste with the export trade in live animals, a ban under European law would be illegal and thus there was little the UK Government could do unilaterally (ironically the trade was abandoned altogether in 1996, an inadvertent product of the BSE crisis and the European ban on British beef quite unrelated to animal welfare considerations; see chapter 8 below).

In the face of such 'direct' and often passionate forms of grassroots protest, official responses have tended to be out of touch with the public mood, frequently caught out by the scale and intensity of the protests and the considerable public support commanded by the protesters (Erlichman et al. 1995). The dominant state response to the 'new environmental protest' has been to treat the unrest within a narrow framework of legislation and public order policing, as if the fitting response is to label such protest activity as 'dangerous' and 'unlawful' and thus appropriate for more intensive policing (Mansfield 1995). Propelled by earlier annual exchanges with new age travellers and the escalating conflicts between hunters and anti-hunt sabo-teurs, the Government, after intense lobbying from the powerful Country Landowners' Association, introduced specific measures into its 1994 Crimi-nal Justice Bill to protect landowners and stop direct action protest. Ironically, while the Act may have contributed to the decline of the new age traveller phenomenon of the 1980s, the effect of the Act appears also to have further energised the protest networks and to have at least initially led to new coalitions with other marginal social networks affected by the Act, including squatters, ravers, the dance party movement and other 'non-organisation' organisations (Travis 1994).

Oil rage

We now turn to an analogous episode which shows how one of the big NGOs responded to and capitalised upon this new effort to rewrite environ-mental discourse. But by comparison with the examples just discussed, Greenpeace's campaign to stop Shell dumping the *Brent Spar* oil platform related to the globalisation of risk and of the ability of the NGO to operate globally.

Greenpeace's campaign to stop Shell dumping the *Brent Spar* began on 20 January 1995. Guys Thieme, who had been newly appointed as coordinator of Greenpeace's North Sea campaign, noticed a copy of Shell's Best Practical Environmental Option (BPEO) proposals for the forthcoming disposal of the *Brent Spar* oil platform. For Greenpeace the disposal of the *Brent Spar* was of huge symbolic importance. Not only was the *Spar* the first of approximately 400 oil platforms in the North Sea due to be decom-missioned over the coming decades, but the proposed method of disposal at sea was viewed as sending the wrong signals to industry that the seas could be used as free dumping grounds for the waste products of industrial society (Dickson and McCulloch 1996). The initial idea was that Greenpeace should stage an occupation on land in protest against the plans for its dumping. However, after discussion with the 'actions' unit, it was decided to occupy *Brent Spar* itself and turn the platform into the headquarters for the campaign. A £600,000 budget was drawn up, and a final decision made to go ahead with the campaign on 11 April. A number of key ingredients thus came together to constitute this dramatic campaign: *Brent Spar* as the symbol of sea pollution; Greenpeace as heroically occupying the platform, thus protecting and bearing witness to the natural world; and huge publicity potential, much of which was facilitated by Greenpeace's communications skills.

The first challenge was to get onto the *Brent Spar*, a sizeable task since Greenpeace only had three weeks before Shell workers were due to move in to sink the platform. Jonathan Castle, veteran Greenpeace protester and former captain of the *Rainbow Warrior*, chartered a boat, the *Embla*, equipped it with six months supply of food and water, and set sail for the *Brent Spar*. On 30 April Operation 'Bees Knees' was executed when a team of climbers and activists climbed aboard the oil platform and set up campaign headquarters. As Pilkington et al. point out, what was hugely significant was the communications technology:

> It may have been a traditional protest, but the communications deployed were second to none. The protesters had satellite telephones and a Mac computer that downloaded photographs and video footage to a media base in Frankfurt. Greenpeace employed its own photographer and cameraman to capture the images that ensured the story was splashed in papers and television screens across the world. (1995: 4)

Before Greenpeace's protest there had not been any protest about Shell's proposals. Indeed, Shell had gone to considerable lengths to convince the UK authorities in private consultations that the deep sea disposal of the rig, in 6,000 feet of water 150 miles from the Outer Hebrides, was the 'best practical environmental alternative'. However, once on board the rig, Greenpeace set about a dual strategy of producing scientific evidence in favour of disposing the oil rig on shore, and in mobilising public opinion.

Reporters from the press and TV stations were invited to join the protesters and given access to their communications facilities. And when Greenpeace activists were eventually evicted from the site they proceeded to shadow the *Spar* by helicopter and rubber dinghies, catching on camera heroic moments of activists hosed down by water pipes before rescaling the platform. A consumer boycott of Shell products developed, starting in Germany and spreading throughout Europe. Unlike previous consumer boycotts, this one was coordinated and sustained and made a very real financial impact on Shell, at one stage costing the company an estimated £5 million a day, and causing certain outlets (especially in Germany) to lose up to 30% on sales. Leading politicians too announced they were boycotting Shell, appeals were made by all of Britain's European partners (except Norway) to dispose of the site on land at the Fourth North Sea Ministerial Conference on 8 and 9 June, and a week later Chancellor Helmut Kohl scored a first by making an environmental issue cause for a diplomatic rebuke when he met John Major at a G7 meeting in June 1995 (Ghazi et al. 1995). The longer-lasting impact on Shell's image was probably greater. Indeed, the scale of public response is reported to have taken even Greenpeace by surprise. On 20 June Shell capitulated and announced its decision to abandon plans to sink the rig in the deep sea. The initial reaction from the UK Government was anger, humiliated that a non-elected pressure group could have outmanoeuvred them, and outraged that Shell (one of Britain's leading and most respected companies) had apparently given in to emotional blackmail. PM John Major immediately responded by accusing Shell of acting like 'a wimp' and stressed that there was no guarantee that the UK Government would grant Shell a licence to dispose of the *Brent Spar* on land. Since *Brent Spar*, other high-profile consumer boycotts have developed, notably against Shell over its environmental record in Ogoni Land in Nigeria and its alleged complicity in the hanging of the Nigerian environmental and social rights campaigner Ken Saro-Wiwa, and against the

French for the policy of continuing nuclear testing in the Pacific in the face of international (including state) opposition.

Thus since Rio we have seen the emergence of new patterns of environmental protest within Britain and elsewhere. Such protest particularly appeals to young people to become directly engaged and personally responsible for a better future. And although such protests have a complex prehistory, from free festivals in the 1960s, to punk in the 1970s, to rave culture in the 1980s and 1990s (see McKay 1996), contemporary direct action has formed partly in reaction to the professionalism and growing elitism of the more established environmental groups – indeed to the environmental discourse which has been so painstakingly invented over the past three decades. Such protest especially emphasises inventiveness in method, including the surprising use of new technologies. It emphasises a sense of fun and self-expression, provocatively deploying the inversions of the carnivalesque. These protests demonstrate a heightened cynicism with official organisations and processes. There is thus a newer generation of environmentalists who are by-passing conventional environmental groups, especially those perceived to have been co-opted by the state and industry and whose commitment to the environment is perceived as mere rhetoric. Such newer environmentalists employ various kinds of non-violent direct citizens' action in the face of the intransigence of what is perceived to be 'the system'. Central to both grassroots direct action and campaigns such as Brent Spar is the striking use of imagery. In the case of the road protester the image is the heroic saviour of each *local* tree about to be felled by the

Plate 2.2   *Tree-hugging (source: with kind permission of Andrew Testa)*

Plate 2.3   *Saving trees from modernity (source: with kind permission of Andrew Testa)*

Plate 2.4   *David and Goliath: Greenpeace activists preparing to board Brent Spar (source: with kind permission of Greenpeace UK/Sims)*

contractors and which is protected by the tree-dweller (see plates 2.2 and 2.3). In the case of Greenpeace it is that of the campaigners who climbed aboard the *Brent Spar* waving to the world through the media, bearing witness to the destruction of *global* nature (see plate 2.4).

However, perhaps even more significantly, the new environmental protests reflect the new experiences of living with global risk in a detraditionalised society. In all cases official bodies have been surprised by the scale of protest and apparently finding such protest outside of existing discourses. As was said about *Brent Spar*, both Shell and the UK Government did not realise that the public does not really care about the arguments of costs versus benefits; they just 'don't like shit being dumped in the oceans' (Ghazi et al. 1995). So too with the behaviour of Shell in Nigeria, the company simply failed to understand that people now expect business to operate in a moral framework, beyond the more limited concerns of their shareholders. Similarly in connection with the road and animal protests, the state failed to comprehend how such protests reflected wider contestation with modernity. Such protests reflect new vehicles for agency in a world in which increasing numbers of people are convinced that governments and business are only concerned with looking after their own interests. We finish by setting out how two *Guardian* columnists articulate the significance of *Brent Spar* and the new environmental protest movement:

> What links the nuclear tests issue with those of pollution, animal rights and others on the protest agenda is not only the fact that Greenpeace has gone so swiftly from its *Brent Spar* triumph in the Atlantic to its confrontation with the French in the Pacific. It is the collision between the anger of people convinced that governments and businesses are every day taking decisions that make the world a more dangerous place and elites who still live mentally in a cosy we-know-best universe in which protest is a problem to be managed rather than a voice to be heeded. (Woollacott 1995)

> The story of *Brent Spar* . . . should be therapy for paranoids. It disposes of the idea of the government-industrial complex. . . . The community of interest between the sinister powers of politics and finance has apparently collapsed. One vast oil company and several democratic leaders, accustomed to agreeing and deciding, have been intimidated into reversing themselves by a single pressure group. Power politics will never the same again. There is business, there is government, and there is what Greenpeace would call the citizenry of the world whose interests it represents against the baleful conspiracies of the other two. (Young 1995)

Hugo Young continues by suggesting that such direct action protests help define the crisis of mainline politics. In chapter 8 below we shall assess further such a perspective and examine the challenges such protests bring for global governance.

Conclusion

We have thus sought to show just how 'nature as environment' has been invented and developed, especially in the British (actually mainly English) context. We have seen just how complex has been this process. There are a number of strands in that story to emphasise in conclusion. First, the contemporary environmental movement and its discursive practices have a complex history, having arisen from diverse factors. These include English Romanticism; the traditions of preservationism; critique of post-war modernisation; science-based critiques of unlimited growth; the expansion in ecology and nature conservation expertise; the counter-cultural movement; the mediatisation of social life; the development of other social critiques and social movements, especially feminism and urban movements; and opposition to the dangers of the Cold War and the search for certain global commonalities. This further entails that the meaning of nature in particular controversies has been multiple and often contested. These include the idea of nature as landscape, as the object of scientific study, as threatened and in need of protection, as providing resources and life support essential to human survival, as a source for spiritual renewal and communion, and most generally as 'the environment'.

Second, there are different kinds of relationship between the state and what can loosely be termed environmental NGOs in the complex evolution of contemporary environmentalism in Britain. Up to the late 1960s, there were specialised and differentiated definitions of nature and the natural. The dominant relationship between the state and the then traditional NGOs, operating with one or other sense of nature, was 'gentlemanly' and consultative. During the 1970s and 1980s, the agenda broadened and new NGOs adopted a campaigning style seeking to demonstrate that there was a more or less single 'environment' which needed protection. And in the 1990s, with the environment clearly on the political and social agenda, the role of the NGOs has become more ambivalent. In particular, instead of struggling to prove the existence of environmental issues, they seek to find solutions. Such a shift, reflected most explicitly by Greenpeace, has led to an increased focus upon industry. The role of NGOs is of special significance in a period where they are often trusted more than government, and where industry is trusted hardly at all (Rose 1995: 9). Part then of their role is to convince the public that they can influence apparently intransigent multinationals, as was achieved so successfully with Shell and the *Brent Spar*. At the same time such NGOs need to employ the marketing and media techniques of the enterprise culture, to develop scientific expertise comparable with government departments, and to work in partnership with local, national and international state organisations.

Third, in particular many environmental groups are working within the new political space afforded by the shared language of sustainability. They have had to learn to work in partnership with the state and industry, often by way of consensus-seeking round-table discussions, striving to influence policy in a practical and incremental fashion. Such perspectives are reflected in the Round Table set up by the UK Government, as well as in the numerous Round Tables set up by local government initiatives as part of Local Agenda 21 initiatives following the Rio Summit. Such Agenda 21 initiatives are designed to encourage wider public participation in officially sanctioned sustainability initiatives. Such initiatives, driven by commitments undertaken at Rio (including the 'Going for Green' initiative), will be critically examined in chapter 7 below.

Fourth, many environmental issues have come to public prominence because they symbolise a broader critique of modern society and of the relations between humans and various kinds of apparently undetectable risk. Thus public opposition to nuclear power in the late 1970s reflected huge disillusionment with technological progress and resistance to the modernising project. Contestation over the English countryside in the mid-1980s reflected concern with the dominance of unregulated markets and their exceptional capacity to destroy people's sense of dwelling, place and identity. Hence the 'environmental agenda' emerged not simply through linear scientific advance but through key events in which states, NGOs and the media came to conceive of the environment as systemic and global, rather than as sporadic and local. The very emergence of nature as the environment is not a linear narrative involving straightforward scientific advance and policy response, but rather one involving complex cultural work so as to connect together often diverse and apparently disparate elements.

Finally, we have seen that new challenges to the emergent environmental discourse have recently emerged, challenges which are as much cultural as they are political. They entail oppositional forms of dress, hair, household, manner, argument, music, sex, drugs, nature, image, and so on. And such protests are not conventionally political but reflect wider cultural shifts of detraditionalisation in that both the intensely local road campaigns and the ingeniously global Greenpeace by-pass national states and their bureaucratically administered attempts at regulation of the environment. It should also be noted that such an anti-statism can take a particularly bleak form, as in the US where American militia groups have articulated a pro-local natureism in order to justify bombing Federal installations.

In the next chapter we consider how these ideas of nature and the environment engage with lay publics, and the effects they have on them. We examine research on how people think, understand, value, worry about and act towards nature and the environment. In subsequent chapters we show that theories of time, space, the senses and cultural change are necessary in order to unravel the complex history of the present reported here.

3
HUMANS AND NATURE

In this chapter we examine in what ways and to what extent the risks and issues now thought of as 'environmental' concern and engage people. How do people comprehend and learn to live with the myriad of risks that seem to absorb daily life? Has environmental concern helped to constitute new forms of human identity and social relations, or led to new public values and worldviews? How concerned are people with environmental threats that can no longer be sensed, and whose effects transcend conventional categories of time? How far has this concern led to shifts in public behaviour, or to a heightened sense of responsibility towards producing a better environment? And does public concern and engagement with environmental matters symbolise wider concerns about contemporary life, including a sense of unease with current trajectories of social change?

These complex questions are currently being interrogated by academics, opinion pollsters and policy analysts. One leading commentator on British environmental issues, Tim O'Riordan, recently stated that 'Environmental concern has become one of the most profound and enduring social themes the world over in the last 25 years' (1995: 4). Other commentators also point to the emergence of new environmental paradigms (Dunlap and Van Liere 1978), to growing postmaterial values (Inglehart 1977), and to the increased numbers of people identifying themselves as environmentalists (Dunlap and Scarce 1991) and of adopting ecologically oriented views and perspectives (O'Riordan 1976, 1989). In this chapter we evaluate the evidence relating to these various claims.

Our aim is first to summarise the survey research relating to public perceptions, attitudes, value orientations and belief structures oriented to the 'environment'. We review such research on what people think and do about the environment and examine the discursive structures upon which the research rests. We try to show this style of research is part of a more general 'polling culture' that has become peculiarly powerful in late twentieth-century societies. It is bound up within the context of the environment with new obligations to affect and to measure 'participation' in a sustainable future. However, we suggest that such polling techniques are not sufficiently powerful to capture the hugely complex and deeply ambivalent ways in which people do in fact engage with what have come to be recognised as environmental issues and behaviours. We then consider certain qualitative methods of research and explore their relevance to those social and cultural dimensions that do appear to structure people's engagements with nature. It seems that since the environment is something understood and experienced through certain social practices, so research will need to reflect or to simulate some at least of the characteristics of those socially embedded practices, noting of course large variations by class, gender, age and ethnicity. Throughout the chapter we demonstrate the diverse conceptions of the 'human' subject implicit within such different methodologies.

These methodological debates have more than mere academic significance since the frameworks and doctrines structuring how we conceptualise environmental concerns and behaviours have clear implications for subsequent policy and collective response to the emerging environmental agenda. For many commentators the framework is simple. Scientific knowledge informs us of the increasing importance of environmental risks – hence people must respond by changing their beliefs and activities so as to reduce such risks and to produce a more sustainable future. Such a view is driven by the combination of all three doctrines of environmental realism, idealism and instrumentalism outlined in chapter 1 above, where realist accounts of the problem combine with an instrumentalist conception of the need to understand what the public is thinking, and where preferred techniques are drawn from survey polls designed to capture underlying attitudes and values. For example, Bob Worcester, founder and chair of MORI and Britain's best-known pollster, suggests that opinion poll research can address the question: 'How must values change for the well being and prosperity of future generations to be secured?' (1994: 1). Similarly, Kempton et al. argue that 'Understanding culture is an essential part of understanding environmental problems because human cultures guide their members both when they accelerate environmental problems and when they slow it down' (1995: 1). Central to both accounts is the realist assumption that while science can inform us about the state of nature, the social sciences enable us to explain and predict how people will respond to that nature and whether they will engage in behaviours which are environmentally benign or environmentally destructive. Such a polling process is then seen as necessary in order to devise appropriate policies. The culture of polling is part of the process of environmental policy determination.

This connection between polling and policy has become of much greater significance within the environmental sphere since the Rio Earth Summit in 1992. Policy makers have now to find ways to change public behaviour and to encourage active participation with government initiatives to further sustainability. The concept of participation has become a core component in environmental policy making, written into action plans and strategy documents at international (CEC 1992b; UNCED 1992), national (UK Government 1994) and local levels (LGMB 1993, 1994a). Whereas previously governments and policy makers could devise environmental policy largely independent from public opinion and the need for public engagement, this is no longer the case. As explored in chapter 7 below, a new discourse is emerging where people are encouraged to change their lifestyles, to participate in government initiatives and to act locally in ways which respect the global environment. As a recent UK Government 'Going for Green' (1996) advertisement stated: 'We can make a difference – together'. In order to aid and monitor such participation the public have to be routinely surveyed as key elements of the 'polling culture' of contemporary societies.

Such a polling culture is itself part of a wider set of reforms which have absorbed most governments in the western world, reforms which the UK think-tank Demos (1995a) has usefully termed 'missionary government'. Such reforms can be seen through the new idioms of 'service provision', 'customer care', 'value for money', 'market testing', 'efficiency savings', and perhaps most spectacularly in the explosion of the 'audit society' (Power 1994). Such reforms reflect a greater desire for states to prove to their electorates their accountability through quantification (or, to use Porter's [1995] phrase, through a 'trust in numbers'). This itself partially reflects the lack of confidence of democratic institutions in the face of mounting public disaffection with mainstream politics. Moreover, as illustrated throughout various parts of this book, the intense desire to understand the public through quantified indicators is likely to be largely self-defeating, since the epistemological and other theoretical assumptions underpinning such techniques are problematic for a number of reasons. Indeed, as we examine in chapter 8 below, crises such as that associated with BSE could not have been predicted through survey polls as currently conceived.

There are three problems with such survey research as the basis of policy. First, the kinds of policies that come to be advocated are those which can in fact be assessed through quantitative techniques, particularly through treating the individual as a polled consumer. The environment is regarded like any other object or experience. The 'consumer' of the environment is viewed as though he or she is similar to the consumer of sweets or the consumer of Switzerland. Thus the assessment of policies is subject to short-term criteria and is not directed to their long-term impact, especially to the evaluation of change in glacial time (see chapter 5 below). Evaluating outcomes in terms of people's immediate responses to being polled in a survey emphasises their more or less instantaneous responses to the questions asked.

Second, we argue in chapter 4 that people come to sense the environment in diverse, multi-faceted and complex ways. Survey questions will weakly capture these different forms in which nature is sensed. They will neglect the passion that people often feel towards nature and local places, or the ambivalence that appears to invade how they respond towards environmental threats, or indeed the cultural factors that have led to the emergence of environmental ideas and perspectives in the first place (including those described in chapter 2). Survey questions are unlikely to capture the sheer density of feeling attached to dwelling in particular environments, and neglect the complex relationships between ideas of nature and wider critiques of progress and societal change.

And third, survey methodology will treat the responses of people to nature in a somewhat linear fashion, as though environmental issues can be set out as 'objects' to which people have particular views and opinions, separate from the social practices in which they are routinely engaged. Surveys proceed with an inappropriate and overly simple model of the human subject. We thus need instead to employ methods of research which at least begin to capture how those concerns that we now take to be 'environmental' are embedded in more wide-ranging arguments and dilemmas facing contemporary societies, including issues of progress, social exclusion, individualism, spirituality, consumerism, security, crime, health, and so on.

The polling culture and the environment

Over the last 20 years or so a mass of data has been gathered on people's attitudes, values and behaviours towards the environment. Most of this research has been dominated by quantitative approaches, usually in the form of opinion polls or attitude surveys. Such surveys typically involve interviews with a representative sample of between 1,000 and 2,000 people within national boundaries. For this chapter we highlight those surveys which have been most influential in *policy making*, including surveys commissioned by public agencies and carried out by market research companies. These include a number of long-running polls in the US and the UK, an international 'Health of the Planet' survey conducted in 24 countries and carried out by Gallup, an international survey commissioned by Greenpeace International and carried out by MORI, and a set of Eurobarometer surveys commissioned by the European Commission.

Many surveys on the environment appear to follow a similar narrative. Surveys often start by asking people how concerned they are about both the environment in general and particular environmental issues; this then is followed by questions asking people about their environmental beliefs and values and how these affect their behaviour in everyday life. Occasionally surveys continue with questions seeking to determine people's levels of awareness, their perceived need for environmental information, their perception of their own sense of personal responsibility towards the environment, their perceptions of the environmental responsibility of other actors including business and government, and very occasionally their perception of the efficacy of personal action. We next set out a résumé of the findings of such recent research.

Measuring environmentalism

In the US a more institutionalised polling culture has led to the tracking of *public concern* with environmental problems since the late 1960s. In the late 1960s there was a reported upsurge of public concern with environmental issues, rising to a peak around the first Earth Day in 1970 (Buttel 1987: 472). Public concern then declined sharply at first and then steadily throughout the 1970s (Dunlap 1991b). During the 1980s and into the 1990s reported levels of public concern rose significantly, partly as an apparent backlash to the lack of environmental policies in the Reagan years, but also propelled by anxieties over air and water pollution, environmental disasters as the *Exxon Valdez* oil spill and the Chernobyl nuclear meltdown, and more focused media attention (Dunlap 1991a).

In the UK and other European societies, survey research indicates that public concern was more constant in the 1970s, that it rose slowly through the mid-1980s, and peaked in mid-1989, at about the time of the European elections when approximately 8% of Europeans voted for green parties (O'Riordan 1995: 8; Rudig 1991: 6; Worcester 1994: 28).

Such expressed levels of public concern have been measured by devising various indicators of 'salience' and 'concern', both absolutely and relative to public concern over other public issues. The most stringent measure favoured in many American surveys is for the volunteered 'most important problem', normally in response to the question: '*What do you think are the two most important problems facing the United States today?*' Results from a 1990 US Cambridge poll suggest that the 'environment' became more salient throughout the late 1980s and rose to 23% in June 1990 (Dunlap and Scarce 1991: 659).

A similar question in a survey commissioned by the UK Department of the Environment and carried out by NOP, inviting respondents to name the most important issues that the Government should be dealing with, elicited 8% who mentioned the environment/pollution in 1986, rising to 30% in 1989, and falling back to 22% in 1993 (Department of the Environment 1994: 133). Similarly, MORI have noted corresponding changes in the public salience of environmental issues through ongoing tracking data. In response to the question: '*What would you say is the most important issue facing Britain today?*', over one third mentioned the environment in July 1989. More recently, this percentage dropped to 9% by September 1990, to 4% in October 1991, and has remained more or less at that level up until late 1995, with expressed worries about jobs, crime, drugs, education and health being more prominent (MORI 1995, cited Worcester 1995: 70).

Less exacting questions have also been asked to measure people's sense of the importance of environmental protection and their level of concern about particular individual environmental problems. In the 1992 Health of the Planet survey conducted across a diverse range of 24 countries, people were asked the question: '*How concerned are you personally about environmental problems?*' In response, exceptionally high levels of concern were reported across both developing and industrialised countries, including majorities (over 50%) in 21 countries who reported a 'great deal' or 'a fair amount' of concern about environmental problems (Dunlap et al. 1993: 11). Similarly, in a Eurobarometer survey conducted in early 1995 in the 15 countries of the European Union, an average 82% of Europeans agreed that protecting the environment is an 'immediate and urgent problem' (CEC 1995: table 1.1).

In the US and the UK, surveys report that environmental issues are now perceived to be becoming more serious and more likely to constitute a threat to contemporary society. For example, a 1989 Roper survey in the US found 62% of respondents agreeing that environmental pollution constitutes a 'very serious threat' to our society, compared with 44% in 1984 (Dunlap and Scarce 1991: 662). A 1990 US Cambridge survey also suggests that there now exists a general perception of deteriorating environmental quality (Dunlap and Scarce 1991: 659).

In the 1993 UK poll by NOP it was found that 30% declared themselves to be 'very concerned' about the environment in general and a further 56% 'quite concerned' (Department of the Environment 1994: 134). When in the NOP survey this was related to specific environmental issues, out of the 27 which were offered, the three top concerns which emerged were chemicals in rivers and seas, toxic waste and radioactive waste. Over 60% of people in 1993 stated that they were 'very worried' about these three environmental issues, well above the three issues which possess global implications, namely global warming, acid rain and traffic. Indeed only about one third of respondents registered strong concern about these issues. However, when questions were subsequently asked about what would be the main problems in 20 years' time, air pollution, global warming and traffic were the top three listed.

Parallel UK survey research also notes the greater sense of the importance of environmental problems when people are invited to conceive of them as concrete and local problems rather than when they are posed in abstract and global terms. In a survey undertaken for the UK response to the World Conservation Strategy, the proportion of respondents who recorded anxiety about environment and resource depletion rose by over 50% (from 16% to 25%) when the question on the issue was asked in relation to daily life activities, as opposed to Britain or the world in general (Johnson 1993). However, other polling data suggest that people are now more concerned with global environmental issues than with local ones. In the last two Eurobarometer surveys, people have expressed higher levels of environmental concern over major systemic and global risks such as major air and water pollution than they do over local and daily nuisance risks such as litter or amenity concerns (see CEC 1992a: chap. 2). In the 1995 survey, when respondents were asked to name four main things that 'cause serious damage to the environment', 68% chose 'factories which release dangerous chemical products into the air or the water', 48% 'global pollution (progressive disappearance of tropical forests, destruction of the ozone layer, greenhouse effect)', 40% 'oil pollution of the sea and coasts' and 39% 'the storage of nuclear waste', as opposed to only 3.7% who chose 'the local environment' (CEC 1995: chap. 2). We will return to the respective significance of global and local issues below.

Survey questions have also sought to probe the resilience of people's environmental concerns by asking people how they would make difficult trade-offs. One example here is a 1994 MORI poll, where twice as many British people said they would choose to protect the environment at the expense of the economy rather than vice versa (Worcester 1994: 2). In the

US a 1990 survey found that 64% of the US public agree that '*I would be willing to pay as much as 10 per cent more a week for grocery items if I could be sure they would not harm the environment*' (Dunlap and Scarce 1991: 669). And perhaps most surprisingly, the 1992 Health of the Planet survey found majorities in all nations surveyed (except Nigeria) choosing the proposition '*Protecting the environment should be given priority, even at the risk of slowing down economic growth*', rather than the alternative: '*Economic growth should be given priority, even if the environment suffers to some extent*' (Dunlap et al. 1993: 33). Such relative prioritising of environmental protection over economic growth has reportedly grown since the mid-1970s. For example, Cambridge polls have shown that respondents who chose '*We must sacrifice economic growth in order to preserve and conserve the environment*', rather than the converse, grew from 38% to 64% between 1976 and 1990 (Dunlap and Scarce 1991: 668).

These data are normally interpreted as suggesting a growing level of environmental concern, at least until the early 1990s. It is also normally presumed that environmentalism is most likely to be a concern for the white middle classes (Hays 1987; Newby 1979; Sandbach 1980; Tucker 1982); and that wealthy industrialised societies are more likely to be concerned with the environment than poorer developing countries (Baumol and Oates 1979). This viewpoint is reflected in the still popular thesis that environmentalism stems from 'postmaterialist values'. Such a thesis follows a Maslowian 'hierarchy of needs' hypothesis which proposes that people become concerned with higher lifestyle and quality of life goals, including the environment, only when more basic goals or needs have been satisfied (such as food, shelter, and economic survival; Inglehart 1977, 1990).

However, the 1992 Health of the Planet survey calls into question the presumption that environmental quality is a higher goal or need. Dunlap et al. argue:

> The idea that environmental quality is a luxury affordable only by those who have enough economic security to pursue quality-of-life goals is inconsistent with the high levels of public concern for environmental problems found in many developing countries. . . . environmental degradation is increasingly recognized as a direct threat to human health and welfare. (1993: 37)

Other studies also show that within industrialised countries concern for the environment is more broad-based than had been previously believed (Mohai and Twight 1987; Morrison and Dunlap 1986). And it also seems that amongst local environmental groups members and even activists are often from relatively underprivileged and minority backgrounds (Bryant and Mohai 1992; Bullard 1990). Indeed, some researchers now claim that environmentalism has become so prominent in society that it constitutes a core value or even a new form of personal identity (Kempton et al. 1995: 4). Such claims are supported by the 1990 US Gallup poll in which 73% of respondents identified themselves as 'environmentalists' (Dunlap and Scarce 1991: 670).

But what do people mean when they refer to themselves as environmentalists? Back in the 1970s Dunlap and Van Liere (1978) argued that American environmental concern reflected a new paradigm, or way of seeing the world, which was incompatible with dominant core American values and beliefs. This 'new environmental paradigm' (or NEP) included such beliefs as limits to growth, environmental protection, a steady state economy and the fragility of nature, all of which were in tension with the 'dominant social paradigm' (or DSM) of American individualism, freedom, abundance, growth and prosperity (Dunlap and Van Liere 1984).

A related distinction has been proposed by O'Riordan (1976) between an 'ecocentrist' orientation and set of values, characterised by a sense of caution, holism, egalitarianism and accommodation, and a more dominant 'technocentrist' perception of the world, characterised by optimism, managerialism, hierarchy and reductionism. More recently MORI UK have devised a new social type of 'Deep Greens'. These agree with the statement that *We should protect the environment at all costs, regardless of economic considerations*' and currently number a stunning 5 million people or 12% of the British adult population (Worcester 1994: 2).

Since the 1970s there appear to have been not only these changes in attitude but also shifts in actions and *personal behaviour* towards the protection of the environment. This shift is reflected in alterations of consumer behaviour, voting patterns and citizens' actions. The 1993 NOP opinion poll attempted to survey such shifts with a set of questions on 26 possible personal actions, including those in the domestic sphere, as consumers and in terms of certain patterns of avoidance. The survey shows that British people claim that on a regular basis they save newspaper for recycling (48%); they keep down the household use of electricity/gas (33%); they avoid using pesticides in the garden (57%); they buy environmentally friendly products (28%); and they limit sunbathing because of increased ultra-violet rays (47%) (Department of the Environment 1994: 143).

Since 1989, MORI UK have devised a number of social types, including the 'Green Consumer' (about 40% of the British population in 1994) and the 'Environmental Activist' (about 28%). Such typologies have been developed with the explicit purpose of tracking different types of environmental behaviour and sentiment across time, and to examine how these different types are related to age, gender and socio-economic class. In broadly similar fashion to British trends of expressed levels of environmental concern, MORI found that Green Consumerism and Environmental Activism rose rapidly from 1988 to 1990, peaked around 1991, dropped a little, and then levelled out through the early to mid-1990s (Upsall and Worcester 1995: 8).

The 'Environmental Activist' typology was set up using a behavioural scale of items indicating an interest in environmental matters. There are 11 activities, and the proportion of environmental activists (defined as those who have taken five or more of the listed actions, such as walking in the countryside, being a member of an environmental group, actual environmental campaigning, giving money to conservation organisations) has more than doubled since 1988. Compared with the UK population as a whole, these green activists are slightly more likely to be female, middle-aged and middle class (Worcester 1995: 73). The same typology was also used in a Greenpeace International-sponsored comparative survey involving 22 countries which was set up to 'obtain objective data about its [Greenpeace's] image in the different countries in which it operates in order to guide its marketing efforts' (Upsall and Worcester 1995: 3). The survey found a positive correlation between Environmental Activism and those working in the service sector, and a negative correlation with those working in manufacturing industry. Moreover, when this typology was further subdivided into a more active 'Environmental Campaigners' type and a less participatory 'Environmentally Friendly' type (EF), the results appeared to confirm the thesis that it is in fact people in richer and more developed societies who are more likely to engage in environmentally friendly behaviour than those in poorer societies:

> A clear pattern appeared, as predicted by Maslow's hypothesis, regarding the EF factor, where the Scandinavian countries, Belgium, Britain, Canada and New Zealand scored much higher while developing countries in the CIS and Latin America, especially, showed dramatically low levels of environmentally friendly behaviour going on. (Upsall and Worcester 1995: 16)

This thesis is supported by the MORI UK 'Green Consumer' study where 17 consumer choices were researched. In 1994 it was found that 66% of the British public now buy 'ozone friendly' aerosols, 52% buy products made from recycled packaging, 52% specifically choose products that have not been tested on animals, and 44% regularly use a bottle bank (Worcester 1994: 11). Across Europe an average 67% now claim to be saving energy, 67% now claim to have sorted out certain types of household waste (glass, paper, motor oil) for recycling, 67% claim to have bought environmentally friendly products even if they were more expensive, and 41% claim to have used less polluting forms of transport such as walking, cycling and public transport (CEC 1995: chap. 3). American research also shows a massive 50% drop in the market share of CFC products largely due to consumer boycotts in the late 1980s (Lyman et al. 1990). These proportions of people who claim to have changed their consumer and domestic habits in various advanced societies are really striking.

With regard to mainstream politics, Hays (1992) has analysed the US House of Representatives voting records between 1971 and 1989. He demonstrates that there has been a gradual increase of pro-environmental voting throughout that period. Voting behaviour in Europe is more complex, not least due to the different constitutional arrangement of different nation-states (Parkin 1989). However, with the notable exception of the German Greens, who gained political support and credibility in the early 1980s, explicitly environmental voting patterns peaked in mid-1989, coinciding with the European elections in which 8% of European Community voters

(11 million people) voted for green parties. Rudig (1991: 6) argues that this was a huge symbolic moment, largely a public response to the perceived lack of effective environmental measures from mainstream parties. However, he also suggests that the 15% UK vote for the British Green Party was more a transitory response to a particular dynamic, rather than a seismic shift in underlying political commitments (see also O'Riordan 1995: 8–9; Worcester 1994: 19).

Survey questions concerning people's level of awareness and *knowledge* of environmental issues are difficult to devise. In recent years, as environmental issues have become more technical and removed from everyday sensory experience, commentators have begun to look at how the public understand such issues as 'global warming', 'acid rain' and the 'destruction of the ozone layer'. All these issues provide considerable problems for pollsters, not least due to the complicated and sometimes contradictory nature of the underlying science, but also due to the mediating roles of the media, government and business. Moreover, as Rudig points out:

> The posing of a question like 'How concerned are you about global warming?' could be seen as sending a message to the respondent that he or she should be concerned with global warming, and thus increase the level of those expressing concern irrespective of whether they have ever heard of, or have any knowledge of, global warming. (1995: 5; also see Sterngold et al. 1994)

In a useful review of archive datasets from Eurobarometer and the 1993 International Social Survey Programme (ISSP), Rudig (1995) has examined questions on people's reported levels of awareness of global environmental issues. A Eurobarometer survey in 1989 found that only about 36% of Europeans felt they were able to discuss 'the greenhouse effect', compared with 61% who were able to discuss 'the destruction of the ozone layer'. By 1992, using a slightly different measure of 'self-perceived knowledge', a Eurobarometer survey found that 90% perceived themselves to have a clear or general understanding of what 'air pollution' meant, 73% 'the hole in the ozone layer', 73% 'global warming' and 73% 'acid rain' (Rudig 1995). Subsequently, the survey sought to test this 'self-perceived knowledge' with 'actual knowledge', asking respondents to give true/false answers to two questions: (1) *The greenhouse effect can raise the sea level* (true), and (2) *The greenhouse effect can reduce the deserts* (false). The results suggested that 'actual knowledge' was slightly less than 'self-perceived knowledge', and that Southern Europeans were less accurate than their Northern counterparts.

The UK Department of the Environment survey on environmental attitudes has also focused on people's knowledge of global warming (1994: 140–1). Carried out in 1993, the survey found that 39% of the public were 'confused' as to the major factors contributing to global warming and a further 24% 'mistaken' (common misunderstandings related to people confusing 'global warming' with ozone depletion). Furthermore, when asked how much individuals, as opposed to business, contribute to global warming in this country, only one third of respondents accurately chose the correct

40% option. Over one half of respondents thought individuals contributed only 10% or 20% of total emissions. Other data, both in international and national surveys, also point to a major confusion in the public mind between global warming and the hole in the ozone layer (see, for example, Lofstedt's [1995] review of public perception studies conducted with publics from Australia, Austria, Sweden and the United States; also see Kempton et al. 1995).

Data produced by MORI UK have also consistently found a public sense of self-conscious confusion and disorientation with respect to environmental issues (Worcester 1994, 1995). In August 1995, 45% of respondents agreed with the statement '*I don't really understand environmental issues*'. Nor do such polls reveal any compensating sense of trust that at least government-funded scientists understand what they are researching. Only 38% of the public responded that they had 'a great deal' or even a 'fair amount' of trust in what scientists working for the government say about environmental issues, compared to 48% who expressed some trust in industry scientists. Thus substantially less than half of those surveyed recorded any trust in what scientists working for industry or government had to say, although an impressive 82% expressed trust in what was said by scientists working for environmental organisations (Worcester 1995: 72). Even more starkly, only 7% of people in socio-economic group AB (professional and managerial people) said they trust industry's scientists 'a great deal', and just 2% government scientists, compared to 37% of ABs who said they trust environmental scientists a 'great deal' on what they have to say on environmental matters.

To look at ways of combating such cognitive disorientation, a number of policy-sponsored surveys now include questions on 'the provision of information'. UK data suggest that over 85% of respondents would like 'much more' or 'slightly more' environmental information to be provided by government and manufacturers (Department of the Environment 1994: 142). However, such information is only likely to be believed in conditions of trust. When asked in the most recent Eurobarometer survey about who were '*reliable information sources on the state of the environment*', only a miserly 2% perceived industry to be trustworthy, 1% political parties and 6% public authorities. These tiny figures contrasted with 28% who perceived the media to be trustworthy, 41% scientists, and 62% environmental protection associations (CEC 1995: 58).

The UK Government's NOP survey in 1993 also asked how people identify their own sense of individual *responsibility* in relation to various official institutions (Department of the Environment 1994: 138). In general, people tended to allocate responsibility for global problems to international bodies (for global warming, the ozone layer and acid rain), and more local problems to central and local government (for toxic waste, traffic congestion and recycling). The survey results showed a marked lack of perceived individual responsibility (only an aggregated average of 10% of people allocated individuals as primarily responsible for a range of 27 environmental issues). Moreover, the issues for which people felt a degree of personal responsibility tended to be either highly local issues (such as litter or dog fouling) or issues which they could affect in immediate ways (such as energy conservation).

A more generalised version of the above was incorporated into the 1992 Health of the Planet survey, which asked who *'should have the primary responsibility for protecting the environment in [their] nation – the government, business and industry, or individual citizens and citizens' groups?'* (Dunlap et al. 1993: 36). In response, respondents from 15 countries were more likely to attribute responsibility to government, in four countries to business (Poland, Korea, the Netherlands and Finland), while in five nations (Chile, Mexico, Uruguay, Brazil and Switzerland) primary responsibility was ascribed to citizens and citizen groups. Interestingly, Britain had the lowest proportion of respondents in the industrialised nations who attributed primary responsibility to citizens and citizens' groups (12%). Here, the allocation of responsibility to citizens and citizens' groups may partly reflect the levels of citizen efficacy in various nation-states – that is, the perceived effectiveness of personal action to contribute to positive change. Thus the low levels of responsibility assigned to citizens in Russia and Poland in the Health of the Planet survey were thought to reflect 'the low levels of citizen efficacy in these formerly totalitarian nations' (Dunlap et al. 1993: 35). A subsequent question dealt more directly with the perceived efficacy of personal action in the form *'How much effect can individual citizens and citizens' groups have on solving our environmental problems?'* Interestingly, respondents from developing countries were more likely to think not only that citizens should be responsible for environmental protection, but also that citizen action was more likely to be effective.

Underlying frameworks

Later in this chapter this powerful set of findings will be counterposed to some qualitative research relating to how people regard and act towards the environment. For the present we will uncover some of the discursive frameworks lying behind such surveys.

We noted above how certain commentators have deployed polling data to contest the still popular wisdom that environmental concern is a luxury which only richer people or nations can afford. Dunlap et al. (1993: 15) suggest that whereas previous applications of Inglehart's postmaterialist thesis had posited environmental concern as a higher goal only entertained when more basic needs have been satisfied, the Health of the Planet survey data suggested that environmental concern is now almost universally recognised. Nevertheless there are clear parallels between the Inglehart thesis that societies are moving towards 'postmaterialist values' and Dunlap and Catton's (1979) distinction between the 'new environmental paradigm' and the 'dominant social paradigm' (later revised to a 'human exceptionalist paradigm'). Both writers as well as their critics imply that there is something which is to be called the 'environmental worldview', that this constitutes a quite separate and fundamentally different 'way of seeing' the world, and that this way of seeing is hermetically sealed within particular interlocking beliefs, values, attitudes and behaviours which are environmental.

Similar notions of a self-contained hermeneutic system are implied by O'Riordan's (1976) 'ecocentric' as opposed to 'technocentric' values. It is also implicit within Cotgrove's (1982) distinction between an 'environmental' as opposed to a 'traditional' paradigm. Merchant's (1992) 'ecocentric ethics' based on a view of nature as organicism similarly is strongly contrasted with both an 'egocentric' (based on a mechanical view of nature) and a 'homocentric' worldview (based on a utilitarian view of nature). Meanwhile, Naess' (1973) highly influential distinction between 'shallow' ecology (retaining a dualistic view of humans as separate and different from nature) and 'deep' ecology (based on a 'oneness' with nature) also implies a distinctive 'environmentalism' which can be differentiated as to the degree of 'greenness'.

This rhetorical move, of positing a preferred and coherent 'paradigm' or 'worldview' as opposed to its repellent 'other', is associated with a presumed process of social change. The environmental agenda seems to involve changing society from an environmentally destructive mode, based on unsustainable values, to one that is based on a new and coherent paradigm of environmentally benign values. The challenge is thus 'how to get from A to B' by ensuring that a higher proportion of the population of any society adopt the environmental as opposed to the technocratic paradigm (Grove-White 1994: 1). Present within such survey research is the doctrine of what in chapter 1 we termed 'environmental idealism'. This revolves around a number of claims: that attitudes and beliefs form consistent, integrated and self-contained wholes; that since around 1970 many people have developed a fundamentally new paradigm of attitudes and core beliefs which can be characterised as 'environmental'; that opposing these beliefs are a distinct set of beliefs and values which are 'anti-environmental'; that environmental improvements will come about if more of the population adopt the former than the latter; and that survey research is adept at 'capturing' these distinct and opposing worldviews (see Pepper 1996: chap. 1 for a recent example of such a rhetoric).

Indeed, such emphases can be found in research which has sought to show that particular groups of individuals adopt certain sets of values which can be identified as *either* environmental *or* anti-environmental. Thus Cotgrove (1982) found that managers, accountants, scientists, skilled manual workers and women in paid employment were more likely to have 'technocentric' attitudes; whereas teachers, academics, unemployed youth, and women in unpaid work were more likely to have 'ecocentric' attitudes. Meanwhile, O'Riordan (1989), from an assessment of recent polling data, has deduced that between 0.1% and 0.3% of people have Gaian ecocentric attitudes towards the environment (advocates of the rights of nature and the needs for co-evolution), between 5% and 10% of people have communal ecocentric attitudes (advocates of the cooperative capacities of societies to establish self-reliant communities on sustainable principles), whereas between 55% and 70% of people have accommodating technocentric attitudes (advocates of the ability of institutions to accommodate environmental demands).

Overall it is interesting to note that the argument being criticised here parallels some feminist claims which posit that there is something about 'women's experience' which produces a distinct, coherent and entirely differentiated way of seeing. Such a women's standpoint is held to be wholly and positively contrasted with that of the male paradigm. And it is this kind of essentialist feminist idealism which recent cultural critiques often also from within feminism have particularly sought to undermine in ways which parallel our analysis here of environmental idealism (see Haraway 1991).

A second presumption of these surveys is that public attitudes towards the environment remain largely stable and consistent over significant periods of time; and that these attitudes underpin and structure how people think and act towards environmental threats and risks. Such an understanding of the separate human subject is derived from what we can loosely term the doctrine of 'methodological individualism'. In this it is asserted that people act as discrete independent beings whose actions are largely isolated from the turbulent, complex and often contradictory practices and discourses which criss-cross contemporary societies. Such a methodological individualism abstracts human subjects out of their spatially embedded practices and the complex interconnections between 'human' and 'non-human' actants which happen to combine together to realise diverse ways of being in and of the apparently 'natural' world.

The third assumption of survey research is that people's innermost values and beliefs can be revealed from their instantaneous responses to sets of questions formulated in advance by the investigator. Thus survey methods assume not merely that individual responses can be meaningfully separated from the social and physical contexts in which they emerge, but that social responses and norms can be derived from aggregating such measured individual actions, beliefs and choices. Bob Worcester states that:

> Survey research measures five things: *knowledge*, what we know; *behaviour*, what we do; and then *opinions*, *attitudes* and *values*. I have defined these latter terms, rather too poetically I fear for scholarly adoption, as '*opinions*: the ripples on the surface of the public's consciousness, shallow and easily changed; *attitudes*: the currents below the surface, deeper and stronger; and *values*: the deep tides of public mood, slow to change, but powerful'. (1994: 1, original emphases)

There is a presumption here of 'non-interference' – that individual values and attitudes are original and independent of forms of social interaction, particularly from those interactions involved in the question and responses of a survey. It is also presumed that individuals can instantaneously respond to questions asked in ways which elicit deeply held and often incoherent beliefs and values that seem to demand a much lengthier process of reflection and deliberation. In chapter 5 we explore some of the temporal dimensions of environmental debate. Clearly the sample survey elicits the kind of instantaneous responses which simulate aspects of a consumer-oriented society which has itself of course been primarily responsible for aspects of current environmental destruction.

But furthermore, implicit in such survey material are tacit assumptions of 'environmental realism': that environmental risks exist 'out there' independently of social practices and beliefs and can thus act as the unambiguous object of individual perceptions, attitudes and values (see also chapter 1 above). It is believed that such risks can be measured and appropriately quantified. Such a view permeates opinion polls which strive to measure public anxieties, concerns and awareness over particular *a priori* specified environmental issues and risks, assuming not simply the independent and consistent nature of people's attitudes, beliefs and values, but also the independent existence of such risks as bounded and framed by the survey question (which is usually taken from conventional 'scientific' understandings of the environment). Such assumptions thus assume that environmental issues can be defined in ways which can transcend the local cultural and historical contexts in which particular issues gain their meaning. This assumption of universal equivalence becomes especially pertinent in an era when commissioning bodies are increasingly likely to seek international comparisons of 'environmentalism' (including radical organisations such as Greenpeace who are now participants within a global polling culture; see Upsall and Worcester 1995).

Finally, we noted above the connections of polling with the development of appropriate policies. Important here is the tacit model of motivation and change embedded in such policy development. In particular, policy programmes related to the environment have assumed that the best way to encourage public identification with government initiatives is through the provision of information; such information then is presumed to lead to concern; and this concern then leads to appropriate changes in personal lifestyle (for UK examples, see Department of the Environment 1986, 1989, 1994; Going for Green 1995; LGMB 1995; Worcester 1994). However, there are some difficulties with such a model. This presumed sequence of stages ignores the processes by which people form a sense of their own agency in environmental matters, and how this sense of agency itself depends on the perceived tractability of environmental issues, itself dependent on people's more general sense of trust in institutions responsible for environmental matters. Each of these may vary very significantly and means that there is nothing inevitable about this sequence. Such a model also treats the environment in an overly cognitivist manner and evades the aesthetic and hermeneutic aspects of reflexivity, and especially the diverse ways in which people 'sense' the environment (Lash and Urry 1994; and chapter 4 below). Not surprisingly, 'environmental policy' actors have found these 'complicating factors' difficult to deal with, significantly because they extend beyond the apparent domain of the 'environment' itself.

Qualitative research

In recent years qualitative research studies have begun to address the limitations of survey research and to provide detailed and embedded accounts of environmental concern and value. Within the policy framework of sustainability and Local Agenda 21 a number of qualitative studies have been commissioned by public agencies to complement survey research. Recent UK examples include a report for the Countryside Commission (HPI 1994), one for the Scottish Office (MORI 1994), one for Hertfordshire County Council (LUC 1994), and one by Harris for the Government's 'Going for Green' initiative (Going for Green 1995). Such qualitative focus group studies provide a level of human interaction which contributes a more complex account of environmental concerns and attitudes than do many quantitative studies. *Inter alia* these studies have found that people are concerned about the environment and agree that it needs protection; that people do not see environmental issues as having much impact on their daily lives, especially by contrast with issues of economy and education; that people commonly do not understand environmental issues, and are particularly ignorant of global environmental issues such as global warming and the concept of 'sustainable development'; and that generally the environmental message endorsed by governments at Rio is not coming across. Such recent reports clearly complement existing polling data. Yet, in various disguises, they adhere to many of the same theoretical frameworks as outlined above and hence are subject to similar limitations.

Thus, for example, the Harris study set out the following findings: that people 'had good intentions, but more support and information were required' to encourage action; that people as individuals 'felt powerless . . . [and] looked to the government and councils to set leading examples'; and that the main barriers to action were 'time/inconvenience and lack of information' (Going for Green 1995: 2–4). Such findings reflect a similar narrative structure to the polling data outlined above; one where environmental issues (and sustainable development) are conceived as a sphere separate and delineated from other issues (such as anxieties over crime, security or jobs), where environmental concern and action is presumed to be limited by information (rather than, for example, by people's sense of the futility of action), and where the key strategy adopted by state institutions to encourage individual environmental responsibility lies in providing information (assuming that people will trust such information as credible). Thus, as with the polling data, the tacit theoretical assumptions delineate the sphere of inquiry of policy-related research, and inadvertently marginalise and inhibit research on the complex and ambivalent ways in which people make sense of environmental issues in daily life, the ways in which people's understanding of environmental change is bound up with other changes in modernity, and the implications of this more complex picture for state institutions.

However, two recent theoretically sophisticated studies on the public understanding of environmental change point to a different relationship between environmental concerns and culture. One study is Kempton et al.'s *Environmental Values in American Culture*, where it is argued:

> Our contribution to an understanding of environmental concern is not in showing that it exists, a task already accomplished by the national polls, but in documenting the reasoning behind that concern. National polls are like satellite photos, giving a broad overview of public opinion. Anthropological research corresponds to exploration on the ground, charting details of the features glimpsed by the national surveys and looking for causal explanations. (1995: 18)

This research, conducted through in-depth interviews and surveys, sought to examine the detail of the ecological worldview that has taken root in recent years. Perhaps most interestingly, the study examined the cultural models and resources Americans use to understand nature and their relationship with it. The study highlights three cultural models of nature which inform and help structure how people conceive of environmental change. These are: a model of nature as fragile and limited, upon which all life depends; a model of nature as in balance and of human action as potentially destabilising such balance with unpredictable effects; and a model of current American ways of living, characterised by industrialism, consumerism and the market, as alienating humanity from nature and endangering nature in the process. Kempton et al. suggest that all three models of nature are more commonplace than currently realised, that each provides strong utilitarian arguments for environmental protection, and that they are now thoroughly embedded within American society. Moreover, they argue that such findings provide 'nothing less than this culture's conceptual basis for environmentalism' (1995: 62). They go on to show how people understand a wide array of environmental issues through appealing to a limited set of cultural models, and how such models can aid or hinder public understanding of the issue in question through providing appropriate or inappropriate cultural resources (in the form of set metaphors, implied relationships, and even folk stories and fables). They also note how the common confusion and ignorance of global warming can be partly explained in terms of the widespread use of an inappropriate cultural model of nature – that of environmental 'bads' as framed through the cultural model of pollution.

The study also provides a number of interesting insights concerning how environmental values are connected with core American values, such as religion and parental responsibility, and how people make sense of environmental issues through an appeal to different underlying cultural models of nature which are now commonplace in American society. Moreover, the research is especially interesting in its suggestion that environmental communication programmes should seek to address the public *within* existing cultural models of nature rather than assume they are writing upon a blank slate. However, the research remains wedded to assumptions of environmental realism and idealism, and in particular to the idea that people have set and stable beliefs and values, that these are organised by underlying cultural models of nature, and that such cultural models can engender or inhibit public understanding depending on their match with external nature (as approximated through current models of science). The latent individualism derives most starkly from their use of 'mental models', a notion taken from cognitive psychology which assumes that people use mental models (simplified representations of the world), built up from past memories and associations, which help them to solve problems by providing inferences. Hence, Kempton et al. suggest that 'such models give an underlying structure to environmental beliefs and a critical underpinning to environmental values' (1995: 11). Set out in this fashion they employ a narrow and restricted definition of culture: culture is what resides in people's heads as a separate and incomplete picture of the external reality which is provided by 'real' science.

A more constructivist account of how people make sense of environmental issues *within* distinct national policy cultures has been provided by Burgess et al. (1995). The research sought to understand the social and institutional factors which influence public definitions of, and responses to, global environmental issues. Burgess et al. compared the structure of attitudes across equivalent populations in the UK and the Netherlands using qualitative and quantitative methods.

They found that people's receptivity to knowledge, as provided by scientific or policy bodies, is strongly shaped by their sense of agency – that is, by their implicit sense of their own power or freedom to act upon or to use that knowledge. The significance of this is that people's inability or unwillingness to assimilate information may frequently be due to tacit political or cultural structures of empowerment or disempowerment which may have no apparent connection with the particular environmental issue in question. Thus Burgess et al. note a general tendency towards greater public awareness and understanding of environmental issues in the Netherlands than in the UK, apparently connected to the greater sense of public agency and involvement within the former.

Equivalent groups in the UK appear to feel more disconnected from political and policy institutions, and this general sense of relative alienation and disempowerment may contribute to a correspondingly diminished sense of active involvement in or responsibility for policies connected with such issues, or with information relating to them. In such circumstances it is hardly surprising to find people apparently less 'informed' about, or attuned to, environmental problems and responses. The crucial point is that it would be misleading to attribute such apparent ignorance to a lack of information, awareness, concern or intelligence. The significant factor lies within the structuring of social relations within different societies. This research shows that the more general characteristics which affect the quality of people's identification with public institutions are fundamentally important in explaining the apparent fluctuations in people's attitudes and behaviours towards the environment.

Our argument is that these dimensions will not become apparent unless they are explicitly built into the design of research. In the next section we outline a relational framework to study the complex ways through which people think about and engage nature and the environment in their daily lives.

A relational framework

Rhetoric, identity and nature

Various social psychologists have developed discursive and relational approaches to the study of human perception and behaviour (see Potter and Wetherell 1987; Shotter 1993a, 1993b). These approaches highlight the embedded and contextual nature of public opinion and thought in daily life, and emphasise the *constitutive* role of discourse and culture in shaping 'attitudes'. Such approaches also problematise the assumption that survey methods do not themselves shape the responses observed. One influential strand of such critique pioneered by Billig (1987, 1991, 1992) is a rhetorical approach to human conduct and behaviour.

Billig draws upon the ancient practices of rhetoric to argue against the methodological individualism within much conventional social psychology, and the embedded assumptions of human thinking, attitudes, values and opinions as internally consistent and coherent, reflecting as is presumed underlying cognitive processes. He questions the extent to which assumptions of internal consistency and 'self-sufficiency' accurately reflect human experience and conduct in everyday life. Using examples of young Conservatives (1991), people talking about the royal family (1992), and the sports pages of the tabloid press (1995), he demonstrates how people's views and opinions are more variable, context-dependent and inherently contradictory than would normally be recognised in attitudinal surveys.

A rhetorical approach to human conduct emphasises the importance of argument in human thought, and the relationship between internal argument and societal controversy. For Billig, the expression of personal views or attitudes is not so much an expression of an internalised, underlying belief, but rather a position whose meaning is only realised when located, however contingently, within wider societal debates. However, public debates are by definition controversial, and people often possess a repertoire of contradictory yet equally persuasive ways of understanding them. To attitude theorists this variability tends to be ignored or suppressed, or treated as a superficial distraction from people's underlying core attitudes and belief constructs (see Potter and Wetherell 1987: chap. 2 for a detailed account). However, for rhetoricians and discourse analysts, this variability reflects much of everyday talk, and provides a key means by which accounts and experience become constituted within social practice. For it is only through our ability to adopt different positions, to take the side of 'the other', to argue with ourselves and with others, that creative and deliberative thought itself becomes possible. Indeed, as Billig points out, if the world did not exist in contradictions, life would be mechanically dull:

> It is because a social group's stock of commonsensical beliefs contains contrary elements that argument, and thereby thought, is possible. . . . If all were clear, undilemmatic and utterly consistent for the members of a society, there would be nothing for them to argue about, and therefore nothing about which to deliberate. (1988b: 12)

Billig (1987) explicitly draws on ancient rhetoricians who understood the dilemmatic nature of common sense, and who were experts in the use of 'commonplaces' in developing argumentative strategies. By 'commonplace' Billig refers to the basic concepts or categories which provide the common resources from which people build arguments. He suggests that the same clash of commonplaces still provides the source of deliberation and contestation in modern life.

A rhetorical approach, sensitive to the role of argument in thought and the dilemmatic nature of everyday life, leads to different interpretations of survey data, especially that which seeks to elicit 'attitudes'. It suggests that individual responses to survey questions will reflect context, a certain understanding of the cultural significance of the question and its broader argument located in time and space. For example, survey questions concerning the relationship between economic growth and environmental quality in Britain in the 1970s had a particular meaning. They reflect an era in which environmental concerns largely stood for amenity and landscape considerations and were largely peripheral in government policy (see chapter 2 above). By the 1990s, by contrast, the idea of the need for a balance between environmental and economic considerations had become 'commonplace' after the signing up of most nation-states to principles of sustainable development, at least in policy rhetoric. Thus, in answering the polling question, the respondent would seek to understand the meaning of his or her response in relation to the perceived political and tactical use of the poll. In other contexts, the respondent will answer in terms of a different logic.

In such ways opinion surveys will often ignore both the importance of ambivalence in people's thought and how such ambivalence may reflect deliberation over the multiple ways in which people can think about and argue through a particular issue. Indeed, we suggest more generally that attempts to categorise and quantify attitudes are likely to say as much about the particular situation in which attitudes are elicited than about supposedly stable social attributes.

It also follows from this approach that the assumed objects of such attitudes should be viewed as more interactively and contextually shaped than is usually recognised. In other words, the *objects* of expressed attitudes, and not only attitudes themselves, are open to interactive or relational processes by which 'the' problem is framed. And most significantly for our argument here, such processes in the scientific domain are also analysable in rhetorical terms.

Scientific knowledges are generally assumed to be above such discursive framing. In particular, environmental issues and risk 'objects' are taken to be objectively given. But recently this assumption that environmental problems exist in nature waiting to be 'read' by evolving scientific knowledge and techniques has been subject to critique (see Grove-White and Szerszynski 1992; Wynne 1987, 1992a; more generally on the contingent, constructed and less than heroic nature of science, see Collins and Pinch 1993). A number of detailed studies now indicate that the relationship between science and policy is subject to interpretation and negotiation (Jasanoff 1990; Latour 1987). Cultural criteria are implicated in both the definition and the trajectories of environment issues, even in apparently physical issues such as habitat protection, acid rain, global climate change and deforestation (Hajer 1995; Shackley and Wynne 1995a; Thomson et al. 1990; Waterton et al. 1995). Survey. approaches have to proceed as if these meanings were simply given in nature, hence they cut out *ab initio* from the public agenda the institutional interactions, behaviours and commitments associated with the establishment and imposition of these as 'given' authoritative findings of science.

This suggests that there is no single 'nature', only natures. And these natures are not inherent in the physical world but discursively constructed through economic, political and cultural processes, including the shaping of issues by NGOs (see chapter 2 above for a more detailed account; Jamison 1996). Recent research has begun to focus on the role of planning discourse and practice in the social construction of competing natures (Healey and Shaw 1994; Whatmore and Boucher 1993); and on how the very concept of environmental change can become a contested concept in arguments over proposed developments of roads (Burningham and O'Brien 1994), a theme park (Harrison and Burgess 1994) and a landfill site (Macnaghten 1993). However, just as discursive processes construct what we tend to identify as 'natural', so too do ideas of nature construct how we think of ourselves. The question emerges as to whether, and in what ways, and through which forms, ideas of nature reconstruct identity and our sense of ourselves as part of, or estranged from, nature.

Grove-White (1993, 1994) argues that much of contemporary environmentalism is located in an argumentative context over fundamental and even existential issues concerned with meaning and the nature of existence, often in opposition to dominant instrumental and economistic accounts. By contrast with most commentators who set out preferred environmental ideologies or paradigms often based on so-called sustainable principles, he argues that 'the most important point is that "sustainability", and argument about its meaning and implications, is best understood as providing a new "space" for political explorations, rather than suggesting an established, unambiguous call for action, the effective implementation of which calls for fresh "values" ' (1994: 1).

Environmental sentiment may thus be found in surprising places, not merely in the membership of environmental groups or through the consumption of 'green' products, but in more commonplace social interactions and practices. Berking argues that one largely inadvertent effect of a highly individualised society has been the intensification of social practices which 'systematically evade the edicts of exchange value and the logic of the market' (1996: 192). Commonplace activities based on reciprocal relations, such as gift-giving, voluntary work, self-help networks and even friendship, gain new symbolic value as sites of resistance to a world increasingly perceived as structured and regulated by global relations, self-interest and the market. Other commentators point to the emergence of flourishing cultural networks and what we have termed 'new sociations' (see chapter 1) around such preoccupations as food, gender, animals, vegetarianism, DIY, pets, alternative medicine, local place, spirituality, festivals, road protests, dance culture and an array of highly specialised leisure practices (Grove-White 1994; Szerszynski 1994). Such social practices may provide important sites of moral renewal in the lifeworlds of human agents, and point to the role of cultural networks in providing the foundations for a more collective response and sense of engagement with the modern environmental problematic (Szerszynski et al. 1996). In later chapters we examine the spaced and timed qualities of such social practices.

To summarise, we have extended Billig's rhetorical perspective and gone on to suggest that the ability of survey data to capture people's attitudes towards the environment is limited. Such data either ignore, or do not recognise as significant, one or more of the following:

- the sheer importance of opinion-making, argumentation and persuasive strategies deployed by people in their day-to-day life to convince others of what really threatens the environment or what could be done to save it;
- the multiple natures that inform discourses which depend upon both how nature is represented and sensed;
- the variability, ambivalence and contradictoriness in how people think and act about such natures;
- the political and cultural dynamics that have contributed to the framing of issues as environmental in the first place;
- the complex ways that individual expressions of environmental concern relate to wider societal controversies;
- the significance of environmental sensibilities as providing new if inchoate forms of personal and collective identity;
- the complex and multi-faceted ways in which people organise around and work through their relationships with nature via diverse social practices;
- the significance of agency and trust within and in relationship to large-scale organisations.

Two provisos in conclusion here. First, surveys about people's actions, such as their patterns of consumer purchase, are not so significantly undermined by the claims made in this section. These claims mainly relate to problems inherent in the surveying of *attitudes* towards the environment and not of people's behaviours (although eliciting the significance of such behaviours is still subject to the points made in this section). Second, in chapter 6 below we actually employ an attitudinal survey to demonstrate what we have asserted here, namely, that attitudes expressed to threats to the English countryside depend upon context and upon the dilemmatic framings within which they are posed.

Globalisation, agency and trust

We have argued that expressions of environmental concern and sentiment are not self-contained but are bounded within wider social, cultural and political contexts. In chapter 1 we identified three broad transformations in late modernity that were structuring the contemporary environmental agenda: changes brought about through the emergence of the 'risk society'; cultural processes of globalisation, individualisation and detraditionalisation; and the emergence of the realm of 'subpolitics' and new sociations. We now examine how these broad shifts may be structuring in complex and ill-understood ways how people understand the significance and 'riskiness' of environmental matters in their daily lives, and in particular how they affect people's sense of agency. We first note two additional dynamics affecting public engagement in environmental change: the role of the media in the production and consumption of environmental meanings; and the increasing levels of public mistrust in 'official' institutions (see also chapter 1 above).

Globalisation has been theorised as the process by which local events and social relations become increasingly shaped by events in faraway places, and vice versa. As this process has become intensified in late modernity, questions of personal agency and of trust between publics and a wide variety of institutions become of growing significance. This dynamic is illustrated in the enhanced role played by both the media and expert systems in people's perceptions as to the nature of environmental risks (see chapter 1 above; Lash and Urry 1994).

Since the mid-1980s a wide variety of environmental issues, including ozone depletion, species destruction, global warming, acidification of lakes and forests, nuclear radiation and chemical pollution, have become widely recognised as risks which are complex, global, long term, often incalculable, and largely invisible to our senses (Beck 1992b; see Yearley 1991: chap. 2 for a useful summary; and see chapter 4 below for a more detailed account on the role of the senses). As risks transcend the boundaries of sensory perception, and as the contours of risk extend to the very distant and the extraordinarily long term, we become dependent on national and increasingly global expert systems for information, knowledge, images and icons to enable such processes to be 'interpreted' (see chapter 5 for a more detailed account of time dimensions and nature). Such expert systems increasingly include environmental NGOs. Indeed, McCormick (1991b: 153–4) points out that those NGOs concentrating upon global issues have recently grown the fastest. Jamison also points to the emerging role of such NGOs as conduits between global environmental problems and the 'non-expert' wider public within the framing of contemporary environmental discourse:

> The public awareness of global environmental problems is inconceivable without a range of middle-men organisations serving as information-conduits between scientists, the media and the public, translating expert discourses into politics, and also recombining specialised expert knowledges into policy-oriented packages. (1996: 224)

In particular, the global media are of major importance to how people understand and make sense of environmental issues (Bell 1994; Burgess 1990; Gamsen and Modigliani 1989; Hansen 1993). This role has been one not only of communicating and disseminating environmental information to the public, but also of actively constructing and even constituting the contemporary environmental agenda partly in conjunction with NGOs. Recent research has begun to note the cultural processes by which environmental meanings are produced and consumed for, and by, the national and international media. This includes the complex interplay of narratives, story-lines, images, icons and metaphors through which environmental issues and events gain meaning. Such research suggests that the media are now an integral part of the cultural process by which environmental meanings are created, circulated and consumed (see Anderson 1997; Burgess 1990; Wilson 1992; Yearley 1991).

Specifically, Ross describes a new 'genre of image' in which the media have tended to frame environmental issues:

> In recent years we have become accustomed to seeing images of a dying planet, variously exhibited in grisly poses of ecological depletion and circulated by all sectors of genocidal atrocities. The clichés of the standard environmental movement are well known to us all: on the one hand, belching smokestacks, seabirds mired in petrochemical sludge, fish floating belly-up, traffic jams in Los Angeles and Mexico City, and clear-cut forests; on the other hand, the redeeming repertoire of pastoral imagery, pristine, green, and unspoiled by human habitation, crowned by the ultimate global spectacle, the fragile, vulnerable ball of spaceship earth. (1994: 171)

Ross argues that the current media forms reinforce a popular understanding of a particular culture of nature, that of nature as not-human. However, media framings of the environment are not always so straightforward. Often the meaning of an environmental story is itself a matter of controversy with different actors seeking to promote opposing media framings of a proposed development, a protest, an action, and so on. Greenpeace, for example, has become expert in packaging environmental action in simple, black and white, media-sensitive fashion, where Greenpeace activism comes to symbolise heroic action pitted against corporate greed and self-interest (Anderson 1997; Jamison 1996). Poorer NGOs and of course environmentalists in the 'South' that are less able to use the media have tended to become marginalised. As Shiva maintains rather more generally, the '"global" thus creates the moral base for green imperialism' (cited Jamison 1996: 236). More recently, as states and corporations have become increasingly sophisticated, they too have sought to frame their actions as environmentally sensible and sustainable, as informed by sound science, while at the same time criticising environmental groups and at times the wider public for being irrational and emotive (this dynamic is especially pronounced in recent environmental controversies over BSE, see chapter 8 below).

This discussion points to the multiple framings and rhetorics involved in environmental controversies. Diverse actors promote particular media framings in order to justify and legitimate their own chosen actions (or inactions) as environmentally sound and benign. Such variable framings have far-reaching implications for how environmental messages and risks come to be understood and consumed by the wider public. Indeed, from the perspective of people experiencing risks of various kinds, being told conflicting things about them, and knowing that future trajectories and hence further risks are uncertain and open-ended, such variable framings become highly problematic. The crucial question then concerns people's relationship with, and dependency on, the mass media and other expert institutions which are supposed to be in control of those risks and their dissemination, but to which most people have little access. Hence, a neglected dimension of research on public perceptions concerns the very basis of trust: 'Who to believe?' and 'How to decide who to believe?' Thus the issue of 'What is the risk?' is not only a matter of technical understanding, but also involves whether the institutions supposedly controlling the risk-generating activity can be trusted to do so, under open-ended future conditions. The dimensions of trust and dependency as *bona fide* questions only entered into the risk assessment and management domain in the early 1980s (Royal Society 1992: chap. 5; Wynne 1980).

In earlier studies it was implied that the public were behaving 'irrationally' if they did not behave in accordance with expert conclusions about particular risks and risk probabilities (Royal Society 1983, 1985). More recent research suggests that the framing of risk problems by experts, including the mass media, employs tacit assumptions about controlling institutions which many people will not share. For example, public environmental information campaigns, by their nature, rely on the public identifying with and trusting such institutions. However, this may conflict with people's experiences, either directly or through the media, of the past behaviour of the same institutions, their honesty, openness, competence, independence, and so on, which 'rationally' influences people's reception of the present claims of those organisations.

Such issues of trust are central to whether or not people believe media stories about environmental matters, and to the extent to which they will be likely to identify with, or participate in, officially defined environmental initiatives. Wynne (1992a) argues that, in excluding this trust dimension from measurements of risk perceptions, official approaches undermine themselves and potentially exacerbate the very problem of public risk perceptions which they are supposed to be addressing. In also obscuring from view the same institutional trust dimensions, many opinion poll surveys of environmental issues and risks similarly misunderstand environmental sentiment, and may indeed even alienate the public from such actions.

We have so far argued that public trust and confidence in the media and in official institutions is a central ingredient in understanding how people make sense of environmental issues. But quantitative and qualitative research suggests that people are particularly sceptical about not just the media but a wide range of hitherto central organisations in certain societies (Burgess and Harrison 1993: 218). Across many western democracies the relationship between governments and their publics has become increasingly fraught because of the apparent growing sense of public disaffection with, and mistrust in, formal politics and mainstream organisations. It has become commonplace for commentators to claim that the public are losing confidence in their politicians (Curtice and Jowell 1995); that people have become more sceptical, even cynical, about the ability of the system to respond to their concerns and anxieties (Jacques 1994); that traditional forms of politics have become largely out of touch with people's everyday lives (Mulgan 1994); that such public disengagement from politics is widespread across Europe (Johnston 1993; but see Kaase and Newton 1996); and that there is a general 'detraditionalisation' of social and cultural life (Heelas et al. 1996).

These processes of distrust and detraditionalisation are clearly linked to an array of globalising processes, which have a double-edged quality. On the one hand, such processes appear to produce a heightened sense of 'insecurity', especially in work patterns and household composition; a sense of perceived powerlessness accentuated by the relentless media reporting of environmental catastrophes around the globe; and the sense that global forces, especially working through money markets, are determining futures in ways largely unrelated to people's more direct wants and aspirations (Ekins 1992; Hutton 1995; Yearley 1996). Yet, on the other hand, they lead to a sense of global connectedness largely due to new information technologies and almost instantaneous media reporting from around the globe, and a heightened reflexivity about different cultures, experiences and forms of life. Ekins (1992) for example, provides many cases of how individuals and small groups develop a sense of agency in environmental and related issues through creative encounters with globalisation and its heightened insecurities.

The intensity of global environmental risks now pervading contemporary societies, and their mediation through abstract systems, not only draw attention to the pivotal role of people's sense of trust in institutions, but also how this affects their personal identity and ontological security. Giddens

(1990: 94) asks how is it, given the immanent possibility of ecological catastrophe and the many forms of risk and danger in today's world, that everyone is not perpetually in a state of ontological insecurity? He suggests that this lack of widespread dread or angst is attained only in conditions of basic trust, trust which is accomplished by a mixture of facework commitments (involving face-to-face interaction) and faceless commitments (involving faith in abstract systems). Such feelings of ontological security can be seen to involve a belief in the ongoing constancy of one's surroundings, a belief in the efficacy of action, a sense of confidence in one's 'being-in-the-world', and a stable self-identity.

However, current levels of disaffection and concomitant mistrust in science and abstract systems may be generating new forms of psychological vulnerability and insecurity. Although the implications of this dynamic have been mainly explored in its implications for personal relationships and the transformation of intimacy, little research has yet focused on its implications for how people make sense of environmental risk in their daily lives, and how this implicates their sense of agency, of hope, of foreboding, their belief in ideas of progress, and their sense of the future (see Giddens 1991 on intimacy). We report on such research that we undertook on the environment, agency and trust in chapter 7 below. This research in part at least seeks to rectify some of the problems we have identified with those produced within the mainstream polling culture discussed in this chapter. In particular we see how processes of globalisation and detraditionalisation affect how people sense, understand, live with and respond to environmental risks.

Conclusion

The survey data reported in this chapter showed the surprising lack of differentiation in expressed environmental attitudes between the rich and poor, both within and across nation-states; the changes in consumer and citizen behaviour attributable to environmental concern; and the interesting movements of opinion on environmental issues in recent years. Such survey data provide fairly crude indicators of such changes of opinion over time and space, and of actual behaviour, such as people's consumer purchases. Overall the quantitative data emphasise the importance to people of the 'global' aspects of the environment. This is by contrast with the findings of the qualitative research we report in chapter 7, which highlights the particular and local components.

We also showed that the use of such survey data is part of a more general polling culture whereby all sorts of organisations increasingly treat their clients as polled consumers. Policies to increase participation, for example, are couched in terms of the polled responses. Because of the increasing significance of such a polling culture within the environmental domain, even now embracing NGOs, the inability of such surveys to capture certain new

dimensions of environmental concern is significant. In particular, detraditionalisation, a lack of trust and the importance of specific localised practices
all possess significant implications for the articulation of contemporary
environmental concerns. Moreover, by not recognising these dimensions,
and yet these being increasingly significant for environmental policy
making, an environmental polling culture may reinforce an increasing
alienation of many social groups from the environment and from agencies
charged with its 'protection'.

These propositions concerning the changing significance of the environment and cultural change inform much of the rest of this book. We conclude
here by setting out four implications of such contested natures.

First, people's particular concerns, attitudes, values, sense of responsibility, environmentally friendly behaviour, and so on, are not distinct and free-
floating, but are powerfully mediated by longer-standing relationships with
expert systems, science, global media, states, global corporations, new forms
of risk, and so on. Research has to capture the complex and mediated
interconnections of the personal and the general.

Second, no *a priori* boundaries can be drawn as to how environmental
issues are to be defined or 'constituted'; these should be derived from
listening to and arguing with people's own categories of experience, value
and agency. This points to the need for qualitative methods to examine the
complex and often ambivalent ways in which people discuss and argue about
environmental matters, and how they connect these to wider concerns in an
increasingly globalised world; a world of intense opportunity and exceptional risk, as we see in chapter 8.

Third, the issue of 'agency' needs to be connected to these institutional
and contextual dimensions. Recent debates suggest that people are continually affected and influenced by their ongoing relationships with institutions such as those of the state and corporations, and that their expressions of
hope or despair, willingness to act or not, trust or mistrust, are inseparable
from their negotiations of such relationships. People's sense of agency,
whether personal or collective, is bound up within these relational issues.

Fourth, this sense of agency relates to changes in the relationships
between humans and nature. The globalisation of risks is one side of the
increasing internalisation of risks, as the borders between the body and the
external world are increasingly breached. Risks flow in and across the
surface of the body; the body ingests substances which humans cannot
sense; the body has implanted prosthetic parts whose long-term effects are
unknown. As nature is increasingly 'culturalised', as we discussed in chapter
1, so the human being is increasingly 'naturalised', being comprised of parts,
substances, liquids and data which are 'inhuman'.

These are some of the considerations which have informed particular case
studies described in later chapters: the importance of the changing ways in
which 'humans' sense nature, including ways in which those senses are
'inhumanly' extended (chapter 4); the emphasis upon small-scale 'spatial

practices' within the English countryside (chapter 6); the role of ambivalence in how people think about the countryside and what threatens it (chapter 6); the particular use of focus group methods (chapter 7); and the analysis of how people talk about the environment in the context of their attachment to local place, their sense of the future, and their relationships with larger-scale organisations (chapter 7).

4

SENSING NATURE

So far we have talked in rather general terms about nature and the environment and of how humans do or do not relate to that nature. But what we have not yet considered are the processes by which we come to know what any such nature is like. In particular we have not considered how nature becomes embodied and embedded in daily life. In the next three chapters we attempt to embed/embody people's responses to nature through an analysis of the role of senses (in this chapter), the analysis of time (in chapter 5), and through an analysis of space and the role of practice (in chapter 6). We argue that such a framework can help unravel how people *make* sense of nature, how space and time combine to produce particular natures, and how spaces come to be produced and consumed as nature. Such analyses pertain both to how people bodily confront nature through direct sensory perception of particular environments, as well as their experiences of nature as it is transmitted and discursively constituted through the more indirect processes of the media and other expert systems.

In this chapter we investigate the contributions made by different senses to our knowledge of different environments. This involves not simply individuals seeing, smelling, tasting and hearing different environments, but also how such odours, sights, sounds and flavours are discursively organised. What, we will ask, are the most important sensory mediators between the 'social' and the 'natural' world? What are the effects of the changing importance of such senses upon 'nature'? Are 'natures' in part constituted by the very operation of the senses? What is the role of the senses in leading people to deem certain environments as 'unnatural' and 'polluted'? How do the various senses enable people to distinguish between acceptable and unacceptable changes in nature? And what is the role of the senses in an age when the long-term impacts of nature increasingly transcend direct sensory experience?

It is our general claim in this chapter that much writing about the 'environment' has not been sufficiently embodied, that it has not addressed the complex, diverse, overlapping and contradictory ways in which people sense the world around them and come to judgements of feeling, emotion and beauty about what is appropriately 'natural' and 'unnatural' about their environment(s). It has also not taken full cognisance of the hierarchies of senses which produce different 'structures of feeling' about different spaces. We thus seek to apply to nature an issue encountered in Popper when he characterises 'closed societies' as a 'concrete group of individuals, related to one another . . . by concrete physical relationships such as touch, smell, and sight' (1962: 173). How do such senses operate not only in closed societies but also more generally in relationship to nature in 'open societies'?

In particular we also seek to show that a central concept involved here is that of 'space' (as well as time, which we discuss in the next chapter). Not only are our feelings and emotions about the environment embodied, they are also spatially embedded. But that of course presupposes a theory of space. We will start here with some of the claims made by Lefebvre in his aptly titled *The Production of Space* (1991). He argues that space is not a neutral and passive geometry. Space is produced and reproduced through human activity and it thus represents a site of struggle and contestation. It is not an empty container simply waiting to be filled. Moreover, all sorts of different spatial phenomena, land, territory, site, and so on, should be understood as part of the same dialectical structure of the production of space or spatialisation. While conventionally these different phenomena are separated as a result of fragmented discipline-based analyses, they need to be brought together in a unified theoretical structure, particularly focused upon the social bases of spatialisation. We discuss Lefebvre's theory of spatialisation in more detail in chapter 6, and apply his categories to the production of the spaces of the English countryside.

Two points emphasised by Lefebvre are particularly germane to our argument in this chapter. First, he notes that for Marx nature is one of the forces of production (Lefebvre 1991: 343). But Lefebvre emphasises a distinction not made by Marx between the domination of nature and the appropriation of nature, and hence between dominated spaces and appropriated spaces. Dominated spaces involving the destruction of nature are commonplace in the contemporary world. Appropriated spaces are those involving its 'consumption'. These are qualitatively distinct regions exploited for the purpose of and by means of consumption. Leisure spaces involving the consumption of supposedly natural phenomena of the sun, sea, snow, and so on, are particularly pertinent examples.

Second, and much related to this consumption of space, Lefebvre emphasises that leisure spaces exhibit an:

> increasingly pronounced visual character. They are made with the visible in mind. . . .The predominance of visualization . . . serves to conceal repetitiveness. People *look*, and take sight, take seeing, for life itself. . . . We buy on the basis of images. (1991: 75–6)

More specifically, he describes the process by which the visual sense gains the upper hand and all impressions derived from the other senses gradually lose clarity and then fade away altogether (Lefebvre 1991: 286). All of social life becomes the decipherment of messages by the eye; and the eye relegates objects to a safe distance which renders them passive. The hegemonic role of visuality overwhelms the whole body and usurps its role. He says that the embodied nature of our relationship to the world has come to be narrowly and regrettably 'focused' upon the visual sense which incorporates the 'spectacularization of life'.

In this chapter we seek to interrogate the above claims by examining in some detail the diverse ways in which humans sense the environment. This is a matter not of individual psychology but rather of certain socially patterned 'ways of sensing'. And we will be concerned not only with sight, as in Berger's (1972) ways of seeing, but also with touch, smell, hearing and, to a limited extent, taste. We argue that these different ways of sensing are organised around the modalities of space and time, which form, mediate and refract the senses in their relationships with 'nature'. These relationships to nature are moreover embodied. We analyse here, hopefully in novel ways, the variety of human senses and their respective contribution to how people bodily confront different physical environments. What senses are involved in the perception, interpretation, appreciation and denigration of different natures? How do we sense what other environments are like? How do senses operate across space? Which senses predominate in different historical periods? Are there hierarchies of value between the different senses? What role is played by different ways of sensing to produce different cultures of nature?

This set of issues should be seen as central to current debates about the so-called 'risk society' (Beck 1992b). In such societies Beck argues that risks have become incalculable, uncompensatable, unlimited, unaccountable and, most important of all, invisible to our senses. The paradigm of such invisible risks is nuclear radiation, a risk which cannot be directly touched, tasted, heard, smelt or especially seen. As Beck argues about Chernobyl:

> We look, we listen further, but the normality of our sensual perception deceives. In the face of this danger, our senses fail us. All of us . . . were blinded even when we saw. We experienced a world, unchanged for our senses, behind which a hidden contamination and danger occurred that was closed to our view. (cited Adam 1995a: 11)

And yet we know from a variety of forms of scientific and other information that nuclear radiation is an astonishingly powerful risk of contemporary society, a risk whose long shadow is cast over everyone, rich and poor, male and female, black and white. It is a risk that has no borders, takes no prisoners, knows no senses. Later in chapter 7 we examine the issue of trust with regard to such risks, and consider in part the degree to which people feel that they can trust their senses as well as key institutions for information and actions about such environmental and other risks.

But over time people have become familiar with such risks, although they do not necessarily believe or trust the institutions mediating such senses. People have heard on radio and seen on TV some of the effects of radiation; it is possible to hear the Geiger counter measuring the degree of personal contamination; the effects of nuclear radiation at Hiroshima have been seen on film; and people can see and touch the outside at least of the buildings which house the nuclear reactors, increasingly because such buildings have been paradoxically transformed into 'leisure spaces'. Thus in order to explain the forms of reflexivity that develop to contest such invisible risks it is this array of senses that need to be first examined and explained. And since there is often widespread mistrust of the institutional mediations of information, there will need to be direct sensual experience of the ways by which such risks are being made visible and openly contested (through the publication of indicators, control mechanisms, TV reports, scientific research, campaigns by environmental groups, and so on) so that people may better imagine the complex spatial and temporal dimensions of such risks.

Overall, Beck's analysis of the responses to such invisible senses is too cognitivist and environmentally realist (see Adam 1995a for a recent reinterpretation; see also Wynne 1996a). It over-emphasises the need for alternative forms of scientific knowledge to compensate for the invisibility of the senses. He argues that because such risks are invisible, only alternative scientific understandings and practice could explain how and why such risks are known about and contested. Like Beck we too will argue that scientific knowledge on its own is an insecure base upon which to explain how risks can be understood and confronted, not least due to the cultural and hermeneutic character of scientific knowledge itself. We will also see in the next chapter that our understandings of science and time need to take account of the transformations of each during the course of the twentieth century. In particular we will see how especially nuclear radiation demonstrates the combination of instantaneous and glacial times that characterises the post-modern period: that in each instant a nuclear reaction can unleash huge amounts of either benign or exceptionally destructive force; and that the effects of such forms of power will remain for thousands of years and almost certainly change the evolutionary development of the human species.

But more than this, Adam (1995b) notes that conventional scientific and social scientific ways of knowing tend to eclipse the body. Again we shall see in the next chapter that this is at odds with the current understandings of time, where bodies are presumed to be thoroughgoingly temporal. We will also see in the next section of this chapter that there have been ways of comprehending the world which have over-emphasised the visualisation of the external world, in particular through what Romanyshyn (1989) terms the 'eye of fragmentation' of linear perspectivism (see also Adam 1995b). And it is this examination of the visual and the other senses which is how we should endeavour to 'embody' the human experience of nature. Such considerations are missing in Beck's otherwise illuminating examination of the 'disempowerment of the senses' induced by nuclear power. We shall try to show in this chapter that the way to articulate the embodied character of our relationship to 'nature' is through considering not just the visual sense but the ways in which that sense intersects with the other human senses; and that these can combine together in unexpected and mutually reinforcing ways. Hence, much of what is involved in our response to environmental risk is a contestation over the discursive organisation of different senses, over sights, tastes, sounds and smells, and this is so even where the risk is invisible outside of increasingly abstract scientific/technological expert systems. Subsequently we will show that it is particular combinations of the senses located within a given set of discourses that may produce what is interpreted as an environmental 'bad'.

Moreover, how and why particular senses are stimulated is not something that is directly determined by the physical characteristics of the external environment but is irreducibly socially and culturally structured. Indeed we should emphasise here that 'nature' is not a self-evident set of entities which are simply there, waiting to be 'sensed'. Rather in part nature is constructed through these various senses, especially as they are given form through institutional and media-generated discourses. They have the effect of producing sets of 'physical environments' which are taken to be components of 'nature', while other features of the physical or social world are presumed to be what we might term 'non-nature'. Many of these cultural processes involved in 'inventing' nature in Britain have been described in chapter 2.

There are two particular implications of this argument. First, to treat as nature what is in fact properly cultural is to generate the kind of ideological distortion originally analysed by Marx in his discussion of market relations (Bermingham 1994; Marx 1973). We examined above some of the important ideological effects which follow from treating market relations as 'natural', as akin to nature (see chapter 1). Such ideological effects are particularly powerful in so far as later nineteenth-century notions of nature as cruel and savage, as tearing and ruthless, of humans as naked apes, have come to occupy a hegemonic position (see Williams 1972). And second, to speak of, write of and sense an exterior nature is partially to collude in the interpellation of subjects who appear to be confronted by a separate and all-powerful nature which simultaneously it seems is able to conceal how it is in fact culturally constructed (see Strathern 1992).

The effects of positing such a nature–subject duality are interestingly examined in Bermingham's analysis of John Constable's 'redesigning' of nature in much of his painting. She proceeds to show that 'naturalization might be seen to organize individual artistic practice and vision, and how this process in turn produces artistic representations that appear to be both highly individual while supporting a shared cultural ideal of the natural' (Bermingham 1994: 238). More generally she argues that at the end of the eighteenth century it became common to argue for particular actions because that was the *natural* thing to do (Bermingham 1986). There was an increasing recourse to discourses of nature and the natural to describe and to justify human activities.

In the next section we will see that one effect of such a construction of nature as separate from and opposed to society is to elevate the role of human vision, as Lefebvre argues. Bermingham says of Constable's naturalisation of the physical and human world:

> Constable's scenes have empirical authenticity because they present a way of being in the world as a way of seeing the world; that is, they posit the point of view of a particular subject position as an objective optical truth. (1994: 249)

We conclude this introduction with a brief examination of Rodaway's (1994) elaboration of a 'sensuous geography' in which he seeks to bring together the analyses of body, sense and space, a kind of prototype for what follows in this chapter. He argues that all the senses are geographical (or spatial). Each contributes to people's orientation in space; to an awareness of spatial relationships; and to the appreciation of the qualities of particular places. This includes those places being currently lived in or visited and those which are more removed in time (Rodaway 1994: 37). It also follows that the senses are intricately tied up with the construction and reproduction of different natures. Natures and their perception are in part produced by specific concatenations of the senses. They receive different emphases within different societies and hence produce what are different 'natures'. Rodaway (1994: 36–7) suggests that there are five distinct ways in which the different senses are connected with each other in producing a sensed environment: cooperation between the senses; hierarchy; sequencing of one sense after another; thresholds of effect of one or other sense; and reciprocal relations of some senses with the environment in question. He also demonstrates that each of the senses has given rise to a rich array of metaphors which attest to their relative importance within everyday life. For example, with regard to what Rodaway terms touch or haptic geographies, these include 'keeping in touch', 'rubbing someone up the wrong way', someone being a 'soft touch', the avoidance of 'touchy subjects', something being a 'touching' gesture, someone being 'skinned alive', and so on (Rodaway 1994: 41).

Nature, space and vision

We now turn to examine aspects of the power of vision and its connections with the other senses. The particular fascination with the eye as the apparent mirror of nature and a more general 'hegemony of vision' has characterised western social thought and culture over the past few centuries, some would argue since Aristotle (Rorty 1980). Such a dominance of the eye, what Bermingham (1994) calls 'optical truth', and of its ambiguous consequences, are part of the process by which subjects are interpellated in the West. This was the outcome of a number of developments in Europe, including ecclesiastical architecture of the mediaeval period which increasingly allowed large amounts of light to filter through brightly coloured windows; the growth of heraldry as a complex visual code denoting chivalric identification and allegiance; the notion of linear perspectivism in the fifteenth century in which three-dimensional space came to be represented on a two-dimensional plane; the development of the science of optics and the fascination with the mirror as both object and metaphor; the growth of an increasingly 'spectacular' legal system characterised by colourful robes and courtrooms; and the invention of the printing press which reduced the power of the oral/aural sense (see Hibbitts 1994 for extensive documentation).

Sight has been long been regarded as the noblest of the senses, as the basis of modern epistemology. Arendt neatly summarises the dominant tradition: 'from the very outset, in formal philosophy, thinking has been thought of in terms of *seeing*' (1978: 110–1). Rorty (1980) has famously demonstrated that post-Cartesian thought has generally privileged mental representations 'in the mind's eye' as mirror reflections of the external world. He elaborates:

> It is pictures rather than propositions, metaphors rather than statements, which determine most of our philosophical convictions . . . the story of the domination of the mind of the West by ocular metaphors. (Rorty 1980: 12–13)

The dominant conception of philosophy has thus been of the mind as a great mirror which to varying degrees and in terms of different epistemological foundations permits us to 'see' nature (see Haraway 1989 on the gendered dimensions of vision).

Of course this primacy of the eye is argued in different ways by different philosophers. Descartes' analysis laid the foundation for modern epistemology by maintaining that it is *representations* of the external world which constitute the mind (Reed 1982; Rorty 1980: 45; generally see Hibbitts 1994). All awarenesses of the external world are, he says, awarenesses of internal brain states. But how, he asks, can people know the world and act towards it when their thoughts are based on awareness of their own body? How do we know that anything which is mental represents anything that is outside the mind? He answers these questions through developing a three-fold distinction between the senses: a physical reaction or sensation of a body in contact with other objects; a set of secondary feelings or qualities such as hunger, pain, colour, and so on; and a mental grade involving perceptions and judgements of the external world. But perhaps most significant for our argument, Descartes conceives of the mind as the *inner eye* which surveys representations for their fidelity. So there is in Descartes a most complex relationship posited between the many scraps of sensory data which we encounter through our different senses, including that of immediate sensation, and the necessity for these to be translated back from physical codes into mental images, in the mind's eye. So although sight is the predominant metaphor in modern epistemology, Cartesian thought does not claim that the external world is seen in a wholly unmediated way through the visual sense which produces straightforward representations of that world in the mind.

Vision has also played a crucial role in the imaginative history of western culture. Jay (1986, 1993) points out how clusters of visual imagery around the sun, moon, the stars, mirrors, night and day, and so on, have helped to make sense of both the sacred and the profane. Indeed, nineteenth-century myths of the American wilderness and its 'loss' and fall from innocence were shot through with religious symbolisms (see Novak 1980). Typical American landscapes were seen to involve the complex intertwinings of God and nature. Nature was presumed to be something which was viewed through the eyes of an all-seeing God and not just through the eyes of humans or even of the landscape artists of the pre-Civil War period. Novak argues that various myths of nature prevailed – that of nature as primordial Wilderness, as Garden of the World, as the original Paradise, and as Paradise regained – derived from Christian theology. Most were based upon two presumptions: that nature and God were indissoluble; and that there was a realm of human practice outside and beyond such a nature that was less worthy in God's eye. Nature and God were thought of as unified in those places of wilderness, where, as we discussed in chapter 1, nature had been cast to the margins, beyond the spheres of human practice. And as Williams (1972) articulates, the effect of such a distinction in Europe was to produce one half of nature which is there waiting to be consumed, and another which remains the site of increasingly intense capitalist production. Each side alters nature to a consumable form. In the wild, barren areas nature is transformed into 'scenery, landscape, image, fresh air' – into sites of visual consumption in which nature is seen as separate from and waiting to be visually consumed (Williams 1972: 160; see Urry 1995b). Overall Jay summarises the significance of this visual sense within the broad sweep of western thought: 'with the rise of modern science, the Gutenberg revolution in printing and the Albertian emphasis on perspective in painting, vision was given an especially powerful role in the modern era' (1986: 179). Fabian (1992) characterises this dictatorship of the eye as that of 'visualism'.

There have been intensely complex interconnections between this visualist discourse and the very discovery of and recording of nature as something which is separate from human practice. Adler (1989a) shows that before the eighteenth century travel to other environments had been largely grounded upon discourse and especially on the sense of hearing and the stability of oral accounts of the world (see also Urry 1995b: 194–6). Particularly important was the way in which the ear had provided scientific legitimacy. But this gradually shifted as 'eyewitness' observation of nature as the physical world became more important. This resulted from the gradual working through of the scientific revolutions of the sixteenth and seventeenth centuries. Observation rather than the *a priori* knowledge of mediaeval cosmology increasingly came to be viewed as the only basis of scientific legitimacy; and this subsequently developed into the foundation of the scientific method of the West (albeit one in which such observations would demonstrate one or other religious truth). Sense-data were typically thought of as those data produced and guaranteed by the sense of sight. And such sight came to be understood within 'science', through what Jenks calls the 'sanitised methodological form of "observation"' (1995a: 3). As Foucault shows in *The Order of Things* (1970), from the eighteenth century natural history came to involve the observable structure of the visible world and not functions and relationships which remain invisible to our senses. A number of such sciences of 'visible nature' developed and these were organised around essentially visual taxonomies, beginning most famously with Linnaeus in 1735 (Gregory 1994: 23; Pratt 1992). Such classifications were based upon the modern epistème of the individual subject, of the seeing eye and the distinctions that it can make. As Foucault strikingly claims: 'man is an invention of recent date', and such a 'man' is one who sees, observes and classifies as the notion of resemblance gives way to that of representation or what Augustine terms the 'lust of the eyes' (1970: 221, 312, 386; see O'Neill 1993: 162–4).

Such scientific observation came to involve the imposition of a European system of classification upon the rest of the world. Pratt summarises the effects of the European-based system of order, what she calls an 'anti-conquest':

> The (lettered, male, European) eye that held the system could familiarize ('naturalize') new sites/sights immediately on contact, by incorporating them into the language of the system. (1992: 31)

So scientific observation eliminated the multiple forms of difference between diverse natures and imposed European-based systems of classifications throughout the world (partly of course because of the claim that such observations were closer to both nature and God).

At the same time, the increasing eighteenth-century emphasis upon the scientific eye meant that travellers to other countries could not expect that their observations of nature would become part of the scientific or scholarly understanding of that nature. No longer did mere travel to another environment, normally beyond 'Europe', provide that 'scientific' authority. The first ever international scientific expedition took place in 1735. After that moment mere travel elsewhere did not provide *scientific* legitimacy for the observations that the travellers made and reported (see Pratt 1992: chap. 2).

The scientific understanding of nature organised through 'scientific' travel and observation thus came to be structurally differentiated from travel as such. The latter required a different discursive justification. And this was increasingly focused around not science but connoisseurship, of being an expert *collector* of works of art and buildings, of rare and exotic flora and fauna and of imposing and majestic landscapes. In particular, travel became more obviously bound up with the comparative aesthetic evaluation of different natures and less with eyewitness scientific observation. Travel entailed a different kind of vision and hence of a different visual ideology. Adler summarises:

> travellers were less and less expected to record and communicate their emotions in an emotionally detached, impersonal manner. Experiences of beauty and sublimity, sought through the sense of sight, were valued for their spiritual significance to the individuals who cultivated them. (1989a: 22)

The amused eye increasingly turned to a variety of natures which travellers were able to compare with each other and through which they developed a discourse for what one might term the comparative connoisseurship of nature (see Urry 1995b: chap. 13 on its implications for the invention of the 'Lake District'). Barrell argues that such upper-class travellers: 'had experience of more landscapes than one, in more geographical regions than one; and even if they did not travel much, they were accustomed, by their culture, to the notion of mobility, and could easily imagine other landscapes' (1972: 63).

Various further developments took place during the course of the later eighteenth and early nineteenth centuries, first in Britain and then throughout Western Europe and North America. These served to constitute the new and distinctive discourse of the 'visual consumption of nature', which has been so significant for the past century or so. First, there were huge increases in travelling to various places in England, Scotland and then Europe, which contained natures which were deemed sufficiently entertaining for the informed and amused eye. This pattern grew especially after the highly innovative and influential 'package tour' devised by Thomas Cook in 1841 (see Brendon 1991). Infrastructures developed which permitted many environments to become sites for 'scenic travel' on a mass scale (see Ousby 1990 on ruins, natures, literary landscapes, and so on; and Pemble 1987 on the 'Mediterranean passion'). Especially important was the railway, which involved the subduing of nature and the new aesthetic of the swiftly passing countryside. Guidebooks, travel maps, landscape paintings, postcards and snapshots all led to an increasing visual objectification of an external and consumable nature, one in which the poor, agricultural labourers and environmental 'eyesores' were generally excluded (see Novak 1980 on the aesthetics of painting nature in nineteenth-century America).

Beginning with Margate in 1815, piers and promenades were built so as to enable 'promenading' and the visual appreciation of the sea (see Corbin 1992: 264). New practices developed by which nature was increasingly gazed upon, particularly the practices of leisurely walking both by the sea and over hills and mountains, as well as Alpine and other climbing (see Urry 1995b; Wallace 1993; chapter 6 below).

Elsewhere garden designers were employed to produce new landscapes to surround the houses of the affluent – gardens which were intended to be visually consumed and thereby to convey civilised images of a now-tamed nature (see Pugh 1988 on the eighteenth-century garden). As Tuan (1993: 67) points out, such gardens were viewed as though they were landscape paintings and did not particularly emphasise or develop other senses, especially that of smell (see also Corbin 1986: 189; although one can also note the popularity of scented plants and in particular the rose especially from the nineteenth century). Indeed, with the extensive enclosures of the land beyond the garden there was often a continuity of scenery between the garden inside and the tamed nature outside (Bermingham 1986). Much landscape painting showed the owner of the land exhibiting visual mastery over it. Such developments contributed to what we term the 'possessive' gaze, that is, the new-found ability to look at the world *as if* it could be owned (see also Berger 1972).

This increasing hegemony of vision in European societies and its ability to organise the other senses produced a transformation of nature as it was turned into spectacle. Paglia makes this point in dramatic fashion:

> There is, I must insist, nothing beautiful in nature. Nature is a primal power, coarse and turbulent. Beauty is our weapon against nature . . . . Beauty halts and freezes the melting flux of nature. (1990: 57)

Certainly up to the later eighteenth century nature was generally perceived as hugely inhospitable. Such areas consisted of impenetrable forests, fearsome wild animals, unscalable mountains and ravines, hostile demons, unhealthy peasants and appalling odours issuing from the bowels of the earth, especially through the orifices of swamps and marshes (Tuan 1993: 60–1). Even those areas of nature which were the first to be turned into the 'beautiful' had been regarded as a turbulent power only a few decades earlier. In the early years of the eighteenth century the English Lake District was viewed by Daniel Defoe as 'the wildest, most barren and frightful' of any that he had visited (Nicholson 1978: 25). And yet by the end of the century it had become the first such nature tamed for aesthetic consumption; nature turned into spectacle (see Urry 1995b: chap. 13).

Important in such a spectacularisation of nature were the development of various visual discourses, especially that of the sublime, which enabled the more terrifying aspects of nature to be reinterpreted as part of a meaningful aesthetic experience. This discourse of the visual derived from the writings on aesthetic judgement of Kant, and especially in the British context, Burke. For the latter the experience of the sublime is one of simultaneous terror and delight; he was particularly concerned with how both these feelings can be physiologically experienced at the same time (see Furniss 1993). Burke laid particular emphasis upon how the threatened self would be able to overcome danger through effort, through strenuous action which produces an act of removal from the terrifying threat.

In England such notions of the sublime came to be applied to the subterranean caverns of the Peak District, the Craven region in Yorkshire with its Gothic-like scars and gorges, and then in its most elaborate form to the Lake District (see Ousby 1990: chap. 4; see also Corbin 1992: chap. 5 on the sublime terrors of the seaside). The emphasis in the sublime involved an intense emotional reaction to landscape, to the dizzying claustrophobic fear induced by height, the rapid movement of water and especially overhanging rocks and crags that were seen as immensely threatening to visitors. A bewildering simultaneous mixture of excitement and horror is experienced. The discourse of the sublime includes the widespread use of terms such as desolate, wild, primaeval, hideous, frightful, tremendous, dreadful, and was perhaps most graphically captured by Gray's description of his journey from Derwentwater to Borrowdale, through what were sometimes known as the Jaws of Borrowdale (see plate 4.1). And interestingly this was not a purely visual experience since part of the intensity of emotion was thought to be produced by the sound of thunder and storms, and subsequently, in the case of Ullswater, by the *sound* of reverberating cannon fire set off across the lake. Such a discourse (minus the cannon fire) helped to make a spectacle out of nature, to attribute value to what had previously been considered repellent about nature, and to further organise the other senses around the visual. Subsequently through the poetry and travel writings of particularly Wordsworth, aspects of the sublime became incorporated into English Romanticism, together with some features of the so-called 'cult of the

Plate 4.1   *The Jaws of Borrowdale (source: John Urry)*

picturesque', as outlined by the Rev. Gilpin and Uvedale Price (see Bermingham 1986 on the latter).

During the nineteenth century there was a general growth in viewing nature as spectacle. This was one of the most visual periods in western culture. Ruskin, as the most significant commentator writing in English, claimed that the 'greatest thing a human soul ever does in this world is to see something. . . . To see clearly is poetry, prophecy, and religion' (cited Hibbitts 1994: 257). Nature came to be understood, according to Green, as scenery, views and perceptual sensation. He suggests that partly because of the writings of the Romantics: 'Nature has largely to do with leisure and pleasure – tourism, spectacular entertainment, visual refreshment' (1990: 6). The different discourses of the visual legitimated the turning into spectacle of different 'natures': in England, the awesome sublime landscapes of the Lakes; the sleek, well-rounded beautiful landscapes of the Downs; and the picturesque, irregular and quaint southern villages full of thatched roofs.

Green proceeds to demonstrate some of the effects of this spectacularisation of nature in the region surrounding Paris in the mid-nineteenth century, a period in which there was a prolonged 'invasion of surrounding regions by and for the Parisian spectator' (1990: 76). Two developments facilitated this invasion: the short trip out of the city; and the increased ownership of country houses. These combined to generate around Paris what he terms a 'metropolitan nature'. These are spaces outside the city which can be easily accessed. Such spaces are turned into safe sites for leisure and recreation for the city dweller to visit from time to time. They produce what the visitors believe is an individualised experience of nature as the rejuvenating or refreshing antidote to the city.

Green notes that much of the advertising for houses in the countryside near Paris in this period emphasised the importance of the visual spectacle:

> The language of views and panoramas prescribed a certain visual structure of the *nature* experience. The healthiness of the site was condensed with the actual process of looking at it, of absorbing it and moving round it with your eyes. (1990: 88)

The establishment of various artists' communities represented such a shift of an increasingly mobile middle class into the countryside surrounding Paris, and provided images of a 'metropolitanised' nature which led to extensive further colonisation of rural space by many other visitors. Elsewhere we have described a similar civilising and metropolitanising of nature that occurred in the English Lake District, although in this case its location 'in the north' away from the metropolis meant that its cultural construction required more complex discursive justifications (see Urry 1995b: chap. 13; and chapter 6 below). In such cases the constructed nature can often seem too perfect, too knowing in its spectacularisation, too far from innocence, too distant from sets of real social relations.

This apparent loss of innocence is even more striking in the twentieth century where the sense of sight and its power over the other senses has been stunningly changed by what Sontag (1979) calls the promiscuous practices of photography (see Crawshaw and Urry 1997 on the following). The visual sensing of nature has been transformed by the widespread adoption of such novel discourses. Adam summarises:

> The eye of the camera can be seen as the ultimate realisation of that vision: monocular, neutral, detached and disembodied, it views the world at a distance, fixes it with its nature, and separates observer from observed in an absolute way. (1995a: 8)

Photography has been enormously significant in democratising various kinds of human experience. As Barthes (1981: 34) says, it makes notable whatever is photographed. Photography also gives shape to the very processes of travel so that one's journey consists of being taken from one 'good view' to capture on film, to a series of others (see Urry 1990: 137–40). It has also helped to construct a twentieth-century sense of what is appropriately aesthetic and what is not worth 'sightseeing'; it excludes as much as it includes (see Parr 1995; J. Taylor 1994 for some recent photographic attempts to contest such a dominant aesthetic). Wilson, whose analysis of various cultures of nature we encounter in chapter 6, summarises its impact on 'nature':

> the snapshot transforms the resistant aspect of nature into something familiar and intimate, something we can hold in our hands and memories. In this way, the camera allows us some control over the visual environments of our culture. (1992: 122)

In subsequent chapters we will consider various contestations over different uses and senses of nature, contestations in which the notion of the passive sightseer/snapshooter who is able to 'hold' nature in his/her hands, as well as the active user of the environment, are dominant tropes. The photograph involves an emphasis upon instantaneous results rather than upon process. There is minimisation of performance, compared with other ways in which nature can be represented (such as through music, sketching, painting, singing, sculpting, potting, and so on). Ruskin, for example, considered that the proper seeing of landscape could only come about through sketching or painting and not through anything as instantaneous as composing a photograph. In the next chapter we examine the more general importance of instantaneous post-modern time in the context of what some view as a 'throwaway society'. And later in this chapter we consider the sense of hearing and the way that according to Ingold: 'what I hear is *activity*', while an object to be seen 'need do nothing' (1993b: 162; the relationship between the camcorder and the hierarchy of the senses is not an issue that we have time to explore here).

Photographic practices also reinforce and elaborate dominant visual gazes, especially that of the male over the landscape/bodyscape of the female. Irigaray summarises:

> Investment in the look is not as privileged in women as in men. More than other senses, the eye objectifies and masters. It sets at a distance, and maintains a distance. (1978: 50)

More generally, photography produces the extraordinary array of circulating signs and images which constitutes much of the visual culture of the late twentieth century. Heidegger (1977) argues that what characterises the modern world is the 'modern world picture'. This does not mean a picture of the world, but that the 'fundamental event of the modern age is the conquest of the world as picture' (1977: 134). Visual 'mastery' thus comes to be exerted over both nature and society.

This transformation of vision into a modality of surveillance and discipline stems from the more general nineteenth-century process by which there is a 'separation of the senses', especially of the visual sense from that of touch and hearing, and where the visual sense increasingly determines and organises the other senses as subservient (see Crawshaw and Urry 1997). The autonomization of sight enabled the quantification and homogenisation of visual experience, as radically new objects of the visual began to circulate (including commodities, mirrors, places, photographs). These objects display not spiritual enchantment but a visual enchantment, an enchantment in which magic and spirituality have been displaced by visual appearances and surface features. Slater terms this the 'sanctification of vision'; modernity's disenchantment being based upon the two doctrines of 'seeing is believing' and 'believing is seeing' (Slater 1995: 220, 226). In subsequent chapters we examine the degree to which current environmental

protest is organised around opposition to abstraction, separation and homogenisation which in the late twentieth century takes a particularly intense
form within Heidegger's 'modern world picture'.

Photography has come to enjoy exceptional legitimacy because of its
power to present the physical and social world through what appear to be
unambiguously accurate modes of representation. Slater notes, for example,
that in the mid-nineteenth century Fox Talbot's first photography book was
entitled *The Pencil of Nature* (1995: 223). Nature appears to represent itself.
Photography came to be characterised as 'natural magic'.

However, the development of photography should not to be viewed as a
gradually unfolding and continuous history of visual representation. Rather
it is a crucial element in a 'new and homogenous terrain of consumption and
circulation in which an observer becomes lodged' (Crary 1990: 13). It is one
of a number of nineteenth-century techniques which involved the simultaneous 'industrialisation of image making' *and* the individualisation of the
subject. It is the most significant component of a new cultural economy of
value and exchange in which visual images are given extraordinary mobility
and exchangeability. Such visual experiences involve 'non-veridical' theories of vision – by contrast with the veridical theories which authorised the
camera obscura. Photography is ineluctably bound up with the modern world
and with the subjectivity of the observer and the extraordinary proliferation
of signs and images that that world ushers in during the first half of the
nineteenth century, a process incidentally which begins well before the
'modernist' Impressionism of the 1870s and 1880s (as Crary [1990: 149]
points out).

Sharratt interestingly describes 'the present image economy' in which past
objects and images are 'now seen, looked at, predominantly if not exclu-
sively, as potential mental souvenirs, as camera material, as memorable
"sights"' (1989: 38). He suggests that there are a number of different ways
in which this sense of sight operates, so as to produce such memorable
'sights'. He distinguishes between three such modes: the glance, the gaze
and the scan (Sharratt 1989; and see Bryson 1983). In table 4.1 we have set
out six different modes of visual consumption of the environment; modes
which derive from these different modalities of the visual. We will return to
these distinctions in chapter 6 when we consider different discourses
surrounding what are deemed to be appropriate and inappropriate activities
within the countryside, as reflected within various discourses of leisure.

In passing it is interesting to note how the apparent importance of the
visual partly undermines the distinction between popular tourism and
academic travel. Academic work in many fields increasingly consists of
producing and interpreting visual data. There are interesting parallels
between academics and tourists in the ways in which they produce and
interpret the 'visual', especially as the former increasingly deploy photographic, filmic, televisual and other multi-media material. These parallels are
even closer in the case of those very disciplines which involve travel as a

Table 4.1   *Modes of visual consumption*

Romantic	Solitary
	Sustained immersion and sense of awe
	Gaze involving the sense of the auratic landscape
Collective	Communal activity
	Series of shared encounters
	Gazing at the familiar with people who are also familiar
Spectatorial	Communal activity
	Series of brief encounters
	Glancing and the collecting of many different signs of the environment
Possessive	Solitary or paired
	Habitual encounters
	Scanning over the familiar landscape as if it could be owned
Natural history	Collective organisation
	Sustained and didactic
	Scanning to surveille and inspect nature
Anthropological	Solitary
	Sustained immersion
	Scanning and active interpretation of the 'culture'

key element of the research method, particularly anthropology and geography. In anthropology there is of course a specialist sub-discipline of visual anthropology, the array of recent work being well captured in the recent *Visualizing Theory* (L. Taylor 1994).

Gregory (1994) brings out the historical significance of the conception of the 'world-as-exhibition' for the emergence of the discipline of geography in the eighteenth century. This discipline appears to have developed on the basis of the visual representation of the world, through the world conceived of and grasped as though it were a picture (Gregory 1994: 34). It is presented as an object on display, to be viewed, investigated and experienced (see Mitchell 1988). This process of 'picturing' the world for travel or for imaginary travel or for the travel of others is particularly reflected in two of the tools through which geography has organised its visualisation of space, namely, landscapes and maps. Such technologies of enframing have served to constitute not only the object framed but also the observers who are involved in the very framing (see Gregory 1994: 37).

Landscapes have of course played a wide-ranging role in the cultural history and memory of western societies. Two different senses are worth noting. First, there is the aesthetic sense of landscape, a particular way of seeing, in which artists have been able to reduce three-dimensional visual experiences of scenery to two-dimensional images. Such images appear to be mimetic of the scene in question seen from a given point of view. The eye, indeed the single eye, is regarded as the centre of the visual world. Cosgrove says that 'Visual space is rendered the property of the individual, detached observer' as a result of what we have characterised as the possessive gaze (1985: 49; and see Barrell 1972; Berger 1972; Bryson 1983; Cosgrove 1984; Jay 1993). In the nineteenth century this conception of landscape as linear perspective was augmented by Romantic conceptions of other natures, of sublime and barren landscapes in which a more multi-sensual relationship of the individual to the physical world was to be experienced and represented. In both cases, though, what was important was the presumed power relation between viewer/artist and the viewed/observed. It is the former who have the privileged viewpoint and power to compose the view and to see the painting. Landscape implies mastery and possession of the scene and of its representation (see Crawshaw and Urry 1997 on such notions within the history of photography).

Second, a putatively scientific sense of landscape developed in the nineteenth century associated with the developing discipline of geography (see Barnes and Duncan 1992; Gregory 1994; Rodaway 1994: 130–2). Landscape came to be understood as the particular synthesis of physical and human elements that serve to constitute a distinct region. More recently humanistic and cultural notions have augmented the sense of landscape (as in the notion of a 'cultural landscape'; see Relph 1981; Tuan 1974, 1979). Also some such landscape notions in geography have in fact combined scientific and aesthetic conceptions, such as Vidal de la Blache's examination of the landscapes of different *pays*, in which landscape is taken to be 'that part of the country that nature offers up to the eye that looks at it' (Gregory 1994: 39). Meinig (1979) has noted more generally that implicit in what is supposedly the same scene can be at least 10 different senses of landscape. These he characterises as nature, habitat, artefact, system, problem, wealth, ideology, history, place and aesthetic.

Although maps are a related means of visual representation and are especially connected to the increased observation and surveillance of diverse landscapes, they are a very specialised form of representation (Harley 1992; Rodaway 1994: 133–42). They are quite different from paintings/pictures. As a particular mode of visual representation they possess a number of characteristics: maps take an imaginary bird's-eye view of the world rather than that of an actual or imagined human subject; they involve a scale drawing and do not endeavour to realise an exact or realist reproduction of the landscape; maps involve the deliberate exclusion of many aspects of the landscape; they are intensely symbolic, with the use of all sorts of apparently arbitrary signifiers, of figures, lines, shapes, shadings, and so on; they mostly emerged as practical tools for merchants, government officials and especially armies; and their emergence in the 'West' represents a peculiarly modernistic process of visual abstraction (Rodaway 1994: 133–4).

Both landscapes and maps are culturally specific visual strategies which have reinforced a particular 'Western' view of the world. Both reduce the complex multi-sensual experience to visually encoded features and then organise and synthesise these into a meaningful whole. They both capture aspects of nature and society through visual abstraction and representation; both express distance and objectivity from what is being sensed; and both organise and articulate control or mastery over what is being viewed and thus usher in new ways in which visuality is complicitous in the operation of power.

Thus landscapes and maps deploy the visual sense as a means of control and surveillance. Both therefore bring out what may be called the dark side of sight, the ways in which the visual is associated not only with metaphors of light or understanding or a clear view, but with notions of surveillance, control and mastery over both nature and society. Indeed much of western philosophy can be seen as wrestling with this very contradiction between vision as lightness and vision as darkness; and this has been true of both the Anglo-American and continental traditions (this is well demonstrated in Levin's [1993b] analysis of 'modernity and the hegemony of vision'; and see Jay 1993). Such a contradiction is also present in much policy debate over the uses of and access to 'nature', as we examine in chapter 6 below.

In the twentieth century three of its most significant philosophers, Derrida, Heidegger and Foucault, have all described the continued privileging of sight and the different ways of how such sight produces dark and destructive consequences. Derrida's examination of the metaphysics of presence pre-supposes a critique of ocularcentrism (see Jay 1993: chap. 9). And he is particularly hostile to the privileging of the eye, indeed to any attempt to hierarchise the senses. He wishes rather to examine the interdependence between the senses, and especially to examine the significance of hearing and touch for deconstructionist practice. But this is not simple to achieve, partly because of the power of the metaphors of light and dark, of the visual inheritance of the so-called Enlightenment (Derrida 1983).

Heidegger (1977), although noting how the hegemony of vision had its origins in Greek philosophy, suggests that its latest phase has particularly ominous characteristics (and see Levin 1993a, 1993b). He sees all experiences as being reduced to the ocularcentric ideology of subject-relevant images or representations. This new era is one in which 'what-is' has become 'what-is in representation'. In this ocularcentric metaphysics our being in the world has become equated with images and representations. Heidegger (1977: 134) is not so much opposed to vision as such as to the particular form that it has taken in the modern age, with the framing of the world picture; with the world transformed into 'pictures', or 'structured images'.

Somewhat similarly, Foucault (1977) analyses disciplinary power and the way that it gradually replaces sovereign power. Such disciplinary power functions through normalisation, surveillance and observation, and gradually dispense with some of the more obviously authoritarian processes which had been employed up to the eighteenth century. Napoleon's regime is transitional in this transformation to modern societies which are organised around surveillance through the omnipotent gaze. Foucault's analysis of the power of the gaze shifts in emphasis from the primacy of the individual knowing eye, to its spatial positioning especially via the panopticon and of the relationship of that social vision to the operation of power (Jay 1993;

Urry 1992). He disagrees with Debord and his concept of the 'society of spectacle' in which there is the 'spectacularization of everyone', maintaining rather that 'our society is one not of spectacle, but of surveillance. . . . We are neither in the amphitheatre, nor on the stage, but in the panoptic machine' (Foucault 1977: 217; Jenks 1995b: 155).

This analysis clarifies how sight, which is often seen as producing illumination and clarity (en*light*enment), also produces its dark side. Many of the most powerful systems of modern incarceration in the twentieth century involve the complicity of sight in their routine operations of power. As Deutsche powerfully writes of the voyeur who takes real pleasure in looking and victimizing:

> Distancing, mastering, objectifying – the voyeuristic look exercises control through a visualization which merges with a victimization of its object. (1991: 11)

Indeed it is often now argued that we live in a surveillance society, even when we are apparently roaming freely through the shopping centre or even the countryside. Amongst others, Virilio (1988) has particularly emphasised the novel importance of video surveillance techniques to changing the morphology of the contemporary city and hence of the trust that the public have to invest in such institutions of surveillance (see also Barry 1995: 44; and the recent film *Sliver* organised around the power and ambiguity of video surveillance). It has been estimated that during a normal stroll through a major city centre in Britain one is likely to be captured on film at least 20 times.

The fascination with *and* denigration of the visual which particularly characterises French social thought has its counterparts in the diverse discourses surrounding travel to experience various places. We are aware that much travel involves, at least in part, the activity of sightseeing. In most of the discourses surrounding travel, there is an emphasis upon the seeing and collecting of sights; the operation of what we have just characterised as the 'spectatorial' mode of visual consumption. In that sense we do live in a society of spectacle; we have noted many ways in which nature has been transformed into diverse and collectable spectacles. Nature thus comes to be divided up and collected by the sightseer as a set of discrete, atomised sights. Indeed it often appears to be little more than the aggregation of relatively unconnected sights, each of which is given objectified form in photographs, postcards, models, guidebooks, brochures, and so on. In many cases, the process of collecting such sights comes to dominate the process of travel (see Urry 1990: 138–40).

In these discourses of 'travel' the mere sightseer of different environments, who only lets the sense of sight have free rein, is particularly ridiculed. Such sightseers are generally denigrated; they are seen as superficial in their appreciation of environments, peoples and places. And many people in response are often embarrassed about mere sightseeing. As with much French social thought, there is the denigration of the purely visual. Sight is seen not as the noblest of the senses but as the most superficial, as getting in the way of real experiences that involve other senses and necessitate much longer periods of time in order to be immersed in the site/ sight (see Boorstin 1964). For example, Wordsworth argued that the Lake District demands a different eye, one which is not threatened or frightened by the relatively wild and untamed nature. It requires 'a slow and gradual process of culture' (Wordsworth 1984: 193). In the next chapter we examine how such a culture of slowness becomes threatened by the speed and violence brought about by processes of instantaneous time in highly globalised societies. Cultural criticism gets levelled both at the tourists who are mere sightseers and at the companies and organisations that pander to such notions by constructing places for such superficial, quick and often commodified visual consumption (see Buzard 1993 on the history of those discourses organised around the tourist/traveller distinction). In later chapters we will of course see how pressures of commodification are particularly strong; and also how many policy initiatives inadvertently tend to encourage such commodification by measuring success through quantitative measures of visitor experiences and rights.

Surveillance is powerfully involved here. The visitor to various environments is subject to extensive monitoring. In Britain visitors to the countryside are subject to an extensive 'country code' which is partly implemented by countryside rangers or wardens. Often there is no general right to roam and one is enjoined not merely to walk in particular directions but even to keep rigidly to the footpath – otherwise one may contribute to environmental damage. In relationship to this almost sacred nature there are strict ways of behaving in order to practise 'quiet recreation'. And at the same time those people living in such places in nature are themselves expected to behave in particular ways. They live in a panopticon, not knowing whether crowds of 'nature-worshippers' will be passing their front door each time they venture out. They can be subject to an almost constant 'threat of surveillance' unless they are able to restrict the visiting-season to particular times of the day, the week or the year. More recently the UK Government's Going for Green campaign has introduced the 'green code' aimed at encouraging individuals to change their lifestyles and so help save the environment. The green code aims to install new elements of self-surveillance into everyday behaviour, for example, by cutting down personal waste, saving energy, keeping cars properly tuned, and so on.

In recent debates, some of the objects seen by the sightseer, including paradigmatically Disneyland, are taken as illustrating so-called hyper-reality, forms of simulated experience which have the appearance of being more 'real' than the original (Baudrillard 1981; Bryman 1995; Eco 1986; Rodaway 1994). Such places rest upon hyper-sensory experiences in which certain senses, especially that of vision, are reduced to a limited array of features, are then exaggerated and come to dominate the other senses. This hyper-reality is characterised by surface – such that a particular sense is seduced by the most immediate and constructed aspect of the scene in question, whether this is the 'eye' at a Disneyland or the 'nose' and the sense of smell at a Fishing Heritage Centre (as at Grimsby in north-east England). This is a world of simulation rather than representation, a world where the medium has become the message.

What is not experienced in such hyper-real places is a rather different visual sense, what Jay (1992) characterises as the baroque (see also Buci-Glucksmann 1994). This involves the fascination for opacity, unreadability and indecipherability of place which has operated as an alternative ocular regime within modernity. Jay talks of celebrating:

> the dazzling, disorientating, ecstatic surplus of images in baroque visual experi-
> ence . . . [the] rejection of the monocular geometricalization of the Cartesian
> tradition. . . . the baroque self-consciously revels in the contradictions between
> surface and depth, disparaging as a result any attempt to reduce the multiplicity of
> visual spaces into any one coherent essence. (1992: 187)

Jay (1992: 192) talks of baroque planning being addressed not to reason but to the engagement and indulgence of all the senses, as in some carnivals and festivals, and not to the dominance of any single one, or to the separation and hyper-real exaggeration of one of them. The baroque can also be seen in nature as the unexpected, the surprise, the unplanned, the incongruous, what we characterise in chapter 6, using Lefebvre's theory of spatialisation, as collective resistances to dominant social practices, especially those practised by the state.

A critique of some ocularcentric regimes has also been developed within feminist theorising. It is argued that the concentration upon the visual, or at least the non-baroque versions of the visual, over-emphasises appearance, image and surface. Irigaray argues that in western cultures 'the preponder-ance of the look over the smell, taste, touch and hearing has brought about an impoverishment of bodily relations. The moment the look dominates, the body loses its materiality' (1978: 123; Mulvey 1989).

Thus the emphasis upon the visual reduces the body to surface and marginalises its sensuality. In relationship to nature it impoverishes the relationship of the body to its physical environment and over-emphasises masculinist efforts to exert mastery, whether over the female body or over nature, which is typically seen as taking a feminised form (see Plumwood 1993). McClintock (1995) demonstrates the extraordinary intertwining of male power over colonised nature and the female body in the history of Empire. The male look over both can be seen as endlessly voyeuristic. She describes the tradition of male travel as an erotics of ravishment, as the western traveller conquered or fantasised the conquering of both. She talks of the tradition of converting non-European nature, the virgin territory, into a feminised landscape, as the 'porno-tropics' (McClintock 1995: chap. 1). Much of the writing on the conquering of nature as an 'untouched' wilderness employs sexual metaphors – of mastery, domination, thrusting into the unknown, and so on.

By contrast it is claimed that a feminist consciousness less emphasises the dominant visual sense and seeks to integrate all of the senses in a more rounded consciousness which does not seek to exert mastery over the 'other'

(Rodaway 1994: 123). Especially significant is the sense of touch to female sexuality. Irigaray argues that: 'Woman takes pleasure more from touching than from looking, and her entry into a dominant scopic regime signifies, again, her consignment to passivity: she is to be the beautiful object of contemplation' (cited Jay 1993: 531).

In this section we have therefore shown the historical development of the sense of sight during the course of the eighteenth and nineteenth centuries; the enormously influential circulation of visual images in the twentieth century and the impact of particular modes of visual representation – especially maps and landscapes; the different types and modes taken by the visual sense; and the gendered nature of the particular domination of visuality over the other senses. It is these other senses to which we shall now turn, before more generally evaluating some implications of these diverse senses for current contestations over 'nature'.

Nature and the other senses

We will approach these other senses by returning briefly to nineteenth-century Britain – to the very period in which photography and mass tourism were emerging at the end of the fourth decade (between 1839 and 1841 to be precise; see Crawshaw and Urry 1997). The House of Commons Select Committee of 1838 argued that because there were whole areas of London through which no thoroughfares passed, the lowest class of person was therefore secluded from the *observation* and influence of 'better educated neighbours' (Stallybrass and White 1986: 134). Engels likewise noted how the social ecology of the industrial city had the effect of 'hiding from the eyes of wealthy gentlemen and ladies . . . the misery and squalor that . . . complement . . . their riches and luxury' (cited Marcus 1973: 259). And it was claimed that such classes would be transformed and improved once they did become *visible* to the middle and upper classes, both through surveillance of their behaviour and through the inculcation of politeness. There were of course some crucial parallels between this argument and the rebuilding of Paris with its hugely enhanced visibility, to see and be seen, which resulted from the replacement of the street layout of mediaeval Paris by the grand boulevards of the Second Empire (see Berman 1983).

These references in the mid-nineteenth-century British Parliament demonstrate how visibility was increasingly viewed as central to the regulation of the lower classes within urban areas. But at the same time as the 'other' class were now seen in the massive cities of nineteenth-century Britain, they were not to be touched. Indeed Stallybrass and White (1986) argue that the notion of 'contagion' and 'contamination' were the tropes through which much nineteenth-century city life was apprehended (note incidentally the continued significance of the rhetoric of 'open air' for those living in the inner city). As the 'promiscuity' of the public space became increasingly unavoidable, so it was insisted that the upper and middle classes should avoid touching the potentially contaminating 'other', the 'dangerous classes'.

Instead, they could be observed, at a safe distance, in novels and newspaper articles.

There were two dichotomies which operated here: gaze/touch; desire/ contamination. The upper class mainly sought to gaze upon the other, while for example standing on their balconies. Stallybrass and White suggest that the balcony took on special significance in nineteenth-century life and literature as the place from which one could gaze but not be touched, could participate in the crowd yet be separate from it. According to Benjamin (1969: 173) what this did was to demonstrate superiority over the crowd as the observer 'scrutinizes the throng' via the 'perambulating gaze' (see also Shields 1995). The later development of the skyscraper in 1880s Chicago with their panoramic windows also enabled those inside to gaze down and across the crowd, while being insulated from the smells and the potential touch of those below. In Chicago the avoidance of the smells of the meat processing industry was a particularly important spur to building skyscrapers up into the light. And there are parallels with the way in which the contemporary tourist bus gives a bird's-eye view, in but not of the crowd, gazing down on the crowd in safety, without the heat, the smells and the touch. It is as though the scene is being viewed on a screen, and sounds, noises and the contaminating touch are all precluded because of the empire of the gaze effected through the screen of the bus.

In another contemporary parallel, this time to the way in which the late twentieth-century backpacker travels to the dark side of the towns and cities of the global marketplace, younger sons of the nineteenth-century rich would often travel to areas of lowlife in the city in order to gaze at sailors and prostitutes. Indeed, some men moved beyond the gaze to seek out the touch and feel of the other in brothels, opium dens, bars and taverns.

More generally we have become familiar with the nineteenth-century discovery of the urban *flâneur*, immortalised by Baudelaire and then by Benjamin, who sought to immerse himself in the crowd and to wallow in its rush of sensory information, but even so is not entirely at home (see Tester 1995). How different travellers and visitors relate to the diverse sounds and sense impressions of the crowd of strangers remains one of the defining conditions of the modern experience, involving an array of technologies, memories and selective use of the range of human senses. In the nineteenth century it was thought that the newly constructed spaces of the panoramas, department stores, exhibition halls, electric lights, the arcades, and so on, involved a bombardment of the senses that created a neurosis or sensory distraction at the same time that it was visually consumed as an exotic spectacle (Boyer 1995). Modern states have of course sought to intervene to both stimulate *and* to control such leisure and tourist sites and the bombardment of the senses that visitors may experience.

One sense which was very significant in the cultural construction of the nineteenth-century western city was smell. It demarcated the unnaturalness of the city. Stallybrass and White argue that in the mid-nineteenth century the city . . . still continued to invade the privatised body and household of the bourgeoisie as smell. It was, primarily, the sense of smell which enraged social reformers, since smell, whilst, like touch, encoding revulsion, had a pervasive and invisible presence difficult to regulate. (1986: 139)

Smells, sewers, rats and the mad played key roles in the nineteenth-century construction of class relations within the large cities (and see Orwell 1937: 159 on the odours along the road to Wigan Pier). Moreover, it was partly to avoid the smell of the city that led to the popularity of the English seaside resort, which emphasised the apparently natural clean air to be found there. These were some of the first urban places to introduce major public health interventions.

Stallybrass and White (1986) note that as the nineteenth-century upper class repressed reference to their lower bodily functions, so they increasingly referred to the simultaneous dangers *and* fascinations of lowlife: the smells of the slum, the rag-picker, the prostitute, the sewer, the dangers of the rat, below stairs, the kneeling maid, and so on (and see Shields 1991 on lowlife in nineteenth-century Brighton). The upper class in nineteenth-century British cities experienced a specific 'way of sensing' such cities in which smell played a particularly pivotal role. The Romantic construction of nature was powerfully forged through the odours of death, madness and decay, which by contrast with nature were ever-present within the industrial city (Tuan 1993: 61–2; see Classen et al. 1994: 165–9 on the class and ethnic structuring of such 'smellscapes'; Corbin 1986: chap. 9 on the 'stench of the poor' in Paris).

More generally here, what Rodaway (1994: 61) terms the 'geography of the nose' has not been particularly developed within the western academy (but see Classen et al. 1994; Corbin 1986; Porteous 1985, 1990). This is partly because of the denigration of the sense of smell within western culture and the related view that smell is much more developed amongst so-called savages than amongst those who are apparently civilised (see Tuan 1993: 55–6). However, Lefebvre for one argues that the production of space is crucially bound up with smell. He says that 'where an intimacy occurs between "subject" and "object", it must surely be the world of smell and the places where they reside' (1991: 197). Olfaction seems to provide a more direct and less premeditated encounter with the environment; and one which cannot be turned on and off. It provides a rather unmediated sense of the surrounding environment, and hence can often figure in contemporary environmental discourse. Tuan (1993) argues that the directness and immediacy of smell provide a sharp contrast with the abstractive and compositional characteristics of sight.

What thus needs investigation are the diverse 'smellscapes' which organise and mobilise our feelings about particular places (including what one might also call 'tastescapes'). The concept of smellscape effectively brings out how smells are spatially ordered and place-related (Porteous 1985: 369). In particular, the olfactory sense seems particularly important in evoking memories of very specific places; as Tuan (1993: 57) notes, the momentary smell of seaweed was sufficient to invoke his childhood memories while sights from his childhood haunts were not. And even if we cannot identify the particular smell, it can still be important in helping to create and sustain our sense of a particular place. It can generate both revulsion and attraction; and as such it can play a major role in constructing and sustaining major distinctions of taste. Rodaway effectively summarises what he describes as the geography of smell:

> the perception of an odour in or across a given space, perhaps with varying intensities, which will linger for a while and then fade, and a differentiation of one smell from another and the association of odours with particular things, organisms, situations and emotions which all contribute to a sense of place and the character to places. (1994: 68)

He summarises a variety of literary writings which seek to characterise different places in terms of their apparent smells, including many drawn from 'nature'. G.K. Chesterton, for example, writes of 'the brilliant smell of water, the brave smell of stone, the smell of dew and thunder, the old bones buried under' (cited Rodaway 1994: 73); while Tolstoy describes the smells following a spring thunderstorm: 'the odour of the birches, of the violets, the rotting leaves, the mushrooms, and the wild cherry' (cited Tuan 1993: 62). More recently, Salmon Rushdie, in his epic *Midnight's Children*, talks of how through the power of the nose he was able 'to learn the secret aromas of the world, the heady but quick-fading perfume of new love; and also the deeper, longer-lasting pungency of hate', and more broadly of 'the powers of sniffing-out-the-truth, of smelling-what-was-in-the-air, of following trails' (1995: 307).

More generally, McClintock (1995: chap. 5) provides a powerful examination of the nineteenth-century development of soap and the actual and metaphorical role of cleanliness in the growth of the British Empire (her book is entitled *Imperial Leather*). She quotes a Unilever Company Slogan from the period: 'Soap is Civilization' (1995: 207)! Soap advertising had two main effects. First, it reinforced the British cult of domesticity and made this definitive of national identity, through what McClintock terms 'domesticating Empire'. And second, the advertising generated notions of cleanliness and hygiene which would civilise the unwashed natives who had still to learn that smelling of Imperial Leather was the marker of the civilised world! Pears advertising in particular was characterised by ideas of hygiene and purification (in which white is presumed to be hygienic). So the politics of smell not only enabled the production of new commodities for the mass market, but it also helped to construct the nature of the colonial encounter, to domesticate and purify it, and to invest it with intimate distinctions of bodily smell. The effect was that new imposed notions of the natural hygienic body came to be imposed by the colonial power. But Ruark captures the paradoxical smellscape of this colonial power when he describes 'the smell of white man, the white man's food and drink and clothing, the greasy stink of the white man's petrol fumes and belching diesel exhausts' (cited Rodaway 1994: 72).

The final issue to consider here is whether, and in what ways, the sense of smell has become less significant in modern western societies, as Lefebvre (1991) and others appear to argue. It is clear that in many pre-modern societies the sense of smell was very significant, particularly in the 'West' with the significance of aroma within the classical world (Classen et al. 1994). And in modern societies there is an apparent dislike of strong odours, as evidenced by the following: the development of public health systems which separate water from sewerage; the view that a lack of smell indicates personal and public cleanliness; the favouring of very frequent baths and showers; the restriction of the use of perfume to adult women; the preference for simpler rather than complex body perfumes and cooking spices; the favouring of domestic arrangements in which animal and other smells are excluded so as to keep the air 'fresh'; and the requirement to be sensitised to different smells and to have some ability to organise the elimination of those smells deemed to be 'unnatural' (which may of course include many smells such as rotting vegetables which are 'natural').

More generally, Bauman further develops this argument by claiming that 'Modernity declared war on smells. Scents had no room in the shiny temple of perfect order modernity set out to erect' (1993b: 24). For Bauman, modernity sought to neutralise smells by creating zones of control in which the senses would not be offended. Zoning became an element of public policy in which planners accepted that repugnant smells are in fact an inevitable by-product of urban-industrial society. Thus refuse dumps, sewage plants, meat processing factories, industrial plants, and so on, are all spaces in which bad smells are concentrated, and are typically screened-off from everyday life by being situated on the periphery of cities. This notion of the war on smells in modernity was of course carried to the extreme in the Nazi period, where the Jews were routinely referred to as 'stinking', and their supposed smell was associated with physical and moral corruption (Classen et al. 1994: 170–5).

But Bauman (1993b) argues that smell is a particularly subversive sense since, as we have argued, it cannot be wholly banished. It reveals the artificiality of modernity. The modern project to create a pure, rational order of things is undermined by the sweet smell of decomposition which continuously escapes from control and regulation. Thus the 'stench of Auschwitz' could not be eliminated even when at the end of the war the Nazis tried to conceal what had happened (Classen et al. 1994: 175). This is why Bauman submits that decomposition has 'a sweet smell'. Such smells bring out how the modern world cannot be totally controlled. As one of the liberators at Auschwitz wrote:

The ovens,
the stench,
I couldn't repeat
the stench. You
have to breathe.
You can wipe out

what you don't want
to see. Close your
eyes. You don't want
to hear, don't want
to taste. You can
block out all the senses
except smell. (cited Classen, Howes and Synnott 1994: 175)

It seems that some of the attempts to restrict and regulate smell have gone into reverse in the past couple of decades in the 'West', as the cultural turn to 'nature' has become more pronounced (see Strathern's *After Nature* [1992]). Recent trends include the increased attraction of spicy 'oriental' foods (a matter of smell and taste); the increased use of natural and often eastern perfumes both for the body for both genders and for the home; a reduced emphasis upon antiseptic cleanliness and a greater use of materials and smells that are deemed to be 'natural' (such as lemon); much greater knowledge of and sensitivity to the smells of nature, especially flowers; a greater awareness of the malodorous smells of the motor car and of the many chemicals identifiable in rivers and seas which may be taken as metonymic of much wider and long-term risks; and some appreciation that the preservation of landscapes involves not just issues of visualisation but also threatened smellscapes. The cultural shift to nature has increased the power of smell over and against that of sight; but this does not mean that all smells are presumed to be equally acceptable (cigarette smoke, nitrates and sewage are increasingly not). The cultural shift to the natural thus ushers in new contestations over diverse smellscapes as they interact in complex ways with the dominant processes of visualisation. We will see in subsequent chapters some important metaphors of smell within contemporary environmentalism.

Finally, we consider acoustic space. Rodaway points out that while the visual world can be turned on and off, rather like seeing the photographs in a book, a TV or on the computer screen, acoustic space cannot. Our ears cannot be closed. Ihde (1976) argues that while we are at the edge of the visual sense, which in a way always remains partially distant from us, we cannot avoid being at the centre of acoustic sense. It is simply all around us, even when there is a poignantly ominous silence (such as when an engine cuts out or when camping in the middle of the arctic or when an ecosystem dies; see Hibbitts 1994: 273; Tuan 1993: 75).

We consider three points here. First, as with smell, there appears to have been a major historical shift from, in this case, oral to visual cultures. Tuan (1974) notes that before people began to live in large cities, noise was nature's prerogative. While people could shout and scream and play musical instruments, these noises could never match those of nature, of the roar of thunder, of a galeforce wind, or a river in full flood. And these were overwhelming sensory mediators between human society and the physical world. Thus, for example, aboriginal space is often interpreted as acoustic while contemporary Western space is more visual. However, much more recently there appears to be something of a reinvigorated aural culture within the West. This is reflected in the ubiquity of muzak, loudspeakers, ghetto-blasters, telephone bells, traffic, motor boats, and so on (see Hibbitts 1994: 303 on the increasing need for 'aural distraction'). As a consequence it is now difficult to find supposedly natural places which are devoid of any sound, or devoid at least of the sounds that are not 'natural'. The Council for the Protection of Rural England reports that there are now only three areas of 'tranquillity' left in England, that is, areas which are out of earshot of urban developments, street lighting and road noise. These areas are north Devon, parts of Herefordshire and the north Pennines (see CPRE 1995).

Second, however, some sounds can be particularly comforting. Morley (1995) in this context, presents an interesting examination of the importance of sound in the viewing of television. He notes how the television as object has become incorporated into normal domestic space and domestic routines. He suggests that the dominant visual mode of viewing the TV is through the *glance*, or perhaps an oscillation between the glance and the gaze as people skilfully move in and out of a regime of watching, rather than the more sustained *gaze* that appears to characterise how people attend to the cinema screen (see Sharratt 1989; and discussion above). But more importantly he claims the predominant sense involved in relationship to the TV is listening. An enormous array of other activities are engaged in while the TV set is on; activities which are mainly carried on with the sound available in the background. So although obviously TV is a component of a visual culture, it may also be an important counter to the more general phenomenon of visual mastery. Perhaps this is a case of sound organising sight. Its soundscapes are part of the domestic life of most households, and increasingly of various 'private' public spaces (such as bars, clubs and cafés).

Third, in the past couple of decades in the West much of this aural culture has come to be viewed as itself unnatural and environmentally polluting. So it is common to designate certain sounds as separate from nature, as involving 'sound pollution'. This designation often involves employing a distinction of taste against those producing what are deemed to be partic-ularly polluting soundscapes. Much conflict in urban and rural areas derives from contestations over soundscapes. Indeed part of the appeal of certain places is because of their presumed sound characteristics. The English countryside is said to attract people partly because it is thought to present a quite different soundscape from urban areas. Rural planners have regularly employed the notion of 'quiet recreation' to exclude many kinds of activity that are deemed not to fit in with historically transmitted conceptions of what are appropriate sounds, activities and peoples in the countryside (see Clark et al. 1994a). However, the use of such a distinction of sound is often inconsistently applied since the countryside does in fact contain very many sounds, especially the car and the tractor, as well as animals, water, the wind, birds, insects, and so on. A countryside without sound would be a dead countryside. One could note that one person's sound pollution may on occasion constitute another person's sign of nature!

So touch, smell and sound are all involved in how we sense nature. Further examination is necessary in order to work out how and in what ways such senses are deployed to identify what are deemed to be environmental 'bads' in particular cultures, and how such senses interconnect with the dominant sense of sight. It will also be necessary to determine how the mobilisation of different senses leads to the different overlapping spatial scales of the environmental issues which happen to be identified and critiqued within a given society or across many such societies.

Conclusion

The most obvious conclusion to draw from this analysis is that an extraordinary power has been historically exerted by the sense of sight and of its ability to organise the other more subordinate senses. Its impact on how we approach, understand and sense nature has been immense. There are various aspects of this: visual observation as the basis of epistemology and western scientific method; the influence of sight over the other senses and the consequences of this upon class, gender and ethnic relations; the role of sight in relationship to travel and to the aesthetic appreciation of the scenic; the specialisation of the senses and especially sight in the later nineteenth century; the industrialisation of the visual sense and the enormous impact of visual images and later of simulations; the more general importance of visual technologies, especially photographs, electronic images, maps and land-scapes; and the role of vision in the disembodying of people's relationships with nature.

But vision has not got its own way without contestation. There have been some counter-tendencies: the twentieth-century critique of the visual so actively pursued by French social theorists; the existence of alternative visual paradigms, especially that of the baroque; the sheer impact of the other senses and especially that of smell; the importance of memory to place and the difficulty of confining this solely within a visual straitjacket; the complex, mediated and contested character of contemporary 'natures' which make them difficult to sense in a simple fashion; and how the exceptional array of spaces that characterise the post-modern world now militate against any direct and unmediated connections between a particular vision and a given slice of nature (unlike the period in which the landscape aesthetic initially emerged).

What we will go on to examine in subsequent chapters is whether the processes described in this chapter can help explain how and why particular environments are thought to be threatened with various kinds of damage, why different social groups sense different environmental 'bads', what the connections are between such senses and the variety of social and cultural responses by different publics, and how such responses are embedded in specific social/spatial practices, especially those involving people's dwellings. We will consider how on occasions a recourse to the senses is employed to contest the abstracted and planned character of the treatment of nature; and what the connections are between the increasing significance of scientific/technological expert systems and the importance of certain of these more immediate senses. At the heart of many environmental disputes between lay and expert forms of knowledge lie contestations over different senses, and over the relative role of the senses, as opposed to more abstract and cognitive forms of knowledge.

But also cross-cutting these distinctions are various spatialisations, to return to Lefebvre (1991). In particular the senses normally pertain to a presumed locality, to some sense of 'acting locally'. We shall see below that there are many such locals, which are constituted in terms of different sense-scapes. But also we shall examine just how the theme of *global* environmental change has emerged and the degree to which this entails modes of understanding which by-pass the senses analysed in this chapter. We have mostly focused here upon what Ingold calls the 'dwelt-in world, in the practical business of life, rather than on the detached, disinterested observation of a world apart' (1993a: 40). But we shall go on to consider some of the complex connections between the emergence of the 'global' level in the environment, and the simultaneous importance of developing a 'dwelling perspective'. In proceeding to look further at global levels of analysis we will need to do full justice to the power, ambiguity and diversity of the human senses.

5

NATURE AND TIME

In the last chapter we focused on how nature, viewed as essentially spatial, is subject to a variety of human senses. In this we attempted to correct the largely unembodied view of nature and the environment which is present in much of the existing literature. But it is also our argument in this book that nature and the environment are not only spatial but also temporal; and indeed that twentieth-century science has anyway shown that such a distinction is itself inappropriate. In now introducing 'time' into our investigation of contested natures, we shall endeavour to retain the analysis of the sensing of space.

We examine below how the temporality of different natures connects to this analysis of the senses provided above. Are the senses differently positioned with regard to time, and if so what are the consequences of this? In particular we shall analyse how the senses are involved in memory, since this is one obvious way in which time has come to be embedded within nature. We go on to consider how space and time combine to produce particular natures. Overall we examine a variety of ways in which different times are reflected within different responses to and configurations of the environment: that is to say, contestations over nature are in significant part contestations over differing times of nature.

There are four sections in this chapter: a brief history of some of the main social science approaches to time; an interrogation of different times and of their insertion within various natures; an analysis of how natures are variably remembered; and a conclusion which develops an analysis of time in terms of a 'dwelling perspective' which transcends many of the deficiencies of both environmental realism and environmental idealism as set out in chapters 1 and 3 above.

The social sciences and time

We begin with a brief sketch of the main social scientific approaches to the investigation of time. Although the very word 'time' designates disparate concepts, most social scientific accounts have presumed that time is in some sense social and hence separate from and opposed to the realm of nature. They have adopted some version or other of the 'French' school's approach, following that of Durkheim. He famously argued in *Elementary Forms of the Religious Life* (1968) that only humans have a concept of time and that time in human societies is abstract, impersonal and objective, and not simply individual. Moreover, this impersonality is socially organised; it is what Durkheim refers to as 'social time'. Hence, time is a 'social institution' and the category of time is not natural but social. Time is conceived of as an objectively given social category of thought produced within societies, and one which may vary considerably between societies. Social time is different from and opposed to the time(s) of nature, including the temporal processes and rhythms that inhabit or order the natural world. In this section we briefly consider the contributions to the analysis of time of Sorokin, Merton, Bourdieu, Marx, Weber, Mead, Giddens, Harvey and Adam.

Sorokin and Merton (1937) go on to distinguish between societies as to whether or not there is a separate category of clock-time, over and above that of social time. The Nuer, for example, do not make that distinction. Time for them is not a resource; it is not something that passes, that can be wasted or saved (Evans-Pritchard 1940). To the extent to which there are expressions of time, these take place by reference to social activities based on cyclical changes in nature. Those periods devoid of significant social activity are passed over without reference to time.

Sorokin (1937) also notes that while most societies have some form of 'week', this may consist of anything from three to sixteen days (see also Colson 1926; Coveney and Highfield 1991: 43–4; Hassard 1990). No other animal appears to have adopted the week as a temporal unit; and no other animal appears to have developed a unit so independent of astronomic divisions. In many societies such divisions reflect some particular social pattern. The Khasi, for example, have an eight-day week since they hold a market every eight days. The seven-day week derives from the Babylonians, who in turn influenced the Jews. There have been various attempts to change it – most noticeably by the French after 1789 with a decimal ten-day week and by the Soviet Union with a five-day week – but almost all societies have returned to the totally arbitrary yet apparently 'natural' seven-day week.

Much anthropological writing on time has been concerned with the relationship between time which appears to be based on 'naturally' determined social activities, such as birth and death, night and day, planting and harvesting, and so on, and that which is 'unnaturally' imposed by the clock (Gell 1992). Bourdieu (1990) argues that the Kabyle of Algeria have constructed a social-time system which is hostile to clock-time. The clock they refer to as 'the devil's mill'. The Khasi are scornful of haste in social affairs, lack any notion of precise meeting points and have no set times for eating. However, such explicit rejections of clock-time are not only found in pre-modern societies. Roy (1990) famously shows in a study of a machine room the importance of a variety of times: 'peach-time', banana-time', 'window-time', and so on – times that had no particular connection with the clock except that some occur in the 'morning', some in the 'afternoon'.

Nevertheless, there is little doubt that time in modern societies is not so structured in terms of social activities which appear to be necessitated by 'nature'. Clock-time seems to be central to the organisation of modern societies and thus to their constitutive social activities. Such societies are centred on the emptying out of time (and space) and the development of an abstract, divisible and universally measurable calculation of time. The first characteristic of modern machine civilisation is thus temporal regularity organised via the clock, an invention in many ways more important than even the steam engine. Thompson (1967) argues that an orientation to time rather than to task or social activities becomes *the* crucial characteristic of industrial capitalist societies based upon the maximal subjection of nature.

This argument depends upon the classical writings of Marx and Weber. Marx shows that the regulation and exploitation of labour time is the central characteristic of capitalism. The exchange of commodities is in effect the exchange of labour times. Capitalism entails the attempts by the bourgeoisie either to extend the working day or to work labour more intensively. Marx and Engels say: 'man is nothing; he is, at most, the carcase of time' (1976: 127). If the working class is not able to resist such pressures, competition will compel capitalists to extend the work period beyond its social and physical limits. There will be 'over-consumption' of labour-power and it will be in the interests of the bourgeois class as a whole to introduce limits on continous extensions of the working day. However, this collective need does not ensure that reductions on the length of the working day will in fact be realised. Capitalist competition has to be constrained in its own interests (and of those of the workforce). And hence during the history of the first industrial power, Britain, factory hour legislation, the intervention of the state, was particularly important in preventing continuous extensions of the working day and heralded the shift from the production of absolute surplus-value to relative surplus-value production. And it is this form of production, with what Marx calls 'denser' forms of work as compared with the more 'porous' longer day, that led to the staggering increases in measured productivity and the intense subjection of nature that have mostly charac-terised capitalist industry since the mid-nineteenth century.

Many later writers have noted more generally how much social conflict in industrial capitalism is focused around time, around capital's right to organise and extend the hours of work and labour's attempt to limit those hours, often describing them as 'unnatural' (see Adam 1990: 110; Thompson 1967). Disputes have focused on duration ('10-hour day', '35-hour week'), intervals ('tea breaks'), sequencing ('flexible rostering'), synchronisation ('wakes weeks') and pace ('time and motion studies'). All these disputes focus around the standardised units of clock-time. Such units of time separate work from its social and physical context. Time itself becomes commodified and constitutes the measure of work and the relationship of humans to their physical environment (see Adam 1998: chap. 2 on 'indus-trial time').

What Marx did not pursue much further is how this dominance of clock-time ('man . . . [as] the carcase of time') transforms people's subjectivities.

Various processes in modern societies constitute people as temporal sub-jects, as having both an orientation *to* clock-time, as well as being dis-ciplined by such time. Weber provided the first sociological analysis of these processes. He said of the Protestant ethic:

> Waste of time is thus the first and in principle the deadliest of sins. The span of human life is infinitely short and precious to make sure of one's own election. Loss of time through sociability, idle talk, luxury, even more sleep than is necessary to health . . . is worthy of absolute moral condemnation. (1930: 158)

And the spirit of capitalism adds a further twist to this. As Benjamin Franklin maintained, 'time is money' – to waste time is to waste money (cited Weber 1930: 48). People therefore have taken on the notion that it is their duty to be frugal with time, not to waste it, to use it to the full and to manage the time of oneself and that of others with the utmost diligence (Adam 1990: 113). Not only work but also leisure has become organised in a similar fashion. It is now increasingly planned, calculative, sub-divided and worthwhile (Urry 1994). Nature too has become subject to similar calculations; it is planned, monitored, sub-divided, and so on.

However, for all the importance of Weber's argument, in most senses time is in fact not like money. Time can be shared to a limited degree (in a baby-sitting circle, for example), time can be stored up and exchanged (in time-share holiday accommodation, for example), and people vary enormously in their capacity to use time effectively (hence the importance of 'time-management'). But these are very limited opportunities. Mostly time, unlike money, cannot be stored up and saved, whatever sense we are employing. Time constrains human activity more firmly than does money since it inevitably passes and subjects everyone and everything to its passage: humans, animals and other organisms cannot escape the movement of time. Indeed Adam suggests that rather than time being like money, money is time. In many cases having a lot of time is of little value to people without money, such as the poor, the unemployed and inmates of total institutions (see Goffman 1968). What is important is access to money which enables time to be put to good use (even if it still inevitably passes). Time therefore varies as to the differential possession of money, as well as to differentials of status and power: 'the wealthy can buy the labour, service and skills of others *as* time, while agents of state and persons in positions of authority have the right to time-structure the lives of those under their control' (Adam 1990: 114).

We have so far mainly considered time in terms of what McTaggart (1927) terms the B-series, that is, the sense of time as 'before and after' (and as social and objective). Events are seen as separate from each other and strung out along the fourth dimension (of time) such that they can be located before or after each other (see Gell 1992; Ingold 1993b). Each event in the B-series is viewed as separate and does not change its relationship to other events. Time is taken to be an infinite succession of instants, each identifi-able before or after the other. In other words, if we take event y, this was after x, is after x, and will always be after x, whatever else happens.

Statements about such phenomena are thus timelessly true. Many analysts have presumed that the physical world can be examined through the prism of the B-series.

This sense of time can be distinguished from what McTaggart terms the A-series, which is the sense of time as in 'past–present–future'. Here past events are in part retained within the present and carried forward into the future. The present has duration and is not conceptualised as an instant. The past is incorporated into that present and it also embodies certain expectations of the future, most famously in Heidegger's (1962) anticipation of death as the transcendental horizon of human temporality (see also Osborne 1994). In the A-series events can be differentiated in terms of their pastness, presentness and futurity; time depends upon context.

One writer who particularly examines the A-series conception is Mead (1959), who adopts a consistently 'temporal' viewpoint (see also Adam 1990). He focuses upon how time is embedded within actions, events and roles, rather than seeing time as an abstract framework. Mead regards the abstract time of clocks and calendars, of the B-series, as nothing more than a 'manner of speaking'. What is 'real' for Mead is the present, hence his major work on time is *The Philosophy of the Present*. As he says: 'Reality exists in the present' (1959: 33).

What we take to be the past is necessarily reconstructed in the present, each moment of the past is recreated afresh within the present. So there is no 'past' out there, or, rather, back there. There is only the present, in the context of which the past is being continually re-created. It has no status except in the light of the emergent present. It is emergence which transforms the past and gives sense and direction to the future. This emergence stems from the interaction between people and the environment, humans being conceived by Mead as indissolubly part of nature. This emergence is always more than the events giving rise to it. Moreover, while the present is viewed as real, the past and future are ideational or 'hypothetical'. They are only open to us through the mind. Finally, it should be noted that Mead's view is fully twentieth century in that he emphasises the relative nature of time. There is no universal time standard but any standard is viewed as relative to the organism undertaking the measuring.

Heidegger was likewise concerned to demonstrate the irreducibly temporal character of human existence. He stresses in *Being and Time* (1962) that philosophy must return to the question of 'Being', something that had been obscured by the western preoccupation with epistemology. And central to Heidegger's ontology of Being is that of time, which expresses the nature of what humans subjects are. Human beings are fundamentally temporal and find their meaning in the temporal character of human existence. Being is made visible in its temporal character and in particular the fact of movement towards death. Being necessarily involves movement between birth and death or the mutual reaching out and opening up of future, past and present. Moreover, the nature of time (and space) should not be confused with the ways in which it is conventionally measured, such as intervals or instants.

Measurable time-space has, he says, been imposed on time–space relations in western culture.

However, feminist critics have argued that Heidegger's 'being unto death' signifies a masculine approach to time and one which excludes birth, the time-generating capacity of procreation and the need to protect the environment for future generations (see Adam 1995b: 94). Especially important is the emphasis in women's lives upon establishing and maintaining (sustainable) links between the generations; as opposed to the individual fear and anxiety built into a masculinist view of time which is seen as inevitably moving unto death.

Heidegger provided some of the inspiration for Giddens (1981, 1984, 1991), who elucidates five ways in which, because of their temporal character, human subjects are different from other animals and material objects in nature. First, only humans live their lives in awareness of their own finitude, something reinforced by seeing the death of others and of how the dead make their influence felt upon the practices of the living. Second, the human agent is able to transcend the immediacy of sensory experience through both individual and collective forms of memory; through an immensely complex interpenetration of presence and absence (this will be examined further below). Third, human beings do not merely live in time but have an awareness of the passing of time, which is embodied within social institutions. Furthermore, some societies develop an abstract concept of rational, measurable time, radically separable from the social activities that it appears to order. Fourth, the time-experience of humans cannot be grasped only at the level of intentional consciousness but also is to be found within each person's unconscious, in which past and present are indissolubly linked. And fifth, the movement of individuals through time and space is to be grasped via the interpenetration of presence and absence, which results from the location of the human body and the changing means of its interchange with the wider society. Each new technology transforms the intermingling of presence and absence, the forms by which memories are stored and weigh upon the present, and of the ways in which the long-term *durée* of major social institutions are drawn upon within contingent social acts (see the critique of Giddens' substantive theory in Lash and Urry 1994: chap. 9).

Somewhat similar analysis is provided by Harvey (1989), although his starting point is more Marx than Heidegger. He is concerned with how capitalism entails different spatial fixes pertaining to different historical periods. By this he means that within each capitalist epoch space is organised in such a way so as to best facilitate the growth of production, the reproduction of labour-power and the maximisation of profit. But it is through the reorganisation of time-space that capitalism is able to overcome its periods of crisis and lay the foundations for a new period of capital accumulation and transformation of space and nature. In particular, Harvey examines Marx's thesis of the annihilation of space by time and attempts to demonstrate how this explains the complex shift from 'Fordism' to the

flexible accumulation of 'post-Fordism'. The latter involves a new spatial fix
and most significantly new ways in which time and space are represented.

Central to this analysis is what Harvey terms 'time-space compression' of
both human and physical experiences and processes:

> the processes that so revolutionize the objective qualities of space and time that
> we are forced to alter . . . how we represent the world to ourselves. . . . Space
> appears to shrink to a 'global village' of telecommunications and a 'spaceship
> earth' of economic and ecological interdependencies . . . and as time horizons
> shorten to the point where the present is all there is . . . so we have to learn how
> to cope with an overwhelming sense of *compression* of our spatial and temporal
> worlds. (1989: 240)

More specifically, this compression involves the accelerating turnover time
in production; the increased pace of change and ephemerality of fashion so
that products, places and people go rapidly in and out of fashion; the greater
availability of products almost everywhere; the increased temporariness of
products, relationships and contracts; the heightened significance of short-
termism and the decline of a 'waiting culture'; the greater importance of
advertising and rapidly changing media images to social life, the so-called
'promotional culture' which increasingly applies to nature and nature
conservation bodies; the increased availablity of techniques of simulation,
including buildings and physical landscapes; and the extraordinary proliferation of new technologies of information and communication which instantaneously transcend space at the speed of nanoseconds (Adam 1990; Brunn
and Leinbach 1990 on such a 'collapsing space and time'; Harvey 1989:
chap. 17; Lash and Urry 1994). Some theorists have suggested that this
results in the very disappearance of time and space as materialized and
tangible dimensions of social life. But Harvey argues that this collapse of
many spatial boundaries does not mean that the significance of space
decreases. As spatial barriers diminish, so we become more sensitized to
what different places in the world actually contain. Moreover, there is
increasing competition between places to present themselves as attractive to
potential investors, employers, tourists, and so on, to promote themselves, to
sell themselves as service-, skill- and nature-rich places (see Kearns and
Philo 1993). Harvey notes the paradox: 'the less important the spatial
barriers, the greater the sensitivity of capital to the variations of place within
space, and the greater the incentive for places to be differentiated in ways
attractive to capital' (1989: 295–6). In later chapters we examine this in
more depth and especially analyse the effects on modern subjectivities
brought about by mobilities of environmentalism, as well as those brought
about by the intensive restructuring of place brought about by global
capital.

Thus there are many senses of time analysed by different commentators.
The word 'time' designates disparate concepts and different relationships
with nature. However, for all these differences, there are some common
features of these analyses of time. First, few writers have analysed the
specific time-space organisation of particular places or societies. There is a

tendency even in contemporary writers to treat all traditional and all industrial societies being more or less the same in their organisation of time (but see Gell 1992). An example of this tendency is Thompson's thesis (1967) that industrial capitalism ushers in a transformation from an orientation to *task* with regard to nature to an orientation to *time*. But Thrift (1990) in particular argues that the transformation from task to time was of greater complexity than this simple dichotomy suggests. In the case of Britain, he argues, only up to the sixteenth century was daily life task-oriented; the week then was not a very important unit of time, and the seasons and related fairs and markets and the church calendar were by contrast the bases for temporal organisation. Between the sixteenth and eighteenth centuries this orientation began to change along with some growth in the ownership of domestic clocks; the increasing use of public clocks and bells; the growth of schooling for the upper and middle classes where activities began to be timetabled; the efforts by Puritans to organise work on a weekly basis; the increasing development of a cash economy which implied the need to calculate days of work and rates of pay; and the introduction of the term 'punctuality' into popular vocabulary. By the eighteenth century, time had become more clearly 'disembedded' from social activities. Partly this was due to innovations within the world of work concerned to instil a new time discipline for the emerging industrial workforce. But it was also to do with changes within the leisured English upper class, which developed visiting and social patterns of Byzantine temporal complexity. There were also developments outside work: the growth of Sunday Schools, of rational leisure and of Greenwich Mean Time. The last of these, a mathematical fiction signalling the total disembedding of time from social activity, developed so as to facilitate new kinds of social practice, namely, mass travel and mobility, not just within a city, as Simmel discussed, but between cities, and, from the later nineteenth century, between countries (also see Lash and Urry 1994: 228–9). Gamst (1993) in particular brings out the importance of railway journeys and work practices in generating the further standardisation of time during the nineteenth century. Overall, then, this material suggests that the spreading of the paradigm of 'clock-time' occurred more unevenly than Thompson's thesis suggests; it involved more diverse social practices than those of industrial capitalist enterprises; and it came to operate on an even wider spatial scale (see Glennie and Thrift 1996).

There is also a tendency in much of the literature to conceptualise time as a measure of chronological distance and stacked information, a measure of stretching across societies (see especially Giddens 1984 on time-space distanciation). But time in modern societies also functions as a centrally important resource. Indeed Adam (1990: 120) argues that time is only conceptualised as a resource in societies such as ours; societies which have not only created clock-time, but relate to that creation as actually being time and organise their social life by it. Or as Lefebvre suggests, with modernity lived time experienced in and through nature gradually disappears. It is no longer visible and is replaced by measuring instruments, clocks, which are separate from both natural and social space. Time becomes a resource, differentiated from social space, and is consumed, deployed and exhausted as nature is put to work (Lefebvre 1991: 95–6). The emergence of time and space as resources apparently independent of each other and of society and nature is one of the defining characteristics of modern society.

Further, time is not much analysed in relationship to pleasure. There has been little recognition that the particularly slow or the particularly fast passing of time can themselves be enjoyable. The pleasures of time are especially intertwined with the embodied (sensed) nature of our relationships with the environment. We explore in chapter 6 below the role of specific spatial practices in contributing to people's enjoyment of and engagement within the English countryside. This ignoring of the pleasures of time can be seen in most academic analyses of travel (see by contrast Schivelbusch 1986). Such analyses are typically concerned with the saving of time or the covering of more space; most strikingly in the discipline of 'time-geography'. But one obvious reason for travel is for pleasure – it enables people to visit other environments, places and people and to do so in particular stylised kinds of way (Urry 1990). Travel is a performance and some categories of aesthetic judgement are pertinent to its comprehension (see Adler 1989b on travel as 'performed art'). Further, one key aspect of many kinds of travel is that one enters a liminoid space where some of the rules and restrictions of routine life are relaxed and replaced by different norms of behaviour, in particular those appropriate to being in the company of strangers. This may entail new and exciting forms of sociability and playfulness, including what one might call 'temporal play' while on holiday (see Shields 1991). It is necessary to investigate how time-space changes will often have the consequence not merely of heightening distanciation, but also of encouraging anticipation, resistance, opposition, pleasure, autonomy or a sense of deprivation in relationship to both physical and built environments.

Finally, most of these social scientists have tended to operate with a conception of 'social time' which is separate from and opposed to the sense of time which the natural sciences have employed. It has been held that natural and social times are wholly different from each other. In the next section we examine this distinction in some detail, beginning with a brief consideration of how time has been conceived of within philosophy.

Different times in and of nature

There has been a longstanding dispute as to whether time and space are absolute entities, possessing their own natures or particularities. Is time something which is itself productive? Is it to be distinguished from matter since it possesses its own properties, or is it merely relative, a way of characterising the relations between the constituents of the physical world? The latter view was particularly expressed by Leibniz in the eighteenth century, who argued that space is 'time as an *order* of successions' (cited Körner 1955: 33). According to this relational view, the universe simply consists of pieces of matter, composed of various substances, and these pieces of matter exhibit temporal relationships between each other and between their own constitutive parts. Generally relationists argue that if any statements appear to assign properties to time it will be logically possible to reduce these properties to the relations between the objects concerned. By contrast, absolutists argue that time does designate particulars, such as the view that time 'flows' and that there are irreducible effects which are a consequence of its passage: for example, that there is an arrow of time (Coveney and Highfield 1991; Smart 1963: chap. 7).

Neither of these two positions can be simply accepted here. Temporal relations are so varied that no simple or predictable outcomes can be said to follow from the identification of the 'temporal relations' which hold between two or more social or physical entities. The outcome depends on what notion of time is being employed. And yet there do seem to be some irreducible aspects of time that need elaboration, even if one would doubt that time 'on its own' does anything or possesses powers which are wholly separate from the entities under interrogation.

Why does time seem to cause us such difficulties? First, unlike some aspects of space, time is invisible to the senses (Elias 1992: 1). Thus we always have to view time through various indicators, especially of course the clock and the calendar. But the relationship between these indicators and that of 'time' itself is unclear since the relationships are highly mediated. In particular the times implicit within environmental hazards are singularly inaccessible to the senses (Adam 1998).

Second, the thesis of this chapter is that there is no one time, only times; and that this has been the overall conclusion of twentieth-century science. Hawking neatly summarises: 'there is no unique absolute time, but instead each individual has his [*sic*] own personal measure of time that depends on where he is and how he is moving' (1988: 33; this is normally known as *Eigenzeit*; see Nowotny 1994). If there is one lesson here it is that the meaning of time is relative to its system of measurement; we can imagine as many clocks as we want to, as Einstein argues (cited Nowotny 1994: 20).

Third, the distinction drawn in the social sciences between social and natural time is inappropriate and out-dated. When social scientists have insisted on the radical distinction between natural and social time, this was based on an out-dated understanding of how time is understood in nature. Adam in particular argues that we should dissolve the distinction between natural time and social time (and also the distinctions between subject and object and nature and culture). Most of what social scientists have seen as specifically human is in fact generalised throughout nature. She summarises:

> a comprehensive understanding of time is not possible from a position where nature and society are treated as separate. Not humans and nature, but human

society *as* nature, is the basis from which to understand the multiplicity of times. (1988: 205)

The one aspect which is not generalisable throughout what we call nature is clock-time. Yet it is precisely this time which paradoxically has been taken by the social sciences as the defining feature of natural time, especially from the sixteenth century, when that time came to be historically separated from social time (see Elias 1992; Thrift 1990). Adam again summarises the paradox, noting the social constructedness of what has tended to be thought of as 'natural' clock-time, on the one hand, and the recent rejection of such time in much of the natural sciences, on the other. She argues that:

> Past, present, and future, historical time, the qualitative experience of time, the structuring of 'undifferentiated change' into episodes, all are established as integral time aspects of the subject matter of the natural sciences and clock time, the invariant measure, the closed circle, the perfect symmetry, and reversible time as our creations. (1990: 150; 1988)

Thus the social sciences have tended to operate with an inappropriate and out-dated conception of time taken from the natural sciences, an almost non-temporal time, which can be described as Newtonian and Cartesian. It is Newtonian because it is based on the notion of absolute time, that from 'its own nature, [it] flows equably without relation to anything eternal . . . the flowing of absolute time is not liable to change' (Newton, cited Adam 1990: 50; see Hawking 1988). Such absolute time is invariant, infinitely divisible into space-like units, measurable in length, expressible as a number and crucially reversible. It is time seen essentially as two-dimensional space, as invariant measurable lengths which can be moved along, forwards and backwards. There is no distinction between past and future, such conceptions barely existing within such notions of time. Coveney and Highfield note the paradox that the 'great edifices of science would all appear to work equally well with time running in reverse' (1991: 23). There is no arrow of time. And it is Cartesian space because it is premised upon the dualisms of mind and body, repetition and process, quantity and quality, form and content, subject and object, and so on.

However, twentieth-century science has largely transformed such notions of time in nature. Time is no longer predominantly Newtonian and Cartesian, although this is of course hugely contested. Hawking summarises:

> Space and time are now dynamic qualities: when a body moves, or a force acts, it affects the curvature of space and time – and in turn the structure of space-time affects the way in which bodies move and forces act. (1988: 33)

The social sciences have largely failed to see this transformation of time within the 'natural' sciences. This causes two problems. First, it reinforces the natural time/social time dichotomy, although Elias trenchantly argues that reflection upon time shows how 'nature, society and individuals are embedded in each other and are interdependent' (1992: 16). And second, it means that some of the extraordinary insights of twentieth-century science have not been incorporated into the social sciences (see Adam 1990, 1995b, 1998 on the a-temporality of the laboratory).

Six major scientific 'discoveries' of the twentieth century have transformed the understanding of time in nature. First, there is no fixed time independent of the system to which it is refers – time is thus a local, internal feature of the system of observation. Second, time and space are fused into four-dimensional time-space entities and such a fused time-space is curved under the influence of mass. Third, according to quantum theory, matter cannot be separated from its activities and notions of cause and effect no longer apply within such a microscopic indivisible whole. Quantum physicists describe a virtual state in which electrons seem to try out all possible futures instantaneously before settling into particular patterns. The position and momentum of an electron cannot be known with precision. Fourth, thermodynamics has shown that there is an irreversible flow of time because all systems show a loss of organisation and an increase in randomness over time. Fifth, rhythmicity is a crucial principle of nature both within the organism and in its relationships with the environment. Humans and other animals are not just affected by clock-time but are themselves affected by multiple rhythms. And finally, the time of one's body is not simply the period between birth and death but should be extended to include the entire evolutionary history of the human species (Adam 1988, 1990: 166, as well as chaps 2, 3, 7; Coveney and Highfield 1991; Hawking 1988; Rifkin 1987: chap. 2).

Thus, according to twentieth-century sciences, nature is intrinsically temporal and there are many different times in nature. Especially important is the way that physical time is now conceptualised as irreversible and directional – as Eddington says: 'The great thing about time is that it goes on' (cited Coveney and Highfield 1991: 83). The clearest example of this can be seen in the irreversibility of the process by which the universe has expanded – through the cosmological arrow of time following the singular historical event of a 'big bang' (see Coveney and Highfield 1991). There are many mundane examples of irreversibility in nature: coffee always cools, organisms always age, spring follows winter, and so on. Laws of nature are thus historical (see Prigogine 1980). It is incorrect to construct a simple dichotomy between nature as time-free or time-less or having a reversible concept of time; and society as being fundamentally temporal. That time is not reversible is neatly adumbrated by Adam when she points out that:

> In real interactions with the environment . . . machine time becomes irreversible: there can be no unmoving, no unpolluting, no reabsorbing the heat and carbons back into the engine from which they emanated. (1995b: 95)

Moreover, biologists have shown that it is false to assert that only human beings experience time or organise their lives through time. Biological time is not confined to ageing but expresses the nature of biological beings as temporal, dynamic and cyclical – humans as having a life-cycle. And of course, even 'dead things' like machines or buildings or physical landscapes are not merely 'natural' and time-free but are both of particular times and are constructed through temporal processes of entropy, self-organisation, dynamical chaos, decay, and so on (Coveney and Highfield 1991).

If all this is accepted, what are the implications for clock-time, which is now revealed as not intrinsic to nature but as the massively powerful agent involved in the very subjugation of nature, especially from the industrial revolution? Such a time has involved a number of powerful effects, including: the disembedding of time from social activities as it becomes scientifically stripped of meaning; the breaking down of time into a very large number of small units; the emergence of the disciplinary power of time; the increasing timetabling and hence mathematisation of social life; and the emergence of a synchronised measure of time, first across national territories and then later across the globe with the development of Greenwich and 'world time' (see Adam 1990: 116; Luhmann 1982; Rifkin 1987). Nguyen summarises the profound consequences for nature of the last of these developments:

> As gradually all other countries began to adopt the time zone system based on the prime meridian of Greenwich, the specifically western temporal regime which had emerged with the invention of the clock in medieval Europe became the universal standard of time measurement. Indeed its hegemonic development signified the irreversible destruction of all other temporal regimes in the world, the last vestiges of which remain only in the form of historical and anthropological curiosities. (1992: 33; although note that it was not until 1940 that the Netherlands synchronised itself with the rest of the world, see Zerubavel 1988)

Greenwich time is thus a mathematical fiction signalling the attempted emasculation of the human experience of time (and space). Modern (or clockwork) time hence involves the mastery of the global sense of nature, as all phenomena, practices and places become subject to the disembedding, centralising and universalising march of Greenwich clock-time. World time was established in 1913 with the first signal from the Eiffel Tower to be sent across the globe.

However, what we will now consider in the following is the claim that this once hegemonic clock-time is now having to contest with two other times, both of which have major implications for how nature is being currently conceived of and contested (see Lash and Urry 1994 for more detail). These two new types of time can be approached through reconsidering the very nature of science and technology as social practices. These practices have two features which are not at all characteristic of clock-time. First, science and technology have resulted from a very long, imperceptibly changing process, occurring over thousands of years, and involving various forms of gradual and even evolutionary adaptation. The 'mastery of nature' has been a centuries-long process. It has not been planned or designed but has happened as the outcome of millions of small changes and tiny advances, which in a non-deterministic fashion has resulted in massive transformations of the relationship of humans and 'nature' (as we now are able to appreciate; see Adam 1990: 86–7).

And second, such transformations in the mastery of nature have resulted in a contemporary science and technology which is based upon time-frames that lie beyond conscious human experience:

If telephones, telex and fax machines have reduced the response time from months, weeks and days to seconds, the computer has contracted them down to nanoseconds. The time-frame of a computer relates to event times of a billionth of a second. (Adam 1990: 140; see Peters 1992 on the 'nanosecond nineties')

Rifkin (1987: 14) notes that nearly 50% of American workers use electronic equipment at work based on such nanoseconds. It follows that when many important activities take place below the threshold of human consciousness, social time as structured by the clock becomes progressively less relevant to the contemporary organisation of human society. Never before has time been organised at a speed beyond the feasible realm of human consciousness. Rifkin talks of how computers in the next century will be able to make decisions in nanosecond time. Hence:

The events being processed in the computer world exist in a time realm that we will never be able to experience. The new 'computime' represents the final abstraction of time and its complete separation from human experience and rhythms of nature. (Rifkin 1987: 15)

There are thus two transformations of time, what Adam refers to as the 'unimaginably slow' and the 'imperceptibly fast' (1995b: 128; and see Ermath 1995). In the following we will generalise such notions. On the one hand, there is the realisation of an immensely long, imperceptibly changing, evolutionary or glacial time; and on the other hand, there is a time so brief, so instantaneous, that it cannot be experienced or observed. The time of modernity, clock-time, lies in-between the two. To the extent that we are passing into an era of post-modern disorganised capitalism, then we are moving to time as glacial or evolutionary *and* to a time that is instantaneous (see Lash and Urry 1994 for more detail on much of this). While the conflicts of modernity were fought out around the significance of clock-time, around efforts to expand or contract the length and sequencing of waged-labour, conflicts within disorganised capitalism have more focused upon contradictory temporal principles, between concepts of time as glacial and as instantaneous. Such conflicts are fought at different spatial levels, from the local to the global. These disjunctions will be especially examined in the analysis of people's felt anxieties over the environment discussed in chapter 7 below.

Indeed we might suggest that one of the processes which activated the momentous recent transformations of Eastern Europe was the inability of such countries to cope with the combined consequences of instantaneous and glacial time. Eastern Europe was stuck in modernist clock-time. It was unable to respond either to the long-term concern with nature, the environment and the reassertion of history and place, or to the extraordinary speeding up of time and space especially as represented by instantaneous fashion, image and the microcomputer. Such countries thus seemed caught in a time-warp, in a forced modernisation around clock-time (note of course the appeal of scientific management to Lenin and of Fordist principles more generally to Soviet planning), while recent transformations of time, nature and society have made such islands of modernist clock-time unsustainable.

Borneman (1993: 105) suggests that time in the GDR was 'petrified', rather than 'quickening' as it was in the West. There was no incentive to speed it up and there was little or no chance of acquiring status through conspicuous consumption. Borneman analyses the transformations of time (and space) consequent on the exceptionally fast and media-directed events of 1989. Moreover, the process of unification had the effect of demonstrating that East Germans were inferior in space and behind in time, stuck in clock-time as the times of the West have literally moved on.

We will now elaborate on these two new kinds of time under disorganised capitalism, beginning with instantaneous time. We are not trying to suggest that clock-time disappears through positing yet another version of a modernity–post-modernity dualism. Nor are we suggesting that the characteristic medium of clock-time, the written word, simply disappears. But what we would claim is that there are two new times which are wrestling for dominance alongside clock-time within late twentieth century-societies, especially within those societies that once constituted the 'centre'.

We begin with examining a number of ways in which it seems that the future is dissolving into the present, that 'we want the future now' has become emblematic of a panic about the apparently collapsing 'future' and a search for the instantaneous. Gross summarises such a time as 'the immediate over the temporally distant, the new over the old, the present over the past' (1992: 59). Subsequently what we call glacial or evolutionary time will be examined.

There are a number of characteristics of the contemporary media which reveal elements of instantaneous time. First, there is the collage effect: once events have become more important than location, then the presentation in the media takes the form of the juxtaposition of stories and items that share nothing in common except that they are 'newsworthy' (Giddens 1991: 26). Stories from many different places and environments occur alongside each other in an often chaotic and arbitrary fashion, such stories serving to abstract events from context and narrative. The experience of news is thus a temporally and spatially confused collage – a collage in which time as instantaneous is paramount.

Second, the mediated experience of disorganised capitalism involves the 'intrusion of distant events into everyday consciousness' (Giddens 1991: 27). Events often of an appallingly tragic character are dramatically brought into people's everyday experience. There is thus a literal time-space compression, as this collage of disconnected stories about famines, droughts, slaughters, nuclear accidents, and so on, intrudes and shapes everyday life. There has been the production of a 'global present' in which seemingly instantaneously people are 'transported' from one tragedy to another in ways which seem out of control. This can be characterised as a world of 'instantaneous ubiquity' (Morley and Robins 1995: 131). The world appears to be particularly risky and there is little likelihood of even understanding the temporally organised processes which culminate in the newsworthy tragedies that are routinely represented. Such time-space compression magnifies the sense that we inhabit a world of intense and instantaneous riskiness.

At the same time those charged with decision-making have to respond to this exceptionally risky world instantaneously. And as in the case of say the worldwide stock exchange crash in 1987, the effects of individual events upon the rest of the world are hugely magnified, as Wark (1994) elaborates in detail. This increasing instantaneity of response has its roots in the early years of this century. Kern (1983) for one notes that new technologies emerging at that time had the effect of playing havoc with the established arts of diplomacy which had been based upon customary times for reflection, consultation and conciliation. More recently, the effect of instantaneous reporting and of a new range of environmental risks with uncertain and even indeterminant consequences over very many years, coupled with a regulatory framework still locked into industrial clock-time, has contributed to a number of recent crises in governance. We examine this further in chapter 8 in connection with the striking case of the BSE crisis and how it was dealt with by the British state.

These collage and compression effects are in turn connected to the development of the so-called three-minute culture: for example, that those watching TV/VCR tend to hop from channel to channel and that they rarely spend time in following through a lengthy programme. Indeed many programmes are now made to mimic such a pattern, being composed of a collage of visual and aural images, a stream of 'sound bites', each one lasting a very short time and having no particular connection with those coming before and after (according to Cannon 1995: 32 there can be up to 22 separate images in a 30-second commercial). This instantaneous conception of time can be re-characterised as 'video-time', in which visual and aural images of the natural world are juxtaposed with multiple images of 'culture'. Recent research in Japan suggests that this restructuring of time is generating curiously new cognitive faculties among the young. The so-called fifth generation of computer-youth 'are able to see several programmes on video screens simultaneously, and to grasp the narrative structures; they develop their own games who's [sic] rules provide for a continuous switching on and switching off, and patterns of temporal perception combining speed and simultaneity' (Nowotny 1994: 39). Tyrrell (1995: 24–5) speculates that such 'multi-media' skills based on the simultaneity of time may be more important in the future than conventional skills which are based upon linear notions of time.

These developments in the media have led various commentators to argue that there will be a decline in the trust that people will exhibit in the future. Deferred gratification involves people having a trusting relationship to the future and this will characterise those whose position is secure within the social structure (see Adam 1990: 124–5). However, it is argued that there may have been some decline in the significance of such deferred gratification, partly because many institutions are singularly untrustworthy, as we now know much better because of improved informational flows, and partly because the future has become an alien concept in a world increasingly characterised by a plethora of insecurities. Instantaneous time dissolves the future – 'I want the future now', as the T-shirt expresses it, although interestingly hunting and gathering societies often exhibit a similar orientation to immediate gratification. Nowotny summarises:

> we are about to abolish the *category* of the future and replace it with that *of the extended present*. . . .The category of the future is shrinking towards becoming a mere extension of the present because science and technology have successfully reduced the distance that is needed to accommodate their own products. (1985: 14–15; and see 1994)

Thus as a result of the need for instantaneous responses, particularly because of the speed implied by the telephone, telex, fax, electronic signals, and so on, the future as such increasingly appears to dissolve. It no longer functions as something in which people appear to trust. Qualitative research reported in chapter 7 suggests that almost all groups of British citizens are pessimistic about living conditions in the future and feel that the pace of life and the development of new life-styles are generating increasing stress, pressure and short-termism. There are two consequences. First, trust and commitment over time appear to be less geared to institutions, which our research suggests are hugely distrusted, and more to how individuals can themselves create their own subjective time of life narratives.

Second, the lack of trust in the future means that it is less likely that gratification will be deferred. Clearly though there are marked differences between western economies, with the Anglo-Saxon countries, rather than Japan or Germany, placing a stronger emphasis upon instantaneous time. Table 5.1 sets out some of the main indicators that suggest that disorganised capitalism, especially in North America and parts of Europe, does indeed involve a collapse of a waiting culture and the permeation of instantaneous time (see Demos 1995b; Heelas et al. 1996; Lash and Urry 1994: chap. 9; Schor 1992).

Overall it appears that there is an increased sense of speed in social life which replaces the clear distances of time and space. There is a 'violence of speed', whether of the military, the media or cities, and this transcends and destroys the subtleties of place and particularity (see Virilio 1986). Recent small-scale research by Cannon (1995) suggests that young people conceptualise the future as extremely short and becoming even shorter (see also Macnaghten and Scott 1994; and chapter 7 below). This generation does not seem to have long-term plans or dreams of the future. It believes that

> most organisations . . . [are] simply incapable of delivering future promises with any certainty. . . . Barings is just one more name on a long list which convinces young people that mortgaging one's life is a dangerous strategy. (Cannon 1995: 31)

The corollary of this lack of a perspective into the future is an enhanced emphasis upon what Nowotny (1994) calls the 'extended present'. Cannon goes on to suggest that the young generation lives in 'real-time', seeing the

Table 5.1 *Indicators of instantaneous time*

- technological and organisational changes which break down distinctions of night and day, working week and weekend, home and work, leisure and work;
- increased rates of divorce and other forms of household dissolution, and the rise in the rate at which men and especially women undertake affairs within marriage;
- a reduced sense of trust, loyalty and commitment of families over generations;
- the increasing disposability of products, places and images in a 'throwaway society';
- the growing volatility and ephemerality in fashions, products, labour processes, ideas and images;
- a heightened 'temporariness' of products, jobs, careers, natures, values and personal relationships;
- the proliferation of new products, flexible forms of technology and huge amounts of waste;
- the growth of short-term labour contracts, what has been called the just-in-time workforce, and how this generates new forms of insecurity;
- the growth of 24-hour trading so that investors and dealers never have to wait for the buying and selling of securities and foreign exchange;
- extraordinary increases in the availability of products so that one does not have to wait to travel anywhere in order to consume some new style or fashion;
- an increasing sense that the 'pace of life' has got too fast and in contradiction with other aspects of human experience;
- increasingly volatile political preferences.

day as having 24 hours in which to eat, sleep, work, relax and play, a kind of student ordering of time writ into the rest of one's life! Bianchini (1995) describes the attempts to develop new and imaginative urban timetables which more closely reflect such patterns of social life. Both Manchester and Leeds have for example recently hosted 24-hour city conferences. The development by young people of a rave culture especially at weekends involves the timing of activities more or less unrelated to conventional divisions of night and day.

Finally, the emphasis here upon instantaneous time means that the time-space paths of individuals are increasingly desynchronised. There is a greatly increased variation in different people's times which are spread, if not over 24 hours, at least over longer periods. People's activities are less collectively organised and structured as mass consumption patterns are replaced by more varied and segmented patterns. There are a number of indicators of such time-space desynchronisation: the increased significance of grazing, that is, not eating at fixed meal times in the same place in the company of one's family or workmates, and hence of fast-food consumption (see Ritzer 1993 on McDonaldization); the growth of 'free and independent travellers' who specifically resist mass travel in a group where everyone has to engage in common activities at fixed times; the development of flexitime, so that groups of employees no longer start and stop work at the same time; and the growth of the VCR which means that TV programmes can be stored, repeated, and broken up, so that little sense remains of the authentic, shared watching of a particular programme.

We suggested earlier that there are two post-modern times, the instantaneous and the evolutionary. We turn now to the latter (see the related
analysis in Rifkin 1987: part 5 on the 'democratization of time').

First, many appeals encouraging people to act in some way to save the
environment crucially depend upon a shared concept of global citizenship. If
people are supposed to reduce fossil fuel use to avoid global warming, or use
only sustainable wood, or limit toxic wastes that are dumped at sea, then it
would seem that they must have some concept of duty towards and sense of
belonging to, not just their locality, but humanity or nature and the planet as
a whole. But what has received little attention has been the way that such a
putative global citizenship is itself a kind of culture. Just as national cultures
need cultural resources – symbols, narratives, rituals – from which a sense of
common destiny can be woven (Smith 1990), so too does a culture of
cosmopolitanism and global responsibility. The shifts of concern from the
local and immediate to the global require the creation, circulation and
consumption of the cultural resources and a glacial sense of time which is
necessary to create an 'imagined community' at the global level, and the
translation of this community into actions (Anderson 1989).

The notion of 'citizenship', encapsulating ideas of membership, rights and
responsibilities, has been subject to much recent reconceptualisation. One
context for this has been the apparent decline in the relative importance of
the nation-state, which has formed the dominant framework within which
notions and institutions of citizenship have operated for a century or more
(Archibugi and Held 1995). The reality of the nation-state as a territorially
defined, coherent unit with control over its own destiny and organised
through the dynamics of clock-time has been under pressure from both
ethnic and regional claims from within the national unit, but also, increasingly, from transnational or global dynamics, institutions and temporalities.
The growing importance of transnational corporations and global markets
has apparently eroded the ability of nations to control their own economies.
The proliferation of information technology, mass media and international
tourism seems to be creating what is in some sense a 'global culture',
transcending what are seen as increasingly local national cultures (Featherstone 1990; Luke 1995). Even where 'small media' play a crucial role in
change, these local media may define themselves and their audiences
through or against the flood of global imagery (Sreberny-Mohammadi and
Mohammadi 1994). Environmental risks are more and more seen as flowing
across national boundaries, creating a sense of global environmental threat
(Beck 1992b). Because of these proliferating global flows (of people, risks,
money, images, and so on), signs of 'global governance' have started to
emerge, from bureaucratic cooperation and integration between states to
summit-level agreements on global problems, such as the Rio Summit in
1992, to global campaigns by transnational environmental groups such as
Greenpeace, the World Wildlife Fund and Friends of the Earth (see chapters
7 and 8 below).

Thus it seems that the emptying of time and space establishes something of a single world, in which, through the extraordinary institutions of the global media, people have begun at least to imagine themselves as part of a single 'community' and indeed even to share some conditions in common with those of non-human animals (see Wark [1994] on the notion of 'virtual geography'). Giddens says that 'humankind in some respects becomes a "we", facing problems and opportunities where there are no "others"' (1991: 27). Or as Beck argues:

> With nuclear and chemical contamination, we experience the 'end of the other', the end of all our carefully cultivated opportunities for distancing ourselves and retreating behind this category. (1992a: 109)

Of course, as we outline further in chapter 7, one reason for the surge of interest in global citizenship lies in the fact that since the Rio Summit in 1992 most nation-states and multi-national corporations have publicly endorsed the concept of sustainability, including the notion that 'we' all must live within the finite ecological limits of the planet. Such formal endorsements rely on everybody conceiving of their practices, lifestyle choices, consumption patterns, aspirations, and so on, in relation to the same glacially fragile planet which we all inhabit.

In later chapters we examine whether it is reasonable to expect that the public will develop such a global sense of citizenship or whether too many institutions have already become so untrustworthy to deliver on the glacial commitments of 'sustainability' to exert much impact (see Macnaghten et al. 1995a; as well as chapter 7). Global citizenship might constitute an integral component of the cultural assumptions of many different local communities at the end of this millennium. Or we may find that it is restricted to a cosmopolitan elite, a kind of ghetto tied to very specific policies and interests. Or indeed we may find the very category of the global fragmenting into a multiplicity of globals, with competing notions of global citizenship inside and outside official institutional discourse.

One consequence of these various developments is that there appears to be for some a re-evaluation of nature. According to Beck (1992b: 80), global-isation undermines the dichotomy of 'nature' and 'society' or the division between what is 'natural' and what is 'artefactual'. Nature comes to be viewed as more of a historical product, and of course subject to laws which are themselves historical. The most striking of these is the Big Bang theory of the beginning of the universe; a theory which implies that there may well be another singular event, namely, the ending of that universe. Hawking expresses this by arguing that: 'Einstein's general theory of relativity implied that the universe must have a beginning and, possibly, an end' (1988: 34). One overwhelming consequence has been some re-evaluation of the physical world especially as western societies are rediscovering the complexity of their interdependence with that world. It no longer seems to constitute 'the other', out there and merely waiting to be 'mastered'. It now seems at least for some groups some of the time as intimately bound up with human experience, with culture, and much less simply exploitable and disposable. Indeed because of this complex interdependence it seems as though humans have an especial responsibility for nature's long-term preservation. Griffiths expresses this well in talking of how 'our pace far outstripping nature's speed – we pollute far faster than nature can clean, and we plunder more than it can renew' (1995). It is therefore necessary to reject such an obsession with speed, to walk and cycle rather than to drive or fly, and to see, hear and feel how slowly nature works and to tailor our actions to the slowness or glacial character of time's nature.

Many such writers go on to claim that people who are as yet unborn should possess extensive rights of inheritance of a particular quality of the environment, one which is certainly no worse than that which is enjoyed by the world's current population. Such a notion has even entered government rhetoric and is embodied in the officially sanctioned Brundtland definition of sustainable development as 'development that meets the needs of the present without compromising the ability of future generations to meet their own needs' (see chapter 7 below). Notions of this sort have existed before, through for example the idea that farmers should exercise stewardship of their land for later generations. But what is distinct about the current epoch is that it appears to be fairly widely believed that future generations *throughout the world* have rights of inheritance of a particular 'nature'. And this is a nature which includes not only the surface of the earth but also a particular condition of the ozone layer. That there might be holes in that layer is of course something which nobody can observe and rests upon the most arcane of scientific theorising. Moreover, the realisation of the interests of future generations ('our children and their children') will almost certainly harm the interests of significant numbers of the current inhabitants of the earth.

Also as part of this glacial sense of time, not only non-human animals but also other components of nature, such as rain forests, are seen as having extensive rights – in the view of some the same rights as humans (Benton 1993; Porritt 1984: 208). Nature has come in part to be viewed not as an object but as a subject. This has been carried to an extreme version in the Gaia hypothesis (see Lovelock 1988). This states that the entire range of living matter on earth should be viewed as constituting a single living entity, a particular kind of subject or superorganism. It is argued that life on the planet is coordinated to keep it habitable by the totality of life which Lovelock names Gaia after the Greek earth goddess. For example, the amount of carbon dioxide in the atmosphere regulates the earth's temperature. This view emphasises the extraordinary way in which all kinds of phenomena are suffused by life itself, and that the planet has a kind of global purpose which ought to be 'worshipped'.

These various developments therefore entail the taking of a very long-term perspective, extending way beyond the lifetime of anyone presently living. The interests of future generations are being considered, partly under the impact of new age and green philosophies. This appears to be novel. In

Bourdieu's (1990) classic study, the Kabyle demonstrate a particular awareness of the rhythms of nature. But this is the outcome not of an orientation
into the almost unimaginable future, but of a relatively short time horizon
and a kind of submission to the passage of time. Although the Kabyle
demonstrate a dependence upon and solidarity towards nature, there is a
nonchalant indifference towards time.

This appears to constitute a far cry from contemporary evolutionary time
where there appears to be an increasing reflexive awareness of the long-term
relationship between humans, animals and the rest of 'nature'. In such a
reflexive consciousness it is held, first, that humans are no longer simply
superior to all elements of 'nature'; second, that humans have a special
responsibility for ensuring the long-term survival not only of themselves but
of many other species; third, that there is and should be a long-term
historical relationship between humans and nature; and, fourth, that how this
relationship develops in the future is something that can only be evaluated
after many generations, when, for example, it is seen what the effects are of
ozone depletion (see Yearley 1991). Thus this glacial notion of time is one
in which the relation between humans and nature is very long-term and
evolutionary. It moves back out of immediate human history and forward
into an unspecifiable future.

In some formulations it also held that women are more able to develop
such a glacial sense of time. This is partly because women in general have
had to develop shadow times, times that develop in the shadow of clock-
time but are partially distinguishable from it (Adam 1990: 94). Indeed
Davies (1990) shows that the time of a carer is largely open-ended and
outside commodified clock-time, and that this is less the case of men's time.
Women as carers are not only in time but also have to give time (Adam
1990: 99). But also it is argued that because of women's role in the 'natural'
activities of childbirth and childrearing, they are more likely to develop
viable alternatives to clock-time. Clock-time is after all based on the
principles of invariant repetition and perfect repeatability. But as Adam
argues:

> As such it is clearly at odds with the rhythms of our body and the 'natural'
> environment where variations and the principle of temporality are a source of
> creativity and evolution. (1995b: 52)

Specifically Fox argues with regard to childbirth that the woman in labour is
'forced by the intensity of the contractions to turn all her attention to them,
loses her ordinary, intimate contact with clock time' (1989: 127). More
generally, feminists argue that because of the role of most women in
procreation, childbirth and childrearing they are necessarily tied into a
longer-term sense of time, certainly of time as inter-generational (see Adam
1995b: 94).

We will now consider an example of a 'deep green ecofeminist' who
articulates such a sense of glacial time. Macy talks of current time as being
'like an ever-shrinking box, in which we race on a treadmill at increasingly

frenetic speeds' (1993: 206). This allows us only 'the very briefest experience of time' (1993: 206). But it is necessary to 'break out of this temporal
trap' caused by what we have termed instantaneous time. She advocates the
inhabitation of 'time in a healthier, saner fashion. By opening up our
experience of time in organic, ecological or even geological terms and in
revitalizing relationships with other species' (1993: 206). In her advocacy of
what we have termed glacial (geological) time, she criticises this 'disregard
for the future', the 'pathetically shrunken sense of time, that amounts to a
pathological denial of the reality and ongoingness of time' (1993: 207).
Macy suggests that a number of factors have contributed to the present
generation's disregard for the future, which is contrary to the way that all
other species exhibit a 'time-thrust' into the future. First, there is the growth
of nuclear weapons, which ruptures the sense of biological continuity
between past and future and has broken our connections with previous
generations. She talks of how this 'biological severance' generates numbing
and feelings of powerlessness. Second, there were the effects of US
government policies in the 1980s which emphasised the present and the
belief that we did not need to look to the future. And third, there is the more
general 'time-squeeze' generated by the contemporary lifestyle of increasing
speed, where we suffer, she says, from the disappearance not only of past
and future but also of the present. Time as an organically measurable
experience has been lost and this results in what she discusses as 'hurry
sickness' (1993: 209–11). Such speed is inherently 'violent' since it is in
contradiction with the slower rythms of the ecosystem. And the more we try
to escape from time, the more we are its slave. Such speed and the need for
instantaneous responses is carried to the extreme in nuclear war-making, a
truly remarkable example of the potential instantaneous destruction of place
with unimaginable glacial consequences; indeed, a threat which was
intensely resonant in the early 1980s.

So what does she advocate as a way of developing glacial time, or, as she
expresses it, as 'eternity' as opposed to 'time'. We need a new narrative
which includes the whole universe, all its beings, and our evolutionary
history. We need a 'bridge to the far future', especially because of the
extraordinary time-scale of nuclear waste, a time-scale that 'pulls us into
league with the future' (1993: 221). Macy provides an exceptionally clear
summary of the relationship between such waste and glacial time:

> the most lively link to beings of the future centuries and millenia [sic] is provided
> by nuclear waste. My involvement with this issue has altered my experience of
> time . . . for the radioactive isotopes generated by our nuclear energy and weapons
> production extend the effects of our actions into vast reaches of time, into *their*
> life spans of thousands or even millions of years. . . . The toxicity of these wastes
> requires them to be kept out of the biosphere for many times longer than recorded
> history. (1993: 215, 221; Adam 1995b: 138 on how we do not have storage
> materials for nuclear waste with a life-span equivalent to such waste)

Macy proceeds to describe how she developed 'time workshops' in order in
a sense to generate a glacial conception of time, of 'eternity' or what she

calls 'deep time', as opposed to what we have termed instantaneous time. Macy describes how in such workshops she used the imagination in order to look forward in time so that people could then reflect back at our present situation with a fresh perspective from the imagined far future:

> the distant, unborn ones to whom they were addressed became more and more real and present to us. We began to inhabit large stretches of time. The NIMBY response evaporated and was replaced by a willingness to care for the waste in order to protect future generations. (1993: 216)

She argues that we need communities to guard these centres of radioactivity that the current generation is handing on to future generations. These she calls Guardian Sites, centres of reflection and pilgrimage. She argues that it is particularly undesirable to try to hide nuclear waste away from our senses and especially away from the senses of future generations who may well not believe what extraordinarily toxic materials were handed on from the current generation. Macy even goes on to propose a third House of Congress, a House of Spokespersons for the Future. It would speak for the rights of such coming generations.

What this somewhat lengthy account of Macy shows is both the significance of glacial time and the way in which it is part of a more general process of increasing reflexivity as people increasingly come to understand that there are many times and many spaces and not just their own society and its rhythms and previous history (see Lash and Urry 1994). To be reflexive is to have some sense of the diverse paths and patterns travelled by different societies in different periods; and to be in part able to evaluate different outcomes somewhat into the future. What is striking about parts of the environmental movement is that this assessment applies to the fate of the earth as a whole and not just to individual communities or even societies. And it may also apply to the realisation that globally coordinated action takes an immense amount of time. While environmental outcomes are glacial, the actions needed may be quick. But because of the necessity for global cooperation, the political and policy responses are likely to be hugely delayed (Adam 1995b: 132).

Of course, such reflexivity does not necessarily lead to an enhanced sense of empowerment. Political and policy time-scales may themselves be constrained by more instantaneous considerations. Indeed, in chapter 7 we analyse empirical research which suggests that such reflexivity may be more commonplace than tends to be realised. But we will also suggest that such notions of reflexivity need to be connected to people's sense of agency, that is, to their felt ability to structure or influence events through their actions. We will question the degree of trust people invest in states or corporations as either willing or able to respond to such glacial concerns, and thus whether such enhanced reflexivity tends to induce a sense of hope and empowerment or merely fatalism and apathy. In particular we examine how people sense the potency of their glacial desires and aspirations in the face of the apparent power and violence of instantaneous time in shaping both local and global spaces.

But reflexivity also reaches inwards. People come to understand that although all human existence involves movement towards death, there are ways of prolonging or hastening that movement and indeed they can evaluate and implement different options. In the most extreme cases almost every item eaten or every place visited is evaluated in relationship to the reflexive project of life-prolongation (a kind of Peter Pan syndrome). Moreover, people's capacity to evaluate places in terms of their environmental quality is significantly affected by their capacity now to 'travel in time', to move into the future or back into various pasts and to simulate such periods through complex and sophisticated encounters with the cultural products, images, physical environments and displays of different times. The proliferation of environmentally oriented theme parks especially leading up to the coming new millennium will further develop and reinforce this capacity to imagine other worlds in 'other' times. Some sense of the changes involved here can be seen in the growing time perspectives that scientists and policy makers can now envisage. In the 1960s Grove-White (1996b) suggests that an orientation to a mere quarter of a century in the future was about the most that could be envisaged; now it is more common to take a view of up to at least a century. However, he also suggests that such priorities are also increasingly in tension with evaluating methodologies and regulatory frameworks aligned to inappropriate and truncated time frameworks, driven not least by the power of market principles and instantaneous time.

One difficulty with the argument just mounted, however, is that it appears to rest upon too strong a distinction between humans and the rest of 'nature'. There is a danger in an apparent humanist claim that only humans can be reflexive. Such a notion is present in Moore's (1963) suggestion that it is solely humans who can use time to control, regulate, order or synchronise their social life and in so doing are able to cheat, structure, make or measure time. We seek to evade such a charge of humanism in the following by noting that reflexivity is a historically specific capacity of humans and has nothing to do with them qua species; that reflexivity is significantly a property of certain institutions as much as it is of individuals; and that we do not rule out the possibility of the non-human world exhibiting similar features.

Such processes of reflexivity are in turn related to the reassessment of place and various forms of resistance to the 'placelessness' which is apparently generated by the modes of instantaneous time that we have elaborated (see Meyrowitz 1985 on the role of media in generating such an apparent placelessness; and see Lefebvre 1991: 343 on the 'interchange-ability of place'). Some efforts are made by individuals and organisations such as Common Ground to remake spaces as sites for 'strolling' and 'living in', and not just for passing through as fast as possible ('instantaneously'). Common Ground has developed the idea of community-based 'parish maps'. Clifford summarises what is involved here: the 'belief that local people together know more and care more than they are ever credited with; that they can make brave decisions, guide change and keep the strands of history and

richness of nature healthy and vibrant' (1994: 2). This slowing down of
place or perhaps the capturing of place by its 'community' presupposes a
glacial sense of time, in which people feel the weight of history, of all those
memories of that very particular place, and to believe that it can and will still
be there in its essence in many generations' time. This glacial attachment to
place can occur in relationship to where one was born or brought up, to
one's place of current residence, or especially to where one has visited or
even where one might visit. In particular, for Common Ground such places
can be anywhere, not merely those places which have the right look, which
are not 'eyesores'. Clifford summarises the determinants of 'local distinctiveness' as 'the patina and detail which makes up ordinary places giving
them identity and particularity' (1994: 3). And particular objects of nature
can be taken as particularly emblematic of that locality, even a particular tree
or type of apple.

Relph says that the phenomenology of what we have called glacial time
results from   .

> improving geographical and social knowledge and especially because of a
> growing intensity of involvement and commitment. The result of such a growing
> attachment, imbued as it is with a sense of continuity, is the feeling that this place
> has endured and will persist as a distinctive entity even though the world around
> may change. (1976: 31)

Lefebvre (1991: 97–9) suggests, as we saw in the last chapter, that certain
kinds of space unleash desire and this stems from the dominant logics of
visualisation and metaphorisation. Time, by contrast, is not desired. He
asserts that people are not seduced by time, but different times can clearly be
deployed to reconfigure place. In the next section we shall elaborate further
on glacial time in relationship to the complexities of socially organised
memories of place.

It should also be noted that the effects of glacial time do not mean that
places are always positively viewed. There can be a 'drudgery of place', the
sense of being inexorably tied to a particular place which cannot be escaped
from and which seems to have been forever unchanging (certainly compared
relatively with other places that are known about). Some places are heavy
with time, but not necessarily those which have been subject to museumifi-
cation (see Lowenthal 1985: 243–4). The growth of instantaneous time, time
induced by Virilio's (1986) 'speed', means that other places may often seem
left behind, left in the 'slow lane' of contemporary life. Advocates for a new
road will often employ claims that such a road will connect a particular place
to the motorway network, so ensuring that that place can become part of the
system of instantaneous time, while opponents may well employ glacial
claims about how a place has prospered for centuries outside such flows of
instantaneous time.

Strolling in some such places 'out of time' is almost itself subversive. The
flâneur seeks the essence of a place while at the same time consuming it –
there is both consumption and subversion (Game 1991: 150). This way of
walking, as though one had 'all the time in the world', 'is oppositional to the

counting of time, Taylorism, the production process. . . . Scrutinising, detective work, and dreaming set the *flâneur* apart from the rush-hour crowd' (Game 1991: 150). It also seems that some places of glacial time particularly invite visiting in order that people may stroll. They are, as Sennett puts it, 'places full of time' (1991: chap. 7). In the next chapter we shall go on to consider how various spatial practices (walking, sitting, photographing, driving, and so on) are deployed within different environments and some of the consequences that they may have.

Finally, aspects of glacial time can be seen in the contemporary fascination with history and heritage. Now it seems nostalgia for the past is everywhere, engulfing almost every experience and artefact from the past, even the 'dark satanic mills' of the industrial revolution or 1950s jukeboxes. Lowenthal characterises such nostalgia as 'memory with the pain taken out' (1985: 8). And Hewison (1987) has argued that Britain has come to specialise in manufacturing nostalgia or heritage rather than on manufacturing goods. Such an institutionalisation of heritage is said to deflect attention away from social deprivation and inequality in the present (see Urry 1990). It is generally reckoned easier to get funding for projects if a discourse of restoration is employed, even if there is no simple and unambigous 'past' – even of nature – waiting to be 'restored'.

More generally, there appears to be an increased aesthetic sensibility with regard to old places, crafts, houses, countryside, and so on. Almost everything that is old or has a certain patina of age is thought to be valuable, whether it is an old master or an old cake tin. Pretty well all such objects can be part of a national heritage. The sense of a unique part of such a heritage can now be occupied by 'a phrase of rhyming slang, an old piece of industrial machinery (preferably *in situ*), a hand-painted plate from the turn of the century and a cherished landscape or place' (Wright 1985: 253). Many objects and activities can enjoy the aura of heritage. Under glacial time remnants of the past are treasured as symbols of culture and nature that had value and have been lost, although we should note that the patina of age is somewhat different from the mere wear and tear of age.

Lowenthal suggests that this obsession with the signs of the past is almost a mental complaint:

> Once the menace or the solace of a small elite, nostalgia now attracts or afflicts most levels of society. Ancestor-hunters search archives for their roots; millions throng to historic houses; antiques engross the middle class; souvenirs flood consumer markets. . . . 'A growing rebellion against the *present*, and an increased longing for the past', are said to exemplify the post-war mood. (1985: 11; and see Corner and Harvey 1991; Macdonald 1997; Vergo 1989)

Although some aspects of the heritage industry indicate a growing instantaneity of time and the instant commodification of history, other aspects demonstrate something at least of a glacial sense of time. First, quite a lot of heritage conservation has in fact resulted from popular resistance to the very demolition of derelict buildings, technologies or physical environments (Samuel 1984). People actively seek to save 'their history', and especially those markers of place that have apparently been present for some generations. Adam expresses this as follows:

> the more the future impinges on and predefines our present the more intense seems to become our concern with the past – immediate, mediate and long-term – in print, television and electronic records, in museums and heritage parks, through the collecting of art and artefacts, through the dating of species, the earth, the universe. (1996: 139)

Interestingly in Britain much of the early conservation movement in the 1960s was plebeian in character, concerned to preserve railway engines, industrial archaeology sites, steam traction engines, and so on. The preservation of some derelict coalmines in Wales resulted from pressure from local groups of miners and their families who sought to hold on to aspects of 'their' history, history here being long-term and involving projection from the past through the present, way into the future. In Lancashire there has been a campaign to conserve a slag heap from an extinct coal mine. (Note though that the largest mass organisation in Britain is the non-plebian National Trust with over 2 million members.)

Second, some heritage sites do recognise the history of struggle and opposition which over a lengthy period is worthy of remembrance and recognition (see Macdonald 1997 on the history of the representation of Gaelic culture). The critique of the heritage industry rests upon a rather simple view of the nation and of what might reproduce such a nation. It has been interestingly shown that heritage in Scotland as opposed to England is linked to a more open, pluralistic and fluid future and one which emphasises its physical environment more conspicuously (McCrone et al. 1995).

Finally, it is important to note how people actively use such heritage sites as bases for reminiscence; as Mellor says: 'as the point of departure for their own memories of a way of life in which economic hardship and exploited labour were offset by a sense of community, neighbourliness and mutuality' (1991: 100; and see Urry 1996a). So that while various built and physical sites may have been established in such a way that history is turned into commodified heritage, visitors may then use such sites in diverse and unexpected ways, using the artefacts and texts on display as points of departure for their own long-term memories, hopes, dreams and disappointments. These all constitute attempts to assert a glacial conception of time, as reflexive subjects seek to challenge the profoundly disruptive effects of instantaneous time.

So far we have discussed the relationship of time and nature at a fairly high level of generality. What we have sought to establish is that there are a number of different times, especially clock-, instantaneous and glacial; that these diverse times have enormously impacted upon 'nature' through in effect constituting different natures; and that contemporary contestations of nature derive from and feed into these various times. In subsequent chapters we shall seek to deploy such arguments to make sense of particular contestations, drawing in part on empirical research which seeks to capture *inter alia* the relatively unusual notions of how people orient to and use time (see chapter 7 below). Central to this discussion will be the notion of trust. In particular, we will consider both the degree to which people have a sense of trust in the future, and what the key institutions are that may or may not sustain such a long-term sense.

It should also be noted that there are interesting connections between different times and different media. Ong (1982) has shown the connections between the development of clock-time and the shift from a mainly oral to a mainly written culture. Thus in nineteenth-century Britain and later in other European societies, much culture was written. There was the huge growth of cheap books and daily newspapers – doubling every 15 years or so; there was the extensive development of time-keeping records; the widespread growth of written documentation of citizens through the registration of births, deaths, marriages, travel and later of the passport; the proliferation of transport timetables; and the general employment of written signs to indicate routes, locations, leisure facilities, tourist sites, and so on (see Lash and Urry 1994: chap. 9 on modernity and travel). We might more speculatively suggest that before clock-time was hegemonic, oral media were important in sustaining the diverse forms of social time. And both instantaneous and glacial times are curiously interdependent with the proliferation of new systems of electronic media, and especially the visual, as we noted above. These relationships are set out in table 5.2.

Table 5.2 *The dominant media of communication and forms of time*

Oral media	–	Social time
Written media	–	Clock-time
Electronic media	–	Instantaneous time
	–	Glacial time

We have been careful here not to suggest that whole societies are characterised by a single form of media or a single 'time'. Our view is that societies are more messy than that. In particular, contemporary societies are characterised by all types of time and all media. But there are of course hierarchies of value and power between them.

Also at various points in the argument, and especially in chapter 8, we shall encounter the dialectic of the local and the global which has been central to certain environmental strategies; especially to think globally and act locally. But as we interrogate this dialectic we shall consider whether and in what ways it is not simply a spatial strategy but is in part a contestation over time. Part of the claim about the local seems to involve an invoking of a glacial sense of time as opposed to the clock-time of the national state and the instantaneous time of the global electronic media just discussed. There seem to be two reasons for this which we have not so far elaborated on.

The first of these is connected with the nature of science. If there is increasing interdependence of what have been previously kept apart, namely, nature and culture, then prediction of the future becomes even more uncertain and contestable. 'Science' simply does not know, partly of course for the reason discussed in chapter 4, namely, the invisibility of many environmental bads to our senses. And yet a glacial sense of time appears to increasingly demand such predictive power for science, especially for the environmental sciences. This has become especially pronounced in official sustainability rhetorics which call for development 'to improve the quality of life while living *within the carrying capacity of the living ecosystems*' (IUCN 1991, emphasis added; see chapter 7 below). So one way that people may seek to secure a glacial future (so to speak) is through blanketing out the intensely global problems of, say, modelling global climate change, and concentrating instead upon one particular place, upon securing its future, even if the rest of the globe is subject to uncertainty and lack of control. This does not mean that people are not concerned about such global problems. Rather, as we examine in chapter 7 below, it may be that such problems are outside one's felt sphere of influence and controlled by untrustworthy forces which appear to be impervious to glacial considerations. Thus people may often rely on hope that the global glacial future will come good, and focus their energies alternatively on the one place that can function as a synecdoche for the whole of a globalised nature and culture which otherwise cannot be known and predicted, let alone controlled.

The second reason for this has to do with memory. To argue for particularities of locality or place may be to capture or reassert certain long-term memories of that particular place or that group or that landscape; and these may be memories that appear to endure and appear to be threatened by different times animating different natures. In the next section we shall engage with this issue of memory directly; and this will lead us on to more precise analysis of just how culture and nature come together within the memories of particular times and places.

Memories of nature

We begin with some brief comments about the different ways in which time is 'sensed', to connect this chapter with the last, before turning to more general issues of memory. In Rodaway's (1994: 124–6) discussion of various visual geographies he suggests that sight is more 'temporal' than the other senses. Visual objects exist in both space and time; they have location relative to other objects, and they have duration relative to other objects as well. Rodaway suggests that film provides the closest analogy here. While watching a film we are aware of the movement of subjects and objects, and of time passing. Some details pass us by, while others proceed much more slowly. Visual experiences appear to go past us, we are sometimes able to catch glimpses of this or that scene or person, we can linger on some events, and we may be able to put together a collection of temporally organised images. Rodaway summarises:

> Vision is time-specific, in the sense of when an object is illuminated in a
> particular way at a certain moment, and temporal in the sense that visual images
> persist over time and give continuity to geographical experience. (1994: 125)

The sense of vision provides both a geographical and temporal continuity
and partial unity of our experience of the environment. We should also note
that visual metaphors tend to be implicated in how we tend to conceive of
the future, as for example in such terms as *scen*ario and fore*sight*. Other
senses provide a more fragmented sense of time since they are more
immanent and do not enable the same sense of movement over and through
time.

And yet this is not entirely the case. In the last chapter we noted the
relevance of especially smell to memory, of what Rodaway terms 'olfactory
memories' (1994: 71–2). These appear immensely relevant to our memories
of childhood, places, relationships, other societies, and so on. Likewise
sounds can be important in the evocative remembering of another place that
one thinks one has previously encountered. And Benjamin (1969: 160)
reminds us of the importance that Proust attaches to the *mémoire involun-
taire* induced in one case by eating (tasting) a particular kind of pastry. But
before continuing here with each of the senses we will turn directly to the
question of memory and consider those contributors who have sought to
dispense with the concept of time as being objective, measurable, reversible
and abstract (see Adam 1995b). We turn to those contributors who have
elaborated a broadly phenomenological approach to the analysis of time (see
the critique of such a viewpoint in Gell 1992).

We begin with Bergson (1950, 1991), whose observations on time and the
body are particularly pertinent. He distinguishes between *temps* and *durée*,
the former being the sense of time as quantitative and divisible into spatial
units (the B-series). Bergson argues against such a spatialised conception of
time and maintains instead that *durée* or lived duration is thoroughgoingly
'temporal'. *Durée* or time proper is the time of becoming. People should be
viewed as in time rather than time being thought of as some discrete element
or presence. Time involves the 'permeation' of the supposedly separate
moments of past, present and future; each flows into the other.

Furthermore, time is inextricably bound up with the body. People do not
so much think real time but actually live it sensuously and qualitatively.
Bergson further argues that memory should not be viewed as a drawer or
store, since such notions derive from incorrectly conceptualising time in a
spatial fashion. Time is not 'spatial'. Memory thus can never be a simple
representation of the past, but should rather be viewed temporally. It is the
piling up of the past on the past which has the effect that no element is
simply present but is changed as new elements are accumulated from the
past. A particularly 'sociological' twist is given to this in Halbwachs' (1992)
Bergsonian examination of collective memory, which emphasises the social,
commemorative and festive institutions by which the past is stored and
interpreted for the present and especially for the present generation.

In Bergson's form of analysis time is viewed qualitatively while space is taken to be abstract and quantitative. In the critique of the 'spatialised' conception of memory as a 'drawer', Bergson privileges time over space and views the latter as abstract and quantitative (see Game 1995). Thus space is conceptualised as overly abstract and Bergson's account of duration is somewhat disembodied. He over-privileges time at the expense of space.

Bachelard (1969) in particular endeavours to remedy this failing by developing a conception of space as qualitative and heterogeneous rather than abstract, empty and static. He seeks to integrate such a notion of space back within a broadly Bergsonian conception of time. He maintains that such a sense of space as qualitative, sensuous and lived ought to be central to the Bergsonian comprehension of time. There are three crucial components to this argument (again see Game 1995).

First, Bachelard argues that phenomenology is concerned with experiencing an image in its 'reverberations', not in terms of its visual impact. He thus employs an aural rather than a visual metaphor through the idea of sound waves. This notion of reverberation points to a movement between the subject and object which disrupts any clear distinction between the two. The metaphor of reverberation implies immediacy, which is not necessarily the case with a visual appropriation of memory. Bachelard describes his work of reading images as an ontology of 'reverberation' (1969: xvi).

Second, Bachelard specifically considers the nature of the 'house' and argues that it is not to be seen purely as a physical object. In particular it is the site within which one's imagination and day-dreaming can take place and be given free rein (Bachelard 1969: 6). And the home is also a metaphor for intimacy. Houses are within us and we reside in houses. In particular, all sorts of spaces, such as the house in which one is born, are imbued with memory traces. And that belongingness derives from the materiality of the particular place in question. Hetherington puts this Bachelardian position as follows:

> The smell of the sheets in the cupboard, the slope of the cellar steps, the patch of paint picked off the edge of the window-sill in a moment of childish boredom, all become the material substance through which our memories are constituted. . . . To dwell . . . is, through daydream and memory, to bring back from the past that which has long been forgotten and live within the reverberations of its remembered intimacy. (1995: 18)

Moreover, Bachelard argues that the very duration of time which is Bergson's concern is itself dependent upon such spatial specificity. Space is necessary to give quality to time. Or as Game neatly expresses it: 'Space transforms time in such a way that memory is made possible' (1995: 201). Thus a space such as a house plays a particularly significant role in the forming and sustaining of memory. In particular, it shelters day-dreaming; it is a metaphorical space within which, in a sense, Bergsonian time operates.

Third, and following on from this, Bachelard presents a notion of memory as irreducibly embodied. In particular our bodies do not forget the first house that we encounter. Bachelard (1969: 15) talks of a 'passionate liaison' between the body and the initial house in which one lives. Its characteristics are physically inscribed in us. Memories are materially localised and so the temporality of memory is spatially rooted according to Bachelard. He spatialises the temporality of memory. Houses are lived through one's body and its memories (Game 1995: 202–3). Without lived space the lived time of duration would be impossible.

Recent research has developed such notions in greater depth. The interconnections of memory, time and space/place have become foregrounded in contemporary social analysis. There are a series of points to make here about memory (see Arcaya 1992; Lash and Urry 1994: 238–41; Middleton and Edwards 1990; Radley 1990). First, it seems that memories are not physically locatable in some part of the brain and merely waiting for appropriate activation. Rather they should be viewed as irreducibly social; people basically remember together within particular places. Thus the production of a shared memory of an event, place or person necessitates cooperative work often over considerable periods of time and located within specific locales. Such memory work may be prompted by a single sensory experience – a photograph, a smell, a taste, a sound, a tree, a hilltop, and so on – rather in the way that Bachelard (1969) argued. But what then gets recovered may well involve a variety of senses.

Further, there are forms of institutional commemoration, 'official memories', within societies. These can silence alternative memories of particular places and may involve particular senses, especially sight. Particular landscapes or particular buildings and monuments are often taken to stand for or represent the nation in ways which undermine alternative memories of other social groups, especially of course those of women, subordinate ethnic groups, and so on (Bhabha 1990; Carter et al. 1993; Wright 1985). (We will return below to memories of landscape.) Many social groups, institutions and whole societies can develop multiple and often contradictory memory practices but these can often be excluded from official recognition (see Urry 1996a). Moreover, there is often a complex rhetoric involved in the articulation of a discourse of memory which will almost certainly involve a range of senses working across time and space. Such a rhetoric can result in communities being united only by shared long-term memories and little else.

Finally, memories are often organised around artefacts and particular spaces such as buildings, bits of landscape, rooms, machines, walls, furniture, and so on. It is these different spaces that structure people's capacities to reminisce, to day-dream about what might have been or to recollect about how their own lives have intersected with those of many others. The much-berated heritage industry may in fact play a significant role in such reminiscence, especially where people encounter artefacts from their past which stimulate memories and the dreams that they once had had (Urry 1996a). Places, then, whether in towns or country, are not just seen through the scopic regime of the 'sightseer', but they are experienced through diverse senses. These may make us ache to be somewhere else, or shiver at the prospect of having to stay put in a particular place for long periods (Jay 1992; Urry 1992). Proust famously conveys this embodied character of memory when he says that 'our arms and legs are full of torpid memories' (cited Lowenthal 1985: 203). And these diverse memories are as much about times as about spaces. Lynch (1972) provocatively asks 'What time is this place?' Natures are in time as they are in space.

Conclusion

In conclusion to this chapter, and in a sense to our efforts in these first five chapters to re-theorise nature, we now consider some general features of the relationship between time and landscape. In particular we evaluate a way of approaching landscape through the idea of dwelling that we will develop further in subsequent chapters of this book. We are indebted here to Ingold's (1993b) argument on the need to develop a 'dwelling perspective' with regard to landscape (and see Heidegger 1962, 1977). The development of this perspective enables him to reject two characteristic conceptions of landscape: the realist or naturalistic conception of the real landscape; and the culturalist, interpretivist conception of landscape as sign. We have likewise in chapter 1 above tried also to move beyond senses of nature which parallel these naturalistic and culturalistic senses of landscape. What, then, does a dwelling perspective amount to?

For Ingold, 'the landscape is constituted as an enduring record of – and testimony to – the lives and works of past generations who have dwelt within it, and in so doing, have left there something of themselves' (1993b: 152). This viewpoint enables him to overcome the conventional distinctions between humans and nature and between mind and matter. In developing the sense of landscape as dwelling, Ingold argues that it is to be understood as neither nature or culture, nor mind or matter. Landscape is the world as known to those who have dwelt there, who do dwell there, who will dwell there, and those whose practical activities take them through its manifold sites and who journey along its multidinous paths.

Furthermore, any such landscape is a place of memory and temporality. In order to develop this temporal character of landscape Ingold employs the distinction between the A- and B-series of time. We saw that in the B-series events are viewed as though they are strung out in time rather like beads along a piece of string – an essentially empiricist and objectivist sense of time. It is in the A-series which Ingold adopts that present events involve some pattern of retention from the past and necessitate projections into the future. Such interpenetrations of past, present and future revolve around the practices, or what Ingold calls the 'taskscape', of any physical environment. It is this taskscape which produces the social character of any such landscape. And it is also this context which produces social time as opposed to the artificial distinctions of chronological time. Such a taskscape only persists as long as people actually engage in the manifold tasks and practical activities of dwelling within that particular landscape.

Ingold's analysis of the temporality of landscape in terms of the task-scapes generated by those dwelling in a given place is one which we will broadly deploy in the following chapters, particularly because of the way that it enables us to begin to avoid the Scylla of environmental realism and the Charybdis of environmental idealism. An emphasis upon dwelling brings out the following characteristics of the relationships of people with land-scape: that there are spatially and temporally distributed tasks; that these are organised through a variety of social practices; that relationships with what is taken to be 'nature' are embodied, involving a variety of senses; that there are 'physical' components of walls, textures, land, plants and so on, which partly constitute such 'dwellings'; that the past is continually redefined in terms of the present and projections into the future; that such redefinitions of the past involve forms of collective memory-work; and that landscapes are never completed but are always subject to contestation and renegotiation, using materials, signs and activities from its various pasts as they are projected into diverse futures.

Ingold then proceeds to demonstrate the value of this dwelling perspective through an astonishing analysis of Bruegel's *The Harvesters* (see plate 5.1). This brings out how landscapes are felt, as they are directly incoporated into our bodily experiences. Our eyes are forced to move down and then up, and as a result we feel the valley and its presence. Ingold argues that the contours of the landscape enter into what Bachelard terms our 'muscular conscious-ness', as though 'the road itself had muscles, or rather, counter-muscles' (1969: 11). Particularly illuminating is his analysis of paths, the pear-tree and the church.

Paths show the accumulated imprint of countless journeys that have been made as people go about their daily business. The network of paths shows the sedimented activity of an entire community, over many generations. Ingold says that: 'It is the taskscape made visible' (1993b: 167). And this, we may hypothesise, is why the maintenance of particular networks of paths is so strongly desired and fought for in contemporary politics. People feel that sedimentation of forms of life through glacial time; they imagine themselves treading the same paths as countless earlier generations. Simply redirecting a path, let alone eliminating it, will often be viewed as an 'act of vandalism' against that sedimented taskscape, that community and their memories.

Even worse, from the viewpoint of glacial time, is the elimination of such paths by new roads. Suddenly paths that have for years demonstrated glacial sedimentation are overwhelmed by instantaneous routes which literally seem to 'carve' through the landscape, killing trees, paths, dwellings and the existing taskscape. New roads which 'slice' through the landscape or which take extra land for the building of a roundabout can provoke intense opposition. First, this is because they destroy at a stroke, instantaneously, the existing taskscape, much as the railway did in the nineteenth century with its stunning new forms of engineering which produced 'cuttings', 'tunnels' and 'embankments'. No amount of re-landscaping can make up for that sudden

Plate 5.1   *Pieter Bruegel's The Harvesters (source: The Metropolitan Museum of Art, New York)*

loss (as opposed to gradual change). And second, roads allow means of movement into the landscape (the car and lorry) that demonstrate no 'muscular consciousness'. Descending the valley or climbing the hill are without cost; they are achieved instantaneously (at least in most cars!). And they are achieved promiscuously. Anyone can pass through that landscape without cost of effort or feeling or knowledge of the forms of dwelling that have given rise to it.

Often roads are objected to by conservationist/environmentalists because particular trees or types of tree are destroyed (in chapter 6 we will consider the significance of woods and trees more directly via Schama's stunning investigation of landscape and memory). Centre-stage in *The Harvesters* is an old pear tree around which the whole landscape is ordered. Ingold suggests that the very place is constituted in part by the tree, although pollen analysis has revealed just how dramatic changes are taking place within apparently unaltered ancient woodlands:

> the place was not there before the tree, but came into being with it . . . the people, in other words, are as much bound up in the life of the tree as is the tree in the life of the people. (1993b: 167–8)

Not far off in the picture is a church, and Ingold (1993b: 169) suggests that it too, like the tree, is a monument to the passage of time. In fact, like the tree, the church helps to constitute a place through the particular way in which it brings in the surrounding landscape, especially through the task-scape that it exemplifies and supports (see Wright 1996 on 'the village that died for England'). Overall, Ingold maintains that the tree and the church have more in common than we might imagine. In both cases 'the form is the embodiment of a developmental or historical process, and is rooted in the context of human dwelling in the world' (Ingold 1993b: 170). Clifford expresses Common Ground's viewpoint here with regard to the loss of an orchard:

> When you lose an orchard you sacrifice not simply a few trees . . . but you might lose fruit varieties particular to that locality, the wild life, the songs, the recipes . . . the look of the landscape, the wisdom gathered over generations about pruning and grafting. . . . In short the cultural landscape is diminished by many dimensions at one blow. (1994: 2)

Ingold, in discussing the people in Bruegel's painting, notes very forcibly that we need not only to see them but also to hear them, to imagine the sounds that they are making, of talk, of eating, of snoring, of drinking, and so on. We need to reconstruct the variety of senses that they are deploying in producing this particular landscape. And this is not principally a visual scene being enacted before our senses, although of course it is only available to our visual sense (this would not be the case if this picture were represented through multi-media). But more important than this is that the characters in the picture relate to each other and to their dwelling not just visually but through various senses which span across various times. Ingold again puts this perceptively:

> The landscape, in short, is not a totality that you or anyone else can look *at*, it is rather the world *in* which we stand in taking up a point of view on our surroundings. . . . For the landscape, to borrow a phrase from Merleau-Ponty, is not so much the objects as 'the *homeland* of our thoughts'. (Ingold 1993b: 171; see Morley and Robins 1995: chap. 5 on the notion of homeland)

We will develop these notions below in the light of a number of physical and cultural transformations, transformations which make the concepts of dwelling, taskscape and landscape enormously more complex than in Bruegel the Elder's world of 1565. We seek to elaborate a dwelling perspective more broadly focused on nature (rather than landscape) in the light of the various transformations established here and elsewhere in this book. Such a perspective would be based upon the following:

- the growth of an enormously powerful taskscape of science which operates globally (as well as locally in the laboratory), whose con-sequences for landscapes are often global and indeed where the 'earth' itself sometimes constitutes its very laboratory (see chapters 1 and 4);
- changes in the character of 'human subjects' with changing patterns of reflexivity, resistance and protest partly directed against the very tasks-capes of science and the partial assumptions of the human that such taskscapes presuppose (see chapters 2 and 3);

- the development of visual and electronic communication based upon instantaneous time which increasingly exert a hegemonic role in the sensing of nature (see this chapter and chapter 4);
- the emergence of diverse spatial practices dependent on nature beyond those of agricultural work or indeed of work more generally. These include walking, music, mass travel, climbing, leisure, photography, and so on, each of which enjoys a distinctive taskscape, and some of which involve new and provocative pathways across existing landscapes (see chapter 6);
- the proliferation of new times and associated technologies beyond that of clock-time which have had dramatic effects upon the lived experience of time; especially the development of what we have termed glacial and instantaneous times. Time and space are being re-warped across 'physical' and 'social' environments (as seen in this chapter).

6

NATURE AS COUNTRYSIDE

In this chapter we examine a variety of ways in which nature gets produced as countryside. We thus examine a specific example of the more general processes involved in the production of space (and time). To examine these processes we employ Lefebvre's theory of spatialisation and in particular his three-fold distinction of spaces (Lefebvre 1991: 33–8; and see Soja 1996 on Lefebvre's trialectics of spatiality). First, there are spatial practices. These range from individual routines to the systematic creation of economic and physical zones and regions. Such spatial practices are over time concretised in the built environment and in the enduring character of the landscape. Second, there are representations of space, the various forms of knowledge and practices which organise and represent space, particularly through the techniques of planning, management and the state. And third, there are the spaces of representation, or the collective experiences of space or lived space. These include symbolic differentiations and collective fantasies focused around space; the resistances to the dominant spatial practices; and the various modes of individual and collective transgression of existing spaces. In each historical period the interplay between these different elements produces particular social spatialisations.

Different forms of space succeed each other through time. There has been a succession from natural to absolute to abstract space, the effect being progressively to expel nature from spatiality. Abstract space is the high point of capitalist relations, involving extraordinarily novel and hugely 'unnatural' created spaces. There is only the 'narrowest leeway' for spaces of representation and more generally for the 'users' of such spaces (Lefebvre 1991: 50). Representations of space involve the manipulation of these spaces, such as the beach, the countryside, the sea, the sun, and so on. Such apparently 'natural' spaces are produced. And at the same time that these spaces are socially produced, especially with the move to the extraordinary abstractions of space, the 'social' underpinning of space is systematically concealed from view. Lefebvre also distinguishes between the domination of nature and the appropriation of nature, and hence between dominated spaces and appropriated spaces. Dominated spaces involving the destruction of nature are commonplace in the contemporary world. Appropriated spaces are those involving its 'consumption', as we saw in chapter 4 (Lefebvre 1991: 164–8).

This kind of analysis is further developed by Wilson (1992) when he examines the production of spaces in nature. Such spaces for him include world fairs, nature parks, zoos, nuclear plants, theme parks, countrysides, Disney Worlds, the wilderness, automobile infrastructures, nature interpretation centres, post-war suburbs, national parks, shopping centres, military zones, and so on. He shows that nature is constituted in spatially uneven forms; that global environmental crises are refracted through what happens in particular spaces; that such spaces of nature are economically and culturally produced; and that underlying senses of nature and its meanings are revealed through, and can be deciphered by, what occurs in particular spaces.

Such an account reveals that societies have intersected with their respective 'physical environments' in diverse ways within different historical periods (thus extending the distinction between the destruction and the appropriation of nature). There are four such intersections. First, there is the stewardship of particular areas of land or natural resources so as to provide a better inheritance for future generations who live within a particular local area. Second, there is the exploitation of land and other resources through seeing nature as separate from society and available for its maximum instrumental destruction. Third, the environment is subject to scientisation through treating it as the object of scientific investigation and hence to systematic intervention and regulation. And fourth, there is the consumption of the physical environment, particularly through turning it into a 'landscape' not primarily for production but embellished for aesthetic appropriation. These are ideal types and any particular society will involve some mixture of two or more of such intersections. Furthermore, although there is a loose historical ordering in the emergence of these different configurations of society and the environment, all four are present in contemporary societies. Moreover, such intersections of society and nature are not simply given, natural and uncontested.

In this chapter we will consider the production of the spaces of the countryside by broadly using Lefebvre's typology of spaces. In the next section we consider a schematic history of the idea of the countryside, considering in part how the term became a key element of social spatialisation in England. We also note that some societies do not produce such spaces of the 'countryside'. In the following section we turn to some recent research on the English countryside, bringing out the dialectic of discipline and transgression present within recent official policy documents. In that examination we suggest that such discourses authorise a rather restricted range of countryside practices; they involve a particular representation of space. In the next section we present some survey data which show the ambivalences that people exhibit in relation to the countryside and to the various processes that might be thought to be threatening it. We will see how people's responses are highly context-dependent. In the final section we examine some of the small-scale spatial practices involved in the countryside, and the way in which they show the limitations of official discourses and the merits of developing what we have termed a dwelling perspective with regard to nature, namely, a perspective that captures the interplay of discipline and transgression which the countryside embodies.

Producing countryside spaces

The term 'the countryside' first came into wide usage in England in the eighteenth century. Bunce notes that there is little disagreement in England about what the space of the countryside means: 'the aesthetic and amenity qualities of a universally domesticated rural landscape, and especially to the landscape of agricultural enclosure' (1994: 4; see Short 1991, especially chap. 4 on much of the following). The development of the space of the countryside in eighteenth-century England stemmed from a number of more or less parallel developments. These included the early growth of towns, particularly London by the seventeenth century and the growing industrial towns of the north by the end of the eighteenth, which provided a striking comparison with increasingly aestheticised rural areas. Further, most rural land had been enclosed by the eighteenth century and the classic pattern of landlord–capitalist tenant farmer–landless labourer was well established. This meant, first, that there was massive rural depopulation of landless labourers which resulted in the first ever urban society – nineteenth-century England. And second, there was an increasing power of the large rural landowning class to shape the countryside, to produce new spatial practices and representations of space within rural areas, including of course the development of landscape gardening, well captured in Goldsmith's *The Deserted Village* (Short 1991: 70). Particularly important was the emergence of new forms of leisurely activity, especially hunting, shooting and fishing, as rural areas turned into a landscaped countryside, increasingly spaces of leisure, amenity value and aesthetic quality (see Bunce 1994: chap. 1). During the eighteenth century there was a growing fashion for touring the English countryside and especially visiting country houses ostentatious in their architecture and landscaping (Ousby 1990).

Central to this transformation was the emerging discourse of 'landscape' and its unambiguous association with pictorialism, as opposed to mere visuality. Barrell (1972: 65) indeed notes that there is no word in English for a tract of land which is merely seen but not appreciated pictorially (and see Bell 1993). In the course of the eighteenth century, as we saw in chapter 4, the language of landscape developed as irredeemably painterly. Such landscapes were the product of complex intertextualities and 'artificial' modes of representation, such as the famous Claude glass. They were never purely seen but required various media of communication and representation (see Andrews 1989; Bell 1993). Such notions of a painterly landscape came to cast a deep imprint upon the emergence of various quintessential English landscapes during the extraordinary transformations that occurred in the nineteenth century.

In particular, Williams (1973) showed how such spaces of the English countryside resulted from its contrasts with the town, and especially with the perceived horrors of the English industrial town, the first such spaces ever to have developed. As we discussed in chapter 1, nature came in a sense to be cast out of such urban-industrial spaces and to find its 'home' on the very margins of the emerging industrial society, in parts of the British country-side. And as we saw in chapter 4, this perception of the industrial town was a matter of the sensing of such pathological spaces. So while the countryside came increasingly to be desired because of its visual qualities mediated through the representation of space via the notion of landscape, the industrial town was seen as thoroughly polluted, as unnaturally invading all the human orifices. Cobbett described such towns as 'unnatural embossments; these white swellings, these odious wens, produced by corruption and engendering crime, misery and slavery' (cited Bunce 1994: 14). Likewise Birmingham was seen by Robert Southey as involving: 'noise . . . beyond description. . . . The filth is sickening . . . active and moving . . . which fills the whole atmosphere and penetrates everywhere' (cited Bunce 1994: 15). As we saw in chapter 4, smell is particularly invasive since it is a sense that cannot be turned off. In the nineteenth century it was the smells of the city that became particularly central to the representation of its opposite, the countryside. In *Hard Times* Dickens described the river in Coketown that 'ran purple with ill-smelling dye', while Ruskin described nineteenth-century industrial London as 'that great foul city . . . stinking – a ghastly heap of fermenting brickwork, pouring out poison at every pore' (cited Bunce 1994: 15). However, this was an artificial polarity since nineteenth-century rural England was of course rich with odours, of farm animals, raw sewage, rotting vegetables, smoke, stagnant water and so on.

Ruskin indeed played a more generally significant role in the late nineteenth-century rejection of industrial capitalism and its urban embodi-ments, and the development of what Wiener (1981) has famously described as the 'decline of the English industrial spirit' (on Ruskin see Mallett 1995, who brings out the parallels with Benjamin; as well as Wheeler 1995 more generally). What is interesting is Ruskin's examination of how the new sensibilities of the city undermine certain features of the imagination of artists and of their ability to wander over the mass of treasure stored in their memories. Particularly striking is the contrast between the painting and the photograph. The latter lacks the infinite richness and complexity of the painting. And more generally life in the nineteenth-century city trained the eye to anticipate shock and hence destroyed the ability 'to attend to the infinite richness offered by art and nature alike' (Mallett 1995: 54; note incidentally similarities with Simmel's analysis of the blasé attitude). The city bombards the eye with advertisements and yet offers nothing to be really looked at. There is a poverty of the imagination of the city; and the starkest of contrasts between most urban buildings and the 'grace of nature'. Modern London, according to Ruskin, teaches the 'adoration of chaos', compared with how in the natural world the eye is in perfect repose in the midst of profusion (cited Mallett 1995: 57).

Such critiques of the first industrial society helped to generate a rapid and extensive gentrification of the industrial class and, according to Wiener, its absorption into the conservative values and practices of the rural elite as well as into the structures of the public school, Oxbridge and the traditional professions. Wiener provocatively asks:

> Why did hostility to industrial advance persist and even strengthen in the world's first industrial society? Why did hostility so often take the form of rural myth making? (1981: 204)

Industry and modernity were regarded as inherently un-English until well into the twentieth century. The Great War was fought to defend the traditions of the pre-industrial order *against* modernist ideology; and the Second World War similarly involved defending essentially old-fashioned and rural values against 'an industrial society run amok' (Wiener 1981:77; Bunce 1994: 21). During the interwar period Stanley Baldwin famously stated that 'England is the country, and the country is England' (cited Lowenthal 1991: 205). In a style later plagiarised by PM John Major 60 years later, he characterised the true (natural?) England as:

> the tinkle of the hammer of the anvil in the country smithy, the corncrake on a dewy morning, the sound of the scythe against the whetstone, and the sight of the plough team coming over the brow of the hill . . . for centuries the one eternal sight of England. (cited Bunce 1994: 33)

It hardly needs saying but most of these supposedly eternal or natural sights have long since gone, living on only in rural heritage centres. And it should also be noted that Baldwin was paradoxically writing during a period of intense suburbanisation. The urban area of England and Wales increased by over 25% in the inter-war period (Miller 1995). It was no coincidence, as shown in chapter 2, that what is now known as the Council for the Protection of Rural England (CPRE) was formed in this period and soon became a highly influential body in policy making.

Why, then, has there been such an appeal of the English countryside, of 'England's green and pleasant land'? Why did especially the southern English countryside come to be so valorised within British culture? What were the processes that produced a distinctive set of spaces in the most urbanised and industrialised of societies at the time? Why did 'nature' come to be so effectively transformed into 'countryside' within England? (See Urry 1995b: chap. 13 for some preliminary material; see also chapter 2 above for an account of the role of the countryside in 'inventing' contemporary British environmentalism.) There are four such processes to emphasise.

First and most obviously, there is the role of English Romanticism, which established a particularly powerful way of sensing, experiencing and engaging with nature during the nineteenth century. There were many strands but undoubtedly Wordsworth's role was seminal. Ousby summarises:

> Wordsworth has most influenced our own attitudes to nature, transforming the cults of the Sublime and the Picturesque . . . into that complex of responses we

call Romanticism, which is still part of the intellectual climate we live in. (1990: 178)

From the picturesque Wordsworth developed a visual delight in the irregular, the fleeting and the modest; and from the sublime he took over and developed the importance of the emotions of awe and reverence towards nature (see chapter 4 above). More generally, the seeing of nature as a living force which was able to console, uplift and ennoble the individual played a powerful role in the widespread nineteenth-century critique of industry, science and progress, some aspects of which developed into a proto-environmentalism (see Bate 1991 on Wordsworth; and Wheeler 1995 on Ruskin).

Second, the idealisation of nature by the Romantics in the early nineteenth century was able to develop into a more widespread appeal of the country-side because rural areas had experienced very extensive transformation by the end of the eighteenth century. The English countryside could not be seen as harbouring a peasantry with values and practices which the emergent elites could wholly disparage. The countryside was not to be written off as simply 'barbaric' and 'idiotic', as was the case in much of the rest of Europe. Also we have noted that enclosures meant that capitalist class relations developed in rural areas – with a substantial class of landless labourers. This class dramatically shrank in size over the course of the nineteenth century, as England became a thoroughgoing urban society. The English countryside became the 'other' to the urban areas, full of landscaped estates, capitalist agriculture, concentrated wealth and rural leisure pursuits. It became and has remained, according to Newby, 'the proper place for proper people to live in' (1990b: 631).

Third, we have so far talked as though there is a single such countryside within England (while realising of course that the production of the countryside has been different in Ireland, Wales and Scotland). But this is not the case, since there is an important distinction within England between the metropolitanised home counties countryside, with a somewhat similar relationship to the area around Paris discussed in chapter 4, and the countrysides of the north and west. In particular, English Romanticism, which historically developed on the edges of English life, has been reappropriated to its centre. Romanticism had emerged on the margins of England, in the south west, the Peak and Lake Districts; on the margins of Britain in especially Scotland; and on the margins of Europe in Italy and Greece. Romanticism as a set of beliefs and practices then came to apply to and legitimise the southern English countryside, to valorise it and to assist in imposing its values upon the rest of Britain (see Bunce 1994: 40 on the use of Wordsworth to legitimate a 'cosier' version of nature). Wiener argues that what he terms the southern metaphor had become dominant in England by around 1900. Such a metaphor 'went together with the devaluation of both the locales of, and the qualities that had made, the industrial revolution. Such places and such characteristics became "provincial"' (1981: 42).

This distinction between the southern and northern metaphors partially overlaps with that between town and country so well captured by Williams (1973). But there is one oddity: the hugely dominant role of London, what Cobbett termed 'a kind of monster', within the economic, political and cultural geography of England/Britain/Empire (cited Williams 1973: 180). As early as 1660 its population was half a million, while its growth in the eighteenth century 'was the astonishing creation of an agrarian and mercantile capitalism, within an aristocratic order' (Williams 1973: 181). London is obviously not the countryside but it is also not the town, certainly not a provincial industrial town of the north. It was a city of services 'producing and reproducing, to a dominant degree, the social reality of the nation as a whole' (Williams 1973: 183).

Thus there are two major dichotomies at the heart of English culture: town and country, and the south and the north. They come together to produce a massively important social spatialisation comprising two components. On the one hand, there is the southern countryside of the home counties which is grouped around and oriented to the not quite real city of London, which has for so long dominated the urban landscape of Britain and indeed the world. It was the first world city of the modern era. The symbiosis between that home counties countryside and the city of London was effected through regular carriage transportation and then a suburban rail network. To live in that countryside was to be able to participate in the culture of London ('to go up to town', as London has always been quaintly described). According to Daniels (1991), this symbiosis was principally effected in the twentieth century as the vernacular, agrarian, home counties countryside became central to notions of Englishness. On the other hand, there is the 'north', which is predominantly urban but in which are found the few pockets of 'nature', of rural tracts in north Wales, northern England and Scotland. They are geographically northern, but are not quite of the north (Urry 1995b: chap. 13 on the Lake District). This distinction has resulted in a powerful production of space in which the dominance of London and *its* countryside reinforces the 'north' as other, as economically, politically and culturally peripheralised. George Orwell's observations in *Homage to Catalonia* particularly capture the power of these relations and metaphors, even in the case of someone who travelled to the 'north'. He talked of how he returned from Spain to find 'southern England, probably the sleekest landscape in the world':

> The industrial towns were far away, a smudge of smoke and misery. . . . Down here it was still the England I had known in my childhood: the railway cuttings covered in wild flowers, the deep meadows where the great shining horses browse and meditate, the slow-moving streams bordered by willows, the green blossoms of the elms, the larkspurs in the cottage gardens . . . all sleeping the deep, deep sleep of England. (1938: 314)

Fourth, this countryside of the south has become particularly central to English national identity, which has then functioned to sustain and bolster such a space, long after the originating spatial practices have been swallowed up in urbanisation and industrialisation. Lowenthal argues that because there are few other signs of national identity in England, there developed instead a scenic essence to such identity:

> One icon in heritage has a distinctly English cast. This is the landscape. Nowhere else is landscape so freighted as legacy. Nowhere else does the very term suggest not simply scenery and *genres de vie*, but quintessential national virtues . . . rural England is endlessly lauded as a wonder of the world. (1991: 213, and 1994)

Many commentators have argued for the importance of especially the southern English landscape to English national identity. Kipling wrote in 1902 that:

> England is a wonderful land. . . . It is made up of trees and green fields and mud and gentry, and at last I'm one of the gentry. (cited Short 1991: 73)

Many later writers particularly enlarged on themes poignantly captured by G.K. Chesterton in the 1930s:

> The solid look of the village; the fact that the roofs and walls seemed to mingle naturally with the fields and trees; the feeling of the naturalness of the inn, of the cross-roads, of the market cross . . . in a real sense the Crown Jewels. These were the national, the normal, the English. (cited Lowenthal 1991: 213; and see Daniels 1991; Miller 1995; Thomas 1984; Williams 1973)

Central to this social spatialisation is the English village. Hilaire Belloc believed that the true heart of (southern) England lay in the village, which has acquired almost mythological status as the archetypal English community. In the same period J.B. Priestley similarly commented on the importance of what has been termed the middle landscape – a lovingly cultivated and controlled nature:

> English people . . . do not willingly let go of the country – as the foreign people do – once they have settled in a town; they are all gardeners, perhaps country gentlemen, at heart. (cited Miller 1995: 99)

Howkins, in summarising the dominant discourse here, argues for the importance of the countryside to the very development of English identity:

> the ideology of England and Englishness is to a remarkable degree rural. Most importantly, a large part of the English *ideal* is rural. (1986: 62)

One group which self-consciously developed such an ideology were the Georgians, who just before the Great War set out to celebrate rural England with their relatively straightforward poetry and prose. They included Rupert Brooke and Walter de la Mare (see Miller 1995).

In the inter-war period, Baldwin, self-described as the man in a field-path, played an exemplary role in developing this English ideology of ruralism and in much more sharply distinguishing between the town and country as social spatialisations. Miller (1995) suggests that it was the growth of national radio broadcasting in the 1930s that helped to develop and sustain this increasingly national ideology of ruralism, a ruralism specifically intended for national consumption mainly of course within urban areas. We may further note the role of the long-running BBC radio soap-opera *The Archers* in helping to sustain ruralism in the post-war era. In developing such a space of representation it was exogenous change that was particularly feared and this led to the widespread adoption of images of a supposedly unchanging English countryside, to counterpose the exceptionally rapid and traumatic changes within the town. Constable's *Hay Wain*, for example became popular in the inter-war period as a particular icon of Englishness (see Potts 1989). It is also worth noting J.B. Priestley's unexpected comment that the timeless rural world should be appreciated by the town-dweller because of its visual impressions: 'that people ought to pay just to have a glimpse of, as one of the last luxuries in the world for the ranging eyes' (cited Miller 1995; see chapter 4 above on visuality).

So far in this section we have seen how nature as countryside has come to occupy a particularly significant role in English culture and in the historic dominance of the south over the north. The English landscape has been exceptionally crafted, a nature tamed, adorned and civilised, the consummate artefact. Lowenthal notes how visitors to England often comment on how the countryside is all finished off, apparently without rubbish, cleaned and polished. He summarises:

> It is an English creed that all land needs care. Far from knowing best, nature requires constant vigilance. (1994: 26; and see Urry 1995b: chap. 13 on related focus group research in the Lake District)

Even Cheddar Gorge is periodically trimmed and shaved so that it does not lose its uniqueness and become just another river valley. So too is the New Forest burned every seven years or so to ensure that the characteristic grasses do not succumb to forest. In England the likely withdrawal of millions of acres of arable land induces great concern that its appearance will be changed for the worse. Lowenthal argues that in most other countries such land would simply be left to its own devices. But not in England, where briar and bramble, seedlings and suckers, are viewed as unnatural. Even Raymond Williams (1984: 218) applauds the complex processes of hedging, tending, weeding, ditching, and so on, that are involved in manicuring the English countryside. Otherwise he suggests there would be too much wilderness! But according to Lowenthal, this manicuring of the countryside through a very particular set of spatial practices has recently been taken to the extreme. He talks of much of the English countryside being turned into a branch of the heritage industry; such a heritage landscape has become 'less and less England, more and more "Englandland", Europe's all-engulfing offshore theme park' (Lowenthal 1991: 222). The English countryside is apparently becoming a much more appropriated leisure space used for attracting foreign tourists (as we showed in the case of recent marketing strategies by the British Tourist Authority: Clark et al. 1994a).

So far we have spoken only of the English countryside and its connections with the social spatialisation of English national identity. But this is curious given that the relevant state is that of the UK and to a lesser extent the European Union. In most North Atlantic Rim societies the pretence at least is that the nation and state coincide. In the UK they manifestly do not. And this poses two interesting questions. First, what role do Irish (the area varying of course during different historical periods), Scottish and Welsh countrysides play in both dominant and subordinate spaces of representation within the UK? And second, does the 'countryside' function in the same way and to the same degree in the social spatialisation of other societies?

First, the English countryside abounds with monuments to past achievements, including of course that of domination over the other nations and of the UK. Such monuments include Stonehenge, the site of the Battle of Hastings, Runnymede, Shakespeare's birthplace, Plymouth Hoe, the English country house, sites of English Romanticism, Constable country, the small towns of the industrial revolution, the estates of the heroes of Empire, the small-town universities of Oxford and Cambridge, the English village green, the airfields of the Battle of Britain, National Trust gardens, and so on. These are monuments to England's insularity and to its dominance over other nations. By comparison the countrysides of Ireland, Scotland and Wales are littered with memorials to lost causes and especially to lost battles (Lowenthal 1991: 209–10). Such landscapes are also rich in gendered relations (as shown by Edensor and Kothari 1994 in Scotland). The Scottish landscape is strewn with derelict crofts which are powerfully iconic of the transformation of the Highlands into a colony of England since the infamous battle of Culloden in 1746. According to Short (1991: 58), this had the effect of ending wilderness within the British Isles. Scotland is a landscape of loss.

A further contrast is between what Lowenthal (1994) terms the consummate artefact of the (southern) English landscape compared with the landscapes of other nations. Those other landscapes are no less culturally constructed but they do have a different resonance. The southern English landscapes have been produced as distinct cultivated spaces through a particularly intense and consistent integration of specific spatial practices, representational spaces and spaces of representation, including, as we will see below, touring by car. They cohere seamlessly together. The landscapes of the other nations of the British Isles have been produced in a less consistent fashion and are more ambiguous in what they represent. Do such spaces represent the integration of such nations within the British state? Are they spaces which represent a subordinate Irish, Scottish or Welsh identity? Are they spaces which represent contested and resurgent nationalisms? Or are they simply resources to be represented as tourist sites likely to appeal to visitors who 'add on' a Celtic dimension to their holiday focused upon London and its material and symbolic domination of those other nations?

In the case of Ireland, romantic notions taken from England have played a major role in the various literary and later filmic representations of that countryside (Bell 1993). In particular there has been a striking absence in pre-revolution paintings of Ireland of agricultural workers engaged in manual toil; the landscape was empty of productive work. There developed a 'picturesque' appreciation of the Irish landscape (Slater 1993), and over time the Anglo-Irish landlord class significantly changed the landscape in

order to heighten its picturesque qualities and to signify qualities of what
had been left behind in England. The ideology of the picturesque became a
reality through landscape gardening designed to make natural what was of
course wholly contrived. Such a romantic appreciation of Ireland has been
that of the outsider, of the coloniser, the landlord, the tourist and later the
anthropologist; and it has privileged pictorial appreciation of the countryside
over the language and material culture of Irish people themselves. Moreover,
it evades the role of narration in creating a sense of attachment to local
places. It prioritises the visual consumption of place especially by the
solitary individual undertaking the romantic gaze (see Urry 1990; also Slater
1993: 42–4 on the picturesque as 'essentially a visual phenomenon').

   Of course, following the formation of the Irish Free State such a
romanticism was radically contested and subject to major re-evaluation.
Especially under the influences of De Valera, there has been the formation of
a much more heroic and peopled romanticism, based on idealised notions of
work, toil, Catholicism and the family. Indeed, post-Independence Ireland
became less overtly concerned with the scenic qualities of the countryside:
there is no true equivalent of the UK 1947 Town and Country Planning Act
and the formation of state planning processes dedicated to sustain clear
distinctions between town and country; Ireland has no equivalent campaigning body to the UK's Council for the Protection of Rural England; its
equivalent to the National Trust is not a major landowning body as in
England; Irish poetry and art has often depicted the countryside as a
landscape of 'ruin'; and on visiting Ireland one's 'cultivated' eyes are met
by dilapidated thatched cottages and 'unsightly' new bungalows in locations
which would not have received planning permission in Britain. Yet such
notions of scenic romanticism have still powerfully impacted back on
conceptions of the countryside which are held in part by Irish elites. Catholic
intellectuals have enthusiastically embraced the romantic inheritance (Bell
1993: 19). As with other colonised societies, Irish nationalism has in its
valorisation of the pictorialised Irish countryside internalised components of
the very colonial culture it sought to contest. Thus Ireland reflects a partial
illustration of what Pratt (1992) more generally calls autoethnographic
expressions – these involve the colonised collaborating with and appropriating the idioms of the conquering 'seeing-man' whose imperial eyes have
looked out and possessed so much of the globe (and see chapter 4 above on
the visual).

   And what of other societies? Do they possess the kind of countryside that
we have described in the English case? A number of brief points can be
made. First and obviously, different features of the landscape are celebrated
within different societies: alpine altitude and air in Switzerland, fjords in
Norway, bogs in Ireland, Wild West wilderness in the US, heaths in
Denmark, geysers in New Zealand, and so on (see Lowenthal 1994). In each
case as Schama shows in such depth, these spaces are produced by human
activity, experience and creativity. Even in the case of the American
wilderness it was an act of Congress in 1864 that established Yosemite

Valley as a sacred wilderness (during the war that marked the American fall from grace; Schama 1995: 7). This particular wilderness resulted from the spatial practice and representation by the federal state in its designation of Yosemite as a national park. It also required various spaces of representation involving preachers, painters, photographers and writers who had begun to describe and lyricise Yosemite and especially its stupendous sequoias. It came to be thought of as the site for the rebirth of the nation after the Civil War, as a holy park and as a democratic paradise. And this was to be a managed wilderness in which the animals were kept in and the humans kept out. Even John Muir, the prophet of wilderness, characterised Yosemite as a 'park valley' and celebrated its resemblance to an artificial landscape-garden (Schama 1995: 8, 191). In order to keep the valley pure and wild, a garden of Eden, it had to be carefully regulated and managed.

More generally, Bunce (1994: 35–6) argues that the countryside ideal which is so strong in Europe has been poorly developed in the US. The American landscape was born out of conceptions of the pioneer and survival, individualism and egalitarianism, work and commerce. While the English countryside was being depopulated throughout the nineteenth century, the population of rural America was increasing as farming settlements moved inexorably westwards. Such farms were based on exceptionally formalised land surveys which were laid out to produce a geometric and dispersed pattern of settlement. To the European eye there is no countryside, only land. American farms are not sights of visual enticement, rather it is to the 'natural' scenery of the deserts and canyons, mountains and ravines, that the eye has been mainly drawn.

Second, in some societies it is the very complexity of landscapes that is seen to be nationally emblematic. The best example of this is France, where the mixture of climates, the length of occupance, the complex diversity of product, the role of family and peasant proprietorship, and the maintenance of high employment within agriculture until well after the Second World War have all produced an exceptionally diverse yet nationally resonant countryside. Lowenthal summarises:

> the heterogeneity of French landscapes and ways of life meant strengths surpassing those of any other nation. . . .Vaunted diversity underscores manifold inherited excellences: the infinite rich variety of French wines, cheeses, cuisine, customs, dialects.
> Yet this diversity in no way detracts from French unity. (1994: 19)

To celebrate such a diverse countryside is simultaneously to celebrate the different regions *and* the different peoples that make up such a society.

Third, human cultures are remarkably ingenious and do to similar physical entities quite different things, developing very different spaces of representation. Schama shows this in the case of woods, where extraordinarily powerful and different myths have come to be woven into the roots and branches of various cultures. For example, in Germany forests have long been viewed as representing the spirit of militarism; an embodied memory which the modernising Nazis deployed and much developed (see Schama

1995: chap. 2). Goering subjected large areas of Poland to a 'total landscape plan' in which villages were depopulated and the land was turned into hunting forests; forest themes invaded most aspects of Nazi art and politics; Hitler and his fellow Nazis were regularly photographed in woodland settings; and the most extensive of programmes of woodland protection were brought in while forest ecology was introduced into the school curriculum (see chapter 2 above on the curious significance of environmentalism within Nazism). More recently the image of dying forests found fresh resonance in the German psyche throughout the 1980s and helped crystallise the European-wide debate on acid rain. Elsewhere in Europe forests drew upon and articulated different myths and memories. In England, the forest has long stood for the idea that liberty against the despot could be attained by those who lived under the greenwood tree (as of course in the Robin Hood myth). In France forests have represented the passion for order and the intervention of the state. In Poland forests have stood for the enduring struggle for national freedom. While in the US, although the forests of the east had harboured the godless Indian, the discovery of the Big Trees of California were seen as an American godsend, the revelation of the uniqueness of America and of the particularly chosen character of the American people (Schama 1995: part 1).

Fourth, it is common to argue that cultures are formed in opposition to other cultures, to one or more 'others'. This applies equally to the spaces of landscape; that part of the appeal of one's own particular countryside is the contrast that it exhibits to other landscapes. There are many ways in which such contrasting spaces of representation can be characterised, particularly through metaphor and metonymy. One contrast is between the countryside as empty and the countryside as full. For Baudrillard the whole of America is a desert. He characterises American desert landscape as the 'empty, absolute freedom of the freeways . . . the America of desert speed, of motels and mineral surfaces' (1988: 5). Such an emptiness cannot be properly described as a space of the 'countryside' since that term seems to imply the fullness and profusion of European landscapes (see Bunce 1994). American landscapes are empty and as such they stand for modernity and the rejection of the countrysides of Europe and the complex histories of European societies. Such an emptiness is a metaphor of the American dream. Baudrillard suggests that 'America' undertook to make utopia real, to realise everything through the strange destiny of simulation. Culture in America is therefore 'space, speed, cinema, technology' (Baudrillard 1988: 100).

These empty landscapes of the desert are experienced through driving huge distances across them. Such deserts constitute a metaphor of endless futurity, a primitive society of the future, combined with the obliteration of the past, the triumph of time as instantaneous rather than time as depth (Baudrillard 1988: 6). It is a process of leaving one's past behind, realising a culture of amnesia, in Huyssen's (1995) terms (and see Smith 1992). Such landscapes involve a particular spatial practice, of driving on and on across the desert, seeing nothing (much) but the ever disappearing emptiness framed through the windscreen. It is a spatial practice which is at the heart of American culture and at the same time of opposition to that culture. It is a spatial practice that is premised upon particular ways of 'dwelling', not in one place but through punctuated movement 'on the road', mainly the unending movement of men in their cars conspicuously consuming the planet's carbon resources, which, like much of the rest of the world's resources, are seen as God's gift to Americans.

In the last section of this chapter we return to various spatial practices which are involved in producing particular countrysides/landscapes (such as driving across the desert, walking up hillsides, swimming in freezing waters, and so on). Before doing so, however, we return to the English countryside and report on two pieces of empirical research we undertook in the early 1990s. Both were directly concerned with the complexities involved in the contemporary production *and* appropriation of the spaces of those rich and manicured landscapes.

Landscapes of discipline

Recent surveys show just how symbolically important is the English countryside. It has wide public appeal – it is seen as a place characterised by tradition, stability and permanence. One such survey suggests that these characteristics are powerful metaphors for the countryside, and that the countryside is regarded as a vital component to people's quality of life by over 60% of the British population by contrast with the presumed 'stress and pollution' of the cities (Countryside Commission 1993). In marketing campaigns by the British Tourist Authority and the like, the countryside is seen as one of the most promising ways to sell Britain, both at home and abroad.

So what is the English countryside? How do those public bodies charged with its protection and exploitation conceptualise it? What is involved in such representations of rural space? Our research consisted of a discourse analysis of the most important policy documents in order to examine the 'representations of space' implicit in public policy (for a full account see Clark et al. 1994a, 1994b). The documents analysed include policy statements from three government agencies (Countryside Commission 1991, 1992; English Tourist Board 1991; Sports Council 1991); two Department of the Environment Planning Policy Guidance Notes (Department of the Environment 1991, 1992); and one government-sponsored Task Force (Department of Employment Task Force 1991). They all represent official responses to the rhetoric of sustainability – the new language of public environmentalism endorsed by national governments following the 1987 Brundtland Report and the 1992 Earth Summit at Rio (see chapter 7 below).

One striking theme was a new kind of concern for 'the environment' that would have been unlikely even 10 years before. All the documents conceive of the countryside as space which is vulnerable to threats associated from inappropriate tourism and leisure uses. These tend to be characterised in terms of character and physical appearance. The public agencies involved in countryside leisure and tourism stress the importance of a diverse and high-quality environment which requires active conservation such that they can satisfactorily fulfil their statutory duties. Thus an environmentally healthy countryside is deemed essential for the Countryside Commission (1991) to enable them to fulfil their duties to 'conserve and enhance the beauty of the countryside of England and to help people enjoy it'. The Sports Council (1991) also argue that their statutory duty of promoting countryside activities depends in part on conserving finite natural resources. The English Tourist Board (1991), meanwhile, similarly point to the need to maintain a high-quality environment, without which there would be less long-term opportunities to promote tourism at home and abroad.

At the same time, our research shows that the ways in which 'environmental' concern are being discursively translated into state policy and practice centre on the concept of landscape and techniques of management, and that this process of translation may be inadvertently contributing to new forms of discipline and self-surveillance in the countryside. We show in the following just how such 'environmentally driven' representations of countryside space effectively close off alternative spaces of representation.

The various government agencies commonly conceive of the environment as a set of *non-human* qualities, defined in physical terms, whose conservation is essential for the agencies to fulfil their statutory duties. Such a discourse on the countryside helps shape the future space of the countryside, including the boundaries of appropriate human use and engagement. The definition of nature as non-human qualities (*par excellence* the character of the landscape and its ecological diversity) is then translated into policies aimed at the further conservation of these qualities. The aim is typically to implement such policies through bureaucracies dedicated to new forms of management and planning. But one effect of such an approach, we argue, is to contribute to new and largely unforeseen techniques of discipline for the countryside user; in stark contradiction to alternative responses to and aspirations for 'environmental' use and practice. We briefly highlight three such representations of space below, what we term the representations of vision, management and consumer choice.

First, then, there are documents which demonstrate the dominance of the visual appropriation of the countryside. This can be seen in the strategy documents of the Countryside Commission (1991, 1992; and see chapter 4 above). Thus while the documents state the desire for an inclusive multi-purpose countryside, closer analysis indicates that the Commission are advocating a particular sort of countryside in which only certain sorts of leisure activities are advocated. This can be seen in relation to the outline of the Commission's vision for the future:

> The job of the Countryside Commission is to conserve and enhance the beauty of the countryside of England and to help people to enjoy it. However, we pursue our task within a wider vision of a multi-purpose countryside, managed so that its

environmental qualities are sustained. A sense of direction is all the more important at a time of change. We call on all those interested to share our vision. Key components are an environmentally healthy countryside, a beautiful countryside, a diverse countryside, an accessible countryside and a thriving countryside. (Countryside Commission 1991: 1–2)

This vision is composed of two broad aspects: one, the sustenance and enhancement of England's beautiful countryside; and, two, access to this beauty. As such, the Commission is primarily concerned with the diverse processes which currently threaten the beauty of the English countryside (such as farming, forestry, rural development, tourism and leisure interests) and is currently urging government for an 'integrated strategy for the countryside' which would take account of how these interests could relate in harmony to one another and with the natural environment. Such a strategy would imply a new kind of foundation for agricultural policy (the primary creators of the English countryside), alongside new imperatives for national forestry policy, coastal policy and water policy; emphasising how each of these areas of government policy can be implemented in harmony with the needs for a beautiful and fully accessible countryside. Moreover, in terms of proposed new access to the countryside, the Countryside Commission are currently advocating quick repair of the existing public rights of way network, high priority to be given to common land legislation, and for a new national approach to be given to the sensitive issue of general access to open country (Countryside Commission 1991).

As outlined above, it might appear curious to describe the above policies as in any way 'disciplinary'. However, the disciplinary aspects arise from the overt and constant emphasis by the Commission on beauty and landscape, and from the rather passive and non-engaging leisure uses of countryside space that such an emphasis engenders. In recent years, the concept of 'landscape' has come under sustained investigation from a range of academic disciplines which argue that models of landscape appreciation involve particular 'ways of seeing' which have a variety of social, political and ideological components.

The documents produced by the Countryside Commission favour particular ways of looking at the countryside and the rejection of others. Applying the typology of 'gazes' elaborated in chapter 4, we can see that a repetitive emphasis on the 'beauty of the English countryside' particularly embodies the 'romantic' gaze. Whether alone, or in company, the model of the person presented is of a privatised individual experiencing and consuming qualities associated with a national beauty (true England). Linked to this 'gaze' in such documents are pictures of 'unspoilt' countryside – usually unpeopled, majestic and awe-inspiring. The message implies a celebration of 'Englishness' as a timeless enduring quality of what landscapes were, and of what they should be (unspoilt), and where the method of engagement (or perhaps non-engagement) is that of quietly and unobtrusively acquiring these enduring qualities. Farmers are either hidden from the tourist's gaze *or* simply referred to as 'the makers of the land' (constructing them symbolically as integral to the romantic gaze), while the significance of the vernacular, the familiar and the locally distinctive are downplayed. Similarly, the leisure subject is usually hidden from the texts (since the tourist has no place in the romantic gaze), and no space is allocated for a more intrusive, active or participatory type of engagement in the countryside. In effect, the Commission are advocating a way of acting in the countryside which involves a *de facto* separation between the subject (the gazer) and the object (the gazed upon, the countryside), helping to produce what can be identified as a particularly alienated relationship between humans and the natural world (Cosgrove 1984; Lefebvre 1991; Thomas 1984). In other words, what appears to be taken for granted in the texts is not only the implicit value of a particular gaze, but also what it is about the countryside that is worthy of the gaze.

This dominant visual gaze and its disciplinary consequences can also be seen in the policies and practices promoted by the Countryside Commission. Policies which aim to promote public access to 'the beauty of the English countryside' take for granted a model of the countryside leisure experience related to a landscape aesthetic. An emphasis on passive consumption of 'romantic' qualities leads to a focus on quiet and non-intrusive countryside activities (such as picnicking and walking), and to threats to such qualities (the three environmental threats highlighted in the Commission's strategy being litter, dogs and noise). But such policies fail to communicate with practices and desires for wider engagement in the production and consumption of the countryside, and with the laws and implicit understandings which continually thwart such attempts (the currently highly restrictive laws on landownership being one such area). Thus the Countryside Commission perhaps not surprisingly have been silent on the possible role of the countryside as a space for broader engagement and participation in the processes by which such spaces are produced, including new possibilities to repopulate and rework the countryside in line with a more broadly conceived environmental agenda.

The implications of such policies are not simply exclusionary but disciplinary. People are not only excluded from using the countryside in ways not characterised by the gaze, but are disciplined and denied 'voice' in the process. While overt discipline and surveillance is embodied in current legislation on general rights of access and encampment, a more subtle form of surveillance occurs through codes of self-discipline, much of which is currently produced and reinforced by the Countryside Commission. One particularly powerful code of behaviour lies in the current promotion and possible extension of the 'country code': a code devised in 1957 to ensure that visitors to the countryside did not interfere with the needs of landowners. However, while ensuring a public sympathetic to the concerns of landowners, such a code also helps produce a public who consider their own rights as involving quiet, orderly forms of behaviour which intrude minimally with the current workings and patterns of ownership of the countryside.

The second disciplinary tendency arises directly out of the formal responses by government agencies to current threats to the environmental quality
of the countryside. As outlined above, government agencies commonly
define the environment as a set of non-human qualities. Furthering this
argument, the common response to current environmental threats across all
three agencies involved with countryside leisure is to appeal to strategic
planning and good management as appropriate techniques to ensure harmony between different interests in the countryside (competing farming,
forestry, rural development, tourism and leisure interests) and the natural
environment. The emphasis on planning and management is yet more
pronounced in recent planning policy guidance notes on tourism and
recreation in the countryside, and is embedded in the remit of the government sponsored Task Force on 'Tourism and the Environment':

> The job of the Task Force was to look at how visitors can be better managed to
> ensure that not only will tourism continue to flourish, but that it will continue to
> do so in harmony with the environment, and continue to give the maximum
> benefit for the visitor, as well as serving the well-being of host populations.
> (Department of Employment Task Force 1991: 2)

There are two problems here. First, it assumes that it is in fact possible to
adopt management techniques that can create harmony across a wide variety
of competing pressures and needs currently expressed in the English
countryside. But this is somewhat dubious since different countryside uses
and activities often imply fundamentally different conceptions concerning
what the countryside is and how it should be used. As such, questions
concerning whether the countryside should be managed for economic
regeneration or for conservation, whether hunting and shooting should be
considered legitimate countryside pursuits, whether the countryside should
be primarily for quiet and reflective uses, whether raves and travellers'
festivals should be permitted, all depend on assumptions and commitments
concerning just what sort of space the countryside is. These issues need to be
recognised as cultural dilemmas requiring political responses, before they
can be adequately addressed by management or a planning system primarily
concerned with competing land uses and the negotiation of physical pressures (as we show in detail in Clark et al. 1994a, 1994b).

Second, the increased emphasis on planning and management may result
in unforeseen disciplinary effects. One of the most illustrative examples of
the level and range of management possibilities proposed for the countryside
are the 10 techniques of visitor management proposed by the Task Force's
working group on the countryside – designed to ensure harmony between
tourism, the environment and host populations. These include appeals to
market analysis, an assessment of capacity, further use of marketing, more
use of interpretation, selective management of access, sensitive design
controls and increased zoning of different activities in time and space. While
the use of these techniques is designed to conserve particular *a priori*
defined environmental qualities, such techniques may further structure

collective experiences of countryside spaces. Thus individual leisure experiences become increasingly managed and mediated by institutions and countryside providers. One effect of such a strategy would be to limit the possibilities for the visitor to discover a countryside spontaneously, to restrict spaces where people can create their own worlds and meanings, where people are conceived as more than 'users' or 'consumers', and where the countryside exists, not as pre-defined qualities, but as something essentially mysterious, undiscovered and somehow indescribable – a very different space of representation, to return to Lefebvre's categories.

Paradoxically, while countryside providers tend to be aware of some these motivating factors (the popularity of which is contributing to this newly found institutional desire for visitor management), there remains a lack of institutional sensitivity to how proposed controls may succeed in regulating access to these special qualities, often by transforming what is perceived as special in the first place. In this sense, these new representations of space are a second-order form of discipline to the countryside leisure-use. Here the language of discipline, surveillance and control appears particularly apt in this new rhetoric, capturing a diversity of ways in which recreation and countryside managers, policy-makers and government officials are identifying the environment dynamic as offering new possibilities of representing space, of ordering, managing and controlling the public.

The third disciplinary tendency lies in the commodification of countryside spaces. Such rhetorics are most evident in the Task Force documents (Department of Employment Task Force 1991) and the English Tourist Board's *Planning for Success* (1991; and see UK Cabinet Office 1995). The latter argues, for example, that there are few tensions between the needs for environmentally benign sustainable tourism and the needs for tourism growth within the countryside. Moreover, not only are new opportunities proposed for increased economic exploitation of leisure and tourism, but the English countryside as a set of highly marketable qualities in themselves is itself proposed for greater economic exploitation.

Many of these opportunities arise from the popular conception of the countryside as the object of a 'romantic' gaze. At present, much of the commodifying processes in the open countryside is occuring in indirect forms (for example, in the increased membership of countryside organisations, and the expanding markets dedicated to countryside clothing and equipment) and to a lesser extent in direct forms (for example, in charging for access and car parking to nature reserves and other sites of spectacular natural beauty). New market-oriented policies may further engender added pressures for different modes of spatial and temporal access to the countryside to be linked to direct and non-direct forms of payment, justified not least through the added costs arising from applying new techniques of visitor management. Such tendencies can already be identified in organisations owning large tracts of the countryside such as the Forestry Commission, the National Trust and the privatised water companies.

Further, the application of such policies may lead to the marketing and further economic exploitation of a wide range of rural activities such as hunting, shooting, fishing and golf; the recent growth in the last of these being one area of contention between developers, local authorities and conservation groups such as the Council for the Protection of Rural England. Each course uses up between 125 and 150 acres and contributes to an array of land-use pressures. They may also further legitimate the recent explosion of new and often highly specialised countryside activities, such as war games, mountain biking and jet skiing (for more detail on all of this, see Clark et al. 1994a, 1994b). There is already huge economic potential arising from the associated development of facilities accommodating such heightened interest in the outdoor – in the form of farm accommodation, camp sites and caravan parks, hotels, time-share accommodation and the highly popular type of holiday villages pioneered by Center Parcs. One government-sponsored report estimates potential demand for a dozen of more holiday villages in Britain alone (NEDO 1992). Each 'village' caters for 250,000 visitors a year, is located in a 'rural' location, uses up between 400 and 600 acres, is typically screened from other activities, and is self-contained.

Such commodification of the countryside has far-reaching social effects. It implies that the countryside will be increasingly consumed as spectacle. Potent images and symbols become readily transformed into saleable commodities. One effect of this lies in the divorce of these saleable qualities from their social and historical context, and the subsequent general loss of the local distinctiveness of countryside places. Countryside spaces become spectacles devised by marketing strategies, earmarked as 'attractions', and where the environmental qualities of countryside places become identified as commodities, devised in marketing plans to enhance economic value. This scenario may help to explain the recent appeals to 'green' tourism by corporate interests and government tourist boards, and the apparent ease and slight effort involved in presenting a 'green' and environmentally friendly image by corporate leisure interests, such as British Airways and Center Parcs. Although this new commercial interest in the environment might produce more sensitive design of buildings, the conservation of such habitats and places of rarity, and the preservation of some of the 'look' of the landscape (the physical appearance being one characteristic that the planning system is particularly adapted to), it also involves a less noticeable but much altered cultural landscape of signposted, saleable commodities or attractions which are dotted about the countryside and which increasingly structure people's movement through it.

We also argue that public agencies adopt a narrow conception both of the leisure function of the countryside and of the boundaries of people's countryside needs. This functions to ensure that public agencies see as outside their remit any consideration of how their policies may be structuring the collective experiences of such affordances. For example, the English Tourist Board can claim that there exist few social or environmental problems over current predictions of economic growth in the countryside only through defining the countryside as principally a resource to be utilised for tourism, and through treating people's tourism needs in terms of 'quality and value for money'. Considered this way, people's legitimate concerns are implicitly defined as relating to receiving 'a high quality countryside product expressed via the market place'. In effect, this rhetoric acts as a third level of disciplinary logic where one's relationship to the qualities which tempt people to the countryside in the first place is not only separated from the leisure subject (the visual space of representation); where the public are not only carefully controlled by increasingly sophisticated techniques of leisure management (the managerial representation of space); but where one is also increasingly likely to have to pay for these managed qualities so as to maximise the economic opportunities that exist in the countryside for a growing tourist industry (the spatial practice of commodification).

We have thus identified three disciplinary tendencies and argued that they fit together into an emerging social spatialisation of the countryside. Lefebvre's typology is particularly useful in highlighting the partial and exclusionary aspects of current policy on countryside leisure, and of the potential mismatch between people's broader aspirations for countryside spaces and those most likely to be generated through the techniques of state planning and management and the further intensification of the market. The attempts by the state to develop an environmentally sensitive countryside are seen to coincide with policies to expand tourism by new methods of state and self-surveillance. Such policies share a common rhetoric where the aims and objectives between the different policy organisations coincide more than conflict with each other. In many circumstances this is clearly the case: policies which focus on the beauty of the countryside as opposed to one's freedom over it clearly invite new methods of visitor management, and policies of visitor management can easily lead to new methods of payment for use. In essence, what these documents reveal is that policies of environmental sustainability fit within a reinvigoured instrumentalist doctrine. One's apparent enjoyment of the countryside is increasingly balanced by one's payment for it in this emerging social spatialisation of the English countryside.

We examine such issues from a different direction and methodology in the next section where we focus not on the official discourses of the countryside but on the complex attitudes and values which people exhibit in relation to it and especially to what they perceive as threats to that countryside. In effect the next section begins to unravel some of the complexity in how people conceive of and engage in countryside practices. In particular we examine some of the responses that people exhibit to the landscaping, management and commodification of the English countryside, to various contestations of the diverse affordances of the countryside (see Gibson 1979; Michael 1996: 149–50).

The countryside and ambivalence

Policy-makers increasingly endeavour to detect the changing expectations and motivations of the public. Particularly important is the commissioning of opinion surveys and other forms of attitudinal research in order to determine the changing contours of people's beliefs, values and concerns – the polling culture discussed in chapter 3. The logic of such analysis is that by asking people to respond to certain statements, it is possible to determine people's underlying values and attitudes in order that government agencies or private companies can better provide for such apparent 'needs'. In this section we report on research we undertook designed to examine the framework underpinning such attitudinal surveys within the specific realm of leisure activities in the English countryside (see Clark et al. 1994a, 1994b; and see Macnaghten 1995).

Of the government agencies concerned with rural leisure, the Countryside Commission have been the most concerned to monitor public opinion through attitude surveys. These studies have been used by the Commission as evidence of the general profile of countryside users, of what people do when visiting the countryside, of the main sources of countryside change and threat, and of people's key motivations and expectations from the countryside (see Countryside Commission 1984, 1986a, 1986b, 1987). Such results have been used to confirm the continuing popularity of visits to the countryside; the importance of the local countryside and especially the activity of walking; the strong attitudes people have towards threats and changes to the countryside, shared equally across town-dwellers and country-dwellers; the high level of concern people have towards the conservation of the natural environment; the increasing cultural significance of an attractive and beautiful countryside; the identification of the countryside as a natural place which offers peace and solitude; the high regard in which the countryside is held by people from all walks of life, and the way in which countryside experiences are cherished.

However, attitudinal research has clear limitations in its ability to clarify the complexity of people's views and concerns. In recent years the epistemological foundations of attitudinal research have been criticised for presupposing a one-dimensional model of the person and for suppressing the latent variability in people's thinking (Billig 1987, 1991; Moscovici 1984; Potter and Wetherell 1987, 1988; chapter 3 above). Billig has pioneered a 'rhetorical' approach to analysis in which attitudes are placed in their wider argumentative and historical contexts:

> If the argumentative aspects of attitudes are stressed, then attitudes are not to be viewed solely as individual evaluative responses to a given stimulus object. Instead, attitudes are stances in matters of controversy: they are positions in arguments (Billig, 1987; 1993). Every attitude *in favour* of a position is also, implicitly but more often explicitly, also a stance *against* the counter-position. Because attitudes are stances on matters of controversy, we can expect attitude holders to justify their position and to criticise the counter-position. (1988a: 84)

Thus while attitudinal research has produced data which supposedly reveal the underlying preferences of people towards various issues, it is argued in criticism that people are more ambiguous, contradictory and dilemmatic than this traditional attitude theory supposes. It is also maintained that the contradictions and variabilities of response which are apparently located *within* individuals actually reflect much wider discursive positions (Billig 1989a, 1989b).

These arguments are especially pertinent to people's concerns and views on nature and the environment (including issues around countryside leisure), as an exemplary arena where societal and policy agendas are often contradictory, paradoxical and highly controversial. Instead of assuming that people have stable and consistent views and attitudes to the countryside and appropriate forms of leisure as proposed in traditional attitudinal research, we suggest an alternative epistemological position. For us the countryside exists as a contested social category which reflects ongoing contemporary public disputes. These contested understandings of the countryside are as likely to be present within each individual as within the public sphere of civil society. Hence there are likely to be few stable, consistent and fixed attitudes present within each individual which are simply waiting to be released by the appropriate survey question. Such questions will in part be answered in terms of the discursive understandings within which they are embedded.

From this perspective we developed a research framework in which different primary needs of countryside leisure were devised in terms of three different 'voices' about the countryside and about what processes might be good for its development and what might threaten it. This analysis develops Bakhtin's (1981) claim that all texts exhibit polyphony, that there is no single monologic utterance, but rather there are a variety of voices struggling for dominance. We then employed an attitude survey to identify whether people's expressed views and attitudes to identical issues of countryside leisure would vary in line with alternative arguments currently voiced as to the nature of the English countryside. Attitudes which appear contradictory when out of context are understandable when located within alternative social and political contexts.

To test the extent of expressed public ambivalence, seven controversies over leisure uses of the English countryside were examined. These were identified as the most prominent cultural disputes in the early 1990s over the 'leisured' uses of nature as countryside.

The seven controversies surveyed were:

1 *Whether farmers should be allowed to charge walkers in return for access over their land.* Dilemmas over whether access and use of the countryside should be priced have recently emerged in policy responses to the rising demand for access to the countryside, as we saw above. Using the framework of environmental economics (see Pearce et al. 1989), these

possibilities are currently being debated and assessed not just by academics, but also by government agencies (the Countryside Commission, the Forestry Commission and English Nature), conservation groups (National Trust) and privatised water companies.

2 *Whether people should have more general rights of access over the countryside.* Access debates are part of a much older history of public controversy, often between rural landowners and a largely urban population. Contemporary disputes frequently draw upon wider controversies over ownership, class and public 'rights' (see Shoard 1980, 1987). The Ramblers Association's campaign for more general access over the wider countryside, highlighted in 'Forbidden Britain days' of symbolic mass trespass, has increasing popular support in terms of escalating membership (now nearly 90,000), and is a political and cultural theme of continuing significance in the 1990s.

3 *Whether car use in the countryside should be officially restricted.* Conflicts over the increased use of cars in the countryside and the associated loss of tranquillity and 'ruralness' has emerged as, perhaps, the most tangible and widely recognised dilemma between people's increasing desire for personal mobility and their accumulative social and environmental impacts (see Countryside Commission 1992).

4 *Whether local authorities should encourage new leisure developments in the countryside.* The dilemmas over local authorities and leisure related developments arise from their dual functions of encouraging economic regeneration *and* as protecting 'green space'.

5 *Whether noisy sports and leisure should be permitted in the countryside.* Perhaps the best publicised public controversy surrounding noisy sports is encapsulated in the public inquiry into a 10 mph speed limit on Windermere in the English Lake District, and the competing arguments as to whether the Lake District is the right sort of place for powerboating and the kinds of people who choose such noisy and energetic water sports.

6 *Whether new age traveller festivals are a legitimate use of the countryside.* This issue has become one of the most contentious and high profile sources of countryside conflict in recent years. New age travellers represent an extremely uncomfortable 'leisure' use of the countryside for government agencies, far removed from the sanitised world of theme parks, marinas and informal recreation. However, their undoubted popularity and their own evolving 'tribal' culture suggest a significant new cultural configuration, with latent public sympathy, especially among many young people who themselves occasionally attend raves and festivals in the countryside.

7 *Whether the use of national quality standards is seen to homogenise the distinctive local character of the countryside.* The promotion of 'local distinctiveness' and sense of place has become an issue of growing political significance, which is likely to conflict with increasingly vocal appeals for national standards in the sphere of countryside leisure.

These are seven major examples of current tensions and conflict over leisure in the English countryside. The research we undertook sought to see how each person, as a user or potential user of the countryside, could hold a range of different and even conflicting opinions or 'attitudes' concerning the legitimacy of these countryside uses and of the potential threats to that countryside that they pose. To undertake this analysis three separate 'voices' were devised to reflect different conceptions of the desirable character of the countryside and of what leisure is appropriate within it.

The first voice or context emphasises the economic role of leisure and tourism in rejuvenating local rural economies. This voice was thought to engender attitudes more in sympathy with development in the countryside, charging policies, noisy sports and an increased use of quality standards. It was introduced to interviewees as follows:

> I would now like to talk to you about the British countryside. Many people feel that the countryside is a wonderful place for tourists and visitors. However, many visitors would like better countryside facilities and attractions. These new developments would help local people by bringing in much needed money and jobs into rural areas. I am going to read out some statements which other people have made about tourism and the countryside and would like you to tell me how much you agree or disagree with each one.

The second voice conceives of the countryside as a place of peace and natural beauty which needs strong protection. This voice was thought to engender attitudes which were less sympathetic to charging policies, festivals, noisy sports, the increased use of quality standards, unrestricted car use, general rights to roam, and new leisure and tourist developments:

> I would now like to talk to you about the British countryside. Many people value the peace and natural beauty of the British countryside in an increasingly polluted world. They feel that efforts must be made to preserve the countryside by making sure that people use it carefully and responsibly. I am going to read out some statements which other people have made about conserving the countryside and would like you to tell me how much you agree or disagree with each one.

The third voice thinks of the countryside as a place of freedom and escape. This voice was hypothesised to engender attitudes which were more sympathetic to unpaid access, the opportunity to ramble freely across the countryside, new developments, noisy sports and new age traveller festivals:

> I would now like to talk to you about the British countryside. More and more people want to escape the towns and cities and enjoy the freedom of the countryside. Nowadays there are lots of opportunities to have fun in the countryside and to enjoy the open air. I am going to read out some statements which other people have made about enjoying the countryside and would like you to tell me how much you agree or disagree with each one.

The research examines whether people's expressed attitudes in a survey depended on how the particular issue is framed by the researcher. This was tested by introducing the same countryside leisure dilemmas in surveys conducted in three consecutive weeks with samples that were essentially the same as each other. The predictions were thus concerned less with the actual

content of the expressed 'attitudes' towards the seven leisure dilemmas and
more with the predicted differences between the three voices or contexts
towards the same issues in the different surveys. The predicted 'attitudes'
are presented in table 6.1 (the gaps in the table are where the voices were
deemed to have no direct relationship to the statements and so were not
asked in the research).

Table 6.1   *Predicted attitudes for voices and leisure dilemmas*

Leisure dilemmas	Voice 1 (economic development)	Voice 2 (quiet recreation/ beauty)	Voice 3 (escape and freedom)
1 Farmers allowed to charge for access	More in favour	Less in favour	Less in favour
2 General rights to roam in countryside		Less in favour	More in favour
3 Car use should be unrestricted in countryside	More in favour	Less in favour	More in favour
4 New developments permitted in countryside	More in favour	Less in favour	More in favour
5 Noisy sports permitted in countryside	More in favour	Less in favour	More in favour
6 New age festivals permitted in countryside		Less in favour	More in favour
7 National standards for new developments	More in favour	Less in favour	

The research was carried out by Research Surveys Great Britain (RSGB),
a national opinion poll and survey organisation, on three separate weeks
using a randomised sample of 1,000 subjects for each voice. Each survey
was based on a representative sample of male and female adults in England,
aged 16 or over. They were selected from a minimum of 130 sampling
points and interviewed at home. The respondents had 'the same' composition in each week, although the samples were composed of different
individuals. Before we analysed the data, the scores for the 'don't knows'
were removed and the scores to each of the other responses were presented
so that positive scores and negative scores for the corresponding versions of
each issue referred to agreement or disagreement on the same issue (for
certain questions the + and − scores were inverted to ensure direct
comparison). A scale was devised between +2 and −2 (see Macnaghten
1995 for detailed results).

Overall the hypothesis that the context or voice significantly affects the
expressed attitudes towards key aspects of the countryside and what is
deemed to be threatening it is generally supported by the research. The one
exception occurred over the first issue, as to whether farmers should charge
for access to the countryside. Respondents in the context of all three voices
showed marked opposition to this suggestion to more or less the same

degree. However, with regard to all the other six issues, the research shows substantial variation by voice:

- there is a large difference of expressed opinion over the right to roam policy: the pro-freedom voice producing strong support for the right, the pro-quietness voice generating marked opposition;
- the pro-quietness voice generates pronounced opposition to the unrestricted use of the car in the countryside, seeing it as a significant threat to the countryside; while the other two voices generate much more ambivalent attitudes;
- the pro-development and pro-freedom voices generate support for new tourist developments within the countryside, neither seeing them as particularly threatening; while the pro-quietness voice generates strong opposition to such developments;
- the pro-quietness voice produces very marked opposition both to noisy countryside sports and to new age travellers and festivals, while the other two voices are relatively ambivalent;
- the pro-development voice generates strong support for national quality standards in leisure developments, while the pro-quietness voice produces marked opposition to such standards.

Thus there is a marked variation of response across the three voices. This is a striking set of findings. The same issues are understood in different ways when the issues are contextualised differently. In all but the issue concerning whether farmers should be allowed to charge for access, the differences in expressed opinion across the voices is most significant. The research shows the extent to which the same people will often take on diametrically opposed positions on the very same countryside controversy when such a controversy is conceived of within a different frame or voice.

Elsewhere we have argued that the different agencies of UK government implicitly assume that people have different primary needs in relation to countryside leisure (Clark et al. 1994a). We suggested that the Sports Council assume a need for leisure related to active, competitive, formalised sports; that the Countryside Commission assume a need for leisure related to passive, quiet and solitary activities; and that the English Tourist Board assume a need for leisure related to 'value for money' and standards of service in exchange for consumption of services in the countryside. However, instead of arguing that these needs are complementary (a position currently stressed by government agencies which provide for rural leisure, such as the Countryside Commission [1991], English Tourist Board [1991] and Sports Council [1991]), we maintain that these different needs represent conflicting representations of space stemming from the remits and outlooks of the different agencies involved. And in this section the research briefly reported here supports these arguments by showing that people are much more ambivalent in their needs and expectations from nature and the countryside than has hitherto been presumed in policy-related research.

Our argument here is different from one which suggests that the public's ambiguous responses are simply an indication that people are generally confused in their attitudes. Such an interpretation would give public agencies scope to 'pick and choose' policies, or simply to justify doing nothing very much. By contrast, we argue here that government agencies and the private sector should be more responsive to the public's ambivalences about the countryside and what are appropriate forms of leisure. It is necessary to identify the cultural circumstances that are producing such ambiguous understandings in the first place, as we have sought to achieve in this book. Such an approach can help cast light on the recent controversy over the proposed ban on fox hunting, and on how opponents to the ban effectively framed the debate in terms of a polarised battle between town and country.

In particular, such organisations concerned with 'official' representations of countryside space need to respond to the exceptional variety of people's aspirations for adventure, sport, festivals, surprise, quietness, visual wonder, risk-taking, and so on, and certainly not to treat the countryside primarily as a marketplace where what gets organised is what can be given a price and then allocated through the market. Such heightened reflexivity can only arise when official representations of space respond to a wider range of competing spatial practices and spaces of representation of the countryside. Such official agencies have largely underestimated the depth of the cultural tensions in such key countryside leisure areas (Clark et al. 1994b). The lack of debate in such areas reflects not just how such issues cut across the remits of existing statutory agencies, but of how, in each of these conflicts, are reflected more widespread and intangible anxieties over the space of the countryside in post-industrial societies. Thus conflicts over 'the right to roam', 'new age travellers', or, indeed, 'local distinctiveness' simply cannot be unambiguously captured through idioms of 'beauty', 'landscape', 'sport', or 'service provision'. Rather they require alternative spaces of representation more appropriate to people's multi-faceted and contradictory aspirations and senses.

We endeavour to provide some notion of this in the final section here when we turn to examine a few of the spatial practices that people have sought to develop within the space of the countryside. Such spatial practices are not 'natural' to the countryside. It is no more natural to go walking up a hillside just for the sake of it than it is to drive a speedboat along Lake Windermere or to go skiing in the Alps, even if such practices have hugely divergent physical effects. These are all distinct practices and entail specific spatialisation. Such practices have had to be developed, given institutional form and located within complex processes of discrimination, distinction and taste within contemporary societies. It is those complex organisational and cultural processes which generate and harbour the ambivalences and contradictions that we have shown are part and parcel of the structure of people's feelings about the countryside briefly described in the research reported here.

Spatial practices in the countryside

In this and other chapters we have criticised various pieces of research for their tendency to abstraction – for failing to locate people's expressed attitudes and actions with regard to nature and the environment within the context of the specific social practices with which they are engaged. People's attitudes and actions have thus been abstracted out of the flows of social life. Such social practices are, as we emphasised in chapter 1, embodied, timed and spaced. In conclusion to this chapter we examine certain such practices, and following Lefebvre we will term these 'spatial practices'. It is our broader claim here that there is no single abstract countryside – only the specific countrysides produced and consumed in some societies in the context of diverse spatial practices. These different countrysides often stand in stark contrast with each other.

We encountered this contrast when seeing how certain tracts of land appropriate for the spatial practice of agriculture were transformed into landscapes for visual consumption in parts of England over the course of the eighteenth century. Wordsworth (1984), in his letters written in 1844 objecting to the building of the Kendal and Windermere Railway, emphasises that the development of the idea of landscape was strikingly recent. He notes that earlier travellers to the Alps made no reference to their beauty and sublime qualities. Indeed, with just one exception, every English traveller refers to the 'precipitous rocks and mountains . . . as objects of dislike and fear' (1984: 188). He also quotes a woman from whom he rented a room as a young man who said that everyone nowadays is 'always talking about prospects: when I was young there never [sic] a thing neamed' (Wordsworth 1984: 188). Furthermore, he maintains that well into the eighteenth century barns and other outbuildings were often placed in front of houses, 'however beautiful the landscape which their windows might otherwise have commanded' (1984: 188). Therefore 'a vivid perception of romantic scenery is neither inherent in mankind, nor a necessary consequence of even a comprehensive education' (1984: 188–9). He then proceeds to object to mass tourism, to the 'transferring at once uneducated persons in large bodies to particular spots' largely because such persons will lack the 'processes of culture or opportunities of observation in some degree habitual' (1984: 191, 189). But the main point to emphasise here is that Wordsworth maintains that the very idea of landscape was of recent origins.

Milton (1993b) has developed this distinction between the discourses and practices of what she terms 'land' and 'landscape'. The former entails conceptualising land as a physical, tangible resource which can be ploughed, sown, grazed, built upon. It is a place of work, conceived of functionally rather than aesthetically. As a tangible resource, 'land' can be bought and sold, inherited and especially left to children, either directly or through the rights established through use of the land over time. Such land may be directly owned and worked by the 'farmer' or there may be divorce of ownership and control. In many cases farming work, domestic work and leisure all take place in very close spatial proximity. To dwell on a farm is to participate in a pattern of life where productive and unproductive activities resonate with each other and with very particular tracts of land whose history and geography will often be known in intimate detail. Heidegger's (1977) notion of dwelling well captures the practice of 'land', where human subjects are apparently united with their environment (see also Thomas 1993: 27–9). The world so constructed 'on the land' is part of people's dwelling. There is a lack of distance between people and things, an engagement which arises through the use of land rather than through the distanced and detached relationships of landscape.

But it should also be noted that land also entails patterns of dwelling that are irreducibly internationalised, as we noted in chapter 5 where we set out the lineaments of dwellingness in a global context. Any particular farm and its practices are dependent upon shifts in primary commodity prices on a world scale or the latest directives from the EU. Farms are tied into complex networks of markets and states. Also such 'land' and its dwellingness does not provide exhaustive rights to ownership and control. Complete strangers may exercise historical rights to walk over agricultural land, often close to places of dwelling, or they may seek to prevent the pursuit of particular leisure practices which are viewed by locals as part of land and its dwellingness. Simultaneously other strangers may seek to regulate the look of the land, to make it consistent with particular aesthetic conceptions of 'landscape', whether or not this is functionally appropriate as 'land'.

Thus the spatial practice of 'land' may contradict with that of 'landscape'. The latter entails an intangible resource whose definitive feature is that of appearance or look resulting from one version or other of the gaze (Milton 1993b). The notion of landscape emphasises leisure, relaxation and the visual consumption of the countryside. In the late twentieth century landscapes are held to be communally owned, a 'sort of national property'. They should be available to all those who want to look, either briefly through the spectatorial gaze or lingeringly through a more prolonged gaze. There are many ways in which such landscapes are encountered, while walking, driving, climbing, photographing, and so on. If people can gain access to the landscape through one or more of these spatial practices, then it is presumed that they should be able to consume that landscape visually, as we discussed in chapter 4. The rights embodied in landscape are also those of future generations who constitute potential viewers of landscape, and not just those of the current owners of any particular tract of land. Especially the rights formulated through the environmental movement are concerned with potential observers of landscape in the often distant future and not just the rights of those who currently 'dwell' on the land.

These competing discourses and practices of land and landscape come into the sharpest contradiction through certain spatial practices by which those seeking to experience landscape endeavour to 'dwell' on the land. There are many variations in such practices. We can distinguish between how such 'landscapers' enter the land, how long they stay, what other senses they deploy, what kinds of sensuous intrusion they effect, what they demand while enjoying the landscape, what practices they generate through the market to service them, how they move across the land, and the kinds of gaze they seek to realise. In the rest of this chapter we will very briefly characterise a number of such spatial practices and point to some of the consequences that they have for the countryside and for the relationships of production and consumption that inhabit such spaces. Overall we seek to demonstrate further the spatially embedded processes by which particular 'countrysides' have come to be produced and consumed.

We begin with perhaps the most obvious practice, that of walking. Over the course of the nineteenth century in England walking gradually came to be viewed as a positive choice and not something that people had to undertake because of necessity. Since ordinary people increasingly did not have to walk because of various developments in transport, so walkers were not now regarded as necessarily poor. Likewise women walkers were not considered disreputable, as they had always been presumed to be before (unless on a pilgrimage). Hewison (1993) nicely makes this point about pre-nineteenth-century walkers (that is, 'vagrants'):

> when Shakespeare's King Lear leaves court to wander on the heath, he does not meet bobble-hatted hikers in sensible boots enjoying a refreshing tramp across the moors. He is among the naked, the starving and the mad, the excluded of society in this hostile wilderness.

Wallace (1993) argues that the following factors transformed the material and ideological shape of walking (Bunce 1994: chap. 4). Transport changes from the late eighteenth century onwards, especially the turnpikes and then the railway, gradually removed the association of walking with necessity, poverty and vagrancy. The railway was particularly instrumental in the development of 'rambling' and of socialist campaigns for access to open land. Further, the diversity of modes of transport increasingly enabled people to compare and contrast different forms of mobility, and on occasions to see the virtues of slower ways of overcoming the friction of distance. Agricultural changes threatened existing rights of way that walkers in particular were keen to keep open through regular usage. And there was the development of a new discourse, the 'peripatetic', which increasingly represented excursive walking as a cultivating experience which was capable of refreshing the individual and society. Wallace argues that such a walking practice 'preserves some portion of local topographies against widespread, nationalising physical changes and, by extension, partially preserves the sites in which the ideal values of agrarian England were supposed to have flourished', including of course those of landscape rather than land (1993: 12).

During the nineteenth century there was an increasing appreciation of how aesthetic choice was one of the main reasons why people went walking voluntarily. There was an extensive growth in excursive walking – and this resulted from the widespread belief that walking as travel had personal and social benefits ('rambling' as such is incidentally said to have begun within nineteenth-century towns). Moreover, this was a disciplined and organised mode of walking well reflected in Wordsworth's choice of the term 'the excursion' (see Wallace 1993: chap. 3). This he uses to refer to the walking tour. The walker does not wander aimlessly or in a socially disruptive fashion. The wanderer returns continually along paths that have already been walked. This ensures connection and stability and in particular there is the intention to return. Wallace (1993: 122) interestingly discusses the notion of the 'wanderer' in Wordsworth; that it is not a withdrawal from community but a deliberate, directed labour undertaken to remake the individual and the home. This conspicuous example set especially by Wordsworth and Coleridge in the Lake District stimulated pedestrian activity by their contemporaries and then by many other relatively affluent men in the nineteenth century. The distances walked by the intellectuals of the period were prodigious: William Hazlitt claimed to walk 40 or 50 miles a day; De Quincey walked 70 to 100 miles a week; and Keats apparently covered 642 miles during his 1818 tour of the Lakes and Scotland (Wallace 1993: 166–7). By the middle of the century 'the very highest echelon of English society regarded pedestrian touring as a valuable educational experience' (Wallace 1993: 168). It had become particularly associated with 'the intellectual classes', who had begun to develop quite complex justifications, a 'peripatetic theory' based upon the way that the pedestrian is supposedly re-created with nature.

During the twentieth century this peripatetic theory becomes taken up and transformed by other classes and social groups, especially during the interwar period. Matless (1995) shows that open-air leisure in general and walking in particular took on a new scale and scope. The 'unnatural' character of such leisurely walking can be seen from its particular spatial specificity, as is evident from the English Lake District. Surrounding that 'District' are a string of once-significant industrial towns which are in many senses marginal to the margins of England (Barrow, Cleator Moor, Workington, Whitehaven; see Urry 1995b: chap. 13). Chapman, on the basis of some ethnographic materials, summarises the hyper-marginality of this West Cumbrian area as follows:

> This area is emphatically not part of the Lake District. . . . The great majority of the British population knows little or nothing about this area. . . . The existence of the area is, most importantly, scarcely acknowledged by most people who frequent 'the Lakes'. . . . Hundreds of thousands look out over it, from the summits of Lakeland peaks, but their eyes are on the horizon. (1993: 197)

Their eyes are on the landscape and not on the land and its forms of dwelling. Chapman describes walking into one of these towns, Cleator Moor (plate 6.1), wearing clothing appropriate for walking in the Lake District, that is, breeches, boots, brightly coloured socks, orange waterproofs and a rucksack. Instead of feeling intrepid, as one is permitted to do on descending a modest Lakeland mountain into Ambleside or Keswick, he felt acutely out of place. He was wearing what would be seen as fancy-dress in Cleator Moor – he had literally walked *out* of the Lake District and its particular

Plate 6.1   *Cleator Moor: on the margins of the Lake District (source: John Urry)*

sense of place and of its appropriate spatial practices, namely, leisurely walking. The Lake District is

> the *locus classicus* of high-minded and privileged leisure, wealthy, rural and beautiful, a national playground for the healthy and the thoughtful, with stone-built hotels in parks of rhododendron. West Cumbria, and Cleator Moor particularly, represents a desolate and unregarded landscape of industry declining, industry departed and high unemployment. (Chapman 1993: 205–6)

The most extensive conceptual discussion of walking is that found in de Certeau (1984). He regards walking as constitutive of the city in the way that speech acts are of language. In particular, he contrasts the strategies and the tactics of walking. The former involve the victory of space over time, or what we would call the victory of spatial practice and the scopic representations of space over spaces of representation. Strategies involve disciplining and regimentation, based upon notions of what are proper activities and ways of walking in particular spaces. Tactics by contrast consist of the seizing of opportunities that arise through time within the city. They serve to constitute lived space and are improvisational and unpredictable (see also Edensor 1996). Walking here is privileged – it is stimulated by a plethora of desires and goals stemming from the interrelations between bodily movement, fantasy, memory and texture.

Walkers and walking thus give shape to space, producing new spatial practices and spaces of representation. This production of new spaces has been most effectively shown in the case of the Haussmannisation of Paris (see of course Berman 1983). The city came to belong to those who were able to consume it as they walked along the new boulevards and passed by and into the brightly lit shops and cafés, a kaleidoscope which changes, stirs, bemuses (Green 1990: 75). Such *flâneurs* were able to give themselves ecstatically to the crowd, as Baudelaire poignantly describes. But of course walking was very different for working-class women in late nineteenth-century Paris. For them the crowd was full of risks; such women lived almost literally on the streets; they would have been presumed to be sexually available as prostitutes; and the new city was overwhelming in size and grandeur (see Edholm 1993).

On the basis of research on walking practices at the Taj Mahal, Edensor (1996) argues that de Certeau over-emphasises the subversive and liberating tactics of walking. He suggests that there are quite different walking practices within 'enclavic tourist spaces' as opposed to that across 'disorganised tourist spaces'. In the former walking is relatively smooth and ordered. There is rapid movement and the clear functions of different zones eradicate confusion. Various personnel are responsible for regulating the walking practices of visitors, who anyway have often internalised just how to effect appropriate walking in such areas. Space dominates time and, contra de Certeau, there is little opportunity for fantasy, memory and desire to effect tactical subversion. Walking in the countryside often takes a regulated form, in the UK with a country code, park rangers and many maps, guides and signposts to lead people along the right paths and then to return along those paths. Also the risks of particular routes are often emphasised and visitors to hilly areas are encouraged to reveal to hotel owners the paths that will be walked along. There is thus a remarkable choreography of walking with walking bodies being tutored so that they come to be held in particular ways (see Edensor 1996: chap. 3; Shields 1991: 53).

By contrast, progress through disorganised tourist spaces, especially by backpackers, will normally be less programmed in advance. Walking may be more improvisational and entail vivid encounters with very diverse and disruptive elements. Local people will often seek to interrupt movement through particular spaces, and physical contact will be difficult to avoid. Contact with vehicles and animals will also be unavoidable. The trajectories of visitors will coexist with and criss-cross local pathways. Edensor argues that this engenders less rigid bodily postures and a more casual wandering and lounging, even to an extent of seeking out risky environments and getting lost. One might thus imagine that walking in the Indian countryside would exhibit many of these characteristics, by contrast with the much more enclavic space of the English countryside. However, this too would oversimplify the multiple tactics and strategies that can be employed in spatial practice. One can note, for example, how many backpackers visit the same places even in India, usually in the company of other foreigners, appropriating sights through limited spaces of representation. One can note also the new array of practices which seek to transgress the formalised representations of space of the English countryside, such as those employed at raves and festivals.

Edensor (1996: chap. 6) also brings out the walking practices of domestic Indian visitors to the Taj Mahal. Particularly interesting is his account of Muslim visitors. They tend to stay longer than other domestic Indians and approach the Taj with exceptional veneration. They linger a long time in the grounds, particularly reading the Quranic script on the building (something almost all western visitors will wholly miss, whatever their walking practices). They exhibit a 'reverential gaze' as they slowly circumambulate the mausoleum or sit on the marble terrace in silent contemplation. Edensor summarises their walking practices:

> the movement of Muslim visitors follows a purposive and predictable spatial pattern but one which differs from the directed routes of Western package tourists, the meanderings of the backpackers, and . . . the routes of other domestic tourists. (1996: 247)

Other related walking practices of course involve the ascent of hills and mountains, something originating in Europe in the Alps and then transferred to various other countries. The most striking example of how the process of mountain climbing has become part of mass tourism is in relationship to Mount Everest. Walking up Everest is now on various tourist itineraries, so much so that on one day in the early 1990s 32 climbers reached the summit (Weaver 1992). Even more strikingly, 10,000 trekkers a year make it to the Everest base camp at 18,000 feet. It is reckoned that as a consequence there are currently at least 60 tons of human rubbish on Mount Everest. It has been suggested that trekking to Everest has even become part of the Hollywood identity, a kind of rite of passage for the most thoroughbred of stars.

One feature of both walking and climbing is the idea of effort. It is presumed that only if some natural feature involves effort to climb it or get to it can it be properly appreciated; the term 'travel' after all comes from *travail*, to work (see Buzard 1993). This emphasis upon effort is well-shown in Barthes' (1972) analysis of the *Guide Bleu*. Barthes argues that the *Guide* combines together three characteristics: the cult of nature, puritanism and an individualistic ideology. Morality is associated with effort and solitude. Certain social practices then are only deemed appropriate within nature or to know nature if they entail a more or less solitary achievement, particularly to overcome uneven ground, mountains, gorges, torrents, and so on. Barthes talks of how the *Guide* emphasises 'regeneration through clean air, moral ideas at the sight of mountain tops, summit climbing as civic virtue, etc.' (1972: 74). Such practices therefore cannot overcome the friction of distance unproblematically or effortlessly. The individual must travel in order to appreciate nature, and so these various spatial practices entail lengthy and often very slow movement; to some extent slowness is itself highly valued. It should also be noted that the countryside is itself partly remade out of these practices and the attempts to produce practices which demonstrate such effort.

But of course there are a wide variety of spatial practices, new ways of 'dwelling' in the countryside, which are by no means slow. The stagecoach, the railway, the bike, the motor coach, the motor cycle and especially the car have generated new and disruptive forms of spatial practice within the countryside. Our interest in such developments stems from what Thrift (1996) characterises as a new 'structure of feeling' within the academy focused upon 'mobility'. In various ways these new mobilities all involve machines which propel humans through the countryside. Such machines thus combine with humans to effect a restructured agency which is neither really machinic nor human but a complex interrelationship involving both. They form what Lyotard (1992) terms the 'inhuman'. Theorising the inhuman means that we need to reject the characteristic division of western thought between humans and non-humans; to emphasise that objects are not mere receptacles of the human subject; to draw out that there are various 'actants' in the world and not just humans; to identify many phenomena which combine what have historically been thought of as separate physical and human properties; to reject any sense that the boundaries of the human are given by human skin because of the widespread growth of various prosthetic technologies; to analyse more generally the development of a cyborg culture which disrupts fixed gender and other identifications; to understand how machines are troublesome companions and not to be viewed as simply all-powerful; to realise that so-called objects may in fact possess human-like characteristics (the computer virus); and to investigate what Haraway (1991) terms the 'machinic complexes' of embodied subjects, machines, texts and metaphors which organise and reorganise social practice (see Bijker and Law 1991; Latour 1993; Michael 1996; Thrift 1996).

In the following we consider two new machinic practices: the nineteenth-century invention of the railway; and the early twentieth-century growth of the car culture in Britain and North America. The first of these practices was of course exceptionally important in the structuring of the modern con-sciousness (see Schivelbusch 1986; Thrift 1996; and see chapter 4 above on the related 'invention' of photography). The growth of the railway brought machinery into the foreground of people's everyday experience outside the workplace. An incredibly powerful, moving mechanical apparatus became a relatively familiar feature of everyday life, especially in or perhaps across the countryside. The age of the train generated one of the most distinctive experiences of the modern world, restructuring for many people the existing relations between nature, time and space.

The very building of the railways flattened and subdued the existing countryside in unique fashion. Rail travellers were propelled through space as though they were mere parcels. The train was a projectile slicing through the landscape on level, straight tracks, over bridges and embankments and through cuttings and tunnels. The landscape came to be viewed as a swiftly passing series of framed panoramas, rather than something which was to be lingered over, sketched or painted. As Nietzsche notes about the late nineteenth century: 'everyone is like the traveller who gets to know a land and its people from a railway carriage' (cited Thrift 1996: 286). Passengers were thrown together with large numbers of strangers in an enclosed space and new ways of maintaining social distance had to be developed. The much greater pace of rail traffic meant that the existing patchwork of local times had to be replaced with a standardised time based on Greenwich (see chapter 5 above). And the exceptional mechanical power of the railway appeared to be creating its own space as it linked all sorts of places in more and more complex and extended systems of circulation. Particular places became known as on the way to, or on the way from, somewhere else. One commentator writing in 1839 argued that if railways spread all over England, then the population

> would . . . sit nearer to one another by two-thirds of the time which now respectively alienates them. . . . As distances were thus annihilated, the surface of our country would, as it were, shrivel in size until it became not much bigger than one immense city. (cited Schivelbusch 1986: 34; and see Harvey 1989 more generally on time-space compression)

Huge anxieties were generated as a result of such speeding projectiles racing through the countryside; and this of course provoked Romantic responses to such a 'rash assault'. As Ruskin maintains: 'all travelling becomes dull in exact proportion to its rapidity' (cited Liniado 1996: 6; see Thrift 1996: 264–7).

Speed and its effects were equally at issue when the earliest cars came onto the scene in the late nineteenth century (see Liniado 1996 on the following). This was a period in which various new kinds of speeding machines had come to the fore (Kern 1983). There was a preoccupation with the breaking of records, especially as these were recorded by increasingly precise watches. Life appeared to be accelerating as humans and machines combined in new and intricate 'machinic complexes', of which the auto-mobile was the most dramatic. The shock of seeing cars racing through the English countryside provoked intensely heightened opposition between rustic images of a defenceless countryside already ravaged by the Great Depression, as against images of technological progress and the dominance of a machine culture (Liniado 1996: 7).

There was an obsession with the setting of new speed records as controversy raged over the costs and benefits of speed. Many motorists described their experience of speed in mystical terms, as though this was an experience not so much opposed to nature but as expressing the inner forces of the universe (Liniado 1996: 7). The author Filson Young wrote of the experience of riding in a racing car as 'the exultation of the dreamer, the drunkard, a thousand times purified and magnified' (cited Liniado 1996: 7). He well captures the cyborgised character of such a machinic complex:

> It is, I think, a combination of intense speed with the sensation of smallness, the lightness, the responsiveness of the thing that carries you, with the rushing of the atmosphere upon your body and the earth upon your vision. (cited Liniado 1996: 7)

Elsewhere he writes of the racing driver having to wrestle with the speed, power and dynamism of the car and of the need to tame it rather like a Nietzschean *Übermensch* struggling with the intense natural forces of life and power.

One important discursive feature of the emerging spatial practice of motoring was the idea of the 'open road', especially since in its early years the motor car was regarded as a vehicle for pleasure. Indeed there are diverse ways in which the technology of the car has been organised since it does not constitute a single machinic complex. The concept of the 'open road' legitimated the slow meandering motor tour which became a highly favoured upper-middle-class pursuit in Edwardian England. This was so especially after the exceptional uncertainties of car travel had been partially overcome (Bunce 1994; Liniado 1996; Thrift 1996). Motor touring was thought of as 'a voyage through the life and history of the land'. There was an increasing emphasis upon slower means of finding such pleasures. To tour, to stop, to drive slowly, to take the longer route, to emphasise process rather than destination, all became part of the spatial practice or performed art of motor touring (see Adler 1989b). Filson Young wrote of how 'the road sets us free . . . it allows us to follow our own choice as to how fast and how far we shall go, to tarry where and when we will' (cited Liniado 1996: 10).

Motoring also had some similarities with the emergent practices of leisurely walking in the countryside discussed above (Wallace 1993). It seems that there was a heightened nostalgia for nature as countryside, as walkers, campers, motorists and caravanners increasingly enjoyed the fresh air and lack of Victorian restraint while passing at various speeds along the open road and through the purity and respectability of rural England (Liniado 1996: 10). The car enabled the tourer to re-create the ideal English countryside. The stability of rural England was re-established around a number of discursive features: Tudor architecture, the benign country squire, thatched cottages, sleek southern landscapes, the village green, and so on (see Howkins 1986). Such a novel spatial practice was facilitated by a number of distinctive organisational innovations partially taken over from cycling clubs: a road map industry, motoring organisations, hotel rating systems, road signs, village signposts, a national road building programme after 1910, and so on. These paved the way for the interwar transformation of the motor car, from alien threat to a 'natural' part of the rural scene. The motor car was tamed and the open road made relatively riskless and safe. Light notes how 'the futurist symbol of speed and erotic dynamism – the motor car – [was turned] into the Morris Minor' in the inter-war years (1991: 214). In that period motoring had become a typical and apparently 'natural' way of experiencing landscape. An interesting additional feature was found in North America and that was the way in which the car was enthusiastically adopted by the wilderness camping and touring fraternity (see Bunce 1994: chap. 4). Even by the 1920s motor camps were springing up to cater for the touring motorist. This enabled huge increases in the use of national parks, transforming so-called 'wilderness' from an elite space approached by rail, to a mass space visited and partially lived in by the mass motorist. Four hundred thousand cars a year visited such parks by 1926 (Bunce 1994: 119).

Obviously over the remaining decades of this century varied spatial practices surrounding the car have totally transformed almost all environments throughout the world; although interestingly it was only in the 1970s that the car began to be viewed as more polluting than the train (Liniado 1996: 28). A number of points should be noted: landscapes are now typically viewed on the move through a screen rather than from dwelling within one place; it is often only through rapid movement, on the road/screen, that real pleasures can be experienced; much of the development of car technology has been to minimise the risks of travel, to heighten the comfort and security of the car, and to insulate passengers from all intrusive environments; rural roadways have been lost to cyclists and pedestrians as the car has come to exert its awesome spatial dominance; huge areas of the globe are now devoted to car-only environments which constitute what Augé (1995) terms the quintessential non-place of super-modernity, a non-place that is neither urban nor rural, neither local nor cosmopolitan; and finally it is the modernist motorway which through its visual impact has particularly 'fuelled' recent environmental protest rather than the nature of the speeding car and roadside developments (Baudrillard 1988: 52–3; Bunce 1994; Liniado 1996; Thrift 1996; chapter 2 above on recent road campaigns).

There are various other spatial practices that could be analysed here. Particularly important in the European context has been swimming in the sea and how this led to the development of seaside resorts during the nineteenth century. Byron, for example, wrote of the complex interconnections of body and sea. This is a hugely embodied experience. Byron talks of the thrilling

Plate 6.2   *Walking dogs as a spatial practice (source: Phil Macnaghten)*

sensation of being rolled along on the 'swift whirl of the new breaking wave' (cited Sprawson 1995: 103). One could also note the increasing salience of spatial practices associated with walking dogs in the countryside, especially since local authorities have tightened restrictions on dogs in urban areas (see plate 6.2).

Also important in terms of the scale of rural land-use has been the military deployment of countryside spaces. Wright has undertaken a Benjaminesque decipherment of Tyneham (1996), the 'village that died for England', as it became the forgotten home of firing ranges and military manoeuvres. And more recent developments have enabled the military to assume the unlikely mantle of contemporary conservationism as they have warded off housing, road and leisure developments on 'their' land.

Finally, there are various 'rural' sociations who tend to be marginalised because of their transgression of the discursive dichotomy of work and leisure. We will mention two. First, there are groups of allotment-holders who emphasise cooperation, non-commercialism, recycling and the freedom to work the land directly and bodily. This is a spatial practice which offers a reworking of the spatial practice of 'land' through a partial and temporary dwelling (Crouch 1992a, 1992b). Second, there are travellers, self-styled groupings of young people who choose to spend at least some of the year moving in irregular fashion through the 'countryside'. They live in make-shift lorries, buses and caravans, and their timetable is constituted through various free festivals and sacred heterotopic sites (Hetherington 1990, 1991, 1993). Such 'travelling' seems to generate *Bund*-like identities related to a countryside much less based on the practice of 'landscape'. Indeed travellers' festivals and campsites are often seen as visually polluting to those who permanently dwell in such places and to other visitors who deploy the spatial practice of landscape. Such practices transgress the managerial representation of space currently favoured in policy discourses outlined above. And in their transgression of the dichotomy of work and leisure they contradict the spatial practices of those working the 'land'.

These various spatial practices serve to make and remake different kinds of countryside space, and to involve new or reworked representations of space and spaces of representation. In the next chapter we return to some more national and international debates and to consider various aspects of the notion of a sustainable future. In deciphering how different groups respond to such notions we will argue the necessity to identify and elaborate the diverse spatial practices that we have sought to describe here, practices that form and structure people's often ambivalent responses to nature and the environment.

7

SUSTAINING NATURE

In this chapter we focus on how nature and the environment are being reconfigured within contemporary policy and politics. Using insights from the previous chapters on the sensed, timed, spatialised and embodied dimensions of nature, we seek to recontextualise policy debates on the role of human agency within environmental change.

In recent years the most significant attempt to reconfigure human/nature relations has been through the discourse of 'environmental sustainability' and official pronouncements which advocate more 'sustainable' forms of development. In this chapter we examine how states and other official bodies have come to understand environmental issues within the discourse of sustainability. And we examine how such understandings have structured subsequent attempts to encourage people to participate actively in saving the environment.

We present recent empirical research on how people talk about, value and conceptualise nature in everyday life and how this contrasts with official models of sustainability. Current moves to encourage people to participate in environmental matters – largely in the form of 'sustainability' initiatives promoted by states, business and environmental groups – involve a limited and largely instrumental set of assumptions about human motivation. Such assumptions are embedded in much policy-related research on sustainability and on environmental perceptions generally, as set out in chapter 3. They include the following notions: that environmentally benign behaviour is limited by people's ignorance of the facts; that ignorance of these facts can be rectified by the provision of information by states and corporations; that such information will engender environmental concern; and that such concern will translate into overt personal and political action. But are these assumptions correct? Little research has so far examined to what extent such assumptions reflect how people do in fact understand and make sense of environmental issues in their daily lives, including their own effective participation within environmental matters.

We are concerned here with the contemporary significance of nature: how ideas of nature are permeating the human lifeworld, and how perceptions of environmental 'threat', 'risk' and 'loss' are inextricably bound up with related wider concerns about social life. We pay particular attention to the institutional dimensions of human engagement with nature. In particular, we examine the ways in which environmental risks, concerns, attitudes, values, senses of responsibility, and so on, are mediated by people's sense of their longer-standing 'trust' relationships with those organisations which have formal responsibility for the environment. Our research is informed by ongoing sociological debates on 'risk', 'trust' and 'agency'. In particular, we highlight the importance of people's sense of their own personal agency – that is, how people conceive of their own ability to affect change in the context of prevailing trust relations. And we address the likely impact of such relations upon whether it is thought meaningful and efficacious to act in some sense 'for the environment', through changing one's lifestyle, buying 'green' products, joining environmental organisations, participating in business and government green initiatives, and so on.

Sustainability as new public discourse

Sustainability is the new discourse which frames the formal environmental agenda in the 1990s. Through this prism environmentalists now share a common language and to some extent a common agenda with states and business. No longer is environmental rhetoric solely the preserve of environmental groups. Now corporations routinely advocate sustainable development, as do aid agencies, government departments, the European Union and even insurance firms.

The idea of sustainability can be traced to the United Nations Stockholm conference on environment in 1972 and to 1970s debates over 'limits to growth' (Redclift 1987). But the term gained prominence in the *World Conservation Strategy* as a core concept to call attention to the need to incorporate conservation measures within development plans (IUCN 1980). The link between environmental limits and development was carried forward into the Brundtland Report (WCED 1987), and subsequently endorsed by national governments at the Rio Earth Summit (UNCED 1992). Since 1987 the Brundtland definition of sustainability has become more or less shared by all major institutions committed to sustainable development. Brundtland defined sustainable development as 'development which meets the needs of the present without compromising the ability of future generations to meet their own needs' (WCED 1987). The other often quoted definition of sustainability is that endorsed by the IUCN publication *Caring for the Earth* (1991): 'to improve the quality of life while living within the carrying capacity of living ecosystems'. Both definitions share the underlying belief that economic and social change is only sustainable and thereby beneficial in the long term when it safeguards the natural resources upon which all development depends.

To understand the significance of sustainability within the Brundtland Report it is necessary to situate the term within the wider context of the Cold War. The Brundtland Commission was set up by the United Nations in the early 1980s to define how global environmental problems were to be interpreted. By then environmental problems had come to be recognised as global in scale, thus requiring a concomitant global political response. However, due to the political realities and rigidities of the Cold War, a unified response between East and West on any policy issue appeared unlikely. But Finger (1993: 42) suggests that the rhetoric of a single world which was facing shared environmental problems and hence 'a common future' (also the title of the report) did help to propel the environment to centre stage within the international arena. The global conception of environment thus came to represent a powerful vehicle to promote international dialogue and cooperation among nation-states, including the blocs of East and West. Finger articulates how the Brundtland Commission's approach to global environmental problems subsequently relied on three central components: the 'same boat' ideology; the concept of sustainable development; and an appeal to management as the response to global environmental problems.

The concept of the 'same boat' is that we all share the same finite planetary resources and means to development, and that unless we learn to cooperate as a single global entity we risk common catastrophe. This concept was most salient in the early 1980s in connection with the threats posed by the nuclear winter scenario, but was then used in relationship to other environmental risks such as resource use, acid rain, ozone depletion and greenhouse warming, which were increasingly recognised as transcending national boundaries.

The concept of sustainable development was then presented as the set of principles whereby nations could develop in a way which incorporated environmental considerations. However, because of the imperatives needed to promote the 'same boat' ideology, somewhat loose and non-binding definitions were sought which did not inhibit the aspirations of nations especially in the South to develop economically. Thus sustainable development was presented by the Commission as an apparent 'win–win' situation where environmental sustainability came to be seen as good for economic development, and economic development as good for environmental sustainability. As Finger points out, this reasoning led the Brundtland Commission to highly optimistic conclusions concerning the projected outcomes of sustainable development. The Report began:

> We have the power to reconcile human affairs with natural laws. And to thrive in the process. In this, our cultural and spiritual heritages can reinforce our economic interests and survival imperatives. (WCED 1987, cited Finger 1993: 42–3)

To achieve such outcomes, the Brundtland Commission appealed to 'global environmental management' as the mechanism by which sustainable development would be implemented. Such management was premised on a further three factors: global scientific programmes objectively assessing environmental damage and the 'carrying capacity' of the planet; the transformation of world leaders into new global managers of the global commons, seeking common agreement preferably at international summits; and the education and enlightenment of the world's citizens, who, realising that they were all in the 'same boat', would give their approval and political support to such programes of global management.

Such elements in the Brundtland Commission's approach to sustainable development reflected the political need for an approach which would gain the support of diverse and potentially conflicting interests, including those of business and states, of East and West, and of North and South. The political project therefore was one which was avowedly *a*political, over and above its preoccupations to achieve global consensus amongst both citizens and governments. Moreover, the mechanism which would facilitate such consensus was dialogue, as if sustainable forms of development would best emerge from education, enlightenment and information. Such emphases led to a new rhetoric of partnership and stakeholder democracy, one where environmental groups came to be seen as collaborators within global management alongside states, business and other interest groups. Indeed, the late 1980s and early 1990s saw the build-up of NGO coalitions as key players within the UNCED process.

The culmination of this process was the 1992 United Nations Rio Earth Summit, where the implications of the term 'sustainability' were set out and endorsed by national governments. The Summit resulted in a number of outcomes, including the international action plan Agenda 21 (UNCED 1992), and the creation of a new United Nations body, the Commission for Sustainable Development, through which its implementation is being monitored. As Sachs points out:

> The novelty of Rio was certainly the fact that for the first time, governments of the world jointly acknowledged the threat of global crisis and moved to formulate common obligations for conducting politics in the future. (1993: xv)

Thus, since Rio, working definitions of sustainability have been broadly accepted by governments, NGOs and business. These tend to be cast in terms of living within the finite limits of the planet, of meeting needs without compromising the ability of future generations to meet their needs, and of integrating the environment and development. Indeed, there has been a growing impetus within the *policy-making* community to move away from questions of principle and definition. Rather they have developed tools and approaches which can translate the goals of sustainability into specific actions, and assess whether real progress is in fact being made towards achieving them. Within this framework, the development of indicators of sustainability as tools of measurement is acquiring increasing prominence.

In recent years considerable effort has gone into the development of sustainability indicators: separate initiatives have come from the UN, OECD, the European Union, national governments and non-governmental organisations (see Adriaanse 1993; OECD 1993; WWF and NEF 1994). Interest has perhaps been most marked at local level, with 'sustainable community' projects in several North American cities receiving international attention (Sustainable Seattle 1994; and see Lancashire County Council 1991; Lancashire Environment Forum 1993).

A number of factors explain the current popularity of these indicators and their different roles and functions. The initial impetus for the development of sustainability indicators was largely managerial. It was argued that only if the environment was measured could coherent policy be made, with the right priorities chosen and appropriate targets for improvement specified (see, for example, Department of the Environment, 1996; UK Government 1994; UNCED 1992). Coupled to 'State of the Environment' information, their role is seen as providing information for managers to assist in the setting of targets, the implementation of programmes and the measurement of progress. By devising indicators linked to specific targets, managers can help operationalise sustainability and thereby facilitate action at a local level.

More recently indicators have come increasingly to be seen as tools for *communication* (see MacGillivray and Zadek 1995). It is through such indicators that members of the public can understand for themselves the problems and trends which society needs to address – particularly those not otherwise available to sensory perception, such as energy consumption and waste production. By providing information in this way, it is claimed that indicators will educate the public and engender a sense of social responsibility for the problems. In turn, it is argued, this will encourage people to change their individual household behaviour and their political responses in order to generate solutions. As UK's Local Government Management Board (LGMB) Project Guidance to local authorities argued:

> Indicators can challenge people to explore how the way they live affects their community/world and thus move the indicators in one direction or another. Indicators can illustrate how each individual can make a difference. (1994b: 1)

Such attempts to encourage people themselves to participate in moves towards sustainability reflect a growing recognition that states alone cannot solve the looming global environmental crisis. One of the more striking achievements by NGOs at Rio was to ensure that a new language of 'empowerment', 'citizen participation' and 'multi-stakeholder partnership' became integrated into Agenda 21 – the action plan for sustainable development adopted by world governments (see Holmberg et al. 1993). Programmes of action for sustainability increasingly involve measures for community participation and involvement. Indeed, the role envisaged for the public in the emerging model of sustainability is crucial. Agenda 21 argues that only if ordinary members of the community, particularly those in disadvantaged groups, take part in decision-making processes can the outcomes of those processes be regarded as good. As a recent review of Local Agenda 21 in the UK put it: the goal is an 'active democracy with more people involved in developing and implementing solutions to the problems that society faces' (UNA and CDF 1995: 45).

Such emphases can also be seen in national and local strategy documents (LGMB 1993; UK Government 1994). For example, in 1994 the UK Government launched three new initiatives designed to stimulate lifestyle changes and to create new levels of partnership between government and other environmental actors. These were a 'Government Panel on Sustainable Development'; the 'UK Round Table on Sustainable Development'; and a citizens' environment initiative, 'Going for Green' (UK Government 1994). The aim of these initiatives was to ensure that the ideas and messages identified in the UK strategy on sustainable development became translated into action, and that all sectors of the community are involved in delivering sustainable development.

Even before the 1992 Rio conference, local government bodies across the globe had begun to take initiatives with respect to environment and development issues (such as the global cities initiatives). Such initiatives were given fresh impetus through the UNCED process, and in particular through the idea that local authorities should develop their own action programmes or 'Local Agenda 21s' – action programmes where principles and targets for local sustainability could be developed, implemented and monitored through partnerships between local authorities and local 'stake-holders'. In the UK at local government level, the LGMB has subsequently developed and submitted to national government its own 'Framework for Local Sustainability' (1993), and has recently completed a 'Sustainability Indicators Research Project' as part of a wider 'Local Agenda 21' initiative which aims to advance sustainability at a local level (1994b, 1995).

But the crucial question is of course whether people will in fact participate. Why should they? It is likely that participation will occur only if the public accept or 'believe in' the project in which they are being asked to take part. Do they? It would also seem that people must in some sense identify with the discourse of sustainability. That is, the public must at least in general terms accept the argument being presented, concerning the undesirability and/or unsustainability of the present situation, the desirability of the proposed future, and the practicability of the suggested means of getting from one to the other. In other words, people must identify with global environmental concerns in their daily lives, accept the need to live in ways which respect the finite limits of the planet, be prepared to change unsustainable aspects of their personal lifestyles, and support government and business sustainability initiatives. They must also be receptive to information provided by sustainability indicators, and be prepared to restructure aspects of their personal lifestyles in line with such information. We conclude this section by outlining three dominant assumptions framing how public bodies are seeking to implicate people in contributing towards this more sustainable future.

First, the discourse of sustainable development conceives of nature as a set of issues identified through modern scientific inquiry. Such a conception of nature subscribes to the doctrine of 'environmental realism'. In particular, environmental issues are recognised first and foremost as global/technical issues such as global warming, ozone depletion and biodiversity – issues which rely on increasingly sophisticated scientific programmes to determine the impact of so-called 'anthropogenic' or human effects (the effects of industrial society) on planetary processes. Indeed, a new type of science has emerged in the fields of atmospheric chemistry, oceanography, climatology and geology dedicated to establishing the impacts of industrial activities on the bio-geo-chemical cycles of the planet, and the likely long-term effects of current and predicted trends of industrial growth. Such science has contributed to a 'new global ecological look', the sense that environmental problems may be more global, more serious, more urgent and more interconnected than we previously imagined (Finger 1993: 40). The discourse of sustainable development relies on the efficacy of such global scientific programmes to determine the carrying capacity of the planet, and hence the limits within which future development can take place. People are exhorted to identify their environmental concerns at this global level in ways which transcend their more local, embedded and culturally specific experiences, and to respond to these global concerns through individual local action.

Second, the discourse exposes the assumption of the human as a rational agent. In the dominant view of sustainable development, people are presented as individual agents acting 'rationally' in response to information made available to them. Ignorance about environmental issues can be rectified by the provision of information; information will engender concern; and concern will translate into both personal and political behaviour changes. Both central and local state discourses, as well as those of businesses and non-governmental organisations promoting 'green consumerism', stress the importance of such individual, personal responsibility for environmental change (see Eden 1993; Myers and Macnaghten 1998 forthcoming).

Third, sustainable development relies on an optimistic model of personal 'agency': that is, of people's sense of their ability to change their situation or the wider world. The discourse assumes that people's actions are governed more or less straightforwardly by their knowledge and concern about environmental issues. People's relationships to states in whose environmental activities they are asked to participate and the businesses whose 'green' products they are requested to buy are here seen as unproblematic. Individuals act simply as 'responsible' citizens and consumers; the institutional context in which their behaviour occurs is implicitly assumed to be benign or irrelevant.

These three assumptions can be read as part of a modernist tradition in which the limits of 'natural' processes can be defined unproblematically by science, where public policy and global management strategies can derive from scientific understanding, and where such understandings can engage and mobilise the wider public – the combination of which leads to the ultimate goal of sustainable development. Such assumptions are modernist since they speak of a world in which people have faith in expert systems, including science, in which states command the support of the wider public, and in which people still believe in the project of economic development and the idea of progress (albeit within limits).

However, are such assumptions resonant in the wider population in the light of the critiques of modernity and the supposed shift to the postmodern? It was to explore these assumptions, and to investigate therefore the cultural and political salience of the sustainable development discourse, that two research projects were undertaken. The results are reported and discussed in the following sections.

Sustainability discourse and daily practice

The first study sought to discover how 'citizens' in Lancashire perceived and understood environmental and 'sustainability' issues in daily life, and how as a consequence they would be likely to respond to the publication and dissemination of sustainability indicators (for a full account of the research findings and the methodology see the research report Macnaghten et al. 1995a; see also Macnaghten and Jacobs 1997; the project was funded by Lancashire County Council).

The research consisted of long sessions of open-ended talk derived from focus group discussions where we listened to people's own categories of experience, and to the multiple and ambivalent ways in which they discussed and made sense of the environment (for accounts of focus group methodology, see Agar and McDonald 1995; Kitzinger 1994, 1995; Krueger 1994; for the related methodology of in-depth groups, see Burgess et al. 1988a, 1988b, 1995).

We conducted eight focus groups, each containing approximately eight unacquainted individuals, and representing a different section of the Lancashire population. A market research firm was used to recruit participants. The focus group discussions were conducted over two sessions in late 1994, each session lasting approximately two hours. The eight groups were as follows:

1 *young men*, aged 17 to 19, currently employed on government training schemes;
2 first generation *Asian women*, socio-economic status C2/D, aged 30 to 40, living in an inner urban area;
3 *mothers* not in paid employment, socio-economic status C1/C2, aged 25 to 40, all with at least one child under five;
4 *unemployed men*, all of whom had been unemployed for between one and five years, living in inner-city council estates;
5 *retired* men and women, socio-economic group B/C1, aged 50 to 70;
6 *professional* men and women, socio-economic group A/B, aged 40 to 60, living in rural areas;
7 *working women*, aged 45 to 60, predominantly employed in manual factory work;
8 *young professional* men and women, socio-economic group A/B, aged 25 to 35, with no children.

We began our focus groups with detailed discussions about aspects of people's day-to-day lives: on their relationship to place, on their current concerns and anxieties, and on things that would improve their quality of life. The aim was to examine, without prompting the discussion, whether and how 'environmental' issues entered into people's day-to-day practices and experiences.

All the groups expressed a strong, local attachment to 'place'. For example, the mothers' group identified strongly with Thornton or Cleveleys (both villages in Lancashire) and talked in detail about the character, identity and qualities of these places and the subtle distinctions between neighbouring villages and parts of towns. In this and other groups talk on place focused on what we have termed the 'dwelt-in world' of daily life. Many people spoke of the sense of community in their locality, and its degrees of friendliness, safety (especially for children), and proximity to nearby countryside.

Nature tended to enter these early discussions on place in relation to daily practices such as walking in parks and the wider countryside, swimming, driving and walking dogs. Such practices were seen to contribute to people's quality of life and to their attachment to the area. But there was unease that this local nature was under threat, and that these threats were beginning to affect people's abilities to engage in hitherto taken-for-granted social practices. Such feelings of environmental threat impinging on people's dwelt-in world took the form of threats posed by cars on their children's health and safety, of expressed concerns about litter and dog dirt, of housing being built on local countryside, and of increasing restrictions on the use of local countryside. In such ways, unprompted discussions of nature and the environment tended to be discussed in terms of their emerging impact on localised social practices. Such concerns were most prominently voiced by the mothers' group in relation to the perceived threat of sewage on local beaches. The exchange below (between three female participants [F] and the moderator [Mod]) shows how the mothers' group view dirty beaches as typical of what one is unable to change. The focus was on people's stock assumptions of Lancashire:

F   *Fish and chips and a pint. Wet weather, wet and cold and windy. Dirty sea.*
F   *Yes, you can't get away from that, can you?*
Mod   *You have said that a couple of times – what do you mean, you can't get away from that?*
F   *Well, you wouldn't even let your dog go in the water, you'd be ill the day after.*
        (Mothers)

This perception of environmental issues as somehow beyond people's control was shared in other groups, commonly in connection with people's experience of local and valued green spaces being lost to development. The significance of such threats tended to be discussed not in global or systemic terms (in terms which could be assessed through scientific inquiry) but rather in human-relational terms. For example, the passage above on dirty beaches continued with a discussion of how the existence of dirty beaches contributed to a sense of shame which threatened the self-respect of what was otherwise a clean and tidy locality. The significance of beach pollution was thus discussed using relational criteria (how others would view them) as opposed to more objective ones (their greater risk of disease).

F   *Dirty beaches. But you see these holiday makers paddling and you think, 'Oh my God!' We know what it's like. They'll be sorry the day after.*
F   *They'll go home bloody ill anyway. And they'll blame it on the booze on the prom. Food poisoning. [Laughter] It could be that as well.*
        (Mothers)

To provide evidence for these claims these women relied on knowledge from their direct observation and experience which was evidently perceived as more reliable than official statistics or media reports. On a number of occasions people made sense of environmental changes in their locality through direct sensory perception, and in particular through the senses of smell and sight. However, as the passage below shows, local aspects of pollution could result in a strong and apparently disproportionate emotional response:

Mod   *Is that Blackpool or the whole coast?*
F   *It's the whole coast. People go to Cleveleys and think they are going somewhere cleaner than Blackpool, but it's not. You've still got a horrible tide line, haven't you. You can still smell it. I saw a man down there the other day with gloves on picking up the seaweed on the beach and putting it in a big bin bag. That's cleaning the beach, that.*
F   *It's awful. I know, we walked down South Shore last week and everything was just floating "I'm going to have to go off the beach, I'm going to die', it's awful!*
F   *. . . Years ago it wasn't. It was a proper beach and water. Just outside Jubilee Gardens it used to be lovely . . .*
        (Mothers)

The claim 'I'm going to die' strikingly shows this woman's visceral disgust with the state of beaches. However, it also symbolises a more profound anxiety about change and how environmental considerations were coming to be connected to a sense of unease about living in modern society. Across the different focus groups other concerns were expressed about jobs and job security, and those of crime and drugs, concerns which appeared to be connected to anxieties of deteriorating local environmental quality (including amenities). In relation to all three sets of concerns there was a widespread sense that conditions were getting worse.

Underpinning these anxieties was an apparent loss of social stability and cohesion. Nearly all groups remarked on the emerging climate of uncertainty and the sense that life was becoming increasingly unpredictable. For example, both the young and older professional groups talked about the fear of redundancy, the new climate of short-term contracts, and the general perception that they were less able to control and thereby plan many aspects of their lives. Many of the other groups talked about the lack of jobs with proper wages, and the worsening conditions now experienced in the workplace.

M   *Well I just think it's the general climate all round. I've been made redundant twice in my life when I haven't thought the circumstances*

dictated it. . . . So I don't feel insecure where I am now, but who can ever say what the long-term situation is. You've just got to live with it and just think if something happens, well what the hell. There's nothing you can do about it.
(Rural professional)

Such problems were regarded as both new and increasingly central to people's daily lived experience. They appeared to be related to a growing sense of a world where people were less able to live normal, decent and stable lives. For example, the unemployed men experienced their council estates as having become so dangerous that they were unable to leave their homes empty for fear of burglary. The Asian women were particularly concerned with safety on local streets. The mothers' group and young professionals expressed worries about local beach pollution and how this was impinging upon their sense of living in a decent locality. And nearly all participants expressed concern about the perceived loss of 'community' and neighbourliness.

M   *If I go out I leave somebody in the house. The daughter, or the wife, has to stay in the house, when I go shopping. Because if there wasn't somebody in when we got back there'd be nothing left. We've got to keep a dog, which we don't want to keep, we have to keep a dog in the garden. Watching everything, and everybody that goes by. . . . You shouldn't have to do these things, but you've got to do it. . . .*

M   *I can't [go out]. If I go out, it's either me or my missus has to stay. If you both go out there's a 99% chance of getting robbed. They stand on the corner and watch you.*
(Unemployed men)

This sense of uncertainty became even more pronounced and prevalent in discussions about the future – what life would be like in 30 years' time. The majority of groups talked of these trends intensifying and accelerating. Environmental problems featured more prominently as producing unwelcome developments. For the Asian women the worsening future was depicted in terms of more selfish (Western) attitudes amongst the young, leading to the subsequent breakdown of traditional family structure and loyalties. Many of the other groups talked of a future in which there would be fewer jobs, more crime, more cars and pollution, with less countryside, and where jobs of all kinds would be even more controlled by the needs and interests of 'others' (business and government). Indeed, both the mothers' and the retired group discussed the possibility of global apocalypse, and in both discussions this was viewed as a possible scenario. One of the mothers made the further observation that even if there still existed a world in 50 years' time, it would be uglier and less enchanted. Indeed, for many groups the tone of discussion was exceedingly pessimistic. There was a very general agreement that day-to-day existence would be harder with a reduced quality of life.

F   *I don't think we look into the future for them [the children] too much.*
F   *We've too much feeling for them to look into the future for them, because there's nothing good to look at.*

F   *We don't think about these things, because we've all got grandchildren,
      and we'd crack up if we thought about this all the time.*
      (Working women)

How should we understand this apparently shared and widespread loss of
faith in the future? On the one hand, we can note a historical fear of change
and the appeal to nature as the embodiment of an older and more stable
social order. Williams (1973) has famously commented on how the
centuries-old appeal to nature has in fact reflected nostalgia for a visual and
social world which existed 30 years previously. However, to interpret such
widespread pessimism as part of an age-old fear of change is to fail to locate
such perceptions within the new historical context of globalisation. In
different ways, the new insecurities and in particular those experienced in
the workplace, reflect an increasingly globalised economic and cultural order
where distant happenings increasingly structure local life. In such a context
it is not surprising that people find it hard to imagine life in 30 years' time or
to map out one's life horizons. Indeed, there are very good reasons for
people *not* to think too sharply about the long term, to live life in the 'here
and now', and to rely on fate that the future will come good. This was
certainly the strategy of the young men on government training schemes, for
whom even the term 'quality of life' conjured up alien notions of responsibility and a view of the long term.

Mod   *OK. The term 'quality of life'. Who would be saying it?*
M   *Grandad.*
M   *People who can't speak properly – use posh words you can't understand.
      Posh people.*
M   *What do you mean by 'quality of life'?*
M   *Yes, because posh people have their quality of life, and we have ours.*
M   *Our quality of life is going out and getting pissed and shagging women,
      basically. To posh people, like, it's taking dogs for walks, and –*
M   *It depends whose life it is. You can't talk about lives in general. Because
      everybody has a different life. Some people have no life, eh, David?*
      (Young men)

The passage above shows the cultural specificity of the terms used in the
sustainability discourse (such as 'quality of life'), and how they fail to
capture the lifeworlds of certain groups in society. For example, the
aspiration to 'improve the quality of life' is simply not a salient concept for
these young men, in a world where there are few employment prospects, and
where life is geared towards the here and now, the week-end, clubs, drugs
and other forms of escape and immediate gratification. The 'temporality' of
the term 'quality of life', they claim, may become more relevant at future
stages of their lives, thus reflecting a degree of reflexivity in their current
predicaments:

M   *Quality of life is something you use when you are older. When you have
      like – grandchildren of your own and you say to your children, quality of
      life, and they go 'shut up you old fart' – Basically you think your parents
      are total toss pots, either that or you think they use stupid terms. But it is
      only stupid as we are going to be using it in 20 or 30 years' time.*
      (Young man)

For other groups, the apparently widespread fear of the future and the sense that lived conditions would be harder was also connected to apparently intractable forces of globalisation. Or, to use the visual metaphors set out in chapter 4 above, we might suggest that people were responding to the dark side of modernity. Many people spoke of this in terms of a widespread sense of 'the system' that was geared to serving the interests of business and corporate finance, that was perceived to be driving economic and social life, that was infecting public institutions and the motivations of those employed in them, and that was beginning to structure personal aspects of daily life. Such trends were commonly perceived to be shaped by 'money' and 'self-interest', and to contribute towards an inappropriate 'short-termism' in public policy. Such perspectives were surprisingly shared across age and class variables in the form of pronounced fatalism and even cynicism towards public institutions, and to expressed doubts of the willingness or ability of such institutions to contribute towards a better future. This perspective came to light most starkly in discussions about the role of the state and businesses in contributing towards a better future.

The discussion of people's perceptions of central government was charac-terised by a deep sense of distrust, and a general lack of faith in its ability and willingness to respond to their concerns. Central government was viewed as corrupt, run by quangos and business interests, and increasingly out of touch with the public. To our surprise, this broad analysis was shared by the professional groups as much as the unemployed and working women's group. However, apart from the working women's group, no other group was of the opinion that a change of government would really make much difference. The problem was generally perceived to be more endemic to the system of 'politics' that was emerging in Britain (and elsewhere) today.

There was also almost unanimous agreement that business had little if any sense of social responsibility, and that financial interests were not merely distorting the democratic process, but also contributing to environmental damage. There was widespread support, even in the professional groups, for the proposition that market forces were uncontrollably spreading into the minutiae of people's personal lives, and that this would threaten people's aspirations for a more cohesive, stable and environmentally sustainable society. However, although there was consensus about the spread of market forces, there was more ambivalence about who, if anyone, could control them. As the following passage indicates, this was unlikely to be forth-coming from politicians:

Mod *Let's start with this, big business, what do you think about them – their role in all this, what trust do you have in them?*

M *They are out to make a profit, so they'll cut back on everything else. Just into making money.*

M *They are powerful, because they can bribe politicians. Turn a blind eye to pollution.*

F   *They can afford to pay the fines if they pollute the water. What's the worst*
        that can happen, oh, we'll pay a fine.
        (Young professionals)

By contrast the only group who were mildly supportive of business, the mothers' group, were so not because of any expectation that business might be concerned with 'bettering' their world. Rather, because corruption and greed in public and business life were so endemic it was naïve to suppose that change could result from anything other than money and self-interest.

These various viewpoints can be examined in terms of competing temporalities. The passages above indicate a mounting sense that institutions of government are more geared towards their own 'short-term' interests than with the 'longer-term' concerns and aspirations of the wider public. This reflects what we have termed in chapter 5 the mismatch between timeframes, and in particular the power of 'instantaneous' time. We found that there was considerable discussion of the ways in which 'instantaneous' time impinged upon people's dwelt-in worlds.

Many people spoke of their aspirations to improve their quality of life through devising ways to experience more fully the temporality and sensuality of their attachment to their 'dwelling' places, including the attachment to landscape. People spoke of desires for more time for themselves (away from kids), being able to live life at a slower pace, having a more local job, having more job security, and having peace of mind. They spoke of their desires for a more tolerant society, better amenities (especially for children), a proper community (where you can leave your house unlocked), a cleaner and less polluted environment (including one where public authorities interfered less with nature), and greater sexual equality and solidarity in family life. Such desires seemed to constitute a wider opposition to uncontrolled market forces and instantaneous time. It is through such dwelling times and spaces that we can identify people's aspirations for a safer and cleaner future, one modelled on long-term and even 'glacial' principles of precaution and care. However, in relation to all this, there was a profound sense of powerlessness as to one's own ability actually to contribute towards such a better future.

We now examine how people understood the term 'sustainability' and how they made sense of their own participation in the environment in terms of their own sense of agency. A remarkably high degree of awareness of environmental issues was found in most of the groups (the exceptions were young men and Asian women). People's primary environmental concerns were expressed in local terms (beach pollution, litter and dog mess), although there was also wider anxiety about global problems, particularly among the more affluent groups. There was also a general perception that both local and global problems were getting worse, and that this was likely to impact on people's lives in increasingly direct ways. Asked to list significant environmental issues, one discussion went as follows:

Car exhaust pollution; water pollution; losing green areas; extinction of rare
species; agricultural practices; grubbing up hedgerows; energy; waste; localised

pollution; litter; lack of recycling; ozone layer; industries and their air pollution and fumes; the greenhouse effect; effluent discharges; lack of public transport; nuclear power; sulphur dioxide emissions; wind power.
(Young professionals)

Despite this level of awareness, only two people in all the groups had heard the term 'sustainability'. When introduced into the discussion by the moderator, it was generally seen as a piece of abstract jargon; even 'gobbledygook'. Nevertheless, many of the participants guessed accurately the broad meaning of the term (about keeping things going for the future) and its significance for contemporary society. Indeed, in the exchange above, when participants were asked which of the above issues related to 'sustainability', the discussion went as follows:

Mod   *Which of these have anything to do with sustainability?*
F   *All of them.*
Mod   *Are they the same things then, sustainability and the environment?*
M   *The connection is the length of time.*
F   *It's the hugeness of the impact of it.*
           (Young professionals)

Sustainability relies on the shared concept of global citizenship in which people conceive of their own sense of duty and responsibility on a planetary level. Such a putatively global identity was more available to the younger and better off groups who understood and identified with the principle of a 'shared world' and the need to respect finite environmental 'limits'. Such global identities were also discussed in the retired group, but as symptomatic of a wider culture of greed, one which was storing up unimaginable problems for future generations. The focus here was on what significance sustainability had for everyday life:

M   *We've used up so much of the earth's resources, can we keep going the way we are, chopping down forests, digging up minerals, and oil? And gas*
            . . .
M   *It's a profligate human race at the moment isn't it? We're gobbling up resources each ten years, more than centuries before. And we still want more and more.*
F   *You paint a very gloomy picture.*
Mod   *Is he realistic?*
M   *Realistic. Yes.*
Mod   *So these things are going to run out?*
M   *Not in our time, but in our grandchildren's time.*
            (Retired)

Other groups also acknowledged the cumulative long-term impact of human activities on the environment. There was a general sense within the better off groups that we are all responsible for environmental problems, which were now identified as transcending national boundaries. Indeed, the following passage taken from the rural professional group is a good illustration of the 'same boat' ideology discussed in the previous section, illustrating how commonplace the concept of global environmental citizenship may have become:

Mod	*Sustainability . . . Is this something that concerns you, affects you, has anything to do with you or not?*
F	*Well yes because we're all consumers.*
F	*We all have to live on this planet as well.*
F	*Yes because we have to survive.*
M	*You have to live together.*
F	*We have to inhabit and cohabit.*
F	*I mean if the ozone layer goes, you can't maintain that. The planet won't sustain itself will it, or us? It affects us all.*
M	*. . . You know that you personally are using more of the earth's resources and if it was more fairly distributed there wouldn't be [so many problems].*

(Rural professionals)

By contrast, the groups in lower socio-economic categories (especially the mothers' and the working women's groups) discussed the environment either in local, immediate and highly personal terms, concentrating on issues such as rubbish, dog mess, car fumes and loss of countryside, or in very bleak and terrifying ways, as in apocalyptic scenarios of doom. For these groups, the environment was conceived in terms of what was available to the senses (the visibility of litter, the stench of dirty beaches, the taste of car fumes, the prevalence of asthma in children), or in terms of a more abstract, unimaginable and fear-inducing future. This suggests that the global sense of environment is only one interpretation and that more local understandings of environment may be salient for particular historical/cultural reasons.

For our groups, the conviction that environmental change could be best understood by means of direct sensory experience reflected reliance on 'the self' in the absence of trustworthy 'others'. Such responses reflected a pervasive sense that people were not being told the whole truth. Many agreed that while environmental conditions were bad and likely to deteriorate further, the public just did not know how bad things were. The general explanation given in all but the Asian women's group was that those 'in power' presented biased or selective versions of 'the facts' to serve their own vested and largely short-term interests.

When people were asked about the credibility of official information, they tended to distinguish between information which could be easily correlated with their own direct sensory experiences, and that which depended on 'expert' knowledge (although we note below how even this knowledge cannot always be trusted). The further removed information was from people's immediate dwellingness, the less likely they were to find it credible. An extreme example of this phenomenon was the opinion of some of the young men who claimed not to believe in global environmental problems, simply because they refused to believe anything said by academics, bureaucrats or experts unless they could directly verify this knowledge with their own senses. In less extreme forms this view tended to be shared by participants in the lower socio-economic groups.

F   *They only tell us what they want us to know. And that's the end of that, so*
        you're left with a fog in your brain, so you just think – what have I to
        worry about? I don't know what they're on about.
Mod   *So why do Government only tell us what they want us to hear?*
F   *To keep your confidence going. [All together]*
Mod   *So if someone provides an indicator which says the economy is improving*
        you won't believe it?
F   *They've been saying it for about 10 years, but where? I can't see any-*
        thing!
F   *Every time there's an election they say the economy is improving.*
        (Working women)

Members of the more middle-class groups tended to be caught in a
dilemma, having to rely on information from an array of 'expert' sources
(the media, government, scientists) but perceiving these 'experts' as producing biased and self-serving information. This dilemma dominated much
discussion in the groups concerning their likely identification with, and
acceptance of, sustainability indicators. Again direct sensory knowledge was
the one benchmark that could be trusted:

Mod   *How do we know whether these things are getting better or worse? . . .*
M   *We can see some for ourselves.*
F   *But when you get to a certain age you can compare back to how things*
        used to be.
M   *Judge how many traffic jams you get into. It comes back to local*
        knowledge. . . .
M   *People have said that the beaches are more polluted than what they've*
        been for years. I could have told you that. Because I've seen from upstairs
        for 30 years and looked out the window every day and seen the colour of
        the sand change colour. Whereas it used to be like everybody imagines
        sand, it's now a browny colour.
        (Rural professionals)

Such passages reflect the uncertainty about the significance and scale of
formal scientific assessments of environmental problems, and the appeal of
sensory perception as a more reliable guide. We now assess how the factors
above affected people's sense of their own responsibility and involvement in
environmental change. We have suggested that for the younger and better
off groups there was a sense of shared responsibility in contributing towards
a better environment. Indeed, many people felt that it was 'up to them' to
change and improve their world, including the state of the environment.
Again the exceptions were the young men's group and the unemployed
group, who did not express much direct responsibility, largely due to their
perceived lack of power in relation to their own situation. However, whilst
most people accepted some personal responsibility, most argued that they
could only create change at a very local level through individual action. Yet
expectations of wider change resulting from more collective, 'political'
actions were generally considered unrealistic. For the mothers' group, for
example, there was a general perception that 'they', as working-class
women, had very little power to influence the systems they exist in.
Sustainability was identified as too ambitious a concept for 'them', even

though they had little faith in those with power to look after their interests, including the state of the environment that their children would inherit.

Such feelings of powerlessness were exacerbated by three factors. First, the history of environmentalism was seen as an unending series of problems, where smaller problems are endlessly taken over by larger and even more intractable problems.

Second, there was the sense that the 'environment' as a problem has been produced within people's lifetime. For especially the older groups (the retired, the rural professionals and the working women), there was considerable guilt expressed that their own actions in terms of consumption styles may have contributed towards the worsening environment. Indeed, as one woman perceptively said:

F   *In fact you always thought it was a good thing to be a consumer. That's what they told us, keeping everyone in jobs. And now we realise it's a double-edged sword.*
     (Rural professional)

Such changes in understanding led people to question the 'objectivity' and time-robustness of current understandings of environmental change. The example of CFCs in fridges was used as a poignant illustration of how everyday practices legitimised by current scientific understanding can result in long-term, albeit inadvertent, damage to the global environment. Such examples led people to question the reliability of current scientific information, especially when many people regarded much of science as contaminated by politics.

And third, the common perception of business and government as increasingly geared towards self-interest and short-term goals led people to cynical postures over official measures proposed to advance sustainability and the environment. Such cynicism was evident even in the professional groups where one might have expected most sympathy with free-market ideology and business ethics.

All three factors contributed to a widespread lack of personal agency in relation to environmental matters. People across all socio-economic groups did not sense that personal, individual actions were likely to make a difference, and that collective action was unrealistic given people's sense of the prevalence of 'short-termism' within the state and business. Moreover, most groups regarded voting or seeking to persuade elected representatives as largely ineffective.

However, even though most people were not radically restructuring their lives, or actively engaged in environmental protest, or explicitly concerned with the global state of the environment, this did not indicate a lack of environmental interest or concern. Indeed, even the unemployed men were concerned about issues of pollution, but tended to identify such concerns as inseparable from wider experiences of social marginalisation and a lack of agency. As the following passage shows, the 'non-involvement' of these men was fuelled by the sense of the futility of personal action, since they would not be listened to, the better off and those responsible for pollution should set an example first, and they have anyway much more pressing day-to-day concerns.

> M   *But when you get up in the morning are you bothered about pollution? I'm not. I am at the end of it, but I can't enjoy life if I've got no money.*
>
> M   *You won't get any nice fresh air at Blackpool. It's polluted.*
>
> M   *Well, that's it. We've got the worst in Europe, haven't we? We're told to clean up the waters, clean up the pollution and everything. But there's nothing we can do about it. All we can do is vote. What does it do? . . .*
>
> M   *The Government has paid so much to put the pollution right, but who put the pollution there in the first place? BP, whoever has done it, they should pay for it. They brag about how they make £10 million profit each year, they should put something back into it. Why should it come out of our pockets? At the end of the day that's where it's coming from. What about BP and all these petro-chemical companies? Let them pay for it.*
>
> (Unemployed men)

Thus the bleakness that characterised the discussion around the ineffectiveness of individual action to solve broader, systemic environmental problems largely arose from the widespread perception that those 'in control' were neither likely nor willing to respond to environmental problems. From this perspective, there was considerable latent support for, although unfamiliarity with, the idea of sustainability. The professional groups, the retired group and, to a lesser extent, the mothers' group and the working women's group all liked the concept of 'sustainability' once explained. It seemed to provide people with a vocabulary to talk about the 'long term' in a culture which otherwise appeared remarkably short-term and self-interested.

To conclude, this research suggests that people do express' mounting concern over the current trajectory of their society, including a pronounced and widespread pessimism over the future. There was a notable absence in all the discussions of the view that markets, technological advance or political foresight would ameliorate current or future environmental problems. By contrast, the dominant claim was the inevitability of a more polluted and dangerous environment.

Such findings suggest a widespread shift in how people think about and value nature, with considerable support for Dunlap et al.'s thesis that 'environmental quality is increasingly recognised as a direct threat to human health and welfare' (1993: 37). Furthermore, it suggests support for Inglehart's (1990) thesis of society moving towards more 'postmaterialist' values, and a shift from traditional or technocratic paradigms to more ecocentric or environmental paradigms (see Cotgrove 1982; O'Riordan 1976, 1995; and see chapter 3 generally). Indeed, it would also suggest that there has been a seismic shift in public attitudes between 1989 and 1995, since few respondents were 'advocates in the ability of institutions to accommodate environmental demands' (compared with 55% to 70% reported by O'Riordan in 1989 to have 'accommodating technocentric attitudes'). And practically no-one believed in the 'ability of science, market forces and managerial ingenuity to protect the environment' (compared with between 10% and

35% reported by O'Riordan in 1989 to have 'interventionist technocratic attitudes').

However, to present such findings as providing support for a fundamental shift in attitudes is to fail to recognise how such expressed attitudes are situated historically, and the ambivalence people express between their understandings and concerns about the environment and their own personal practices. We found considerable evidence of environmental concern, including shared predictions of worsening environmental quality, combined with little evidence that people were actually restructuring their lifestyles in line with the discourse of sustainability. The apparent mismatch between concern for the environment and people's lack of overt changes in lifestyle presents an apparent enigma. Most policy research tends to advocate greater public information, as if a more informed public will engender the most appropriate sense of responsibility and hence action. However, our research points to a widespread sense of powerlessness and a perceived lack of political agency. To understand this sense of powerlessness and the related lack of active involvement in environmental programmes, we will set out three assumptions implicit in the official discourse of sustainability that are apparently not widely shared by the public and which mean that their concerns are rarely translated into significant actions.

First, the conception of the role of the state within the official discourses of sustainability was apparently rejected. Institutions of the state were generally seen as part of 'the system' which generates environmental and social problems rather than as benign agents committed to solving them. The lack of faith in the institutions of the state was held across all focus group discussions. These institutions were regarded as theoretically responsible for developing sustainability, but were thought to be very unlikely to do so since they were run for the vested interests of their own members and 'big business'.

Second, and following this, people's own sense of agency in relation to the problems was extremely weak. Most accepted some individual responsibility as morally responsible citizens, but felt that what they could do on a personal level was extremely limited. However, their lack of trust in government meant that 'political' action would also be ineffective. There was little faith in the mechanisms designed to make institutions accountable, such as voting, protest letter-writing or the Citizens' Charter. Since governments and businesses were contributing to the problems rather than solving them, the public's 'participation' in government-sponsored programmes such as Local Agenda 21 or the UK's 'Going for Green' seemed unlikely. Overall there appeared to be a widespread sense of powerlessness in the face of an increasingly risky world.

Third, there was little evidence that information, such as in the form of sustainability indicators, could play the role assigned to them within official discourses. Because governments tend to serve vested interests, the information they provide could not be trusted. Many participants felt that in any case statistical measures could not capture the important issues of concern: in particular, they could not measure the significance of nature as it is embedded in daily practice. Feeling little sense of personal agency and mistrusting the state, few participants would regard the publication of sustainability indicators as an encouragement to change their own behaviour. By contrast, people tended to rely on their own sensory experience as the one benchmark that could be trusted.

These official discourses assume relationships of trust between citizens and responsible institutions, based on a view of the state as benign. It assumes that citizens accept official information as true, and that they feel a sense of personal agency in affecting the world. Such assumptions are central to the 'same boat' ideology reflected in the Brundtland Commission, and in subsequent local, national and international official responses to sustainability. But this research suggests that few of these assumptions can be sustained. Indeed, such feelings of powerlessness appear to be compounded by the apparent mismatch between competing temporalities, with people's longer-term desires and aspirations developing in opposition to the 'short-termism' and instantaneous time imperatives largely brought about by living within a globalised society. The idea of sustainability thus provides a vocabulary with which to talk about the long term, both in the sense of people's 'dwelling' aspirations, and in terms of more 'glacial' concerns necessary for the sustenance of such important and benign aspirations.

In this section we have set out the findings of a research study whose aim was to examine the cultural and political salience of the discourse of sustainability. In this we treated the notion of the 'environment' fairly unambiguously. Yet in arguments developed elsewhere in this book, people's responses to and engagement with nature and the environment are seen as diverse, ambivalent, embedded within daily realities and contested. We now address these issues by reporting on a subsequent related study.

Framing environmental concerns

In this second study we researched how people make sense of environmental concerns in daily life and the social and institutional dimensions that mediate between concern and action. In particular, we sought to examine how people talk about environmental concerns in terms of their identities; the contested and divergent ways in which people conceive of nature; and their sense of power to act with regard to that environment (full findings are in the research report, Macnaghten et al. 1995b; and see Myers and Macnaghten 1998 forthcoming; the project was funded by the ESRC).

We conducted a series of eight focus group discussions in early 1995. Members of groups were chosen according to the specifications set out below and selected by market research recruiters. Four groups were conducted in Lancashire and Manchester, and four were held in West Sussex. Each session lasted approximately two hours.

The four sets of groups were as follows:

1 *young professional* men and women, socio-economic group B/C1, aged 25 to 35, regular readers of the *Guardian* or *Independent* newspapers, with no children;

2 *professional* men and women, socio-economic group A/B, aged 45–60, regular readers of the *Times* or *Telegraph* newspapers, living in rural areas;

3 *mothers* not in paid employment, socio-economic group C1/C2, aged 25 to 40, all with at least one child under five;

4 *working* men, socio-economic group C1/C2, aged 40–55, married with children, regular readers of the *Mail* or *Express* newspapers, living in surburban housing.

At the start of each focus group discussion, participants were asked to choose one or two environmental issues that particularly concerned them. This generated substantial discussion of a wide range of issues. Within this range, participants chose and explained problems in terms related to their daily lives and in relation to the identities they presented to the group. Four main points recurred frequently in these opening discussions: people were concerned with environmental changes that were perceived to interfere with their daily lives, including specific social/spatial practices; they were particularly concerned with unseen and unknown risks, and with the potentially long-term effects of these risks upon human health; they called upon other participants to share in feelings of disgust and loss, including a sense of outrage that the authorities were either unable or unwilling to respond to such concerns; and people recognised the ambivalence of their concerns by engaging in practices often at odds with their beliefs. `

In these discussions, people discussed their environmental concerns as being serious at local, national and global levels. But whatever the level of the problem, most people also presented environmental issues in terms of the ways in which they interfered with their own day-to-day lives. As one man from the professional group from Sussex stated:

M   *I suppose there's pollution of rivers, er, the taking away of the common land, the green land, which our I think our children are going to need, er, the growth of motorways, the growth of pollution, I mean, er, my wife suffers from asthma, and it's the fastest growing, er, one of the fastest growing afflictions for children now. Er, sewage, is another one, I think the loss of farmland, that the small farmers – it's leading us to, er, to lose a way of life which is quite important. I can go on. How many will you need. [Laughter]*

M   *Just leave some for us. [Laughter]*
   (Professionals – Sussex)

The perception of increasingly proximate environmental 'risks' in daily life permeated all the group discussions, often expressed in terms of how conventional and formerly taken-for-granted social practices were now considered dangerous. For example, there was discussion over how they (as parents) no longer permitted their children to swim in the sea, of how they could no longer catch flukes or eat fish from local beaches, of the new dangers associated with canoeing or even leaving your washing outside, of

the risks associated with car fumes and the health of young children, and of
more general local beach, river and car pollution – especially over the last
decade or so. The simple 'affordances' of place, what activities or possibilities an environment provides, furnishes or offers, were beginning to be
shaped and structured by people's perceptions of a deteriorating environment (Gibson 1979).

However, the narrative structure of the passage above is also revealing.
Especially striking is the metaphor of *loss* (loss of a way of life, taking away
of common land, loss of green land). Such metaphors are implicitly temporal
in that they refer to the passing away of valued and cherished ways of life,
with expectations of future absences. Such loss reflects a sense of threat over
one's historical attachment to place, and in particular threats to the collective
memories and reconstructions of place that shape one's sense of continuity
with the past and with the landscape. When places no longer afford simple
pleasures, and when sensory experience no longer reveals age-old meanings
(cows as part of healthy nature, beaches as places for bathing and sunbathing, rivers as places for catching and eating fish, outdoors and sea air as
places for healthy living), it is perhaps not surprising that people felt a sense
of disgust and outrage. This suggests that our senses fail us not simply in
relation to faraway and invisible risks such as nuclear radiation, but also in
more everyday, local and familiar contexts of daily life (Adam 1995a; and
see chapter 4 above).

Such discussions were generally forthright and emotive, as people spoke
of how environmental change had personally affected important aspects of
their daily lives, and clearly expected the other people in the group to agree
with them. Indeed a shared sense of disgust and loss was perhaps the most
common way in which people expressed deteriorating environmental conditions. Two members of the professional group articulate such feelings of loss
below.

M   *Well, my main gripe is the river. You were just told about the pollution of
     the sea. It ends up in the river, comes back in the river, and comes up the
     river, gets even as far as Arundel, and I've had £300 vets fee for my dog,
     who goes swimming in the river, and is getting infections out of the water.
     And all the muck of the day that's coming up from the sea, back up the
     river, lies on the bank, and it's never cleared. . . . And it just – the
     pollution that's lying there, it's just absolutely disgusting. . . . You see the
     very fishes getting washed up dead, fish, crabs, the lot, are just getting
     washed up onto the banks, and when the river rises then it comes up
     above the flood banks over the top and into the fields. And it just lies there
     and ferments. The smell there in the summer is absolutely disgusting.*

F   *Well, mine is sort of the wildlife and the flowers too. Because again,
     because of this – up on the Downs, which they're taking a lot of, obviously
     it affects our wildlife, and we've always walked to the Downs, we've
     always walked, and half the things are missing now. The flowers aren't
     there any more. You've got – er, you've got the cattle which are still
     grazing, but even they don't seem to have as much as they used to. It's just
     been taken away.*
     (Professionals – Sussex)

In this and other groups, a similar narrative of disgust and regret was expressed about the loss of countryside and valued green spaces, particular plants and wildlife, traditional ways of life, and everyday activities such as swimming. This disgust and loss were presented as both highly personal and inevitably shared, needing little further explanation. Such narratives can be read as partly about the loss of 'slowness' in daily life, as well as about threats to one's ability to engage, experience, sense and attune oneself to the lived-in world of one's immediate surroundings. In the previous section we argued that people tend to express considerable pessimism about the future, with adverse trends worsening in most respects. We also argued that this related to people's sense of powerlessness, and to a widespread cynicism about the commitment of public institutions to do anything about them. Such dynamics can help explain the intensity of the narrative of loss, including the shared sense of disgust and outrage expressed above. Indeed, even for the professional group (the group in which one might have expected a high sense of agency), the narrative of loss can be read as a poignant illustration of the mismatch between their own aspirations and the emerging world in which they live. The language of loss and outrage thus illustrates people's sense of their own passivity and powerlessness (as in the quote, 'It's just been taken away') to combat such trends which are commonly experienced as both inevitable and troubling.

Though the group discussions typically started with immediate effects of environmental damage in daily practice, people were also concerned with dangers that were distant, unseen, unknown or delayed. People were remarkably well informed about a wide range of environmental problems, both in this country and abroad. However, such familiarity did not appear to engender a sense of trust or a heightened sense of personal or ontological security (Giddens 1990). It led people to feel overwhelmed by the sheer scale of environmental problems, and to the inchoate sense that not nearly enough was being done. One female young professional from Manchester stated:

F   *Er, there just seems to be so much of it. And you – almost daily you read about, er, oil spillages, and waste going into the sea. Or rivers. Not just in this country, worldwide. It may not happen every day on our doorstep, but it's certainly happening almost daily throughout the world.*

Mod   *Right, so, the sheer scale of all this?*

F   *And nobody seems to – well, people do do things about it, but nothing, there's not enough, er, the rules aren't there to stop people from doing it.*

(Young professional – Manchester)

The difficulty this woman had in translating her rather amorphous feelings into words reflects a more widespread confusion felt by many people as to just how serious environmental problems actually are. Such uncertainties were compounded by a new array of environmental risks that no longer could be seen or sensed, and of how this engendered an increased feeling of dependency upon experts who often failed to tell one the facts. This generated a discussion of the more diffuse sense of risk and insecurity in everyday living. Indeed, if visible signs of environmental risk have unknown and potentially dangerous consequences, the risks associated with invisible and intangible causes are even more troubling. Such fears were voiced by the mothers in connection with a mysterious film of dust that was occasionally deposited upon washing and on the unknown risks associated with canoeing:

> F   *I've got some canoes. . . . I must admit, I've heard that if you fall in the water you can be ill afterwards. . . . It would be nice to know, to be reassured that you could – without being ill.*
>
> F   *I worry about this film you see on your car sometimes, in the morning, from the ICI. . . . We're very close to the ICI, I don't know. This is why it's very worrying. Some mornings you go out and it's like there's a thick layer of dust all over everything. . . . If it was just a bonfire and they were burning rubbish, and it was just – soot, well you'd think, ah, well it's just – but you don't know what it is. It could be anything couldn't it?*
>
> F   *Because you can smell something it doesn't mean it's harmful. I mean, probably the ones that are really harmful are the ones you can't smell.*
> (Mothers – Lancashire)

Such anxieties about the unknown risks again raise the issue that our senses can no longer be trusted to interpret the dwelt-in world. Such anxieties illustrate the salience of the so-called 'risk society' and the fundamental sense of insecurity. These anxieties were also linked to worries about future effects, especially in relation to what life would be like for one's children:

> F   *Because we have young children, we just – you just don't know what their life is going to be like. When they are our age, what is going to happen?*
> (Mother – Sussex)

The worries about what kind of environment we were leaving to our children were also shared by the men's group in Lancashire, who made similar comments about the invisibility and long-term effects of the worst problems, such as heavy metals.

> M   *What bothers me most is – your heavy metal substance, it's not just going to affect us now, the child can pick up asthma, right, but what you don't realise is, what he's taking in heavy metals, which by the time the child today of five gets to 21, his brain is going to stop developing, and this really concerns – But it's never looked upon, nobody is telling you the [truth]- in the water they are getting heavy metals now, in your tap water in your house we're getting it, the fish that you're eating out of the sea you're getting it, shoving it into the drains, it's going out in this orange muck and sludge onto Blackpool promenade – it's sewerage that everyone is screaming about, but that sewerage is contaminated with heavy metals, it's going through the current and it's contaminating the Western Isles of Scotland.*
> (Working man – Lancashire)

Such passages reveal how people identify their concerns about the environment in terms of what we have called 'glacial' or evolutionary time (chapter 5). Also the comment that 'nobody is telling you the truth' is revealing, since this sentiment was shared in most of the other groups. Indeed, as we examined above (see pp. 224–5), such sentiments appeared to be connected to a largely sceptical view of the self-interested character of those organisations charged with caring for the environment, and to massive doubts about their ability to act responsibly in awesomely long 'glacial' time.

Thus while people express environmental concerns in terms of its immediate effects upon daily practice, they were not as parochial and local in their concerns as one might think, nor were they ignorant of large-scale and long-term threats. If they started with immediate problems, including those made available through their senses, this was because other problems were even more difficult to know, to assess, or to do anything about.

The concerns we have quoted show that people recognised the effects of environmental damage in their daily lives, were worried about the unknown and the future, and shared a sense of disgust and loss. However, people in the focus groups had not significantly restructured their lifestyles, nor were they engaged in collective forms of protest or lobbying. The ambivalence of people's responses to environmental threats was time and time again illustrated by their comments about cars. These were identified both as the most visible threat to the environment, and as an essential part of people's daily lives which could not be done without. Most people expressed concerns about car emissions, and how these were affecting their health, referring frequently to the heightened prevalence of asthma in children.

M   *With me it's the air pollution. Er, I drive something like 35,000 miles a year, in my job, increasingly I'm conscious of sitting in traffic jams, the North West is probably one of the worst examples in Britain, and has been for the last couple of years. . . . I am now very, very conscious of breathing in crap all the time. Also, believe it or not, I jog four or five times a week, where I live is half a mile from the M6, a couple of miles from the M61, I'm surrounded by it, and usually I'm jogging maybe about six half past six at night, alongside the traffic, and I can almost taste this stuff. . . . it's more and more cars, cars, cars.*
      (Working man – Lancashire)

This participant and others could express apparently contradictory views on such issues, and expect that the rest of the group would accept and develop this ambivalence. The particular viewpoint adopted depended upon the immediate context of the discussion (here the listing and prioritising of environmental concerns). Burningham (1995) has observed a similar effect, showing that surveying attitudes towards road building can produce radically different responses from the same person, depending upon the context in which the issue is framed (see chapter 6 above on ambivalence and the countryside; and also Macnaghten 1995).

However, there are additional factors which point to motoring as a particularly ambivalent spatial practice. First, there is the undoubted attachment which people feel towards cars. They have become an essential part not merely of daily life but also of modern and especially male identity (note a whole cable TV channel devoted to the theme of 'Men and Motors'). Moreover, as we explored in chapter 6, motoring also represents a way of dwelling in the countryside, of experiencing the beauty of nature and the countryside by way of the 'open road', what Ward (1991) calls the 'freedom to go'. But simultaneously such spatial practices are increasingly viewed as polluting, dangerous and irresponsible, especially in terms of their long-term impact. Car-use symbolises the most obvious and direct example of how everyday commonplace activity can lead to widespread and long-term environmental damage. Indeed, unlike other pollution issues such as acid rain, toxic waste or water pollution, it is less plausible for people to lay the blame elsewhere (with governments or multi-national corporations or privatised industries), especially since the effects upon health and landscape are so evident.

Such ambivalence, using a car while criticising the effects of traffic, is linked to a model of personal agency, that is, of how one conceives of one's sense of power to effect change either directly or through trusted institutions. Models of agency are the framework within which people determine the likely efficacy of future action, a point developed later. Meanwhile, we outline two further factors affecting how people talk about, value and engage with nature – that of how nature is reconfiguring identity, and of how the idea of nature is itself a contested concept.

Official discourses on sustainability rely on individuals defining themselves and their concerns at a global level, as for example the widely quoted IUCN Caring for the Earth definition of 'improving quality of life within the carrying capacity of the planet' (IUCN 1991). A similar appeal to global concerns is implicit in the maxim 'Think Globally, Act Locally' (we discuss this in more detail in chapter 8 below). Recently, research has examined whether people identify their environmental concerns and expectations at this global level, or whether they present themselves and their environmental concerns within other spatial identities. Our research supports the claim of Burningham and O'Brien (1994) that global concerns are in practice localised.

In discussion participants presented their environmental concerns in terms of their sense of their own focus group identity. Some of these identities related to the categories we had used to select participants. So, for instance, both groups of mothers referred to their identities as mothers, and both rural groups referred to the rural nature of their community life. But participants also brought out alternative relevant identities. On occasions people in several of the groups presented themselves as parents, and at other times they presented themselves as representatives of a community, or as incomers, or as people with some special knowledge and expertise. We now look at how contested ideas of nature reconfigured and structured identity.

For both mothers' groups much of the talk focused on issues which had direct implications for their role as mothers. There was considerable anxiety expressed over traffic fumes and asthma, beach effluent, the loss of green spaces, pollution from a local factory, and dog dirt, precisely because these were the local issues that were most relevant to the future health, well-being and safety of their children. Other more global environmental issues, such as whaling and deforestation, were termed 'higher issues'.

F   *You don't tend to talk about the higher environmental [issues] . . . – Well, you know, like deforestation, and whaling, and environmental things like that.*
(Mother – Lancashire)

These 'higher' issues were considered by many mothers as being too distant and of little relevance to their everyday lives. One woman reflected on her own current identity as the mother of young children and how this prioritised immediate and localised concerns. At other stages of her life, she suggested, she would have more time and motivation to become concerned with these wider social and environmental issues.

F   *I mean, if the nuclear power station went up it's a bit more important than perhaps if we've got turds in the sea, isn't it, but I mean as you say, as a mother you tend to step back from it, it's what affects you personally, rather than is the ozone layer still there, and are we sizzling up because the sun's coming through.*
(Mother – Lancashire)

Indeed, both groups of mothers expressed guilt over their lack of overt environmental concern and behaviour. This guilt implied a reconstitution of what it means to be a good mother. The responsibilities of motherhood, which have always implied caring about the future welfare of one's children, have now been extended to embrace an appropriate sense of *long-term* responsibility for the environment as a whole. The identity of parenthood was also used in other groups, mainly in discussions over the long-term impact of current activities and their implications on what life would be like for future generations. Parents were considered to have a personal stake in the future. Such arguments suggest that parenthood may be the most salient identity in which people conceive of their roles, obligations and senses of responsibility consistent with evolutionary or 'glacial' time.

Alternatively, both working men's groups tended to use technical expertise and understanding from their jobs to justify claims as to the severity of current environmental problems and risks, such as resource depletion, heavy metals, global warming, air and oil pollution, and recycling. Here is an engineer talking about the release of cadmium on the sea floor:

M   *So we heat it [the crude oil] on the rig, as it comes up through the head, and then we have, for want of a better word, a sleeve on the draw-pipe. And every 15 seconds we raise this something like 30 mil, and the sludge goes phweuh out of the side, and then we drop it again and ignore it, and this isn't like raw sewage, it can't be seen, it can't be smelled, it can't be touched, and yet it's so deadly, that there's just nothing living within like a hundred miles of that rig.*
(Working man – Lancashire)

Again we note the way in which people were able to realise how our senses are increasingly unable to assess risks. However, by contrast with

other groups, the 'structure of feeling' was different. Not only were these
men more prone to conceive of environmental issues from a global perspective, but they also were more likely to conceive of these concerns
detached from lived experience. Such a perspective led to a more abstract
discussion of the technical problems associated with industrial processes,
and of their systemic and long-term impacts (although, as we note later, in
the Lancashire working men's group moral indignation was expressed
towards local and aesthetic problems). Indeed, although there was some
discussion of the effect of environmental risks on their local environment
(chemicals in rivers, viruses on beaches), such problems tended to be
discussed independent of localised social practices. Or, to use Ingold's
distinctions, environmental problems were conceived as 'the object of
human interest and concern' rather than 'the world of which humans
themselves are conceived to be a part' (1993a: 40). Such detachment or
'undwellingness' is discussed later in relation to official understandings of
sustainability but is illustrated here in the following:

> M   *Same as the last chap. I'm more concerned globally than locally. I think
> things locally can be more controlled, fixed, er, globally, I think the
> politicians of most countries just go through the motions of environmental
> issues. They don't actually do anything about it. Except maybe to put
> another few shillings on petrol, things like that, they're actually encourag-
> ing more cars to be on the road, by building more by-passes and
> motorways, and producing more cars. Etcetera. We were talking about
> river pollution earlier, the main pollutions in the river is not industry, like
> it was a few years ago, but fertilizers, run off from the farm land, into the
> river. And, er, polluting it that way. Killing off rivers.*
> (Working man – Sussex)

Again, by contrast, for both groups of professionals living in rural areas,
environmental threats were discussed in connection with the social practices
afforded by their local countryside. Unlike other identities, ideas of nature
have for some centuries been central to the ideals of the rural landscapes and
rural living. In our discussions people spoke in detail of the various qualities
associated with living in the countryside: the quality of life it offered them,
its beauty, its slower pace of life, its clean air, and its social cohesion and
sense of community (especially important for bringing up children). Environmental concerns tended to be conceived in terms of threats to such
countryside spaces, threats which were relatively place specific and included
road building, urban encroachment on the green belt, loss of common land,
local beach pollution, the increasing fragmentation of the local community,
the pressure of mass tourism and outdoor leisure activities, and for the
Lancashire group of professionals the underlying threat arising from the
proximity of the nuclear industry at Sellafield. Such threats were seen as a
direct infringement of their sense of rural identity, which partly explains the
appeal of rhetorics of loss.

Another identity available to a number of groups in connection with
environmental concerns was that of being British. Usually this identity was
seen as a source of shame or embarrassment, either as a problem lurking

beneath 'our' collective psyche, or more commonly attributed to what the groups saw as the British Government's inactivity within a wider European or international context. Interestingly, the label of Britain as 'the Dirty Man of Europe' appeared to have particularly stuck (see chapter 2 above), resonant with a commonly shared perception that environmental policy in Britain was backward and a source of stigma:

> M   *You mention environment in Britain you'll get, shit, Greenpeace, not again, you know. And that is the problem particularly the last one coordinating use of resources. As part of my degree course we looked at alternative energies, and one thing we found – a case study we looked at – was in Britain people just won't consider alternative resources, because as soon as they put a plan in to the local authority to erect a windmill or a wave turbine or anything you like you can get some crank saying you can't do it because . . . – Scandinavia doesn't have this problem, they've got windmills everywhere, wave turbines at every available bit of water, there's something wrong with the British psyche about this.*
> (Working man – Lancashire)

Britain was often compared unfavourably with France, the Netherlands and Germany (the one counter to this was the appeal to Britain as a nation which cares for animals). However, while participants sometimes questioned or regretted this British identity, there was little development of the global identity encouraged within the sustainability discourse. While global environmental issues were on occasion discussed, most notably in the Lancashire working men's group, people rarely discussed their actions as contributing towards wider, more global environmental issues. By contrast, most people tended to conceive of their own identity – and indeed the impact of their own actions – in more situated, localised and grounded ways, notably in their forms and patterns of dwellingness.

In these passages we have seen that the identities that were adopted shaped how people appeared to understand and discuss environmental concerns within their daily lives. And we have also seen how and in what ways these environmental concerns were in turn reconfiguring such identities. We thus see some illustration of the constructed, polyvocal, contested and situated character of identities. As a consequence, as Pile and Thrift maintain: 'social conflicts are no longer seen as just the epic clash of antagonistic social blocs but as a distributed deconstruction and reconstruction of social identities' (1995a: 9). They also argue that identities are increasingly to be understood as shaped by and through various metaphors of space, not only those of home and place, but also those of travel, in-betweenness, mobility, diaspora and nature. Such identities involve movement in and through various objects which themselves can be said to 'act'. 'Human' identities are formed and reformed, conceptualised and contested in the midst of countless 'subjects' and 'objects' which produce and reproduce different agents and senses of agency.

Such arguments for the diversity of identity challenge the notion that there is an epic clash of green and non-green social blocs. It also contests the notion that there is a single environment or nature 'out there' waiting to be

saved. Burningham and O'Brien (1994), for example, have shown that the
parties involved in the road disputes that they studied did not seem to be
referring to the same environment at all. Different groups with different
identities 'localised' nature in distinct ways. Similarly, the focus group
discussions we studied revealed differing and distinct conceptions of nature,
by contrast with the global and unified conception of nature and the local
and rational conception of action, which are articulated within the official
discourses of sustainability.

Much environmental debate has been divided into local issues (such as
local pollution, traffic or recycling) or global issues (such as ozone depletion, global warming or deforestation). However, we found that the ways in
which people conceived of local issues and action, and their relationship to
more global and systemic issues, was complex and took different forms for
different groups. For some the relationship between the local and the wider
environment arose through metaphors of dirt and purity. The Lancashire
mothers' group saw local pollution, especially sewage on the beach and
industrial emissions in the air, as making their lives more dirty, more risky,
and more dangerous. For them, the environment was localised within their
daily practices, uses and actions, and their disgust at locally intrusive
pollution.

For other groups local issues were discussed in more symbolic and moral
terms. For both groups of professionals living in rural areas, nature was
embodied within the symbolic integrity of the countryside and especially in
rural living. This discourse of nature was framed in terms of the rhythms,
time-scales, quality of life, beauty and character afforded by rural places;
and how these were being threatened by encroaching urban developments
and associated economic growth. The focus on 'rural natures' points to
competing local natures, including those situated and embedded within
contemporary rural practices.

For others, nature was also conceived using symbolic romantic language,
drawing upon immediate sensory experience and recollection, and a corresponding sense of threat and loss. Rhetorics of loss clearly date back to
literary evocations of a Golden Age and Romantic critiques of industrialism
and growing cities. But they have also taken on a new range of examples in
line with contemporary environmentalism, perceptions of social breakdown
and unease with material progress.

Other groups were more explicitly concerned with the 'global' state of the
environment. For the Lancashire working men's group there was common
agreement that the more serious environmental problems were of a global
and systemic basis (such as heavy metals, global warming and other toxic
releases). However, these men still expressed considerable moral anger and
indignation towards local and aesthetic environmental problems, such as
litter and dog mess. These local issues acquired symbolic importance as
reflecting a wider *amoral* disrespect for one's surroundings. Moreover, this
group argued that if we as part of society were unable to deal with such local
and remediable problems, what possible chance had we to manage more

complex, more global and more systemic environmental risks. The focus was on environmental issues that concerned people:

M   . . . *what gets up my nose is intrusive, er, effects on the environment, like litter, discharge pipes on the beach, er, a three-foot discharge pipe giving out orange muck into the river, dog crap, things that shouldn't be there. Piles of litter, piles of junk, people throwing things out of cars, there's no need for it. That can be addressed immediately. Things like this are going to take forever to get right [referring to prior discussion on heavy metals]* (Working man – Lancashire)

Here the perceived intractability of immediate and visible local issues reflected wider unease over the intractability of more global and systemic environmental issues. One might also note that it is harder to construct alibis for local problems, or to rationalise them as being outside one's own responsibility.

Again, by contrast, 'global' constructions of nature were on occasion discussed in moral terms. In the group of young men and women in Manchester, for example, environmental issues were related to people's moral engagement with each other, and the animate world. For them, environmental issues symbolised a new, inclusive and even 'global' morality involving mutual care and respect for others, including animals. Those outside this moral sphere included multi-national corporations (who did not care about people or nature), people who exploit wild animals such as dancing bears (who do so for their own greed and self-interest), a local community who opposed a gypsy site (thus showing a marked lack of tolerance), and a society which had forced people onto the streets (the increased number of homeless people was seen as evidence of how morally corrupt our society had become). For these participants, a concern for any of these moral issues was seen as being connected to a parallel concern for the environment. Thus many campaigns, such as the protection of bears, tigers, dolphins, and so on, could be seen as standing for much wider environmental considerations. Other people also claimed to share a moral concern for nature. It was thought that a society which cares for animals was one which would also care for each other and for the long-term future.

These complex spatial and moral conceptions point to multiple spaces of nature, from the local to the global, and to competing definitions and understandings of such natures from the rational/instrumental to the moral/ romantic. In each case, people's expressed concerns with nature and the environment led to broader concerns over the functioning of society's institutions. Environmental concerns were thus seen to be bounded neither from other concerns nor from people's understandings of how and whether change can occur. To see how these concerns relate to change, we need to examine the relationship between how people talked about environmental concerns and their own sense of power or agency.

Most people accepted that everyone is partly responsible for environmental problems, that solutions might mean far-reaching changes to our personal lifestyles, and that technological and consumer-driven society was not sustainable. However, calls for people to change their individual lifestyles were only occasionally promoted by participants in the focus groups. On such occasions, people tended to stress the need for environmental education, especially of children. The older and rural groups tended to advocate education, with a particular emphasis on teaching young people to care about local and aesthetic environmental issues, such as not throwing litter or letting their dogs mess the pavements.

> M   *It is discipline at home. You turn that light switch off, you don't need that now – go to the fridge and open a bottle of something and drink half and throw the other half down the sink. Or open a can and some take two sips out and say I don't like it, I don't want it. That's waste. And it's total waste of the material it was made with and the waste of the energy as well.*
> (Professional – Sussex)

Other people also spoke of their own personal power to effect change, usually through consumer choices, such as buying dolphin-friendly tuna or aerosols which do not contain CFCs. For some, voting and democratic accountability were still the best means towards a better environment, even though conventional political structures were seen as limited in their capacity to solve environmental problems:

> M   *We can nibble round the edge of the total environmental issue, but at the end of the day, if we don't get the politics right, if we don't get the power, to be able to control our own environment, then we go nowhere. People don't realise the power of their vote. You are absolutely correct. They [referring to politicans] think of today and tomorrow. They don't think of next week, never mind 350 frigging years. That's how short-sighted they are. Now we are going to have to get a grip of it, bloody soon. I think there's a very small, there is a slow awakening as to the environmental issues there, there's a slow awakening, but there is an awakening, I'm a wee bit more encouraged.*
> (Working man – Lancashire)

But this model of agency was largely absent in the focus group discussions. Rarely did people believe that collective action (through participation in political parties, consumer or environmental groups, or trade unions) would help towards a better environment. More common was the belief that voting rarely changed anything, that real power was largely beyond their control, and that the deteriorating state of the environment was a largely intractable by-product of a system increasingly run through financial interests. Such beliefs reflect the widespread distrust of public institutions encountered in the study reported above. For instance, the man who made the ambivalent comment on the usefulness and threat of cars, quoted earlier, continued:

> M   *It's more and more cars, cars, cars. That's from government policy all the way through. And anybody who uses vehicles and has used them for maybe 10 or 15 years must see the massive increase of everything on the road. It's the pollution of the air. And as linked to the previous one [heavy metals] obviously, it's the oil companies again, it's the financial clout of the oil companies.*
> (Working man – Lancashire)

In the same group, there was much discussion concerning whether states still possessed the authority to manage environmental risks in the face of the power of multi-national corporations. The subsequent passage shows just how deep global economic integration has penetrated the national consciousness.

M   *But that's the key to the whole thing, the attitude of the whole thing. It's all politics, it's economics, and it's power. And the power of the multi-nationals who are involved in oil, who are involved in gas exploration, they make and break governments, it's as simple as that. And if in fact the Government is not going to really make it difficult for a company who employ nearly 50,000 people and donate several million to the war chest the next general election, then what chance have you got of real legislation – who will punish someone who's dumping tens of thousands of barrels of crap into the sea? They won't do it.*
(Working man – Lancashire)

This model of increasingly global and hegemonic capitalist interests informed much of the discussion of the environment, including the likelihood of solutions and what people themselves could or should do. For example, many people spoke of how it was unfair to blame individuals when big companies were themselves mostly to blame, of how there was insufficient regulation of industry by governments, and of how environmental degradation in the Third World was possibly even more serious where companies could get away with it more easily. This cynical view of industry and governments was commonplace in all the discussions, frequently in a similar form to the assertion made in the Lancashire mothers' group: 'at the end of the day, it's all down to money, isn't it?'.

In this study we have examined how people make sense of environmental issues and the dimensions that mediate the complex relationship between concern and action. Contrary to much survey research which has suggested a decline in the public salience of 'the environment', we found that people from many sectors of society were aware of a wide range of issues, and were deeply concerned about them. Moreover, these anxieties were exacerbated by a sense of environmental risks becoming increasingly uncertain, unknowable, globalised and dependent upon highly abstract expert systems. Furthermore, there was a common perception that these risks were beginning to impact directly upon people's health and to constrain locally based social practices.

We have emphasised three points in opposition to survey research which we think misreads how people make sense of environmental issues and how this sense becomes incorporated into their daily practices. First, it assumes that environmental concerns exist *a priori*, waiting to be revealed through sample surveys. By contrast, our research points out how people make sense of environmental issues within particular localised and embedded identities. Moreover, people were able to understand environmental issues in terms of how they impinged upon or threatened their sense of identity, for example, as mothers, as rural dwellers, as global or as British citizens. Identity thus provides a framework in which to contextualise oneself in relationship to nature, and thus to interpret the associated risks and issues. For most of our group discussions, environmental issues either posed serious threats to people's sense of personal identity (as mothers or as rural dwellers), or they provided a context in which to clarify the profound dangers associated with growing environmental risks (as technical managers or engineers).

Second, survey research tends to give partial accounts of contemporary environmental concern by ignoring the competing frameworks or discourses of nature that inform everyday life. Environmental issues in the group discussions were distinguished not only by a local and global continuum, but also by rational/instrumental and moral/symbolic dimensions. Thus, again, this points to the need to engage with people's own sense of nature and the environment, including the historical and cultural significance of the countryside and rural living, and with the moral sense of nature that informed much of people's concerns with animals, especially within younger groups. To conceive of environmental issues in global, instrumental and rational terms is simply one out of a number of possible 'natures'. Moreover, it is likely to ignore people's moral attachment to local places such as the countryside, as well as the symbolic significance of particular issues (such as the use of veal crates, or concern over the extinction of species such as tigers, whales or bears).

Third, most existing research has misread the apparent decline in concern for and action on the environment. Official responses tend to identify this lack of action as caused by a lack of environmental awareness. This was not borne out in our focus group discussions. By contrast we found evidence of ambivalent attitudes towards personal action, related to a pervasive lack of personal agency and a marked lack of trust in institutions responsible for managing environmental change. Indeed, the dominant tacit model of social change favoured by our focus group participants was one centred on the all-pervasive power of economic interests, with its internal logic of short-termism, so that even governments were seen as constrained in their possibilities for action, especially as regards adopting a long-term perspective on the environment. Such dynamics are reflected in the now sizeable evidence concerning the lack of trust currently invested in conventional politics, and in the tendency for people to regard environmental groups as more worthy of trust than business and governments (Worcester 1995). It might also be noted, though, that other research of ours suggests that there may also be increasingly sceptical attitudes among young people even to environmental NGOs, as well as to these more established institutions (Macnaghten and Scott 1994; note how the young men's group discussed above refused to believe in the existence of global environmental problems).

Conclusion

In this book we have set out a framework in which to discuss the significance of nature within everyday life in the light of social practices which are spatially distinct, including conflicting senses of local and global natures; temporally discontinuous, including conflicting times in nature from the instantaneous to the unimaginably long term; differentially embodied, including the new array of 'environmental bads' that now enter 'bodies' in ways which transcend direct sensory perception; and discursively ordered, including the contrasts between official rhetorics and everyday talk.

In these final paragraphs we explore the implications of the empirical research for this framework. We do not of course claim that these focus groups are statistically representative. But given the degree of consensus within each of the groups, the strong convergences between the groups and between the two studies on some key issues, the findings do seem to have a significance beyond their particular situated location.

In chapter 4 we examined Beck's (1992b) claim that in the new 'risk society' risks could no longer be directly touched, tasted, heard, smelt, and especially seen. For many participants in our focus groups this was indeed the case; moreover, such risks were now permeating everyday life and contributing to a diffuse sense of unease and insecurity. In these circumstances, 'trust' becomes a crucial mediating factor. In the research, we found that mistrust is even more widespread than previously thought and related to a widespread disaffection with the institutions of science, the media, business, and most significantly the state. Particularly important is the belief that visible signs of environmental risk have unknown consequences, that the senses can no longer be trusted to make sense of daily practice, that all of this belies the true extent of risk on an evolutionary or glacial scale, and that this leads to a fundamental sense of anxiety and pessimism over the future. Such fears are further exacerbated by the strong sense that institutions of the state and business are both unwilling and unable to respond to such concerns.

In chapter 5 we analysed the different times in and of nature, and in particular the distinct cultural shifts towards both a more 'instantaneous' time and a more 'glacial' time. For many participants in our focus groups, there was a mounting awareness of multiple time-horizons and time-scales. On the one hand, there was the experience of an increased pace of life, with associated pressures of short-termism (especially in work patterns); while, on the other hand, there was the realisation of the need to think, act and plan for the long term, not least brought about via the immediacy and scale of environmental problems. However, these two distinct time-horizons were identified as largely conflicting and in tension with each other. Indeed, most people were uncomfortable with the new instantaneous 'short-termism' that now appeared to be structuring increasing aspects of their lifeworlds, as life became more and more tangled in globalising processes. Such pressure not only threatened people's aspirations to plan and act for the future, but also threatened their more everyday 'dwelling' times and spaces, especially the simple and everyday pleasures which contribute to people's quality of life, including local and symbolic spaces of nature.

Finally, we return to the multiple spaces of nature highlighted elsewhere in this book, from the local, to the national and global. For participants in our focus groups we identified multiple natures, variously spaced, but also discursively ordered along moral/symbolic and rational/instrumental axes. The idea of 'global' citizenship, so central to formal rhetorics of sustainability, was employed by some of our focus group participants. However, by contrast with the rational and instrumental spaces of nature within the discourse of sustainability, especially young people tended to identify the global in moral as opposed to instrumental terms, and to conceive of a new embryonic moral 'global' sphere as the counter to instrumental, global short-term rationality. Indeed, the detached idea of sustainability, reflecting as it were the subject gazing upon the globe as if he/she were detached and outside, was only employed by the two working men's groups, both of which contained engineers and middle managers. It is perhaps not coincidental that these two groups were single-sex men's groups, and that mixed-sex and female groups conceived of nature more in relation to their dwelt-in world. Ingold has argued that 'what is perhaps most striking about the contemporary discourse of global environmental change is the immensity of the gulf that divides the world as it is lived, and the world of which they speak under the rubric of "the globe"' (1993a: 40).

However, for some of the groups researched, the lived-in world is now not merely the local but can also be the distant. Through the global media and new technologies such as the Internet, as well as through the environmental groups such as Friends of the Earth and Greenpeace, people can dwell in faraway places, empathise with the plight of distant peoples. And this can be so not just through the use of abstract principles such as those of global equity and justice, but in relation to people's situated cultural concerns so as to engage in protests involving nature and morality across the whole planet. In the final chapter we return to theoretical debates around identity, detraditionalisation and globalisation, in the light of these empirical studies. We examine the challenges that are posed for forms of governance brought about by what we may term the 'globalisation of nature' and new forms of 'global dwellingness' (see Giddens 1995).

8

GOVERNING NATURE

Summarising

In the last two chapters we have empirically examined a range of processes hugely significant both for the theorising of nature, and for developing and implementing policies that reflect how people talk about, value and engage with nature in daily life, and thus the basis for how one might save that nature. These processes constitute the lineaments of an approach which both recognises, and goes beyond, the starting point of this book, namely, that there is no single nature, only natures.

In this concluding chapter we interrogate a major recent issue which has forced itself onto the 'environmental' agenda, namely, the BSE crisis in the UK, since it demonstrates many of the themes addressed in this book. In particular, it shows that governing nature in a global context is well-nigh impossible; and that many interventions by the state or by science generate unexpected and unpredictable reactions which can escalate the issue and the problem far away from what is apparently intended. We will see that issues of science, the senses, time, bodies, space and practices are all part of the sorry story of British beef. Following that account we outline some of the main characteristics that the 'governing of nature' takes within the increasingly globalised context. We thus conclude this book by demonstrating just how the 'globalisation of nature' discussed in chapter 7 and elsewhere has produced a new and equally contested nature, a nature that is more or less ungovernable, at least within available practices and discourses.

But before we encounter mad cows (as well as of course mad politicians) we summarise the approach to nature and the environment adopted in this book, beginning with some of the claims initially made in chapter 1.

First of all, we have sought to reject dominant doctrines of *environmental realism*. By contrast we have emphasised the exceptionally diverse ways in which nature or the environment has come to be constructed, both through different social practices with which the physical environment is hugely intertwined, and through different available discourses and vocabularies, including those produced from within the academy (see Dickens 1996: chap. 5 on the role of the division of labour in 'industrialising nature's powers'). We have seen that what has been viewed as nature has varied enormously and that nature is in some senses as cultural as is say the content of television. Moreover, embedded within different natures are different bodily relationships, as nature has come to be sensed and hence produced in diverse ways. We have seen in chapter 4 that what is nature depends in part on how it is sensed by humans; and how different senses produce what are deemed to be different natures.

We also showed in chapter 2 just how the so-called 'environmental agenda' had to be invented in the post-war period. It was not simply 'out there' waiting to pounce upon the social world. We do not deny the enormously powerful effects that the physical world exerts and in particular its capacity to take massive and often deserved revenge upon human society. But we are denying that there is an already formed and causally powerful set of environmental bads which *in and of themselves* can generate such havoc in the public realm. For example, public awareness of a global environmental crisis is not simply the product of risks becoming global. It is partly that a range of diverse environmental issues have come to be viewed as operating on a global scale, on a scale which presumes that many people living in diverse societies can imagine themselves as inhabiting the same environment, and thus subject to international and even global planetary risks which are to some extent universal and shared (see Beck 1996b; Hajer 1996; Wynne 1994). The perception of environmental threat as of global proportions has relied upon such an imagined community, and from the multiple cultural and economic processes which connected what were hitherto separate and discrete processes.

Second, we have criticised the doctrine of *environmental idealism*. Because we have shown that there are many natures, that each is contested and that no one nature is obviously more natural than any other, so we cannot argue for or justify particular values because they supposedly inhere in nature (see Harvey 1996: chap. 7; O'Neill 1993: chap. 2). We have emphasised how people's orientation to the environment is structured in terms of their temporally and spatially organised social practices, their complexly organised patterns of dwellingness. It is only within the context of such practices, as well as their sensory and temporal organisation, that it is possible to identify and to justify how various values regarding nature may or may not be adopted. We argued against investigating such values in a way abstracted from people's specific, contextual and temporally resonant patterns of life. Many studies have shown that the choice of values supposedly in nature is in fact historically specific and that these values function only as more or less useful metaphors or symbols. As Capra points out: 'We can never speak about nature without, at the same time, speaking about ourselves' (1975: 77).

We have also shown that how people value nature is often highly ambiguous and contradictory; that values only appear to inhere in nature in particular and context-specific ways. In many contexts people's attitudes to nature, science, the countryside and various spatial practices are ambivalent and there is no clear and unambiguous sense of what values can be said to inhere within nature. By contrast, we have shown how values, attitudes and concerns about nature are indissolubly bound up with wider dimensions of living in late modernity. Values are thus not free-floating but intertwined with senses of insecurity, globalisation, anxiety, individualisation, mounting mistrust with politics and scientific expertise, the enhanced role of the media, and so on.

We further emphasised in chapter 6 that some such spatial practices entail particular combinations of humans and machines, what have been called 'machinic complexes'. Many environmental bads appear to stem from such complexes in which specific combinations of 'human' and 'non-human' actants produce powerful and in cases environmentally destructive agency (such as the railway, the car, the plane, the computer, and so on). These complexes contest the notion that particular significance should be attached to humans and to the particular values they believe inhere within nature. The emergence of an 'inhuman' cyborg culture signifies the collapsing of the distinctions between animals and machines and the physical and non-physical worlds (Haraway 1991; Michael 1996). The miniaturization of the machine and its transcendence of the boundaries of the slow-moving human body destroy much remaining sense of an authentic human to nature relationship and value.

Third, we also argued against *environmental instrumentalism*. We have shown that a great deal of policy has been directed towards inducing the public to adopt environmentally benign behaviour. It is often presumed that if people are simply presented with the facts, then they will be motivated to change their behaviour and save the planet since they will see it is in their interest to do so. And sometimes it is presumed that people will only change their behaviour if there is some readjustment of the costs and benefits of actions, so that they are persuaded that it is in their more immediate interests to modify their behaviour (see O'Neill 1993: chaps 4 and 5). In both cases, though, there is a conception of the individual subject who can calculate the costs and benefits of different behaviours and who trusts that each individual action will be matched by those of public institutions. Such policy discourse – such as those promoted by official initiatives aimed at sustainable development – depends on a benign model of agency where people feel empowered that personal individual action can improve the wider situation since everyone is in the 'same boat'. Related initiatives also often presume that we need to increase the number of 'environmentally oriented' members of a society's population as though 'being green' is a once-and-for-all identity.

By contrast we have shown in chapters 6 and 7 that most people's attitudes to the 'environment' are ambivalent. They are not fixed and given, although they are often sustained in particular contexts with exceptional passion and commitment. It seems that relatively few people are simply 'green' in essence. But also equally few people are willing to trust public bodies to undertake the right policies in order to 'save' the planet. Many people are unlikely to undertake behaviours simply because such bodies claim it is in their apparent interest to do so, since there is little belief that public authorities and corporations will also undertake what is necessary in

order to complete the particular environmental task. We have thus emphasised the importance for people of relational dimensions of public attitudes
and practice; of how what people themselves are prepared to do depends on
how they conceive of their relationship to others, including those in
positions of power and authority. It seems that it is only within relationships
of trust that people possess a powerful sense of agency that personal
individual action might meaningfully contribute to 'save the planet'. But in
Britain at least few appear to possess such a sense of agency (see chapters 3
and 7). Although many people are concerned about the environment and the
need for fundamental changes in lifestyle, no amount of hectoring or
financial inducement by states or corporations is likely to lead people to 'go
for green' on as large a scale as may be required. Indeed it is precisely
because states and corporations appear so untrustworthy in their long-term
commitments to the environment that there is a reduced sense of personal
agency and hence less willingness to engage in environmentally benign
behaviour. We examine below how recent putative globalisation has
increased the possibilities of agency on behalf of the planet because of our
expanding knowledge and experience of global environmental change and
the new opportunities to affect events on the far corners of the globe. But it
has simultaneously reduced such a sense because of our awareness of
mounting dependence in daily life upon global forces largely beyond our
control, coupled with the strong belief that states and corporations endlessly
disobey their own environmental directives, fuelled as they appear to be by
intractable short-term economic interests.

One ironic and troubling implication of this book is that 'nature' is not so
different an object of analysis from many of the other topics interrogated by
the so-called social sciences. In some senses, then, there is no special case to
be made for the sociology of the environment, just as unfortunately there is
no special realm of nature from which values and appropriate patterns of the
good life can be simply derived and implemented. Most of our arguments
about time and space, body and sense, local and global, official and lay
discourses, and so on, apply equally across most domains of the physical and
social world. But there are nevertheless four key features of nature and the
environment which undoubtedly turn our analysis in particular and problematic ways.

First and most obviously, to begin even to contribute to the emergent
social science of the environment means that there is some displacement of
the sciences from a previously monopolistic position with regard to nature
(as evidenced by the historic power of the very term 'natural' sciences). It is
therefore not surprising that most social science of the environment has been
heavily 'scientistic', partly to ensure some credibility in the head-to-head
competition with the hugely powerful discourses of natural science. We
investigated the strengths and weaknesses of some such quantitative approaches in chapter 3. The kinds of historical, qualitative and critical approaches
developed in this book are thus on the margins of the margins of the
environmental literature (but see Lash et al. 1996; Milton 1993a).

Second, nature is a hugely significant concept within western culture and therefore any efforts to interpret and even deconstruct its complex and contested senses will almost certainly take one into debates about the nature of the human, the character of the natural world, the relationship of God to that world, the ideological import of 'natural' phenomena, the duties humans owe to the earth and other species, the relations between different generations, the legacy of the Enlightenment, and so on. A social science of the environment cannot but be deeply contested since it engages with and confronts hugely powerful ideological conceptions which have been at the very centre of especially western thought (see Hayward 1994).

Third, to treat nature as like any other 'social' practice/institution does not do justice to its capacity to exert revenge upon human and animal life over exceptional spatial scales and across extraordinary lengths of time. So even if the technologies of investigation are more or less the same as other social practices, there will be a quite insistent pressure to devise, recommend and implement policies on some or other scale that recognise the awesome threats to human and animal life posed now and in the unimaginable future by multiple forms of what are contemporaneously taken to be 'environmental threats'. A social science of the environment cannot therefore be unengaged from current policy and politics, even if much of the time it seeks to deconstruct the policies of especially corporations and states.

Finally, the increasingly global nature of both social and physical phenomena means that apparent differences between nature and society can no longer be sustained. Indeed the very idea of 'social' science now appears to carry much less conviction. Later in this chapter we examine the impact of the variety of global flows that criss-cross contemporary societies, flows which are physical, symbolic and human and where borders and frontiers of the 'social' no longer seem to exert powerful constraints (see Taylor 1996). A social science of the environment almost certainly needs to recognise that societies and their nation-states are no longer to be viewed as the appropriate 'power-container' for many significant kinds of social relationships. Arguably, such environmental inquiry *should* be able to recognise this since many other areas of social science inquiry appear even more trapped within the nation-state–society boundary (see Bauman 1993a: 230 on the crisis of the nation-state).

In the next section we encounter one recent series of events surounding the flows of disease, of image, of scientific finding and of perceived risk which demonstrate many of these points. In the final sections of the chapter we reflect upon what mad cows can tell us much more generally about the problems of managing nature in a globalising and deeply ungovernable world.

Mad cows

The saga of bovine spongiform encephalopathy (BSE) in Britain and Europe is one in which political controversy over how best to regulate a new disease in cattle escalated to such proportions so as to threaten the very cohesion of the European Union (EU). For Beck (1996a), the crisis signifies the emergence of a new kind of society, the famous 'risk society'. Character- istics of such a society are intense public awareness of the riskiness of hitherto mundane aspects of daily life which can as if spontaneously acquire acute political and cultural significance, of the manifest uncertainty of those risks, of people's sense of dependency upon institutions and expert systems responsible for managing and controlling such risks, and of the increasingly untrustworthiness of those same institutions to respond adequately (see chapter 7; see also Beck 1992b; Wynne 1996a). BSE illustrates in dramatic detail such a risk dynamic, one in which the churning of modern industrial innovation led inadvertently to the intensification of risk in everyday practice, and where current reductionist scientific approaches to evaluating such risks led to an extraordinary breakdown of governance in modern policy culture (Wynne 1996b). For Grove-White (1996b), such dynamics signal 'a new stage in the tangled relationships between science, environ- ment and government'.

Yet, the BSE crisis raises wider questions as to how states can govern nature in the increasingly globalised risk society. How can states manage risk when the authority of a policy culture highly dependent on scientific expertise becomes corroded? How can states allay public worries and anxieties when government reassurance couched as scientific fact is met with mounting public scepticism and disbelief? What scope do nation-states have to deal with risk within their national borders in the light of globalising economic realities? And what opportunities exist to manage a risk event objectively when the issue becomes interlinked with a number of other political, social and moral concerns? Wynne sets out the difficulties for experts to capture the risk dynamic by pointing to the multiple and interlinking issues implicated in BSE, just weeks after the crisis exploded into the public domain following the admission by the UK Government of a possible link between mad cow disease and human death:

> Already coursing through the issue are, *inter alia*: the tortured United Kingdom relationship with the European Union; the over-industrialisation of agriculture and food supply; ideological obsessions with deregulation, and government ministries' scandalous proximity to sponsorship of private industrial interests; fast-eroding public identification with official public bodies and their pronouncements; and the distinct whiff of political control of science arising from recent changes in UK research and education culture. (1996b: 13)

Before examining these more general questions of governance we first identify some key elements of the complex history of BSE in Britain, including the response of the UK state to the disease and the state's ironic employment of 'science'.

Agricultural practice in Britain (as in many other western industrial societies) has a long and somewhat unsavoury history of using industrial, cost-cutting methods to produce cheap food. Even though cattle are natural herbivores traditionally fed on grass in summer and hay in winter, as far back as the 1920s farmers unwittingly fed the by-products of slaughtered animals to their herds. This included chicken litter, pig offal, cattle remains and, until July 1988, offal from scrapie-infected sheep. The use of meat and bonemeal feed for traditional herbivores has been made on commercial grounds: it takes 7lb of vegetables to make only 1lb of beef protein while the use of animal protein supplement speeds up the process and allows animals to be reared more intensively, giving savings in cost. The most probable cause of mad cow disease is suspect cattle feed derived from scrapie-infected offal (although see Adam 1998: chap. 5 on rival explanations, including that of organo-phosphates). As early as 1979 (a symbolic year for deregulation!) the Royal Commission of Environmental Pollution warned of the dangers of feeding animal protein to herbivores. But it is now thought that until the 1980s the chemicals used in the processing of animal feed were sufficient to kill the scrapie agent. However, the chemical extraction process was replaced in the 1980s by one involving lower temperatures, which is now thought to have been ineffective at killing the scrapie prion. A relatively minor change in abattoir practice appears to have inadvertently facilitated the transmission of the new disease of BSE in cattle and the new strain of Creutzfeldt-Jakob disease (CJD) in humans (for various accounts, see Adam 1998; Connor and Prescott 1996; Durrant 1996; Highfield 1996; Jacobs 1996; Radford 1996; Wynne 1996b).

BSE is one of a group of separate yet related neurodegenerative diseases that affects animals and humans. Scrapie in sheep has for centuries been causing the symptoms of irritation and itching, a lack of coordination, apprehension, nervousness, aggression, loss of memory and finally death (Radford 1996). The human disease CJD is an extremely rare disorder that until recently affected approximately one in 2 million people. The symptoms of BSE in cattle are very similar to those of scrapie in sheep and CJD in humans.

The first cases of BSE were detected in cattle in 1985, and even though scientists were aware of the disease by late 1986 it was not until June 1988 that UK government scientists formally notified BSE as a new cattle disease. The incidence of BSE in cattle then rose dramatically, peaking at approximately 700 new cases per week in 1992, falling to approximately 70 new cases a week in mid-1996. By July 1993 100,000 cases of BSE in cattle had been confirmed out of a national herd of 12 million, while by 1994 it was predicted that 50% of dairy herds and 13% of beef herds were incubating the disease (Radford 1996).

The initial government response was to set up an expert scientific committee led by Sir Richard Southwood to assess the risks posed by the disease and what measures should be taken to stop it. This committee, which later developed into the Spongiform Encephalopathy Advisory Committee (SEAC), became a permanent advisory group in 1990. The strategy adopted was premised on a number of assumptions derived from experience of the scrapie disease in sheep, the most important of which centred on the extreme unlikelihood of BSE jumping species from cattle to humans. This assumption was based on scrapie having existed in sheep for over two hundred years without causing evident harm to humans through infected lamb or sheep offal. It was considered that cattle would be an end-stage host for the scrapie agent (as in other species), that it could be spread only by contaminated feed, and that there was no risk of transmission from mother to calf, or from cow to humans. Thus in July 1988, the Ministry of Agriculture proposed a ban on ruminant protein (designed to elimate the scrapie-infected sheep offal) for cattle feed, and announced at the same time that BSE in cattle posed 'no conceivable health hazard to humans'.

The dual strategy of strengthening regulations, and at the same time pronouncing British beef as safe, was to characterise government responses between 1988 and 1996. In July 1988 specified bovine offals (or SBO), including brain spinal cord, spleen, thymus, tonsils and intestines, were banned from cattle feed; in August 1988 the UK Government ordered that infected cattle must be slaughtered; in December 1988 milk from cows suspected of having BSE was banned for human consumption; while in November 1989 SBO was banned from all products meant for human consumption. These bans were the cornerstone of repeated claims by government ministers that British beef was safe (Leadbeater 1996). The offals chosen were those thought most likely to contain infectious material by extrapolation of knowledge of scrapie in sheep. This asumed that the BSE agent would act like the scrapie prion and be located within the same tissues. At the time John MacGregor, as Agriculture Minister, proposed that the likelihood of humans contracting the disease was 'remote and theoretical', and that the ban was 'an act of extreme prudence' (cited Radford 1996). Later in May 1990, John Gummer as Agriculture Minister famously fed his four-year-old daughter a beefburger, stating: 'It's delicious. I have no worries about eating beefburgers. There is no cause for concern' (cited Brown et al. 1996).

The particular government strategy aimed at ensuring that BSE did not enter the food chain depended on a number of assumptions of social practice in real-world contexts. Official policy took for granted, *inter alia*, that farmers would comply with official regulations, that abattoir workers would carefully and systematically remove SBO from animal carcasses, and that feed manufacturers would discard mammalian offal in cattle feed. Yet, official assertions that rules would be followed have proved naïve and unrealistic. Leadbeater (1996) gives a worrying exposé of how the culture and economics of the beef industry may have contributed to significant amounts of infectious material passing into the food chain long after the SBO ban in 1989. For example, from 1988 to 1990 farmers were offered compensation for cows with BSE at only 50% of their value, thus giving a clear incentive for farmers to be dishonest and to seek to pass off cows with BSE as healthy. Similarly with the rendering industry, Leadbeater (1996) shows how fierce price competition between abbatoirs, very low profit margins, high volume turnover, and a conspicuous lack of regulation all contributed to an informal culture, suspicious of outsiders and with little respect for the regulating authorities. Indeed, spot checks carried out by the State Veterinary Service in September 1995 showed that 48% of abattoirs were failing on some aspect of SBO regulation, as were 63% of SBO collection centres and a staggering 75% of rendering plants (Ministry of Agriculture, Fisheries and Food 1995). Other research suggests that animal feedstuffs may have been contaminated with ruminant protein well after the 1989 ban, as infectious SBO continued to escape from the abattoirs, via the renderers, to the animal feed manufacturers (Honiville et al. 1995).

Official moves to ensure that BSE did not enter the food chain were viewed as a precautionary move principally to allay public fears (both at home and abroad) since it was largely assumed that BSE could not jump species from cattle to humans. Perhaps such a belief helped bolster the view that SBO regulations need not be taken too seriously. But from 1990 onwards, the assumption that there was no conceivable link between BSE in cattle and its human equivalent began to look increasingly implausible. In May 1990 a cat died from a brain disease with similar symptons to BSE, giving rise to a major food scare fuelled by the strong possibility that BSE could 'cross the species barrier' and so perhaps infect humans. Since then BSE has apparently been transmitted to a number of zoo animals, and experimentally to pigs and primates. Yet in the absence of scientific proof to the contrary, up until March 1996 government ministers in Britain repeatedly dismissed the possibility of any link between BSE and CJD.

Since 1986 ministers have repeatedly justified the formulation of BSE policy as being based on 'sound science'. Durant (1996) characterises such an approach as one more fitting the 1950s rather than the 1990s. He suggests that the UK Government has approached BSE as if we believe in the authority of science to assess, control and manage risk: 'listening to current government pronouncements is like living in a timewarp; it is as if 30 years of questioning and criticism had simply not taken place'. Indeed, before 20 March 1996, government ministers had rigorously stuck to the assumption that BSE could not jump species to affect humans. They had continuously reinforced the view that there was no scientific evidence of a connection between BSE and CJD and thus no cause for alarm. But, as Grove-White (1996b) states: 'repeatedly over the last 10 years ministers have asserted the existence of no "evidence" or "proof" of precise causal connection between BSE and CJD, as the justification for limited action'.

In this context, the astonishing admission by two government ministers on 20 March 1996 that BSE may in fact be transmitted to humans was a complete reversal of the position held for over a decade. The admission followed a report by SEAC that 'the most likely' explanation for a new strain of CJD involving 10 young people was exposure to BSE before the offal ban in 1989. Health Secretary Stephen Dorrell introduced the report as indicating a serious public health concern with a very large uncertainty as to the risks involved. John Pattison as chair of SEAC raised the spectre of a major national disaster, speculating that the numbers of people likely to contract CJD as anywhere between a two-figure number and 500,000. What followed was what has been described as a 'spectacular collapse of public confidence in British beef' on a global scale (*Nature* Editorial 1996: 271). The implications of such an admission were that everyone who had eaten beef in the decade before 1989 was in danger of contracting the disease. Public anxiety was compounded since no-one knew for certain the incubation period of the new disease (estimates were from 5 to 50 years) and thus how many people were at risk. Faced with public panic and plummeting beef sales emergency measures were promised to tighten controls on beef production. PM John Major responded to the crisis once again through the medium of science, seeking to reassure the public that the government would do 'whatever the scientists said was necessary' (cited *New Scientist* Editorial 1996: 3).

But overnight, science appeared to have changed its mind. The very next day, Pattison had changed his interpretation of the likely risks involved. Now he claimed that the public could be reassured that, in the normal sense of the word, British beef was safe to eat. Such a shift reflected the change of tenor of public policy, from Dorrell's precautionary and largely correct account of the uncertainties in the science making it an inadequate base to predict risk, to the Cabinet's position (articulated by the Agriculture Minister, Douglas Hogg) that there were *no* scientific grounds for such concern and that everything was under control. Arguably, the change in emphasis was designed to help the beef industry in conditions of widespread panic and to bolster public confidence at home and abroad. But as we see below such turnabouts were to have troubling implications for the longer-term credibility of science and government.

Adam (1998: chap. 5) has undertaken a comprehensive analysis of the news coverage of BSE in the four days following the original admission. She describes how the issue rapidly shifted from a health crisis to a beef crisis, from one of public safety to anxiety about job losses and the need to safeguard a key industry. She also notes how the conflict over BSE within days became caught up in wider scepticism in Britain over the European project, and of how it became unpatriotic to talk about anything being wrong with British beef, British farming, or the British industrial way of life (Adam 1998). Moreover, even though BSE remained a major news story for 10 days, actual information of the sort that might be useful to parents or to those whose livelihood was threatened became increasingly difficult to extract. What became obvious was not merely the level of ignorance about BSE, but also the narrow and ahistorical contextualisation of the issues both in the media and by government.

The BSE crisis has had profound economic and political consequences. These include, *inter alia*, the effective collapse of a £500 million beef export industry, a longer-term ban on British beef across the European Union, a number of rejections by EU states of UK proposals to ease the beef ban, the slaughter of over a million cattle (ostensibly to improve public confidence in the beef industry), and rising costs of measures to deal with BSE, estimated in late 1996 at over £2.5 billion. For a short time the British Government even set up a UK task force to veto all EU decisions until the EU agreed a clear framework to ease the ban. What to the Government started as a purely technical problem of how to deal with a new disease in cattle escalated to what PM John Major described as 'the worst crisis the Government had endured since the Falklands' (cited *Daily Telegraph* Editorial 1996).

What does the BSE saga tell us about the dynamics of governing nature in the 'risk society'? First, BSE is a compelling example of a domain of science where existing knowledge provides a shaky base for the articulation of public policy. The attempt by governments to defer responsibilities to science – as if science was equipped to provide unmediated and normatively compelling knowledge – was naïve and ultimately damaging. BSE represents a *prima facie* domain of science where current understanding of the risks associated with eating beef is not only open-ended and uncertain but also contingent on multiple assumptions of the social world (such as the working practices of abattoir workers). For example, 10 years after the identification of the disease there remains huge uncertainty over the origins of BSE, the nature of the infectious agent, its host range, its means of transmission, and its relationship with CJD in humans (Durant 1996). Even more starkly, no-one knows how many people have been exposed to the prions, nor how big a dose is required to cause the disease. Such indeterminacy means that it is impossible to know whether the scale of the epidemic is likely to remain at a few score or hundreds of thousands of human deaths. For governments to seek political authority in 'sound science' is to underestimate the structural indeterminacy involved in scientific endeavour.

Moreover, to assume that UK policy has always been premised on independent and impartial scientific understanding of the risks associated with BSE is itself disingenuous. Wynne (1996b) provides a revealing account of the political processes shaping the science, and in particular of how the evidence provided by government scientists was itself 'shaped before it arrived at the policy door, by the scientists' own perceptions of what would be politically digestible'. He outlines the reasons given by Southwood for why SEAC did not advocate the need for a ban on the use of cattle offal in human food until November 1989, two years after government scientists suggested scrapie-infected offal as the likely source of the disease and a full 15 months after a ban had been imposed on cattle feed:

> He [Southwood] recalled that: 'We felt it was a no-goer. MAFF [Ministry of Agriculture, Fisheries and Food] already thought our proposals were pretty revolutionary'. He later pressed for a ban, and it was introduced in 1989. But, at the time, the politicians could say that a ban on scientific grounds was not necessary, when the scientists had ruled it out on tacitly political grounds.

Second, the lack of public trust both in the state and in scientific expertise may remain one of the most significant outcomes of the BSE saga. Unlike other high-profile environmental and food scares (such as salmonella and eggs, *E. coli* and food poisoning, phthalates and baby milk, the pill and certain health risks, and hormone-disrupting chemicals and male infertility),

BSE has hit the public domain for nearly a decade. The history of BSE has provided people with quite considerable insights of the darker side of government, including its apparent inability to safeguard long-term public health and its often ignominious proximity to producer interests. Such mistrust has been fuelled by relentless media exposés of government collusion with industrial interests, of disgraceful practices operating in abattoirs and rendering plants, of unsavoury images of chainsaws to remove offal from carcasses and the infamous concept of 'mechanically processed meat', and of the serious lack of regulation and enforcement. Such factors have undoubtedly contributed to a more general sense of unease with industrial practice in late modernity. Yet because these anxieties have remained largely outside the criteria used in formal risk assessment methodologies, they have tended to be presented in policy culture as irrational, even hysterical, and as based on the misunderstanding of the risks as determined by experts (see Wynne 1996b).

The mismatch between the character of public anxieties over what is implicated in BSE and the narrow criteria used in official risk assessments has a number of troubling implications. It has undoubtedly fuelled public scepticism and indeed cynicism over government pronouncements. Indeed, the more certain the political reassurance that British beef is safe, the more sceptical people have apparently become about the credibility and integrity of the science underpinning such claims. The strongest response by most people to the BSE saga has been to conclude that there has been a cynical cover-up by the state. In other words, people have to some degree accepted the scientific realism advocated by governments (the idea that governments know from science the true nature of the risks associated with such diseases as BSE) but that they are not telling us these facts which they really know. For example, an ICM poll conducted for *The Guardian* showed that nearly three out of four adults agreed with the proposition that 'the government knew there was a risk [with BSE] and tried to hide it' (Linton and Bates 1996).

The long-term effects of the BSE crisis in further corroding people's identification with formal politics is also slowly being realised. For example, in further qualitative research undertaken by the authors in late 1996, many people speak of BSE as having hardened their scepticism as to what politicians generally say, and in particular as to how politicians deploy claims about science to reassure the public across a variety of contexts (Grove-White et al. 1997). This is not to say that people better understand the uncertain character of science. Rather, people appear to view much of science as distorted by commercial interests, leading them to scrutinise carefully the apparent interests underlying scientific claim and counterclaim. Such scepticism in science is not new; rather the effect of BSE has been to intensify existing trends where people refute claims concerning the impartial and independent character of much of official scientific endeavour.

Third, BSE highlights the difficulties for the institutions of the nation-state in managing new forms of risk in the increasingly globalised world, and the more general problems for governance when corporations and politicians refuse to take their responsibility for the outcomes. For some analysts the British Government's inept handling of BSE is a direct by-product of a wider mania for global deregulation, reflecting a declining reluctance of the state to intervene in opposition to apparently overwhelming market forces in order to protect the public interest (see Hutton 1995; Marquand 1996). Deregulation (in the abattoir industry) and traditional Whitehall secrecy and insularity greatly exacerbated the beef crisis. But much of the conflict reflects differences of regulatory culture. More used to a precautionary culture, many of Britain's partners in Europe (especially Germany) have not surprisingly sought to ban British beef from the continent. Until BSE is eradicated from British herds, they argue, continental consumers cannot be sure that it is safe to eat. And with recent revelations suggesting that BSE may be transmitted from mother to calf, and from cow to sheep, the prospects of eradicating the disease look increasingly remote. By contrast, Britain has argued that there is no scientific case for continuing the ban and that it is unjust and unlawful. To David Marquand (1996), the BSE battle is not just about British beef, but about the conflict between Britain's laissez-faire individualist culture pitted against the more regulatory, social democratic culture in Europe:

> The beef war is, in fact, the latest skirmish in a long drawn-out battle between two different economic cultures and two different conceptions of government. On the one hand is the myopic, profit-driven, public-interest-denying culture of de-regulation which has always been latent in British capitalism, and which has swept all before it in the last 15 years. On the other is the regulatory culture associated with the social capitalisms of mainland Europe.

However, the difficulty in handling the crisis points to a more general crisis of institutional authority in the risk society. In hindsight, a small and largely unnoticed change in rendering practice may have contributed to a chain of events which could cost the British taxpayer more than £3 billion. It thus provides a dazzling reminder of the limited ability of nation-states to predict, manage and control risk.

But, is it in fact possible for states to obtain better intelligence of the riskiness of technologies which are associated with the perpetual churning of economic innovation? Wynne (1996b) argues that one current feature that helps ensure that wider moral and social issues are excluded from public debate lies in Britain's reductionist scientific culture of risk assessment. For example, in the case of BSE, the scientific committee assessing the likely risks associated with the disease was structured so as to exclude wider issues from public debate, such as the *morality* of feeding the by-products of dead animals back to natural herbivores, or more general issues of the industrial intensification of food, even though these are the issues that most concern the general public. And by excluding such debates from public scrutiny, 'the politicians ignore the issue claiming the experts are handling it, while the experts define a narrow technical area whose limits are not held in focus' (Wynne 1996b).

In such ways, reductionist science-based methodologies are unable to assess adequately wider social and moral dimensions of risks associated with new innovations and practices. Such concerns gain added weight in the light of current technological innovations – such as recent advances in genetic engineering and neuro-technology – which are now capable of redefining the basic structure of life (Grove-White et al. 1997). Here the BSE crisis illustrates the need for wider participation in how people judge technological innovation, and in what kind of moral, social as well as scientific criteria are used in order to make such judgements. Grove-White (1996b) argues that it is now crucially important to devise new ways to promote wider public participation and more intelligent governance in reaching social judgements:

> The only way forward to contain such crises in future is through a franker shared sense of the new forms of uncertainty in which we are all now embedded in advanced industrial society and wider genuine participation in the far-reaching social judgments to be made under such conditions of chronic indeterminacy. This calls for radical new thinking about institutional reform and innovation, a path along which even the opposition parties have barely begun to advance.

Yet while this points to the need for more inclusive forms of collective responsibility, the BSE saga also highlights the lack of responsibility for alarmingly large potential risks. Beck (1996a) states:

> Politicians say they are not in charge: they at most regulate developments. Scientific experts say they are merely creating technological opportunities but not deciding how they are taken up. Businesses say they are just responding to consumer demand. Risk politics resembles the 'nobody's rule' that Hannah Arendt tells us is the most tryannical of all forms of power because under it nobody can be held responsible. Our society has become a laboratory with nobody responsible for the outcome of the experiment.

Fourth, the BSE saga particularly highlights the timed and sensed dimensions of risk (see chapters 4 and 5 above). Such risks associated with eating beef well illustrate how an everyday and taken-for-granted social practice can have unknown, unsensed and indeterminate effects in the barely imaginable future. And eating beef is a social practice of peculiar significance within English gastronomic and middle-class culture. Roast beef and Yorkshire pudding (see plate 8.1) signifies middle-class suburban taste and this has become widely generalised within English life. Most people in England would always have believed that beef is especially good for one and that it represents all that is good about England. The joint of roast beef is metonymic of English life and of its down-to-earth and solid character. As Roy Hattersley (1996) states: 'beef has always been a symbol of Britain's national superiority'. It is often consumed within the context of the family and is associated with a variety of accompaniments which heighten its sensual and symbolic delights. It would not have occurred to most English people that beef could possibly be contaminated. Beef continued to smell and taste the same during the 1980s. To suggest that it was 'impure' would have been thought of as 'unpatriotic'.

Plate 8.1   *Roast beef and Yorkshire pudding: the meat of English culture*
(source: John Urry)

And yet during the deregulating decade of the 1980s, it appears that British people were placed in a laboratory in which cattle were turned into carnivores and on occasions into cannibals, but where there was no knowledge of when the outcomes of the scientific experiment would be known. It now appears that BSE in cattle may have as long as a six-year gestation period, while estimates for CJD range from six to as many as 50 years (see Adam 1998: chap. 5). Given these exceptionally long periods before the risks could be known, it is clear that no-one should have been exposed to such dangers in the laboratory of the English dinner table. This illustrates the 'evolutionary' quality of risk in daily practice.

A further temporal dimension of BSE concerns the apparently spontaneous collapse in confidence in British beef. Once the fear of the unknown and unsensed danger had been brought to light there was an almost instantaneous fear about what is ingested. Such a momentous quality does not reflect an 'irrational' concern. It rather reflects a moment where a particular concern 'feeds' into and exacerbates existing fears that we highlighted in chapter 7; the fear that current developments stimulated by short-term 'instantaneous' calculations of time are generating unimaginable and unsensed risks in the future. These risks are not open to the senses, except when for example we see on TV a picture of a mad cow (see plate 8.2). Bad beef cannot be sensed as bad and hence people are hugely dependent upon expert systems which have to provide guarantees across time and space. But it is just those guarantees that cannot be provided with

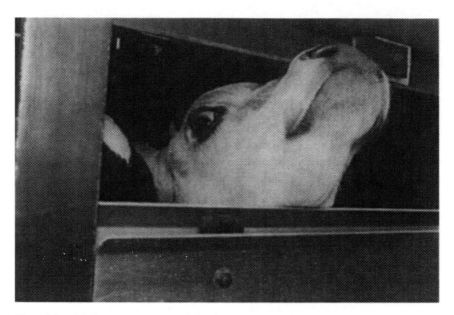

Plate 8.2   *Mad cow (source: with kind permission of Luca Zampedri)*

something so indeterminate as BSE. Many members of the public have
become more sceptical about the ability of such expert systems to provide
long-term environmental health which takes proper account of glacial
time.

Jacobs (1996) describes the functioning of such a dynamic where fears
appear to surface momentarily only to disappear as if without trace:

> These general feelings attach themselves to whatever environmental subjects
> emerge in the news. Specific issues – BSE, veal calves, *Brent Spar* – simply act as
> vehicles propelling a more amorphous environmental anxiety to the surface of
> public life. The problem is that, once they get there, there is nothing to hang on to
> ensure that they stay in public debate. British politics lacks an ideological
> framework through which environmental issues like the BSE crisis can be given
> proper political expression.

Another way to express this is to note the ways in which in contemporary
societies there is little or no way of representing the future and especially the
interests of people and other sentient beings who have yet to be born. The
expert systems are not oriented to what we have termed the politics of
glacial time.

Fifth, public anxieties expressed over BSE can be identified as part of a
wider unease over current 'industrial' practices that are seen as infecting the
most private and innermost aspects of people's lives, especially their food.
Such practices are increasingly viewed as immoral, wrong and 'unnatural'.
The recent realisation that farmers, sanctioned by the state, have been
treating apparently natural herbivores – cows – as carnivores merely

confirms people's worst suspicions of the unnatural character of modern agriculture. CJD in humans appears to confirm people's fears that nature knows exactly how to strike back against such apparently 'unnatural' practices. The increasing belief in the power of nature to be able to extract its revenge in the long term upon the human species is a further paradoxical consequence of the saga of the mad cow. There appears to be some development of a conception of nature as glacial time, as an embryonic moral space outside and largely in resistance to instrumental, market-oriented globalisation.

In the next section we schematically examine the increasingly global context which confronts all nation-states, generalising in part from this strange story of the British cow. In this story we have employed the language of risk, following Beck's concept of the risk society. But in many ways this is incorrect. As Adam (1998: chap. 2) shows, environmental degradation in the contemporary world poses risks which are qualitatively different from those involved in, say, driving a car, having one's house burgled, or of a woman being attacked by a stranger in a different area of a city. These are all side-effects of otherwise reasonable actions and can be subject to a local calculation of appropriate odds (even if such calculations are nearly always bound up with people's sense of the dependency on expert institutions). There is a fairly direct relationship between certain actions within a particular time and space and certain outcomes which will also occur within that same context. These are properly understood as 'risks'.

But BSE is not a risk but a hazard. It is a hazard because it has resulted from an intrinsic or endemic feature of the 'western economy and society' predominantly organised around short-term economic gain highly localised in its temporal and spatial ordering. Such short-term market forces created a hazard which operates at the expense of the long-term well-being of animals and peoples and of those who are geographically distant from where the short-term gain is realised. Adam (1998: chap. 5) points out that corporations take risks which then turn into no-choice hazards for the public; in this case, those poor, benighted consumers of British beef during especially the 1980s.

Such consumers face not the uncertainty of whether they might or might not have an accident if they drive down the M6. They face a massive indeterminacy which cannot be calculated. Neither the past nor the estimation of the future gives people any knowledge of what to do. They are 'guinea pigs' in a laboratory but where there is no clear or specifiable relationship between the starting and the ending of the experiment, in either time or space. This is for Adam a 'hazard' society. People therefore do not take risks when confronted by environmental dangers. Rather they are subject to large-scale and often invisible hazards which are organised outside the local context of action. The putative globalisation of such hazards, as contemporary economies and societies treat the world as a laboratory, induces many new and potentially even more catastrophic hazards.

Globalising the nation

It was a characteristic of the period of organised capitalism (roughly from the 1900s to the 1970s in Europe and North America) that most economic and social problems were thought to be soluble at the level of the nation-state. The concerns of society, including those of environmental risk and health, should be dealt with through national policies, especially through a Keynesian welfare state which could identify and respond to the risks of organised capitalism (see Lash and Urry 1987). These risks were seen as principally located within the borders of each society, and where solutions could also be envisaged as being devised and implemented within such national borders. Nation-states were based upon a concept of the citizen who owed duties to the state via the concept of the nation and who received rights from it, including the rights to predictable and minimum levels of health, welfare and environmental quality (see Held 1995 on democracy and the nation-state; Taylor 1996 on 'embedded statism' and a nationalised social science). Held summarises the nature of citizenship based on a national community of fate:

> Citizenship rights embody a conception of empowerment that is strictly limited to the framework of the nation-state. In modern times, rights have nearly everywhere been enshrined effectively within the institutions of nation-states. (1995: 223; and see Bulmer and Rees 1996 on citizenship debates today)

Historically however, societies in the modern world have always been more complex than this nation-state–society model, as Mann shows in his conception of society as comprising 'multiple, overlapping and intersecting socio-spatial networks of power' (1986: 1; and see 1996: 1964, on the sheer messiness of society). Indeed most people in twentieth-century society have lived within sprawling empires where it was often a foreign nation-state that acted on their behalf and yet failed to provide many or any of the rights of citizenship. The nation-state system really only characterised the dozen or so societies of the North Atlantic Rim, and even here the Vatican in Rome partially dominated the domestic policies of a number of 'Southern' European countries. Most of the rest of the world was subject to colonial domination, and this was true of most of Africa, Asia and Eastern Europe, and indirectly true of much of the Americas. And of course these supposedly bounded nation-states of the North Atlantic Rim were themselves mainly the colonial powers, having all sorts of economic, military, social and cultural ties beyond their borders. These were in very many senses not bounded nation-states since almost all sought to subjugate 'other' peoples. More generally, imperial domination, world wars, famines, flows of refugees, and the like, were risks that crossed national borders and which peoples in most societies were little able to control and regulate. One particular nation-state, Germany, was nearly able to subject most of 'Europe' to its military hegemony. And for much of the twentieth century the most powerful nation-state, the USA, principally functioned as a super-power locked into an escalating diplomatic, political, military, economic and cultural struggle with another massively powerful imperial power, the USSR.

The BSE example, though, shows most graphically that even within the 'centre', what we have termed the North Atlantic Rim, nation-states are no longer able to provide an effective national citizenship and national state solutions, at least in the terms in which they had been originally conceived (Lash and Urry 1994; more generally see O'Brien and Penna 1997 on how the environment changes characteristic static and national notions of welfare and citizenship). Disorganised capitalism disorganises such a national strategy, so that one of the most powerful states in the world cannot ensure that its population eating its home-grown food is not being seriously poisoned. We will now list the extraordinary array of processes which undermine whatever remains of a nation-state–society conceptualisation of the rights and duties of being a citizen at the end of the twentieth century, processes which have, it has been argued, ushered in the beginnings of a new global age (Albrow 1996; Waters 1995):

• The development of new technologies which in dramatic fashion transform time-space and in part at least transcend national control and regulation: fibre-optic cables, jet planes, audiovisual transmissions, digital TV, the Internet, satellites, credit cards, faxes, electronic point-of-sale terminals, portable phones, electronic stock exchanges, high-speed trains, virtual reality, and so on (Castells 1996; Scholte 1996). Global electronic transactions and the growing importance of instantaneously mobile intellectual property undermine national tax-bases, the most important power of nation-states.

• Economic, social and political processes increasingly organised beyond national states and analysable in terms of scapes and flows. The former are the frameworks of actors and technologies through which flows occur; the latter consist not just of the economic flows of money, labour and capital, but also of images, information, migrants, tourists, technologies and noxious substances that flow within and across national territories and which individual states are to varying degrees unable or often unwilling to control (Castells 1996; Lash and Urry 1994). Bauman (1993a: 231) points out that for any particular state most of the economic assets relevant to the well-being of its citizens will be owned outside its borders.

• Huge increases in the flows of nuclear, chemical and conventional military weapons to many different countries and organisations throughout the world and which necessitate, but do not necessarily produce, international regulation and NGO lobbying and campaigns aimed at ensuring reasonable levels of personal and national security (see Mann 1996).

• These scapes and flows do not originate from all parts of the world equally (see Sklair 1990). Such a putative globalisation is based within the leading advanced capitalist economies, what Mann terms the 'tricontinentalism' of the USA, Western Europe and a Japan-led Asia. These three continents account for 85% of world trade, 90% of advanced sector production and almost all the headquarters of the leading corporations (Mann 1996: 1962). Distinctions need also to be drawn between the *international* relations between existing nations; the *transnational* networks which pass straight through national borders; and the *global*, those sets of relations which cover much of the globe (Mann 1996: 1960).

- The inability of most contemporary states to guarantee many of the conditions of citizenship because of the power of these global flows, which are widespread, unpredictable and not subject to national governance (see Held 1995: 223). As a consequence many traditional domains of state action cannot be fulfilled without international collaboration. States have had to increase their levels of integration with each other to offset the destabilising consequences of this global interconnectedness (Held 1995; Lash and Urry 1994).

- Signs or images particularly exemplify the time-space compression of the global world. A worldwide industry produces and markets images, not only for products, but also for peoples, states, NGOs, places, universities, and so on. There are an extraordinary number and transitoriness of different images, including in recent years those of nature and the natural (such as 'one earth'; see Urry 1996b). Intrinsic to such flows are various languages and discursive strategies, of advertising organisations, products and places, of science and alternative science, of the media, of resistance and opposition, and so on.

- The hollowing out of societies: a relatively weaker and increasingly delegitimated state (post-traditional?) that has a reduced set of 'traditional' functions; more powerful market relations which emphasise instantaneous rather than clock-time and which begin to undermine national markets; and a plethora of 'non-traditional' and less traditionalised sociations and NGOs concerned to reflect upon, to argue against, to retreat from, to provide alternatives to, to campaign for, these various flows. There is a complex, overlapping, disjunctive order, a pervasive condition of off-centredness, precipitating new modes of personal and collective self-fashioning as individualisation and cultural formations come to be chronically combined and recombined (see Lash and Urry 1994; but see Mann 1996).

- There is an increasing contradiction between the conception of the global as conceived of by states and by corporations, which is predominantly technical-managerial, and the global notions held by members of the public and some NGOs, who deploy new technologies in diverse ways so as to promote some sense of an imagined global citizenship or dwellingness (see Ingold 1993a; and chapter 7 above). Beck (1996b) usefully distinguishes such perspectives as globalisation from above (mainly involving international actors and institutions) and globalisation from below (deriving from the realm of global sub-politics and involving *ad hoc* participation by-passing formal procedures of political representation).

- These newly salient flows create novel risks and uncertainties, as well as new kinds of opportunities and desires. The latter include overseas travel to the cities of the West or the East; obtaining consumer goods and hence lifestyles from the West; forming internationalised 'new sociations' employing global imagery (Friends of the Earth); participating in global cultural events (World Cup); the development of 'world music', and so on. The former include AIDS, Chernobyl, cultural homogenisation, the loss of economic national sovereignty, migration, exiles and asylum-seeking, BSE, and so on (see Featherstone et al. 1995).
- The increasing importance of the 'global' as ideology. This notion is employed by those with interests in promoting worldwide capitalist relations and undermining national identity and the kinds of social democratic project that such identities underlie and authorise (Ohmae 1990). The global also refers to the kinds of strategies employed by transnational corporations which involve a lack of commitment to particular territories, labour forces or governments (Peters 1992; and see Hirst and Thompson 1996; and Mann 1986 for critiques of a globalisation thesis).
- The widespread movement of peoples across borders makes it far less easy for states to mobilise clearly separate and coherent 'nations' in pursuit of national goals. Through what Gilroy (1993: 195) terms the 'spatial focus', notions of mobility and flow are increasingly seen as constitutive of identity. The hybridisation of cultures, the importance of travelling cultures, some growth of a global dwellingness, the development of global networks, diasporas and other notions of the 'unhomely' all problematise the home-nation and its ability to mobilise for action (Eade 1997; Pieterse 1995; Pile and Thrift 1995a, 1995b).
- The Westphalian model of democracy, that the world consists of and is divided into sovereign national states with no superior authority, is becoming outmoded as a whole array of different kinds of 'state' are developing, some of which exert power above existing nation-states, others below. There are various socio-spatial political entities which do not fit the nation-state model (see Bauman 1993a). And what is also in a fragmented way developing, and what needs to develop further, is a model of cosmopolitan democracy in which the building blocks are groups and associations consisting of multiple and overlapping networks of power that range across national borders, and which have access to a putative 'cosmopolitan civil society' (Beck 1996b; Held 1995). Such a civil society may increasingly be able to escape governance by and through individual nation-states (as with the use of the Internet by paedophiles and protestors, by Marxists and right-wing militias).
- Such globalisation also generates localisation. Harvey claims that the 'collapse of spatial barriers does not mean that the significance of space is decreasing' (1989: 293). The less salient the temporal and spatial

barriers, the greater the sensitivity of firms, of governments and of the general public to variations of place across time and space. As spatial barriers diminish, so people appear to become much more sensitised to what the world's spaces contain (Harvey 1989: 294; 1996). The specificity of place, of its workforce, the character of its entrepreneurialism, its administration, its buildings, its history, and especially its physical environment, become more important as many temporal and spatial barriers collapse. But globalisation changes the local, although the tenor of change depends upon its relationships of inclusion within, and exclusion from, the various global flows.

In the final section we consider some of the implications of these processes just outlined for the governance of nature. Our comments will be highly schematic.

Governing nature

The environmental movement has employed the culturally illuminating motto: 'Think Global, Act Local'. What does this mean? What kind of reworking of the global–local nexus is involved in order that nature can be appropriately governed? Minimally, the motto indicates two processes. First, many environmental problems at the local and regional level do in fact have transnational origins in different parts of the globe and hence need international agreements for states and other actors to propose measures to remedy them and to improve each locality (such as acid rain generated by cars and nationally based power station emissions exported to affect lakes and forests in other nation-states). And second, many large-scale problems require for their solution localised, decentralised actions from vast numbers of people, many of whom will not personally benefit from such a change since they will be spatially or temporally distant from the benefits of such a change (such as reducing the use of carbon fuels). We consider these in turn.

First, most nation-states are now organised in terms of imperfect systems of representative democracy. As Adam notes, they are organised on the basis of boundedness, of both national territory and the elapse of time before the next election (see Adam 1998: chap. 3 for much of the following). So given that most environmental hazards necessarily extend beyond these boundaries, states have a huge incentive to externalise hazards onto other nations and onto future generations and electorates. Many international organisations have developed in part to prevent such externalisation, but few apart from perhaps the 1992 Rio Earth Summit have seriously sought to represent the 'glacial', long-term future. And the capacity of international organisations to prevent 'spatial externalisation' is hugely limited. Even the European Union, which has certainly raised the visibility of environmental issues, has as its primary goal the maintenance of a common market. Environmental policies are only acceptable to the EU to the extent to which they do not interfere with the higher authority of the maintenance and extension of the European economy and of its place within the global market. Indeed, more generally international trade agreements such as GATT and NAFTA are designed and policed with the precise purpose of ensuring the passage of free trade between nation-states on equal bases, one effect being new forms of constraint for nation-states to make moral judgements about future commitments. A recent example lies in the possibilities of a trade war between the US and the EU if the latter proceeds to restrict the import of genetically modified foods.

More generally, there are immense problems of producing appropriate collaboration between individual nation-states since each may have good reasons to free-ride on the presumed actions of others. This is especially true where it is increasingly known that all other states have broken their own environmental directives. There is thus the displacement of environmental crises from the global or transnational level where they should be dealt with to the level of the nation-state (see Hay 1994 on the intensely threatening tendency for 'state-specific crisis management'). Collaboration between nation-states is also rendered difficult because of global divisions, especially between North and South. The scale of the differences between such groupings means that it is almost impossible to generate the sense that we are all in the same boat, although occasionally southern activists such as Chico Mendes (1992) have gained valuable support from NGOs (although rarely governments) in the North. Shiva argues that the global definition of environmental problems by the North causes particular problems for the South; she says that the: 'seven most powerful countries, the G-7, dictate global affairs, but the interests that guide them remain narrow, local and parochial' (1993: 149–50). Beck defines such dynamics as helping to constitute new forms of 'ecological neo-imperialism' where northern actors sustain inequalities by monopolising knowledge and hence the power to determine what constitutes the lineaments of global environmental change. This dynamic is epitomised most starkly in the politics of the Inter-governmental Panel on Climate Change (IPCC) and the expert construction of highly complex and computer intensive 'general circulation models' (Beck 1996b: 6).

But national governments do not have it all their own way. They increasingly have to justify their actions on the environment within the social context of international gatherings. On occasions it is the threat of being shamed by the rest of the international 'community' that constitutes a constraint on the actions of national states. An example of this has been the attempted shaming of the British Government by the EU over the extra-ordinary number of 'dirty beaches' in the UK, the shaming of the French Government over nuclear tests in the South Pacific, the widespread criticism of the German Government for its failure to impose speed restrictions on its motorways, and so on. The shaming is then brought to 'world attention' through the global media, most of whom demonstrate at the most limited loyalty to their own national state and its apparent interests.

Second, 'acting locally' means that many large-scale environmental problems require for their solution decentralised actions from large numbers of people who dwell within different localities. The significance of the local environment and community has long been a major theme of much writing on the environment, most strikingly within bio-regionalism (see Adams 1996: 9; Leopold 1949; Martell 1994: 52–7; Sale 1985). Such a view prioritises dwelling in and respecting the particular local configuration of the land; the acquiring of greater understanding and knowledge of nature; and an emphasis upon the small-scale and the self-sufficiency of each particular place. Although there are few successful implementations of such a bio-regional programme, many of its tenets have been drawn upon to develop and strengthen the emphases upon local forms of dwelling within contemporary environmentalism. Indeed chapter 7 reports on the extensive importance for people of acting in and for their local environment, so much so that some local authorities in Britain are financing 'local distinctiveness officers' following the inspiration of Common Ground. To a significant extent aspects of the threatened 'environment' are only sensed locally; and ways of undoing such damage are often only conceivable at a relatively local level. Hence we have seen the importance of Local Agenda 21 initiatives.

But the 'local' in 'acting locally' is more complex than this (see Dickens 1996: 189–90 generally here). First, the commitment to the 'local' may in fact make it hard to 'govern' nature appropriately. The local as promoted in national or international environmental policies may not resonate with and mobilise people's local concerns and interests. Chapter 7 showed the mismatch between the rational and instrumental spaces of the local in official policy (such as saving energy, recycling bottles or using public transport) as compared with more moral and historically symbolic spaces of the local informing everyday concerns (such as protecting local spaces of the countryside, the right to hunt, concerns over dog mess, or anxieties about dirty beaches). Moreover, such local concerns are themselves being transformed and remade by many of the global processes outlined above. For example, increasing levels of commuting, migration, exile and tourism patterns all contribute to local communities being less based upon geographical propinquity. Indeed the 'local environment' is often most protected by those having little connection with it on a day-to-day basis of dwellingness. Recent research in Britain, moreover, suggests that it is the village/neighbourhood that more people identify with, rather than a broader district or county. In other words, people appear to feel attached to a unit that almost certainly has little power of influence to make much impact with regard to most globally relevant environmental issues (Gosschalk and Hatter 1996).

Such clashes present considerable difficulties for policies aimed at mobilising local action, especially when they are conceived of in national or international fora. Even more problematically, new rhetorics and social practices are emerging which contest conceptions of the local which have been historically based in the North Atlantic Rim and which rely upon the structures of the nation-state (see Eade 1997 for various studies of 'global-ization as local process'). National states are thus confronted by intense contestation over the local, on the one hand, and by delegitimation and the power of the global, on the other (see Lash and Urry 1994: chap. 11; and see Harvey's [1996] efforts to combine Heidegger and Marx). And even if local responses and policies are developed, there is no simple way of ensuring that there is appropriate global coordination between the hundreds of thousands of local communities throughout the world.

But while acting locally may on occasions impede or produce outcomes opposed to thinking globally, there are other instances where acting for the globe may improve the local environment of particular places. An example of this would be a local campaign to reduce the use of cars within a rural area. This not only benefits future generations living elsewhere, providing of course that car drivers do not just transfer their driving onto other roads, but may also benefit local residents, whose air quality and aural environment will be improved. In such cases local–global coordination may be effected.

But more often the beneficiaries of action are spatially or temporally distant from those undertaking actions within particular localities. In many cases those living in particular localities have to act on behalf of populations who are as yet unborn. The collective good to be produced is invisible in time, a further example of the peculiar restructuring of time within the contemporary world. O'Neill (1993) refers to this as the 'temporal tragedy' (and see Martell 1994: chap. 3 on a critique of the main arguments against not taking 'future generations' into account). He provocatively asks:

> Why is it the case that successive generations did not knowingly deplete resources until recently? Indeed, why did they improve the land, even given that they knew they would not reap the benefits? (O'Neill 1993: 39)

O'Neill's answer is that until recently in many societies land across generations was seen as the common property of particular families or particular communities. Each generation possessed a sense of identity over time with past and with future owners. People enjoyed a strong sense of temporal continuity and saw themselves as implicated in a set of projects from the past and linking to the future, what in chapter 6 we termed the 'stewardship' of nature. O'Neill cites the planting and growing of trees as an obvious example of how diverse generations need to participate in the collective process which necessarily proceeds over different generations.

Three features of a globalising world disrupt this continuity of dwelling over time: global agricultural competition which emphasises instantaneous monetary returns at the expense of long-term deterioration; the replacement of family by corporate owners who have little interest in glacial time perspectives; and the increased mobility of landownership which has effec-tively destroyed the long-term links between generations and the sense that anyone really *owns* the earth (Adam 1998: chap. 2 on money and nature; O'Neill 1993: 40–1). Stewardship and associated long-term dwellingness of place have thus been undermined by such global changes. And more generally, a markedly enhanced consumer culture, based on the power of western media conglomerates, has produced huge increases in new and extensive forms of environmental damage. This is because of rapid increases in the turnover of new products, the ways in which products are transported almost everywhere in the increasingly global market-place, and because people travel to very many different places much more frequently.

But what O'Neill does not proceed to consider is whether the growth of these global processes may induce, even in a fragmentary form, another set of inter-generational concerns. This is what we termed in chapter 5 'glacial time', a time to offset the instantaneous time of global capitalism. In conclusion to this book, then, we consider whether certain aspects of globalisation, especially the global media, supranational states, global environmental groups and a kind of global (networked) civil society, could play a crucial role in generating a sense of a 'global village' (see also Beck 1996b). Such a new way of dwelling could conceivably connect together individuals, groups, corporations, nation-states and supranational institutions, North and South, and the present and the glacial future within a putative shared imagined community. Could such a community provide the basis for a transformed governance of a global nature that currently seems literally out of control? What sort of evidence is there for such a possible development?

First, many different kinds of damage in the North did indeed come to be collectively interpreted as 'environmental' and undesirable. We have seen that the very concepts that constituted the environmental agenda in the UK in the 1970s and 1980s necessitated active construction by environmental groups, in response to concerns about the more general character of contemporary society. New forms of environmental protest were related as much to widespread concern about a highly technocratic and modernistic economy and politics, as to the specific evaluation of the health-threatening properties of the physical environment. Such changes came to be viewed as collectively novel and disruptive and not 'naturally' part of the modern project. Many citizens in the North and the South now identify a set of issues as 'environmental' and as damaging either to themselves or to others, and in so doing are expressing at least some semblance of a critique of change in contemporary society.

Moreover, a range of organisations has developed which has begun to generate something of a new global identity. Such bodies include the UN, the World Bank, Greenpeace, the EU, Friends of the Earth, Band Aid, Amnesty, Oxfam, the Commission for Sustainable Development, large media conglomerates, the International Institute for Environment and Development, and so on, what Beck (1996b) terms globalisation from above. Some people are willing to engage in actions on behalf of humanity as a whole, although we have noted huge problems in the relationship of North and South. To the extent to which a post-nation-state concept of citizenship is emerging, then this will be significantly structured by rights and duties which particularly concern the global environment.

Also because of the relatively recent development of the global environmental movement, NGOs have had to become media-wise to reach the imagination of the people (see Anderson 1997; Hansen 1993). Environmental organisations have developed familiarity with the global media, Greenpeace being a paradigm case, as we saw in chapter 2 (Beck 1996b). The movement has in a variety of ways learnt to be reflexive about the implications of the media. In their use of the media such organisations routinely employ global images. Hajer (1995) brings out the way in which the acid rain issue came to be highlighted through the the images of seemingly dead forests and discoloured leaves and trees. Many environmental NGOs develop effective employment of media images, particularly based around the publicising of corporate and state abuse of nature. American NGOs have distributed video cameras to grass-roots groups around the world in order that violations of environmental laws can be accurately recorded and then distributed worldwide (Castells 1997: chap. 3). Many groups have also used the Internet and Web sites. The use of such images and information is developing a globalising imagined community (see Albrow 1996 on new and labile forms of global sociality; Anderson 1989 on the concept of 'imagined community' in relationship to nation).

But at the same time, such a community will not simply and unproblematically save the planet because it is in the interest of everyone that this should happen. We have shown that there is widespread mistrust of most large-scale organisations, including those that supposedly seek to save global nature. For example, in the 'South' the World Bank is probably the most hated of organisations (Shiva 1994). And Yearley points out how the logic of free-market solutions to the problem of debt in lesser developed countries, such as those currently promoted by the World Bank, can inadvertently (and on occasions self-consciously) 'encourage international pollution and restrict the ability of governments to regulate environmental problems' (1996: 76). So it is not true that 'we' are simply all in this together. Much of the strength of the 'we' is in fact oppositional, to states and corporations that make the globe a more hazardous place, to their elites who inhabit a 'we-know-best' universe in which environmental protest needs to be carefully managed, and to various global organisations that deflect and divert global protest (Woollacott 1995). And strikingly, many institutions have been caught out, failing to anticipate the hostility of public opinion to government and the new global order. Set-piece conflicts over particular instances of the 'death' of nature often reflect wider tensions in the contemporary world, symbolising broader and more profound struggles between governments, corporations and citizens. Embryonic and highly 'moral' discourses of a global nature can thus come to signify new spaces for diverse kinds of collective 'agency', what Albrow (1996) terms 'performative citizenship' in the global age, at a time when increasing numbers of people appear to have lost trust in the ability of nation-states, corporations and some NGOs to avoid global catastrophe.

To the extent that a global citizenship may develop, it will be the product of often ill-formed groups and associations seeking to *escape* the 'power-containers' of both national and supranational states and corporations and energised by passionate opposition to those institutions. The UN has calculated that there are 50,000 such NGOs (Beck 1996b). But such a resistance does not produce agreement upon the causes and consequences of global disorder. Indeed such a resistant order especially to global institutions is highly fragmented and disparate. They embrace, according to Castells (1997), the Zapatistas in Mexico, the American militias or the Patriots more generally, Aum Shinrikyo in Japan, environmental NGOs – and, we may add, the women's movement, New Age-ists, religious fundamentalisms, and so on. They are all opposed to aspects of the new global order; and yet they all employ the technologies of that order, so much so that Castells (1997: chap. 3) terms the Zapatistas the 'first informational guerrillas' on account of their widespread use of computer-mediated communication and the establishment of a global electronic network of solidarity groups. Similar widespread use of the Internet is to be found amongst the American Patriots, who believe that the federal state is turning the US into a part of the global economy and destroying American sovereignty. They particularly oppose federal attempts to regulate the environment, as opposed to sustaining local customs and culture. Another sphere of resistance lies in the burgeoning consumer boycott movement, where large numbers of people boycott all sorts of consumer products for ethical reasons, ranging from all products French (due to nuclear testing in the South Pacific), to Faroese fish (because of their whaling practices), to W.H. Smith (targeted for selling soft porn). Indeed, as Beck (1996b: 16) states, what brought Shell to its knees in the *Brent Spar* fiasco was not Greenpeace but a mass public boycott organised through global media networks.

So what may develop is a global citizenship which is endlessly resistant, forever opposing states and corporations, their 'we-know-best' world, and their often self-serving attempts to manage, regulate and order protest, what Beck (1996b) terms globalisation from below. Our notion here is that of a cosmopolitan civil society with no originating subject and no unnegotiated agreement on which objects are to be contested (see Held 1995: chap. 10 on democracy as 'transnational'). One unintended and paradoxical outcome of such resistance, opposition and contestation, which employs all the global gadgetry of the hyper-modern world, is to produce the kinds of global dwellingness that escape from both the nation-state and market deregulation. It is such a cosmopolitan civil society which frees itself from the overarching structures of the contemporary world, an immensely heterogeneous and cosmopolitan civil society which the globe needs instantaneously, in order possibly to survive into glacial time.

Whether such intense globalising processes will facilitate or impede a reasonable environment for 'in-humans' (such as cyborgs) and 'in-animals' (such as carnivorous cows) in the next century is a question of inestimable significance and awesome indeterminacy. What Adams (1996) terms 'Future Nature' and its wonderful wildness may have a short shelf-life. The instantaneous power of mega-corporations, the untrustworthiness of nation-states and the managerialism of supranational organisations may paradoxically generate a global resistance and cosmopolitan citizenship, albeit constituted by highly different and deeply antagonistic groupings. But such developments may also unleash a wildness of nature that takes its revenge upon human society and leaves nothing at all for future global citizens to sense as all contested natures come to an end.

BIBLIOGRAPHY

Abercrombie, P. 1933. *Town and Country Planning*. London: Thornton Butterworth

Adam, B. 1988. 'Social versus natural time', in M. Young and T. Schuller (eds) *The Rhythms of Society*. London: Routledge

Adam, B. 1990. *Time and Social Theory*. Cambridge: Polity

Adam, B. 1995a. 'Radiated identities: in pursuit of the temporal complexity of conceptual cultural practices', *Theory, Culture & Society* Conference, Berlin, August

Adam, B. 1995b. *Timewatch*. Cambridge: Polity

Adam, B. 1996. 'Detraditionalization and the certainty of uncertain futures', in P. Heelas, S. Lash and P. Morris (eds) *Detraditionalization*. Oxford: Blackwell

Adam, B. 1998. *Timescapes of Modernity*. London: Routledge

Adams, J. 1981. *Transport Planning: vision and practice*. London: Routledge

Adams, J. 1995. *Risk*. London: UCL Press

Adams, W. 1996. *Future Nature*. London: Earthscan

Adler J. 1989a. 'Origins of sightseeing', *Annals of Tourism Research*, 16: 7–29

Adler, J. 1989b. 'Travel as performed art', *American Journal of Sociology*, 94: 1366–91

Adriaanse, A. 1993. *Environmental Policy Performance Indicators: a study in the development of indicators for environmental policy in the Netherlands*. The Hague: Ministry of Housing, Physical Planning and Environment

Agar, M. and MacDonald, J. 1995. 'Focus groups and ethnography', *Human Organization*, 54: 78–86

Agarwal, A. and Narain, S. 1991. *Global Warming in an Unequal World: a case of environmental colonialism*. Delhi: Centre for Science and Environment.

Albrow, M. 1996. *The Global Age*. Cambridge: Polity

Anderson, A. 1997. *Media, Culture and the Environment*. London: UCL Press

Anderson, B. 1989. *Imagined Communities*. London: Verso

Andrews, M. 1989. *The Search for the Picturesque*. Aldershot: Scolar

Appadurai, A. 1990. 'Disjuncture and difference in the global cultural economy', *Theory, Culture & Society*, 7: 295–310

Arcaya, J. 1992. 'Why is time not included in modern theories of memory?' *Time & Society*, 1: 301–14

Archibugi, D. and Held, D. (eds) 1995. *Cosmopolitan Democracy: an agenda for a new world order*. Cambridge: Polity

Arendt, H. 1978. *The Life of the Mind*. New York: Harcourt Brace Jovanovich

Arnold, D. 1996. *The Problem of Nature: environment, culture and European expansion*. Oxford: Blackwell

Ashby, E. and Anderson, M. 1981. *The Politics of Clean Air*. Oxford: Clarendon

Augé, M. 1995. *Non-Places*. London: Verso

Bachelard, G. 1969. *The Poetics of Space*. Boston: Beacon Press

Bakhtin, M. 1981. *The Dialogic Imagination*. Austin: University of Texas Press

Barnes, T. and Duncan, J. (eds) 1992. *Writing Worlds: discourse, text and metaphor in the representation of landscape*. London: Routledge

Barrell, J. 1972. *The Idea of Landscape and the Sense of Place: 1730–1840*. Cambridge: Cambridge University Press

Barry, A. 1995. 'Reporting and visualising', in C. Jenks (ed.) *Visual Culture*. London: Sage

Barthes, R. 1972. *Mythologies*. London: Cape

Barthes, R. 1981. *Camera Lucida*. New York: Hill and Wang

Bate, J. 1991. *Romantic Ecology: Wordsworth and the environmental tradition*. London: Routledge

Baudrillard, J. 1981. *For a Critique of the Economy of the Sign*. St Louis, MO: Telos

Baudrillard, J. 1988. *America*. London: Verso

Bauman, Z. 1989. *Modernity and the Holocaust*. Cambridge: Polity

Bauman, Z. 1992. *Intimations of Postmodernity*. London: Routledge

Bauman, Z. 1993a. *Postmodern Ethics*. London: Blackwell

Bauman, Z. 1993b. 'The sweet smell of decomposition', in C. Rojek and B. Turner (eds) *Forget Baudrillard?* London: Routledge

Baumol, W. and Oates. W. 1979. *Economics, Environmental Policy and Quality of Life*. Englewood Cliffs, NJ: Prentice Hall

Beck, U. 1987. 'The anthropological shock: Chernobyl and the contours of the risk society', *Berkeley Journal of Sociology*, 32: 153–165

Beck, U. 1992a. 'From industrial society to risk society: questions of survival, structure and ecological enlightenment', *Theory, Culture & Society*, 9: 97–123

Beck, U. 1992b. *Risk Society: towards a new modernity*. London: Sage

Beck, U. 1993. 'Individualization and the transformation of politics', Detraditionalisation Conference, Lancaster, July

Beck, U. 1996a. 'When experiments go wrong', *The Independent*, 26 March

Beck, U. 1996b. 'World risk society as cosmopolitan society? Ecological questions in a framework of manufactured uncertainties', *Theory, Culture & Society*, 13: 1–32

Bell, A. 1994.'Climate of opinion: public and media on the global environment', *Discourse & Society*, 5: 33–64

Bell, D. 1993. 'Framing nature: first steps into the wilderness for a sociology of the landscape', *Irish Journal of Sociology*, 3: 1–22

Bender, B. (ed.) 1993. *Landscape: politics and perspectives*. Oxford: Berg

Benjamin, W. 1969. *Illuminations*. New York: Schocken

Benton, T. 1993. *Natural Relations: ecology, animal rights and social justice*. London: Verso

Berger, J. 1972. *Ways of Seeing*. Harmondsworth: Penguin

Bergson, H. 1950. *Time and Free Will*. London: George Allen and Unwin

Bergson, H. 1991. *Matter and Memory*. New York: Zone Books

Berking, H. 1996. 'Solidary individualism: the moral impact of cultural modernisation in late modernity', in S. Lash, B. Szerszynski and B. Wynne (eds) *Risk, Environment and Modernity*. London: Sage

Berman, M. 1983. *All That Is Solid Melts Into Air*. London: Verso

Bermingham, A. 1986. *Landscape and Ideology*. London: Thames and Hudson

Bermingham, A. 1994. 'Redesigning nature: John Constable and the landscape of enclosure', in R. Friedland and D. Boden (eds) *Nowhere: space, time and modernity*. Berkeley: University of California Press

Bhabha, H. (ed.) 1990. *Nation and Narration*. London: Routledge

Bianchini, F. 1995. 'The 24-hour city', *Demos Quarterly. The Time Squeeze*, 5: 47–8

Bijker, W. and Law, J. (eds) 1991. *Shaping Technology/Building Society: studies in socio-technical change*. Cambridge, MA: MIT Press

Billig, M. 1987. *Arguing and Thinking: a rhetorical approach to social psychology*. Cambridge: Cambridge University Press

Billig, M. 1988a. 'Rhetorical and historical aspects of attitudes: the case of the British monarchy', *Philosophical Psychology*, 1: 83–104

Billig, M. 1988b. 'Social representation, objectification and anchoring: a rhetorical analysis', *Social Behaviour*, 3: 1–16

Billig, M. 1989a. 'The argumentative nature of holding strong views: a case study', *European Journal of Social Psychology*, 19: 203–23

Billig, M. 1989b. 'The rhetoric of social psychology', in I. Parker and J. Shotter (eds) *Deconstructing Social Psychology*. London: Routledge

Billig, M. 1991. *Ideology and Opinions: studies in rhetorical psychology*. London: Sage

Billig, M. 1992. *Talking of the Royal Family*. London: Routledge

Billig, M. 1993. 'Studying the thinking society: social representation, rhetoric and attitudes', in G. Breakwell, and D. Cantor, (eds) *Empirical Approaches to Social Representations*. Oxford: Blackwell

Billig, M. 1995. *Banal Nationalism*. London: Sage

Bookchin, M. 1980. *The Ecology of Freedom*. Palo Alto, CA: Cheshire Books

Boorstin, D. 1964. *The Image: a guide to pseudo-events in America*. New York: Harper

Borneman, J. 1993. 'Time-space compression and the continental divide in German subjectivity', *New Formations*, 21: 102–118

Bourdieu, P. 1990. 'Time perspectives among the Kabyle', in J. Hassard (ed.) *A Sociology of Time*. London: Macmillan

Boyer, C. 1995. 'The great frame-up', in H. Liggitt and D. Perry (eds) *Spatial Practices*. Thousand Oaks, CA: Sage

Bramwell, A. 1989. *Ecology in the 20th Century*. New Haven, CT: Yale University Press

Bramwell, A. 1994. *The Fading of the Greens: the decline of environmental politics in the West*. New Haven, CT: Yale University Press

Brendon, P. 1991. *Thomas Cook: 150 years of popular tourism*. London: Secker and Warburg

Brown, P., Smithers, R. and Boseley, S. 1996. 'Beef warning sparks panic', *The Guardian*, 21 March

Brunn, S. and Leinbach, R. (eds) 1990. *Collapsing Space and Time: geographic aspects of communications and information*. London: HarperCollins

Bryant, B. and Mohai, P. (eds) 1992. *Race and the Incidence of Environmental Hazards: a time for discourse*. Boulder, CO: Westview Press

Bryman, A. 1995. *Disney and His Worlds*. London: Routledge

Bryson, N. 1983. *Vision and Painting*. London: Macmillan

Buci-Glucksmann, C. 1994. *Baroque Reason: the aesthetics of modernity*. London: Sage

Bullard, R. 1990. *Dumping in Dixie: race, class and environmental quality*. Boulder, CO: Westview Press

Bulmer, M. and Rees, A. (eds) 1996. *Citizenship Today*. London: UCL Press

Bunce, M. 1994. *The Countryside Ideal*. London: Routledge

Burgess, J. 1990. 'The production and consumption of environmental meanings in the mass media: a research agenda for the 1990s', *Transactions of the Institute of British Geographers*, 15: 139–62

Burgess, J. and Harrison, C. 1993. 'The circulation of claims in the cultural politics of environmental change', in A. Hansen (ed.) *The Mass Media and Environmental Issues*. Leicester: Leicester University Press

Burgess, J., Limb, M. and Harrison, C. 1988a. 'Exploring environmental values through the medium of small groups: 1. Theory and practice', *Environment and Planning A*, 20: 309–26

Burgess, J., Limb, M. and Harrison, C. 1988b. 'Exploring environmental values through the medium of small groups: 2. Illustrations of a group at work', *Environment and Planning A*, 20: 457–76

Burgess, J., Harrison, C. and Filius, P. 1995. 'Making the Abstract Real: a cross-cultural study of public understanding of global environmental change', *UCL Report*, Geography Department, London

Burningham, K. 1995. 'Attitudes, accounts and impact assessment', *Sociological Review*, 43: 100–22

Burningham, K. and O'Brien, M. 1994. 'Global environmental values and local contexts of action', *Sociology*, 28: 913–32

Buttel, F. 1987. 'New directions in environmental sociology', *Annual Review of Sociology*, 13: 465–88

Buzard, J. 1993. *The Beaten Track: European tourism, literature and the ways to culture 1800–1914*. Oxford: Clarendon

Cannadine, D. 1995. 'The National Trust: the first hundred years', in H. Newby (ed.) *The National Trust: the next hundred years*. London: National Trust

Cannon, D. 1995. 'Post-modern work ethic', *Demos Quarterly. The Time Squeeze*, 5: 31–2

Capra, F. 1975. *The Tao of Physics*. Berkeley: University of California Press

Carson, R. 1962. *Silent Spring*. Boston: Houghton Mifflin

Carter, E., Donald, J. and Squires, J. (eds) 1993. *Space and Place*. London: Lawrence and Wishart

Castells, M. 1996. *The Rise of the Network Society*. Oxford: Blackwell

Castells, M. 1997. *The Power of Identity*. Oxford: Blackwell

Catton, W and Dunlap, R. 1978. 'Environmental sociology: a new paradigm', *The American Sociologist*, 13: 41–9

CEC (Commission of the European Communities) 1992a. *Europeans and the Environment in 1992: Eurobarometer 37.0*. Brussels: European Commission

CEC (Commission of the European Communities) 1992b. *Fifth Environmental Action Programme for the Environment and Sustainable Development*. Brussels: European Commission

CEC (Commission of the European Communities) 1995. *Europeans and the Environment in 1995: Eurobarometer 43.1*. Brussels: European Commission

Chapman, M. 1993. 'Copeland: Cumbria's best-kept secret', in S. Macdonald (ed.) *Inside European Identities*. Oxford: Berg

Chaudhary, V. 1994. 'Anti-lobby stirs nationwide', *The Guardian*, 14 June

Cherry, G. 1975. *Environmental Planning 1939–1969. Vol II. National parks and recreation in the countryside*. London: HMSO

Clark, G., Darrall, J., Grove-White, R., Macnaghten, P. and Urry, J. 1994a. *Leisure Landscapes: background papers*. London: CPRE

Clark, G., Darrall, J., Grove-White, R., Macnaghten, P., and Urry, J. 1994b. *Leisure Landscapes: main report*. London: CPRE

Classen, C., Howes, D. and Synnott, A. 1994. *Aroma: the cultural history of smell*. London: Routledge

Clifford, S. 1994. 'Pluralism, power and passion', BANC Conference, St Anne's College, Oxford, December

Clifford, S. and King, A. (eds) 1993. *Local Distinctiveness: place, particularity and identity*. London: Common Ground

Cloke, P., Doel, M., Matless, D., Phillips, M. and Thrift, N. 1994. *Writing the Rural*. London: Paul Chapman

Collins, H. and Pinch, T. 1993. *The Golem: what everyone should know about science*. Cambridge: Cambridge University Press

Colson, F. 1926. *The Week*. Cambridge: Cambridge University Press

Commoner, B. 1972. *The Closing Circle: nature, man and technology*. New York: Knopf

Connor, S. and Prescott, M. 1996. 'BSE: a scandal of dither and delay', *The Sunday Times*, 24 March

Corbin, A. 1986. *The Foul and the Fragrant*. Leamington Spa: Berg

Corbin, A. 1992. *The Lure of the Sea: the discovery of the seaside in the western world, 1750–1840*. Cambridge: Polity

Corner, J. and Harvey, S. (eds) 1991. *Enterprise and Heritage*. London: Routledge

Cornish, V. 1930. *National Parks and the Heritage of Scenery*. London: Sifton Praed

Cosgrove, D. 1984. *Social Formation and Symbolic Landscape*. London: Croom Helm

Cosgrove, D. 1985. 'Prospect, perspective and the evolution of the landscape idea', *Transactions of the Institute of British Geographers*, 10: 45–62

Cotgrove, S. 1982. *Catastrophe or Cornucopia: the environment, politics and the future*. Chichester: Wiley

Countryside Commission 1984. *National Survey of Countryside Recreation*. Cheltenham: Countryside Commission

Countryside Commission 1986a. *Motivations behind Visiting the Countryside*. Unpublished

Countryside Commission 1986b. *The Greenwich Open Spaces Project*. Unpublished

Countryside Commission 1987. *A Compendium of Recreational Statistics*. Cheltenham: Countryside Commission

Countryside Commission 1991. *Caring for the Countryside: a policy agenda for England in the nineties*. Manchester: Countryside Commission

Countryside Commission 1992. *Enjoying the Countryside: policies for people*. Manchester: Countryside Commission

Countryside Commission 1993. *United Kingdom Day Visits Survey*. Cheltenham: Countryside Commission

Coveney, P. and Highfield , R. 1991. *The Arrow of Time*. London: Flamingo

Coward, R. 1989. *The Whole Truth: the myth of alternative health*. London: Faber and Faber

CPRE (Council for the Protection of Rural England) 1995. *Tranquil Areas for England*. London: CPRE

Crary, J. 1990. *Techniques of the Observer*. Cambridge MA: MIT Press

Crawshaw, C. and Urry, J. 1997. 'Tourism and the photographic eye', in C. Rojek and J. Urry (eds) *Touring Cultures*. London: Routledge

Crouch, D. 1992a. 'British Allotments: landscapes of ordinary people', *Landscape*, 31: 1–7

Crouch, D. 1992b. 'Popular culture and what we make of the rural, with a case study of village allotments', *Journal of Rural Studies*, 8: 229–40

Curtice, J. and Jowell, R. 1995. 'The sceptical electorate', in R. Jowell, J. Curtice, A. Park, L. Brook and D. Ahrendt (eds) *British Social Attitudes: the 12th report*. Dartmouth: SCPR

Daily Telegraph Editorial. 1996. 'How far will he go?' *The Daily Telegraph*, 22 May

Daniels, S. 1991. 'Envisioning England', *Journal of Historical Geography*, 17: 95–9

Davies, K. 1990. *Women and Time: weaving the strands of everyday life*. Aldershot: Avebury

Davis, M. 1995. 'Because cars can't dance', *The Guardian*, 19 July

de Certeau, M. 1984. *The Practice of Everyday Life*. Berkeley: University of California Press

Demos 1995a. 'Missionary government', *Demos Quarterly*, 7: 1–8

Demos 1995b. *Demos Quarterly. The Time Squeeze*. London: Demos

Department of Employment Task Force 1991. *Tourism and the Environment: maintaining the balance*. London: Department of Employment and English Tourist Board

Department of the Environment 1986. *Digest of Environmental Protection and Water Statistics, No. 9*. London: HMSO

Department of the Environment 1989. *Digest of Environmental Protection and Water Statistics, No. 12*. London: HMSO

Department of the Environment 1991. *Planning Policy Guidance on Sport and Recreation: PPG17*. London: Department of the Environment

Department of the Environment 1992. *Planning Policy Guidance on Tourism: PPG 21*. London: Department of the Environment

Department of the Environment 1994. *Digest of Environmental Protection and Water Statistics, No. 16*. London: HMSO

Department of the Environment 1996. *Indicators of Sustainable Development for the United Kingdom*. London: HMSO

Derrida, J. 1983. 'The principle of reason: the university in the eyes of its pupils', *Diacritics*, 13

Deutsche, R. 1991. 'Boys town', *Environment and Planning D: Society and Space*, 9: 5–30

Devall, W. and Sessions, G. 1985. *Deep Ecology: living as if ecology mattered*. Salt Lake City, UT: Peregrine Smith

Dickens, P. 1991. *People, Nature and Alienation: an alternative perspective and a case study*. Brighton: Sussex University, Centre for Urban and Regional Research, Working Paper 82

Dickens, P. 1992. *Society and Nature*. Hemel Hempstead: Harvester Wheatsheaf

Dickens, P. 1996. *Reconstructing Nature*. London: Routledge

Dickson, L. and McCulloch, A. 1996. 'Shell, Brent Spar and Greenpeace: a doomed tryst', *Environmental Politics*, 5: 122–9

Dobson, A. 1990. *Green Political Thought*. London: HarperCollins

Douglas, M. 1966. *Purity and Danger: an analysis of the concepts of pollution and taboo.* London: Routledge

Douglas, M. 1985. *Risk Acceptability According to the Social Sciences.* New York: Russell Sage Foundation

Douglas, M. 1990. 'Risk as a forensic resource', *Daedalus*, 119: 1–16

Douglas, M. 1992. *Risk and Blame.* London: Routledge

Douglas, M. and Wildavsky, A. 1982. *Risk and Culture: an essay on the selection of technological and environmental dangers.* Berkeley: University of California Press

Dunlap, R. 1991a. 'Public opinion on the environment in the eighties: a decade of growing concern', *Environment*, 33: 10–15, 32–7

Dunlap, R. 1991b. 'Trends in public opinion towards environmental issues: 1965 to 1990', *Society and Natural Resources*, 4: 285–312

Dunlap, R. and Catton, W. 1979. 'Environmental sociology', *Annual Review of Sociology*, 5: 243–73

Dunlap, R. and Catton, W. 1994. 'Struggling with human exemptionalism: the rise, decline and revitalization of environmental sociology', *The American Sociologist*, 25: 5–30

Dunlap, R. and Scarce, R. 1991. 'The polls – poll trends: environmental problems and protection', *Public Opinion Quarterly*, 55: 651–672

Dunlap, R. and Van Liere, K. 1978. 'The "new environmental paradigm": a proposed measuring instrument and preliminary results', *Journal of Environmental Education*, 9: 10–19

Dunlap, R. and Van Liere, K. 1984. 'Commitment to the dominant social paradigm and concern for environmental quality', *Social Science Quarterly*, 65: 1013–28

Dunlap, R., Gallup, G. and Gallup, A. 1993. 'The health of the planet: a global concern', *Environment*, 35: 7–15, 33–9

Durkheim, É. 1952. *Suicide.* London: Routledge

Durkheim, É. 1968. *Elementary Forms of the Religious Life.* London: Allen and Unwin

Durant, J. 1996. 'Once men in white coats held the promise of a better future. Why have we lost our trust in them?' *The Independent*, 1 April

Eade, J. (ed.) 1997. *Living the Global City.* London: Routledge

Eco, U. 1986. *Travels in Hyperreality.* London: Picador

Ecologist 1972. *Blueprint for Survival.* Sturminster Newton: Ecologist

Eden, S. 1993. 'Individual environmental responsibility and its role in public environmentalism', *Environment and Planning A*, 25: 1743–58

Edensor, T. 1996. *Touring the Taj.* PhD, Dept of Sociology, Lancaster University

Edensor, T. and Kothari, U. 1994. 'The masculinisation of Stirling's heritage', in D. Hall and V. Kinnaird (eds) *Tourism: a gender analaysis.* Chichester: Wiley

Eder, K. 1990. 'Rise of counter-culture movements against modernity: nature as a new field of class struggle', *Theory, Culture & Society*, 7: 21–47

Eder, K. 1996. *The Social Construction of Nature.* London: Sage

Edholm, F. 1993. 'The view from below: Paris in the 1880s', in B. Bender (ed.) *Landscape: politics and perspectives.* Oxford: Berg

Ehrlich, P. 1968. *The Population Bomb.* New York: Ballantine Books

Ekins, P. 1992. *A New World Order.* London: Routledge

Elias, N. 1992. *Time: an essay.* Oxford; Blackwell

Elkington, J. and Hailes, J. 1988. *The Green Consumer Guide.* London: Gollancz

English Tourist Board 1991. *Planning for Success.* London: English Tourist Board

Erlichman, J., Vidal, J. and Keeble, J. 1995. 'A new political animal is born', *The Guardian*, 7 January

Ermath, E. 1995. 'Ph(r)ase time: chaos theory and postmodern reports on knowledge', *Time & Society*, 1: 91–110

ESRC [Economic and Social Research Council] 1990. *Global Environmental Change Programme.* London: ESRC

Evans-Pritchard, E. 1940. *The Nuer.* Oxford: Oxford University Press

Eyerman, R. and Jamison, A. 1991. *Social Movements: a cognitive approach*. Cambridge: Polity

Fabian, J. 1992. *Time and the Work of Anthropology: critical essays 1971–1991*. Chur, Switzerland: Harwood

Featherstone, M. (ed.) (1990) *Global Culture: nationalism, globalization and modernity*. London: Sage

Featherstone, M., Lash, S. and Robertson, R. (eds) 1995. *Global Modernities*. London: Sage

Finger, M. 1993. 'Politics of the UNCED process', in W. Sachs (ed.) *Global Ecology: a new arena of global conflict*. London: Zed

Fitzsimmons, M. 1989. 'The matter of nature', *Antipode*, 21: 106–20

Flood, M. and Grove-White, R. 1976. *Nuclear Prospects*. London: NCCL

Foucault, M. 1970. *The Order of Things*. London: Tavistock

Foucault, M. 1977. *Discipline and Punish*. London: Allen Lane

Fox, M. 1989. 'Unreliable allies: subjective and objective time', in J. Forman and C. Sowton (eds) *Taking Our Time: feminist perspectives on temporality*. Oxford: Pergamon

Furniss, T. 1993. *Edmund Burkes's Aesthetic Ideology*. Cambridge: Cambridge University Press

Game. A. 1991. *Undoing the Social*. Milton Keynes: Open University Press

Game, A. 1995. 'Time, space, memory, with reference to Bachelard', in M. Featherstone, S. Lash and R. Robertson (eds) *Global Modernities*. London: Sage

Gamsen, W. and Modigliani, A. 1989. 'Media discourse and public opinion on nuclear power: a constructivist approach', *American Journal of Sociology*, 95: 1–37

Gamst, F. 1993. ' "On time" and the railroader – temporal dimensions of work', in S. Helmers (ed.) *Ethnologie der Arbeitswelt: Beispiele aus europäischen und aussereuropäischen Feldern*. Bonn: Holos Verlag

Gell, A. 1992. *The Anthropology of Time: cultural constructions of temporal maps and images*. Oxford: Berg

Ghazi, P., McKie, R. and Narayan, N. 1995. 'Now let the fight for the Pacific begin', *The Observer*, 25 June

Gibbons, J. 1995. 'Tactics that crippled the veal industry', *The Sunday Telegraph*, 5 February

Gibson, J. 1979. *An Ecological Approach to Visual Perception*. Boston: Houghton Mifflin

Giddens, A. 1981. *A Contemporary Critique of Historical Materialism*. London: Macmillan

Giddens, A. 1984. *The Constitution of Society*. Cambridge: Polity

Giddens, A. 1990. *The Consequences of Modernity*. Cambridge: Polity

Giddens, A. 1991. *Modernity and Self-identity: self and society in the late modern age*. Cambridge: Polity

Giddens, A. 1995. 'Government's last gasp?' *The Observer*, 9 July

Gilroy, P. 1993. *The Black Atlantic: modernity and double consciousness*. London: Verso

Glacken, C. 1966. 'Reflections on the man–nature theme as a subject for study', in F. Darling and J. Milton (eds) *Future Environments of North America*. Garden City, NY: The Natural History Press

Glacken, C. 1967. *Traces on the Rhodian Shore: nature and culture in western thought from ancient times to the end of the eighteenth century*. Berkeley: University of California Press

Glennie, P. and Thrift, N. 1996. 'Reworking E.P. Thompson's "Time, Work-Discipline and Industrial Capitalism" ', *Time & Society*, 5: 275–300

Goffman, E. 1968. *Asylum*. Harmondsworth: Penguin

Going for Green 1995. *The Harris Final Report*. Richmond: Harris

Going for Green 1996. *We Can Make a Difference – Together*. National UK newspaper campaign, April

Gosschalk, B. and Hatter, W. 1996. 'No sense of place? Changing patterns of local identity', *Demos Quarterly*, 9: 13–16

Green, N. 1990. *The Spectacle of Nature*. Manchester: Manchester University Press

Gregory, D. 1994. *Geographical Imaginations*. Cambridge, MA: Blackwell

Griffiths, J. 1995. 'Life of strife in the fast lane', *The Guardian*, 23 August

Gross, S. 1992. 'Reading time – text, image, film', *Time & Society*, 1: 207–22

Grove, R. 1990. *Green Imperialism: colonial expansion, tropical island Edens and the origins of environmentalism, 1600–1860*. Cambridge: Cambridge University Press

Grove-White, R. 1991a. 'The emerging shape of environmental conflict in the 1990s', *Royal Society of Arts*, 139: 437–47

Grove-White, R. 1991b. *The UK's Environmental Movement and UK Political Culture. Report to EURES*. Lancaster: CSEC, Lancaster University

Grove-White, R. 1992. 'Land use law and the environment', in R. Churchill, J. Gibson, and L. Warren (eds) *Law, Policy and the Environment*. Oxford: Blackwell

Grove-White, R. 1993. 'Environmentalism: a new moral discourse?' in K. Milton (ed.) *Environmentalism: the view from anthropology*. London: Routledge

Grove-White, R. 1994. 'Society and Culture', *Values for a Sustainable Society*, World Environment Day Symposium, 2 June

Grove-White, R. 1995. 'Environment and society: some reflections', *Environmental Politics*, 4: 264–75

Grove-White, R. 1996a. 'Environmental knowledge and public policy needs: on humanising the research agenda', in S. Lash, B. Szerszynski and B. Wynne (eds) *Risk, Environment and Modernity: towards a new ecology*. London: Sage

Grove-White, R. 1996b. 'Life in a "risk" society', *The Financial Times*, 29 March

Grove-White, R. 1997. 'The environmental "valuation" controversy: observations on its recent history and significance', in J. Foster (ed.) *Valuing Nature: economics, ethics and the environment*. London: Routledge

Grove-White, R. and Szerszynski, B. 1992. 'Getting behind environmental ethics', *Environmental Values*, 1: 285–96

Grove-White, R., Macnaghten, P., Mayer, S. and Wynne, B. 1997. *Uncertain World: genetically modified organisms, food and public information in Britain*. Lancaster: CSEC and Unilever.

Haigh, N. 1976. 'The national organisations: the birth of a movement', Civic Trust (ed.), *The Local Amenity Movement*. London: Civic Trust

Haigh, N. 1986. 'Public perceptions and international influences', in G. Conway (ed.) *The Assessment of Environmental Problems*. London: Imperial College

Haigh, N. 1987. *EEC Environmental Policy and Britain*. London: Longman

Haigh, N. and Lanigan, C. 1995. 'Impact of the EU on UK policy making', in T. Gray (ed.) *UK Environmental Policy in the 1990s*. London: Macmillan

Hajer, M. 1995. *The Politics of Environmental Discourse: ecological modernization and the policy process*. Oxford: Clarendon

Hajer, M. 1996. 'Ecological modernisation as cultural politics', in S. Lash, B. Szerszynski and B. Wynne (eds) *Risk, Environment and Modernity: towards a new ecology*. London: Sage

Halbwachs, M. 1992. *On Collective Memory*. Chicago: University of Chicago Press

Hall, A. 1986. *Nuclear Politics: the history of nuclear power in Britain*. Harmondsworth: Penguin

Hall, C. 1976. 'The amenity movement', in C. Gill (ed.) *The Countryman's Britain*. Newton Abbot: David and Charles

Hall, P. 1973. *The Containment of Urban Britain. Vol 1. Urban and metropolitan growth processes*. London: Allen and Unwin

Hansen, A. (ed.) 1993. *The Mass Media and Environmental Issues*. Leicester: Leicester University Press

Haraway, D. 1989. *Primate Visions: gender, race, and nature in the world of modern science*. New York: Routledge

Haraway, D. 1991. *Simians, Cyborgs, and Women. The reinvention of nature*. London: Free Association Books

Hardin, R. 1968. 'The tragedy of the commons: the population problem has no technical solution; it requires a fundamental extension in morality', *Science*, 162: 1243–8

Hardy, D. 1979. *Alternative Communities in Nineteenth Century England*. London: Longman

Harley, J. 1992. 'Deconstructing the map', in T. Barnes amd J. Duncan (eds) *Writing Worlds: discourse, text and metaphor in the representation of landscape*. London: Routledge

Harrison, C. and Burgess, J. 1994. 'Social constructions of nature: a case study of the conflicts over Rainham Marshes SSSI', *Transactions of the Institute of British Geographers*, 19: 291–310

Harvey, D. 1989. *The Condition of Postmodernity*. Oxford: Blackwell

Harvey, D. 1996. *Justice, Nature and the Geography of Difference*. Oxford: Blackwell

Hassard, J. (ed.) 1990. *The Sociology of Time*. London: Macmillan

Hattersley, R. 1996. 'Beef as barometer of the national psyche', *The Guardian*, 1 April

Hawking, S. 1988. *A Short History of Time*. London: Bantam

Hay, C. 1994. 'Environmental security and state legitimacy', in M. O'Connor (ed.) *Is Capitalism Sustainable?* New York: Guilford Press

Hays, S. 1959. *Conservation and the Gospel of Efficiency: the progressive conservation movement 1890–1920*. New York: Atheneum

Hays, S. 1987. *Health, Beauty and Permanence: environmental politics in the United States, 1955–1985*. New York: Cambridge University Press

Hays, S. 1992. 'Environmental political culture and environmental political development: an analysis of legislative voting: 1971–1989', *Environment History Review*, 16: 1–22

Hayward, T. 1994. *Ecological Thought*. Cambridge: Polity

Healey, P. and Shaw, T. 1994. 'Changing meanings of "environment" in the British planning system', *Transactions of the Institute of British Geographers*, 19: 425–38

Heath, A. 1995. 'Polite pickets defy farmer's "cruel trade"', *The Independent*, 13 January

Heelas, P., Lash, S. and Morris, P. (eds) 1996. *Detraditionalization*. Oxford: Blackwell

Heidegger, M. 1962. *Being and Time*. Oxford: Blackwell

Heidegger, M. 1971. *Poetry, Language, Thought*. New York: Harper and Row

Heidegger, M. 1977. *Basic Writings*. New York: Harper and Row

Held, D. 1995. *Democracy and the Global Order*. Cambridge: Polity

Hetherington, K. 1990. *On the Homecoming of the Stranger: new social movements or new sociations?* Lancaster Regionalism Working Group no. 39, Lancaster University

Hetherington, K. 1991. *The Geography of the Other: Stonehenge, Greenham and the politics of trust*. Lancaster Regionalism Working Group no. 42, Lancaster University

Hetherington, K. 1993. *The Geography of the Other: lifestyle, performance and identities*. PhD, Dept of Sociology, Lancaster University

Hetherington, K. 1995. 'Technologies of place', Labour of Division Conference. Keele: Keele University

Hettena, P. and Syer, G. 1971. *Decade of Decision: report on the Conservation Society's conference 'Conservation 1970s'*. London: Conservation Society

Hewison, R. 1987. *The Heritage Industry*. London: Methuen

Hewison, R. 1993. 'Field of dreams', *The Sunday Times*, 3 January

Hibbitts, B. 1994. 'Making sense of metaphors: visuality, aurality, and the reconfiguration of American legal discourse', *Cardozo Law Review*, 16: 229–356

Highfield, R. 1996. 'Sorry sight of ministers hiding behind the skirts of science', *The Electronic Telegraph*, 22 March

Hirst, P. and Thompson, G. 1996. *Globalisation in Question*. Cambridge: Polity

Holmberg, J., Thomson, K. and Timberlake, L. 1993. *Facing the Future*. London: Earthscan, IIED

Honiville, L., Wilesmith, J. and Richards, M. 1995. 'An investigation of risk factors for cases of bovine spongiform encephalopathy born after the introduction of the "feed ban"', *Veterinary Record*, 136: 312–18

Howard, E. 1965. *Garden Cities of Tomorrow*. London: Faber

Howkins, A. 1986. 'The discovery of rural England', in R. Colls and P. Dodd (eds) *Englishness: politics and culture 1880–1920*. London: Croom Helm

HPI 1994. *Sustainability and the Countryside: exploratory final report to the Countryside Commission*. London: HPI (unpublished)

Hutton, W. 1995. *The State We're In*. London: Jonathan Cape

Huyssen, A. 1995. *The Culture of Amnesia*. New York: Routledge
Ihde, D. 1976. *Listening and Voice*. Athens, OH: Ohio University Press
Illich, I. 1973. *Deschooling Society*. Harmondsworth: Penguin
Illich, I. 1975. *Tools for Conviviality*. London: Fontana
Inglehart, R. 1977. *The Silent Revolution: changing values and political styles among western publics*. Princeton: Princeton University Press
Inglehart, R. 1990. *Cultural Shift in Advanced Industrial Societies*. Princeton: Princeton University Press
Ingold, T. 1993a. 'Globes and spheres: the topology of environmentalism', in K. Milton (ed.) *Environmentalism: the view from anthropology*. London: Routledge
Ingold, T. 1993b. 'The temporality of the landscape', *World Archaeology*, 25: 152–74
Ingold, T.1996. 'Life beyond the edge of nature? Or, the mirage of society', in J. Greenwood (ed.) *The Mark of the Social*. London: Rowman and Littlefield
Irigaray, L. 1978. 'Interview with L. Iragaray', in M.-F. Hans and G. Lapouge (eds) *Les Femmes, la pornographie et l'érotisme*. Paris
Irvine, S. and Pontin, A. 1988. *A Green Manifesto: policies for a green future*. London: Optima
IUCN (International Union for Conservation of Nature) 1980. *World Conservation Strategy*. Gland, Switzerland: IUCN, UNEP and WWF
IUCN (International Union for Conservation of Nature) 1991. *Caring for the Earth*. Gland, Switzerland: IUCN, UNEP and WWF
Jacobs, M. 1996. 'Sheepish about safety', *The Guardian*, 24 July
Jacques, M. 1994. 'The end of politics', *The Sunday Times*, 18 July
Jamison, A. 1996. 'The shaping of the global environmental agenda: the role of non-governmental organisations', in S. Lash, B. Szerszynski and B. Wynne (eds) *Risk, Environment and Modernity*. London: Sage
Jasanoff, S. 1987. 'Contested boundaries in policy-relevant science', *Social Studies of Science*, 17: 195–230
Jasanoff, S. 1990. *The Fifth Branch: science advisors as policymakers*. Cambridge, MA: Harvard University Press
Jay, M. 1986. 'In the empire of the gaze: Foucault and the denigration of vision in twentieth-century French thought', in D. Hoy (ed.) *Foucault: a critical reader*. Oxford: Blackwell
Jay, M. 1992. 'Scopic regimes of modernity', in S. Lash and J. Friedman (eds) *Modernity and Identity*. Oxford: Blackwell
Jay, M. 1993. *Downcast Eyes*. Berkeley: University of California Press
Jenks, C. 1995a. 'The centrality of the eye in western culture', in C. Jenks (ed.) *Visual Culture*. London: Routledge
Jenks, C. (ed.) 1995b. *Visual Culture*. London: Routledge
Johnson, B. 1987. 'The environmentalist movement and grid/group analysis: a modest critique', in B. Johnson and V. Covello (eds) *The Social and Cultural Construction of Risk*. Dordrecht: Reidel
Johnson, B. 1993. *The Conservation and Development Programme for the UK: a response to the World Conservation Strategy*. London: Kogan Page
Johnston, M. 1993. 'Disengaging from democracy', in R. Jowell, L. Book and L. Dowds (eds) *International Social Attitudes; the 10th BSA Report*. Dartmouth: SCPR
Kaase, M. and Newton, K. 1996. *Beliefs in Government*. Oxford: Oxford University Press
Kearns, G. and Philo, C. (eds) 1993. *Selling Places: the city as cultural capital, past and present*. Oxford: Pergamon
Kempton, W., Boster, J. and Hartley, J. 1995. *Environmental Values in American Culture*. Cambridge, MA: MIT Press
Kern, S. 1983. *The Culture of Time and Space, 1880–1914*. London: Weidenfeld and Nicolson
King, A. and Clifford, S. 1985. *Holding Your Ground: an action guide to local conservation*. London: Temple Smith

Kitzinger, K. 1994. 'The methodology of focus groups: the importance of interaction between research participants', *Sociology of Health and Illness*, 16: 103–21

Kitzinger, K. 1995. 'Introducing focus groups', *British Medical Journal*, 311: 299–302

Koestler, A. 1964. *The Sleepwalkers: a history of man's changing vision of the universe*. Harmondsworth: Penguin

Körner, S. 1955. *Kant*. Harmondsworth: Penguin

Krueger, R. 1994. *Focus Groups*. Thousand Oaks, CA: Sage

Kwa, C. 1987. 'Representations of nature mediating between ecology and science policy: the case of the International Biological Project', *Social Studies of Science*, 17: 413–42

Lancashire County Council 1991. *A Green Audit*. Preston: Lancashire County Council

Lancashire Environment Forum 1993. *Lancashire Environment Action Plan: local agenda 21 for Lancashire*. Preston: Lancashire County Council

Lash, S. 1995. 'Risk culture', Australian Cultural Studies Conference, Charles Stuart University, New South Wales, December

Lash, S. and Urry, J. 1987. *The End of Organized Capitalism*. Cambridge: Polity

Lash, S. and Urry, J. 1994. *Economies of Signs and Space*. London: Sage

Lash, S. Szerszynski, B. and Wynne. B. (eds) 1996. *Risk, Environment and Modernity: towards a new ecology*. London: Sage

Latour, B. 1987. *Science in Action*. Milton Keynes: Open University Press

Latour, B. 1993. *We Have Never Been Modern*. Hemel Hempstead: Harvester Wheatsheaf

Latour, B. and Woolgar, S. 1996. *Laboratory Life*, 2nd edition. Princeton: Princeton University Press

Leadbeater, C. 1996. 'Meat and money: why the beef industry has led itself to slaughter', *The Observer*, 22 December

Lean, G. 1994. 'New green army rises up against roads', *The Observer*, 20 February

Lefebvre, H. 1991. *The Production of Space*. Oxford: Blackwell

Leopold, A. 1949. *A Sand County Almanac*. London: Grafton Books

Levin, D. 1993a. 'Decline and fall: ocularcentrism in Heidegger's reading of the history of metaphysics', in D. Levin (ed.) *Modernity and the Hegemony of Vision*. Berkeley: University of California Press

Levin, D. (ed.) 1993b. *Modernity and the Hegemony of Vision*. Berkeley: University of California Press

Lewis, C.S. 1964. *The Discarded Image: an introduction to medieval and renaissance literature*. Cambridge: Cambridge University Press

Lezard, N. 1993. 'The battle of Twyford down', *The Independent*, 3 July

LGMB (Local Government Management Board) 1993. *A Framework for Local Sustainability*. Luton: LGMB

LGMB (Local Government Management Board) 1994a. *Local Agenda 21 Guidance Notes: community participation*. Luton: LGMB

LGMB (Local Government Management Board) 1994b. *Sustainability Indicators – guidance to pilot authorities*. Luton: LGMB

LGMB (Local Government Management Board) 1995. *Sustainability Indicators Research Project: consultants' report of the pilot phase*. Luton: LGMB

Light, A. 1991. *Forever England: feminity, literature and conservatism between the wars*. London: Routledge

Liniado, M. 1996. *Car Culture and Countryside Change*. MSc Dissertation, Geography Dept, University of Bristol

Linton, M. and Bates, S. 1996. 'Public suspects cover-up', *The Guardian*, 3 April

Lofstedt, R. 1995. 'Why are public perception studies on the environment ignored?', *Global Environmental Change*, 5: 83–5

Lovejoy, A. 1936. *The Great Chain of Being: a study of the history of an idea*. Cambridge, MA: Harvard University Press

Lovelock, J. 1988. *The Ages of Gaia: a biography of our living earth*. Oxford: Oxford University Press

Lowe, P. 1976. 'Amateurs and professionals: the institutional emergence of British plant ecology', *Journal for the Society for the Biography of Natural History*, 7: 517–35
Lowe, P. 1983. 'Values and institutions in the history of British nature conservation', in F. Gloversmith (ed.) *Conservation in Practice*. Chichester: Wiley
Lowe, P. and Goyder, J. 1983. *Environmental Groups in Politics*. London: Allen and Unwin
Lowenthal, D. 1985. *The Past is a Foreign Country*. Cambridge: Cambridge University Press
Lowenthal, D. 1991. 'British national identity and the English landscape', *Rural History*, 2: 205–30
Lowenthal, D. 1994. 'European and English landscapes as national symbols', in D. Hooson (ed.) *Geography and National Identity*. Oxford: Blackwell
LUC (Land Use Consultants) 1994. *Hertfordshire Soundings Exercise: focus groups – report to Hertfordshire County Council*. London: LUC
Luckham, B. 1990. *Questions of Power*. Manchester: Manchester University Press
Luhmann, N. 1982. *The Differentiation of Society*. New York: Columbia University Press
Luke, T. 1995. 'New world orders or neo-world orders: power, politics and ideology in informationalizing glocalities', in M. Featherstone, S. Lash and R. Robertson (eds) *Global Modernities*. London: Sage
Lury, C. 1993. *Cultural Rights*. London: Routledge
Lury, C. 1996. *Consumer Culture*. Cambridge: Polity
Lyman, F., Mintzer, K. and McKenzie, J. 1990. *The Greenhouse Trap*. Boston: Beacon Press
Lynch, K. 1972. *What Time is this Place?* Cambridge, MA: MIT Press
Lyotard, J.-F. 1992. *The Inhuman: reflections on time*. Stanford, CA: Stanford University Press
Mabey, R., Clifford, S. and King, A. (eds) 1984. *Second Nature*. London: Jonathan Cape
McClintock, A. 1995. *Imperial Leather*. New York: Routledge
McCormick, J. 1991a. *British Politics and the Environment*. Chichester: Wiley
McCormick, J. 1991b. *Reclaiming Paradise: the global environmental movement*. Bloomington: Indiana University Press
McCormick, J. 1995. *The Global Environmental Movement*, 2nd edition. Chichester: Wiley
McCrone, D., Morris, A. and Kiely, R. 1995. *Scotland – the Brand*. Edinburgh: Edinburgh University Press
Macdonald, S. 1997. 'A people's story: heritage, identity and authenticity', in C. Rojek and J. Urry (eds) *Touring Cultures*. London: Routledge
MacGillivray, A. and Zadek, S. 1995. *Accounting for Change: indicators for sustainable development*. London: New Economics Foundation
MacIntyre, A. 1985. *After Virtue: a study in moral theory*. London: Duckworth
McKay, G. 1996. *Senseless Acts of Beauty*. London: Verso
McKibben, W. 1990. *The End of Nature*. New York: Viking
Macnaghten, P. 1993. 'Discourses of nature: argumentation and power', in I. Parker and E. Burman (eds) *Discourse Analytic Research*. London: Routledge
Macnaghten, P. 1995. 'Public attitudes to countryside leisure: a case study on ambivalence', *Journal of Rural Studies*, 11: 135–47
Macnaghten, P. and Jacobs, M. 1997. 'Public identification with sustainable development: investigating cultural barriers to participation', *Global Environmental Change*, 7: 1–20
Macnaghten, P. and Scott, J. 1994. 'Changing worldviews of students', *ECOS*, 15: 2–7
Macnaghten, P. and Urry, J. 1995. 'Towards a sociology of nature', *Sociology*, 29: 203–20
Macnaghten, P., Brown, B. and Reicher, S. 1992. 'On the nature of nature: experimental studies in the power of rhetoric', *Journal of Community and Applied Social Psychology*, 2: 43–61
Macnaghten, P., Grove-White, R., Jacobs, M. and Wynne, B. 1995a. *Public Perceptions and Sustainability: indicators, institutions, participation*. Preston: Lancashire County Council
Macnaghten, P., Myers, G. and Wynne, B. 1995b. *Public Rhetorics of Environmental Sustainability: ambivalence and effects*. Lancaster: CSEC, Lancaster University

McTaggart, J. 1927. *The Nature of Existence. Vol 2, Book 5.* Cambridge: Cambridge University Press

Macy, J. 1993. *World as Lover, World as Self.* London: Rider

Maddox, J. 1972. *The Doomsday Syndrome.* London: Macmillan

Mallett, P. 1995. 'The city and the self', in M. Wheeler (ed.) *Ruskin and the Environment.* Manchester: Manchester University Press

Mann, M. 1986. *The Sources of Social Power. Vol. 1.* Cambridge: Cambridge University Press

Mann, M. 1996. 'Neither nation-state nor globalism', *Environment and Planning A*, 28: 1960–4

Mansfield, M. 1995. 'Case without compassion', *The Guardian*, 14 April

Marcus, S. 1973. 'Reading the illegible', in H. Dyos and M. Wolff (eds) *The Victorian City: images and realities. Vol 1.* London: Routledge and Kegan Paul

Marquand, D. 1988. *The Unprincipled Society: new demands and old politics.* London: Fontana

Marquand, D. 1996. 'Time to take sides', *The Guardian*, 27 May

Martell, L. 1994. *Ecology and Society: an introduction.* Cambridge: Polity

Martin, B. 1981. *A Sociology of Contemporary Cultural Change.* Oxford: Blackwell

Marx, K. 1973. *Grundrisse.* Harmondsworth: Penguin

Marx, K. and Engels, F. 1976. *Collected Works. Vol. 6.* London: Lawrence and Wishart

Marx, L. 1964. *The Machine in the Garden: technology and the pastoral ideal in America.* New York: Oxford University Press

Matless, D. 1990. 'Definitions of England, 1928–1989: preservation, modernism and the nature of the nation', *Built Environment*, 16: 179–91

Matless, D. 1995. 'The art of right living: landscape and citizenship, 1918–39', in S. Pile and N. Thrift (eds) *Mapping the Subject.* London: Routledge

Mead, G. 1959. *The Philosophy of the Present.* La Salle, IL: Open Court

Meadows, D., Meadows, D., Randers, J. and Behrens, W. 1972. *Limits to Growth.* London: Earth Island

Meinig, D. 1979. 'The beholding eye', in D. Meinig (ed.) *The Interpretation of Ordinary Landscapes.* New York: Oxford University Press

Mellor, A. 1991. 'Enterprise and heritage in the dock', in J. Corner and S. Harvey (eds) *Enterprise and Heritage.* London: Routledge

Melucci, A. 1989. *Nomads of the Present: social movements and individual needs in contemporary society.* London: Radius

Mendes, C. 1992. *Chico Mendes in His Own Words.* London: Zed

Merchant, C. 1982. *The Death of Nature: women, ecology and the scientific revolution.* San Francisco: Harper and Row

Merchant, C. 1992. *Radical Ecology: the search for a livable world.* New York: Routledge

Meyrowitz, J. 1985. *No Sense of Place: the impact of electronic media on social behavior.* New York: Oxford University Press

Michael, M. 1996. *Constructing Identities.* London: Sage

Middleton, D. and Edwards, D. (eds) 1990. *Collective Remembering.* London: Sage

Miller, S. 1995. 'Urban dreams and rural reality: land and landscape in English culture, 1920–45', *Rural History*, 6: 89–102

Milton, K. (ed.) 1993a. *Environmentalism: the view from anthropology.* London: Routledge

Milton, K. 1993b. 'Land or landscape: rural planning policy and the symbolic construction of the countryside', in M. Murray and J. Greer (eds) *Rural Development in Ireland.* Avebury: Aldershot

Milton, K. 1996. *Environmentalism and Cultural Theory.* London: Routledge

Ministry of Agriculture, Fisheries and Food 1995. *Bovine Spongiform Encephalopathy in Great Britain: a progress report.* London: Ministry of Agriculture, Fisheries and Food

Miss Pod 1993. 'Fine young radicals', *Pod: for DIY culture*, 5: 7–11

Mitchell, T. 1988. *Colonizing Egypt.* Cambridge: Cambridge University Press

Mohai, P. and Twight, B. 1987. 'Age and environmentalism: an elaboration of the Buttel model using national survey evidence', *Social Science Quarterly*, 26: 2048–56

Moore, W. 1963. *Man, Time and Society*. New York: Wiley

MORI 1994. *Environmental Education: is the message getting through?* Edinburgh: Scottish Central Research Unit

MORI 1995. *MORI Business and the Environment Survey*. London: MORI

Morley, D. 1995. 'Television: not so much a visual medium, more a visible object', in C. Jenks (ed.) *Visual Culture*. London: Routledge

Morley, D. and Robins, K. 1995. *Spaces of Identity*. London: Routledge

Morrison, D. and Dunlap, R. 1986. 'Environmentalism and elitism: a conceptual and empirical analysis', *Environmental Management*, 10: 581–9

Moscovici, S. 1984. 'The myth of the lonely paradigm: a rejoinder', *Social Research* 51: 939–67

Mulgan, G. 1994. *Politics in an Antipolitical Age*. London: Sage

Mulvey, L. 1989. *Visual and Other Pleasures*. London: Macmillan

Myers, G. and Macnaghten, P. 1998 forthcoming. 'Rhetorics of environmental sustainability: commonplaces and places', *Environment and Planning A*

Naess, A. 1973. 'The shallow and the deep, long-range ecology movement: a summary', *Inquiry*, 16: 95–100

Nature Editorial. 1996. 'Lessons from BSE for public confidence', *Nature*, 380, 28 March: 271

NEDO 1992. *Tourism: competing for growth*. London: NEDO

Newby, H. 1979. *Green and Pleasant Land? Social change in rural England*. London: Hutchinson

Newby, H. 1987. *The Countryside in Question*. London: Hutchinson

Newby, H. 1990a. 'Ecology, amenity and society: social science and environmental change', *Town Planning Review*, 61: 3–20

Newby, H. 1990b. 'Revitalizing the countryside: the opportunities and pitfalls of counter-urban trends', *Royal Society of Arts Journal*, 138: 630–6

Newby, H. 1993. *Global Environmental Change and the Social Sciences: retrospect and prospect*. Swindon: ESRC (unpublished)

New Scientist Editorial 1996. 'Give us the beef about beef', *New Scientist*, 2023, 30 March: 3

Nguyen, D. 1992. 'The spatialisation of metric time', *Time & Society*, 1: 29–50

Nicholson, M. 1987. *The New Environmental Age*. Cambridge: Cambridge University Press

Nicholson, M. 1989. *CPRE/Shell Oral Archive*. London: CPRE

Nicholson, N. 1978. *The Lake District*. Harmondsworth: Penguin

Novak, B. 1980. *Nature and Culture: American landscape and painting, 1825–1875*. London: Thames and Hudson

Nowotny, H. 1985. 'From the future to the extended present: time in social systems', in G. Kirsch, P. Nijkamp, K. Zimmerman (eds) *Time Preferences: an interdisciplinary theoretical and empirical approach*. Berlin: Wissenschaftszentrum

Nowotny, H. 1994. *Time: the modern and postmodern experience*. Cambridge: Polity

O'Brien, M. and Penna, S. 1997. *Theorising Welfare: Enlightenment and modern society*. London: Sage

OECD 1993. 'Core set of indicators for environmental performance reviews', *Environment Monographs No. 83*. Paris: OECD

Ohmae, K, 1990. *The Borderless World*. London: Collins

Olwig, K. 1989. 'Nature interpretation: a threat to the countryside', in D. Uzzell (ed.) *Heritage Interpretation. Vol. 1. The natural and built environment*. London: Belhaven

O'Neill, J. 1993. *Ecology, Policy and Politics*. London: Routledge

Ong, W. 1982. *Orality and Literacy: the technologizing of the word*. London: Methuen

O'Riordan, T. 1976. *Environmentalism*. London: Pion

O'Riordan, T. 1989. 'The challenge for environmentalism', in R. Peet and N. Thrift (eds) *New Models in Geography*. London: Unwin Hyman

O'Riordan, T. 1995. 'Frameworks for choice: core beliefs and the environment', *Environment*, 37: 25–9

O'Riordan, T. and Jordan, A. 1995. 'British environmental politics in the 1990s', *Environmental Politics*, 4: 237–46

Orwell, G. 1937. *The Road to Wigan Pier*. London: Victor Gollancz

Orwell, G. 1938. *Homage to Catalonia*. London: Secker and Warburg

Osborne, P. 1994. 'The politics of time', *Radical Philosophy*, 68: 3–9

Ousby, I. 1990. *The Englishman's England*. Cambridge: Cambridge University Press

Ovitt, G. 1987. *The Restoration of Perfection*. Brunswick, NJ: Rutgers University Press

Paglia, C. 1990. *Sexual Personae*. Harmondsworth: Penguin

Parkin, S. 1989. *Green Parties: an international guide*. London: Heretic Books

Parr, M. 1995. *Small World*. Stockport: Dewi Lewis

Patterson, W. 1984. 'A decade of friendship: the first ten years', in D. Wilson (ed.) *The Environmental Crisis: a handbook for all Friends of the Earth*. London: Heinemann

Peach, H. and Carrington, N. 1930. *The Face of the Land*. London: Allen and Unwin

Pearce, D., Markandya, A. and Barbier, E. 1989. *Blueprint for a Green Planet*. London: Earthscan

Pearce, F. 1991. *Green Warriors: the people and politics behind the environmental revolution*. London: Bodley Head

Pemble, J. 1987. *The Mediterranean Passion: Victorians and Edwardians in the South*. Oxford: Clarendon

Penman, D. 1995. 'It's eco-war. And you can be a winner', *The Independent*, 23 June

Pepper, D. 1984. *The Roots of Modern Environmentalism*. London: Croom Helm

Pepper, D. 1996. *Modern Environmentalism: an introduction*. London: Routledge

Peters, T. 1992. *Liberation Management*. London: Macmillan

Pieterse, J. 1995. 'Globalization as hybridization', in M. Featherstone, S. Lash and R. Robertson (eds) *Global Modernities*. London: Sage

Pile, S. and Thrift, N. 1995a. 'Introduction', in S. Pile and N. Thrift (eds) *Mapping the Subject*. London: Routledge

Pile, S. and Thrift, N. 1995b. 'Mapping the subject', in S. Pile and N. Thrift (eds) *Mapping the Subject*. London: Routledge

Pilkington, E., Clouston, E. and Traynor, I. 1995. 'How wave of public opinion bowled over the Shell monolith', *The Guardian*, 22 June

Plumwood, V. 1993. *Feminism and the Mastery of Nature*. London: Routledge

Popper, K. 1962. *The Open Society and Its Enemies*. London: Routledge

Porritt, J. 1984. *Seeing Green: the politics of ecology explained*. Oxford: Blackwell

Porritt, J. and Winner, D. 1988. *The Coming of the Greens*. London: Fontana

Porteous, J. 1985. 'Smellscape', *Progress in Human Geography*, 9: 356–78

Porteous, J. 1990. *Landscapes of the Mind: worlds of sense and metaphor*. Toronto: Toronto University Press

Porter, T. 1995. *Trust in Numbers*. Princeton: Princeton University Press

Potter, J. and Wetherell, M. 1987. *Discourse and Social Psychology: beyond attitudes and behaviour*. London: Sage

Potter, J. and Wetherell, M. 1988. 'Accomplishing attitudes: fact and evaluation in racist discourse', *Text*, 8: 51–8

Potts, A. 1989. ' "Constable country" between the wars', in R. Samuel (ed.) *Patriotism. Vol. 3*. London: Routledge

Power, M. 1994. *The Audit Explosion*. London: Demos

Pratt, M. 1992. *Imperial Eyes*. London: Routledge

Prigogine, I. 1980. *From Being to Becoming: time and complexity in the physical sciences*. San Francisco: W.H. Freeman

Pugh, S. 1988. *Garden–Nature–Language*. Manchester: Manchester University Press

Radford, T. 1996. 'BSE controls reluctantly', *The Guardian*, 1 July

Radley, A. 1990. 'Artefacts, memory and a sense of the past', in D. Middleton and D. Edwards (eds) *Collective Remembering*. London: Sage

Rattray Taylor, G. 1970. *The Doomsday Book*. London: Thames and Hudson

Redclift, M. 1987. *Sustainable Development: exploring the contradictions*. London: Methuen

Redclift, M. 1993. 'Sustainable development: concepts, contradictions, and conflicts', in P. Allen (ed.) *Food for the Future: conditions and contradictions of sustainability*. London: Wiley

Redclift, M. 1995. 'The UK and international environmental agenda: Rio and after', in T. Gray (ed.) *UK Environmental Policy in the 1990s*. London: Macmillan

Redclift, M. and Benton, T. (eds) (1994) *Social Theory and the Global Environment*. London: Routledge

Reed, E. 1982. 'Descartes' corporeal ideas hypothesis and the origin of modern psychology', *Review of Metaphysics*, 35: 731–52

Reich, C. 1970. *The Greening of America*. New York: Random House

Relph, E. 1976. *Place and Placelessness*. London: Pion

Relph, R. 1981. *The Modern Urban Landscape*. London: Croom Helm

Richards, J. 1995. 'The role of the railway', in M. Wheeler (ed.) *Ruskin and Environment: the storm cloud in the 19th century*. Manchester: Manchester University Press

Rifkin, J. 1987. *Time Wars: the primary conflict in human history*. New York: Henry Holt

Ritzer, G. 1993. *The McDonaldization of Society: an investigation into the changing character of contemporary social life*. London: Sage

Robertson, G., Mash, M., Tickner, L., Bird, J., Curtis, B. and Putnam, Y. 1996. *FutureNatural: nature, science, culture*. London: Routledge

Rodaway, P. 1994. *Sensuous Geographies*. London: Routledge

Romanyshyn, R. 1989. *Technology as Sympton and Dream*. London: Routledge

Rorty, R. 1980. *Philosophy and the Mirror of Nature*. Oxford: Blackwell

Rose, C. 1984. 'Wildlife: the battle for the British countryside', in D. Wilson (ed.) *The Environmental Crisis: a handbook for all Friends of the Earth*. London: Heinemann

Rose, C. 1993. 'Beyond the struggle for proof: factors changing the environmental movement', *Environmental Values*, 2: 285–98

Rose, C. 1995. 'Future of environmental campaigning', *Royal Society of Arts*, 6 December

Roseneil, S. 1995. *Disarming Patriarchy*. Buckingham: Open University Press

Ross, A. 1994. *The Chicago Gangster Theory of Life: nature's debt to society*. London: Verso

Roszak, T. 1970. *The Making of a Counter Culture: reflections on the technocratic society and its youthful opposition*. London: Fontana

Roszak, T. 1981. *Person/Planet: the creative disintegration of industrial society*. St Albans: Granada

Roy, D. 1990. 'Time and job satisfaction', in J. Hassard (ed.) *The Sociology of Time*. London: Macmillan

Royal Society 1983. *Risk*. London: Royal Society of London

Royal Society 1985. *Public Understanding of Science Report*. London: Royal Society of London

Royal Society 1992. *Risk: analysis, perception, and management*. London: Royal Society of London

Rubin, N. 1989. 'Environmental policy and environmental thought: Ruckelshaus and Commoner', *Environmental Ethics*, 11: 27–51

Rudig, W. 1991. 'Green party politics around the world', *Environment*, 33: 6

Rudig, W. 1995. 'Public opinion and global warming', *Strathclyde Papers on Government and Politics*, 101:1–38

Rushdie, S. 1995. *Midnight's Children*. London: Vintage

Ruskin, J. 1985. 'The nature of gothic', in Clive Wilmer (ed.), *Unto This Last and Other Writings*. Harmondsworth: Penguin

Sachs, W. (ed.) 1993. *Global Ecology: a new arena of global conflict*. London: Zed Books

Sachs, W. 1994. 'The blue planet: an ambiguous modern icon', *The Ecologist*, 25: 170–5

Sale, K. 1985. *Dwellers in the Land*. San Francisco: Sierra Club Books

Samuel, R. 1994. *Theatres of Memory*. London: Verso

Sandbach, F. 1980. *Environment, Ideology and Policy*. Oxford: Blackwell

Savage, M., Barlow, J., Dickens, P. and Fielding, T. 1992. *Bureaucracy, Property and Culture: middle-class formation in contemporary Britain*. London: Routledge

Schama, S. 1995. *Landscape and Memory*. London: HarperCollins

Schivelbusch, W. 1986. *The Railway Journey: trains and travel in the nineteenth century*. Oxford: Blackwell

Scholte, J. 1996. 'What are the new spaces?', *Environment and Planning A*, 28: 1965–9

Schor, J. 1992. *The Overworked American*. New York: Basic

Schumacher, E. 1974. *Small is Beautiful: a study of economics as if people mattered*. London: Abacus

Schwarz, M. and Thompson, M. 1990. *Divided we Stand*. Hemel Hempstead: Harvester Wheatsheaf

Sennett, R. 1991. *The Conscience of the Eye: the design and social life of cities*. London: Faber

Shackley, S. 1997. 'The intergovernmental panel on climate change', *Global Environmental Change*, 7: 77–9

Shackley, S. and Wynne B. 1995a. 'Global climate change: the mutual construction of an emergent science-policy domain', *Science and Public Policy*, 22: 218–30

Shackley, S. and Wynne B. 1995b. 'Integrating knowledges for climate change: pyramids, nets and uncertainties', *Global Environmental Change*, 5: 113–26

Shackley, S., Wynne, B. and Waterton, C. 1996. 'Imagine complexity: the past, present and future potential of complex thinking', *Futures*, 28: 201–26

Sharratt, B. 1989. 'Communications and image studies: notes after Raymond Williams', *Comparative Criticism*, 11: 29–50

Shields, R. 1991. *Places on the Margin*. London: Routledge

Shields, R. 1995. 'Fancy footwork: Walter Benjamin's notes on flânerie', in K. Tester (ed.) *The Flâneur*. London: Routledge

Shiva, V. 1988. *Staying Alive: women, ecology and development*. London: Zed Books

Shiva, V. 1991. *Ecology and the Politics of Survival: conflicts over natural resources in India*. New Delhi: Sage

Shiva, V. (1993) 'The greening of the global reach', in W. Sachs (ed.) *Global Ecology: a new arena of political conflict*. London: Zed Books

Shiva, V. 1994. *Close to Home: women reconnect ecology, health and development*. London: Earthscan

Shoard, M. 1980. *The Theft of the Countryside*. London: Temple Smith

Shoard, M. 1987. *This Land is Our Land: the struggle for Britain's countryside*. London: Paladin

Short, R. 1991. *Imagined Country: society, culture and environment*. London: Routledge

Shotter, J. 1993a. *Conservational Realities: studies in social constructionism*. London: Sage

Shotter, J. 1993b. *The Cultural Politics of Everyday Life*. Milton Keynes: Open University Press

Sklair, L. 1990. *Sociology of the Global System*. Hemel Hempstead: Harvester

Slater, D. 1995. 'Photography and modern vision: the spectacle of "natural magic"', in C. Jenks (ed.) *Visual Culture*. London: Routledge

Slater, E. 1993. 'Contested terrain: differing interpretations of Co. Wicklow's landscape', *Irish Journal of Sociology*, 3: 23–55

Smart, J. 1963. *Philosophy and Scientific Realism*. London: Routledge

Smith, A. 1990. 'Towards a global culture', *Theory, Culture & Society*, 7: 171–92

Smith, J. 1992. 'Writing the aesthetic experience', in T. Barnes and J. Duncan (eds) *Writing Worlds*. London: Routledge

Soja, E. 1996. *Thirdspace*. Cambridge, MA: Blackwell

Sontag, S. 1979. *On Photography*. Harmondsworth: Penguin

Sorokin, P. 1937. *Social and Cultural Dynamics. Vol. 2*. New York: American Books

Sorokin, P. and Merton, R. 1937. 'Social time: a methodological and functional analysis', *American Journal of Sociology*, 42: 615–29

Sports Council 1991. *A Countryside for Sport: a policy for sport and recreation*. London: Sports Council

Sprawson, C. 1992. *The Black Masseur*. London: Jonathan Cape

Sreberny-Mohammadi, A. and Mohammadi, A. (1994). *Small Media, Big Revolution*. Minnesota: University of Minnesota Press

Stacey, J. 1997. *Teratologies: a cultural study of cancer*. London: Routledge

Stallybrass, P. and White, A. 1986. *The Politics and Poetics of Transgression*. London: Methuen

Sterngold, A., Warland, R. and Herrmann, R. 1994. 'Do surveys overstate public concerns?', *Public Opinion Quarterly*, 58: 255–63

Strathern, M. 1992. *After Nature: English kinship in the late twentieth century*. Cambridge: Cambridge University Press

Sustainable Seattle 1992. *Indicators of Sustainable Community 1992*. Seattle

Szerszynski, B. 1993. *Uncommon Ground: moral discourse, foundationalism and the environmental movement*. PhD, Dept of Sociology, Lancaster University

Szerszynski, B. 1994. *The Politics of Dependence: the self and contemporary cultural movements*. Lancaster: CSEC Working Paper, Lancaster University

Szerszynski, B. 1995. *Environmental NGOs in Britain: communication activities and institutional change*. Lancaster: CSEC Working Paper, Lancaster University

Szerszynski, B. 1996. 'On knowing what to do: environmentalism and the modern problematic', in S. Lash, B. Szerszynski and B. Wynne (eds) *Risk, Environment and Modernity: towards a new ecology*. London: Sage

Szerszynski, B., Lash, S. and Wynne, B. 1996. 'Introduction: ecology, realism and the social sciences', in S. Lash, B. Szerszynski and B. Wynne (eds) *Risk, Environment and Modernity: towards a new ecology*. London: Sage

Taylor, J. 1994. *A Dream of England*. Manchester: Manchester University Press

Taylor, L. 1994. *Visualizing Theory: selected essays from V.A.R. 1990–1994*. New York: Routledge

Taylor, P. 1996. 'Embedded statism and the social sciences: opening up to new spaces', *Environment and Planning A*, 28: 1917–28

Tester, K. (ed.) 1995. *The Flâneur*. London: Routledge

Thomas, J. 1993. 'The politics of vision and the archaeologies of landscape', in B. Bender (ed.) *Landscape: politics and perspectives*. Oxford: Berg

Thomas, K. 1984. *Man and the Natural World: changing attitudes in England 1500–1800*. Harmondsworth: Penguin

Thompson, E. 1967. 'Time, work-discipline and industrial capitalism', *Past and Present*, 36: 57–97

Thomson, M., Ellis, R. and Wildavsky, A. 1990. *Cultural Theory*. Boulder, CO: Westview Press

Thrift, N. 1990. 'The making of a capitalist time consciousness', in J. Hassard (ed.) *The Sociology of Time*. London: Macmillan

Thrift, N. 1996. *Spatial Formations*. London: Sage

Toogood, M. 1995. 'Representing ecology and highland tradition', *Area*, 27: 102–9

Toogood, M. 1997. *Natural State: the culture of conservation in Britain, 1949–1973*. PhD, CSEC, Lancaster University

Travis, A. 1994. 'Eco-warriors to step up battle against Howard's bill', *The Guardian*, 6 August

Tuan, Y.-F. 1974. *Topophilia: a study of environmental perception, attitudes, and values*. New York: Prentice Hall

Tuan, Y.-F. 1979. 'Sight and pictures', *Geographical Review*, 69: 413–22

Tuan, Y.-F. 1993. *Passing Strange and Wonderful*. Washington, DC: Island Press

Tucker, W. 1982. *Progress and Privilege: America in the age of environmentalism*. New York: Anchor Press

Tyrrell, B. 1995. 'Time in our lives: facts and analysis on the 90s', *Demos Quarterly. The Time Squeeze*, 5: 23–5

UK Cabinet Office 1985. *Pleasure, Leisure and Jobs: the business of tourism*. London: HMSO

UK Government 1994. *Sustainable Development: the UK strategy*. London: HMSO, Cm 2426

UNA (United Nations Association) and CDF (Community Development Foundation) 1995. *Towards Local Sustainability: a review of current activity on Local Agenda 21 in the UK*. London: UNA

UNCED 1992. *Agenda 21*. Conches, Switzerland: United Nations

Upsall, D. and Worcester, R. 1995. 'You can't sink a rainbow'. WAPOR Conference, The Hague, 21 September

Urry, J. 1990. *The Tourist Gaze*. London: Sage

Urry, J. 1992. 'The Tourist Gaze "revisited"', *American Behavioral Scientist*, 36: 172–86

Urry, J. 1994. 'Time, leisure and social identity', *Time & Society*, 3: 131–49

Urry, J. 1995a. 'A middle class countryside', in T. Butler and M. Savage (eds) *Social Change and the Middle Classes*. London: UCL Press

Urry, J. 1995b. *Consuming Places*. London: Routledge

Urry, J. 1996a. 'How societies remember the past', in S. Macdonald and G. Fyfe (eds) *Theorizing Museums*. Oxford: Blackwell Sociological Review Monographs

Urry, J. 1996b. 'Is the global a new space of analysis?', *Environment and Planning A*, 28: 1977–82

Vallely, P. 1994. 'Are animals losing their innocents?', *The Independent*, 22 April

Vergo, P. 1989. *The New Museology*. London: Reaktion Books

Vidal, J. 1994. 'The real earth movers', *The Guardian*, 7 December

Virilio, P. 1986. *Speed and Politics*. New York: Semiotext(e)

Virilio, P. 1988. 'The work of art in the age of electronic reproduction', *Interview in Block*, 14: 4–7

Wallace, W. 1993. *Walking, Literature and English Culture*. Oxford: Clarendon

Ward, B. and Dubos, R. 1972. *Only One Earth: the care and maintenance of a small planet*. New York: Penguin

Ward, C. 1991. *Freedom to Go: after the motor age*. London: Freedom Press

Warde, A. 1994. 'Consumers, identity and belonging: reflections on some theses of Zygmunt Bauman', in R. Keat, N. Whiteley and N. Abercrombie (eds) *The Authority of the Consumer*. London: Routledge

Wark, M. 1994. *Virtual Geography: living with global media events*. Bloomington: Indiana University Press

Waters, M, 1985. *Globalization*. London: Routledge

Waterton, C., Grove-White, R., Rodwell, J. and Wynne, B. 1995. *Corine: databases and nature conservation – the new politics of information in the European Union*. Lancaster: CSEC, Lancaster University

WCED (World Commission for Environment and Development) 1987. *Our Common Future*. Oxford: Oxford University Press

Weale, A. 1992. *The New Politics of Pollution*. Manchester: Manchester University Press

Weaver, M. 1992. 'The world's top tourist attraction', *The Daily Telegraph*, 14 May

Weber, M. 1930. *The Protestant Ethic and the Spirit of Capitalism*. London: Unwin

Welsh, I. and McLeish, P. 1996. 'The European road to nowhere: anarchism and direct action against the UK roads programme', *Anarchist Studies*, 4: 27–44

Whatmore, S. and Boucher, S. 1993. 'Bargaining with nature: the discourse and practice of "environmental planning gain"', *Transactions of the Institute of British Geographers*, 18: 166–82

Wheeler, M. (ed.) 1995. *Ruskin and the Environment*. Manchester: Manchester University Press

Whitehead, A. 1926. *Science and the Modern World*. Cambridge: Cambridge University Press

Wiener, M. 1981. *English Culture and the Decline of the Industrial Spirit 1850–1980*. Cambridge: Cambridge University Press

Williams, R. 1972. 'Ideas of Nature', in J. Benthall (ed.) *Ecology: the shaping enquiry*. London: Longman

Williams, R. 1973. *The Country and the City*. London: Chatto and Windus

Williams, R. 1976. *Keywords: a vocabulary of culture and society*. London: Fontana

Williams, R. 1984. 'Between country and city', in R. Mabey (ed.) *Second Nature*. London: Cape

Williams-Ellis, C. 1928. *England and the Octopus*. London: Geoffrey Bles

Williams-Ellis, C. (ed.) 1938. *England and the Beast*. London: Dent

Wilson, A. 1992. *The Culture of Nature: North American landscape from Disney to the Exxon Valdez*. Cambridge, MA: Blackwell

Woolf, M. 1995. 'Green protesters give up scraps of paper for the Internet', *The Independent*, 26 February

Woollacott, M. 1995. 'War in the Pacific', *The Guardian*, 7 July

Worcester, R. 1994. 'The sustainable society: what we know about what people think and do', *Values for a Sustainable Society*, World Environment Day Symposium, 2 June

Worcester, R. 1995. 'Vital statistics: green gauge of Britain', *BBC Wildlife*, 13: 70–3

Wordsworth, W. 1984. *The Illustrated Wordsworth's Guide to the Lakes* (P. Bicknell ed.). London: Book Club Associates

Worster, D. 1985. *Nature's Economy: a history of ecological ideas*. Cambridge: Cambridge University Press

Wright, P. 1985. *On Living in an Old Country*. London: Verso

Wright, P. 1996. *The Village that Died for England: the strange story of Tyneham*. London: Vintage

WWF (World Wildlife Fund for Nature) and NEF (New Economics Foundation) 1994. *Indicators for Sustainable Development*. London: WWF and NEF

Wynne, B. 1980. 'Technology, risk and participation: on the social treatment of uncertainty', in J. Conrad (ed.) *Society, Technology and Risk*. London: Academic Press

Wynne, B. 1982. *Rationality and Ritual: the Windscale inquiry and nuclear decisions in Britain*. Chalfont St Giles: British Society for the History of Science

Wynne, B. 1987. *Risk Management and Hazardous Wastes: implementation and the dialectics of credibility*. London: Springer

Wynne, B. 1989. 'Understanding public risk perceptions', in J. Brown (ed.) *Environmental Threats: perception, analysis and management*. London: Belhaven

Wynne, B. 1991. 'After Chernobyl: science made too simple', *New Scientist*, 1753: 44–6

Wynne, B. 1992a. 'Misunderstood misunderstandings: social identities and the public uptake of science', *Public Understanding of Science*, 1: 281–304

Wynne, B. 1992b. 'Risk and social learning: reification to engagement', in S. Golding and D. Golding (eds) *Theories of Risk*. New York: Praeger

Wynne, B. 1994. 'Scientific knowledge and the global environment', in M. Redclift and T. Benton (eds) *Social Theory and the Global Environment*. London: Routledge

Wynne, B. 1996a. 'May the sheep graze safely', in S. Lash, B. Szerszynski and B. Wynne (eds) *Risk, Environment and Modernity: towards a new ecology*. London: Sage

Wynne, B. 1996b. 'Patronising Joe Public', *The Times Higher Education Supplement*, 12 April

Wynne, B. and Crouch, D. 1991. *Responsiveness of Science and Technology Institutions to Environmental Change: a UK case study. Report to OECD*. Lancaster: CSEC, Lancaster University

Wynne, B. and Mayer, S. 1993. 'How science fails the environment', *New Scientist*, 1876: 33–5

Wynne, B., Waterton, C. and Grove-White, R. 1993. *Public Perceptions and the Nuclear Industry in West Cumbria*. Lancaster: CSEC, Lancaster University

Yanagisako, S. and Delaney, C. (eds) 1995. *Naturalizing Power: essays in feminist cultural analysis*. New York: Routledge

Yearley, S. 1991. *The Green Case: a sociology of environmental issues, arguments and politics*. London: HarperCollins

Yearley, S. 1996. *Sociology, Environmentalism, Globalization*. London: Sage
Young, H. 1995. 'Democracy ditched in waves of escapism', *The Guardian*, 22 June
Zerubavel, E. 1988. 'The standardisation of time: a sociohistorical perspective', *American Journal of Sociology*, 88: 1–23

INDEX